A WIZARD
A TRUE STAR

TODD RUNDGREN IN THE STUDIO

A WIZARD A TRUE STAR

TODD RUNDGREN IN THE STUDIO

PAUL MYERS

A Wizard, A True Star

TODD RUNDGREN IN THE STUDIO

PAUL MYERS

For Liza, my true partner, spiritual backbone, travel companion, and the instigator of all things fun and exciting in my life.

A Jawbone Book
First Edition 2010
Published in the UK and the USA by Jawbone Press
2a Union Court,
20–22 Union Road,
London SW4 6JP,
England
www.jawbonepress.com

ISBN 978-1-906002-33-6

ART DIRECTOR: Paul Cooper
DESIGN: Elizabeth Owens
EDITOR: John Morrish

Printed by Regent Publishing Services Ltd.

1 2 3 4 5 14 13 12 11 10

Contents

Todd Rundgren (Lead Guitar)

NAZZ

CLOCKWISE FROM LEFT: **A Todd-centric Nazz publicity shot from 1968; a previously unseen photograph taken by engineer James Lowe during sessions for *The Ballad Of Todd Rundgren* at Rundgren's LA home; Rundgren with his dog, Furburger, his mother, Ruth, and Moogy Klingman in Lake Hill, New York; playing a used Les Paul in Woody's Truck Stop, 1966.**

CLOCKWISE FROM TOP LEFT: A **Utopia session at Secret Sound, New York, 1974, featuring John Siegler, Ralph Schuckett, Rundgren, Bebe Buell, Moogy Klingman, and John Siomos; the Secret Sound exterior today; a 1972 ad for *Something/Anything?*; Rundgren (center) with Jerry Nolan, Sylvain Sylvain, David Johansen, Johnny Thunders, and Arthur Kane of The New York Dolls, 1973; a 1975 Bearsville promo shot, featuring Roger Powell (center).**

"Go ahead. Ignore me."

Take no chances.
Something/Anything?,
a twin-pack of
Todd Rundgren albums
on Bearsville Records.

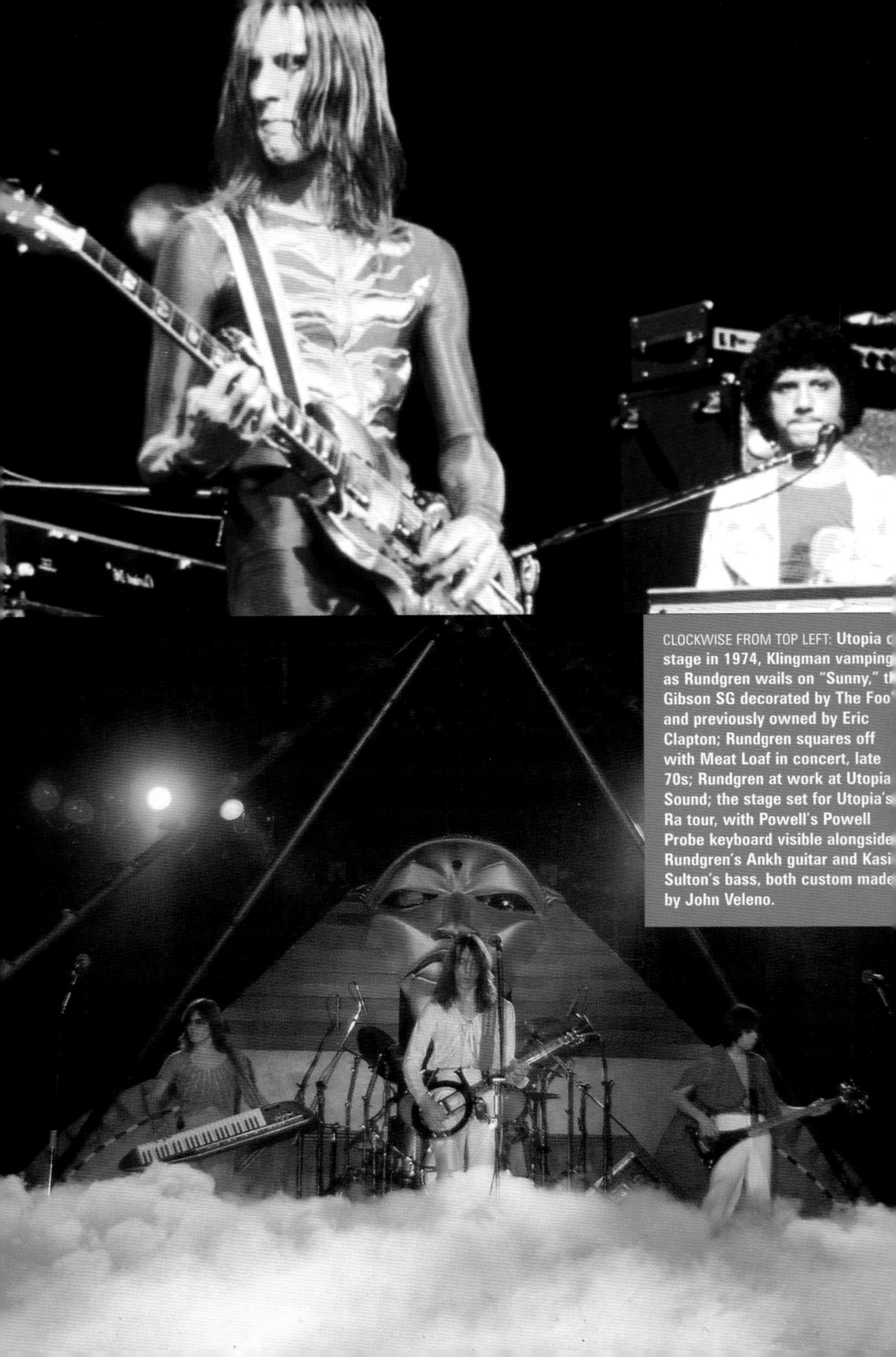

CLOCKWISE FROM TOP LEFT: **Utopia o[n] stage in 1974, Klingman vamping as Rundgren wails on "Sunny," th[e] Gibson SG decorated by The Foo[l] and previously owned by Eric Clapton; Rundgren squares off with Meat Loaf in concert, late 70s; Rundgren at work at Utopia Sound; the stage set for Utopia's Ra tour, with Powell's Powell Probe keyboard visible alongside Rundgren's Ankh guitar and Kasi[m] Sulton's bass, both custom made by John Veleno.**

AIN PICTURE: **The final Utopia line-up, mprising Rundgren, Willie Wilcox, Roger well, and Kasim Sulton, posing on an urban oftop, 1983.** RIGHT: **Rundgren and "Sunny" on e Deface The Music tour, 1980.**

CLOCKWISE FROM TOP LEFT: **Rundgren with Dave Gregory during sessions for XTC's *Skylarking* at Utopia Sound, 1986; with XTC's Andy Partridge; rehearsals for *2nd Wind*, 1991; the *A Capella* live ensemble (left to right): Doug Legacy, Michele Rundgren, Doug Howard, Todd Rundgren, Robert Redding, Kasim Sulton, Shandi Sinnamon, Briz, Mary Lou Arnold, Gary Windo, Bob Leinbach, and Steve Petrone, October 1985; Rundgren at work on *Nearly Human*, 1989; the Utopia Sound exterior.**

ABOVE: **Rundgren opens his A Wizard, A Tr Star Live show by singing 'International Fe in a space suit, 2009.** BELOW: **There's alwa more ... Rundgren with "Foamy," unleashe his inner *Johnson*, 2010.**

Introduction Couldn't I Just Tell You

At one point during an interview for this book, Patti Smith's guitarist Lenny Kaye summed up Todd Rundgren's production philosophy better than anyone I'd spoken to over the course of my year and a half of research.

"Todd's aphorism," Kaye told me, sitting in the kitchen of in his New York City pied-à-terre in St Mark's Place, "was, 'If you know what you want, I'll get it for you. If you don't know what you want, I'll do it for you.'"

That may be easy enough to say, but over Todd Rundgren's 40-plus years as a producer, he has been one of the few musicians with the facility to back it up. A self-taught guitarist, he willed himself into being a serviceable multi-instrumentalist. But as good as he became as a drummer, singer, vocal arranger, and keyboard player, his ultimate instrument is the recording studio (both the old-fashioned bricks-and-mortar kind and today's virtual kind). Arguably continuing in the tradition of multi-track pioneer Les Paul, Rundgren would himself come to inspire a generation of self-contained geniuses like Prince.

Throughout his storied career, Rundgren has ping-ponged between the worlds of producer and recording artist with varying degrees of critical and commercial success and financial reward. For many, myself included, their first sense of Rundgren's studio wizardry came after hearing the spoken word 'Intro,' from his 1972 tour de force, *Something/Anything?* After two full album sides, where Rundgren played and sang everything himself, the wizard allowed us a peek behind his sonic curtain as he playfully demonstrated a litany of audio gaffes one might have encountered on the albums of the day. He couched all of this in the sarcastic premise of a "game," inviting the listener to play along with him on their home stereo system.

"Before we go any further," Rundgren announced as side three began, "I'd like to show you all a game I made up. This game is called 'Sounds Of The Studio,' and it can be played with any record, including this one … You can even play it with your favorite record; you may be surprised. Now, if you have a pair of headphones, you better get 'em out and get 'em cranked up, 'cause they're really gonna help you on this one."

Rundgren's guided tour of things like 'P' popping, bad editing, and other common recording flaws told me more about him as both producer and artist than anything I've read about him since. Rundgren's recordings could be seriously masterful, whimsically sarcastic, poppy and progressive, sweet and hard, often at the same time.

As a producer and engineer, Todd Rundgren is the product of both Les Paul's recording innovations and the studio experimentations of 60s trailblazers like The Beatles and The Beach Boys. As such, he was born at the perfect time to flourish as a rock producer in the 70s and 80s, the golden age of the studio, when his reputation was largely cemented by a span of work stretching over 20 years. While he continued, and continues, to make recordings, Rundgren's attentions were frequently diverted over the 90s into new fields of technology. Ironically, some of his innovations would come to liberate the recording artist in such a way as to lessen the perceived value, or need, for a record producer at all. His evolution into a significant digital artist of the 21st century milieu is covered rather broadly in this volume, and I have intentionally dwelled upon the first 20 years, when Todd Rundgren made his name as a studio producer, working in big rooms and, predominantly, on analog tape.

After learning his craft as a songwriter and arranger for Nazz, and then gaining major attention for his engineering skills with The Band, Rundgren began to demonstrate a latent genius for pulling off hit productions with acts like Badfinger, The New York Dolls, and Grand Funk Railroad. All the while he was pushing the boundaries with his solo albums and those made with the various versions of his performance-based group, Utopia. We'll look at some of his more underappreciated albums for Sparks, Hall & Oates, The Tubes, and Cheap Trick as well as iconic releases by Meat Loaf, Patti Smith, The Psychedelic Furs, and XTC. Along the way, we'll touch on some of Rundgren's other work for artists like Steve Hillage, Shaun Cassidy, Jules Shear, Alice Cooper, Tom Robinson, and Bourgeois Tagg.

In describing Rundgren, the word that most frequently came to the lips of his clients and associates, the majority of whom talked to me for this book, was "genius." The second most frequent, however, was "sarcastic," with "aloof" running close behind. But while most artists only worked with Rundgren once – with notable exceptions being Grand Funk, The New York Dolls, The Tubes, The Hello People, and The Pursuit Of Happiness – rarely do any of his single-time clients bemoan the final results.

A case in point is Bad Religion's Greg Graffin, who reportedly had a fraught experience working with Rundgren, his boyhood idol, on the band's 2000 album, *The New America*. When it was over, Graffin still managed to praise Rundgren's methods to a writer from *Rolling Stone*.

"He's a prick in the studio ... an egomaniac," Graffin told Jennifer Vineyard. "It's his way or the highway ... but if you don't like hearing the truth about your own shortcomings, don't talk to Todd ... Most producers suck your dick: 'You're the greatest, you rule.' That's why most records suck: You're not challenged. But we were legitimately challenged. He would be very honest. We got along great. He has a sharp tongue, and so do I. He has a resilient character, and so do I. He used to be my hero, and now he's just my friend. But what I learned, it's like having a good editor to be a great writer. He challenged me to be as clear as possible. And he and I spent more time laughing than anything else."

Jim Steinman, composer of Rundgren's most commercially successful production, *Bat Out Of Hell*, echoed that sentiment for this book. At one point during our two-hour conversation, Steinman began laughing as he described Rundgren's constant browbeating and sarcastic taunts. Then, in the same moment, Steinman insisted that Rundgren, who put himself on the line financially to get *Bat Out Of Hell* made, was "the only true genius" he'd ever met in his life.

The most legendarily combative sessions of Rundgren's production career were undoubtedly those for the XTC album *Skylarking*. Yet, in each of their interviews for this book, the three members of XTC express, in hindsight, their admiration for the final results. Dave Gregory, admittedly a fan, credited Rundgren for doing exactly what he'd been hired to do. "Against all the odds," said Gregory, "he got the band a hit in America with 'Dear God.' Todd Rundgren saved XTC's career."

As you will see, over the course of the first-hand remarks, post-mortems, and personal opinions expressed by the many players in Rundgren's professional world, he is not always the hero in his own story; but he is frequently the most compelling character. Contrary to the myth, Todd is not God; in fact he's nearly human. Good social skills may make for a more pleasant life, but they are not a prerequisite for good art. Having said that, Rundgren nonetheless has legions of friends and admirers and enjoys a uniquely close relationship with his fans, many of whom he invited to camp out in his backyard in Kauai, Hawaii, for his 60th birthday festivities.

What has become clear to me, over my year and a half researching this project, is that Todd Rundgren is a true pioneer who has rarely received the acclaim he deserves. That he has yet to be inducted into the Rock And Roll Hall Of Fame, for example, beggars belief. Not that he himself seems to care.

But before we go any further, I feel it is appropriate to tell you a bit about what this book is and isn't. When asked, I have described it as "an anecdotal history of the recording world of Todd Rundgren, centered on the golden age of studio recording, when real people made records by hand in the big rooms." What this means is that, while there will be relevant background about the personal life of Todd Harry Rundgren, we are more concerned with what happened in the studio during the early years, when Rundgren earned his reputation as a studio whiz.

In light of this studio-only mandate, most live albums, personal family scandals, and tragedies are only touched on obliquely in the text. Likewise, tales of protracted litigations, bankruptcies, and all manner of bad business decisions – and there have been a few – are only referred to when they are deemed germane to the purview of this book, which is the making of studio recordings.

I have chosen to cover Rundgren's own work, as a solo artist and with Utopia, rather broadly. There are not specific chapters dedicated to each and every Rundgren album, and certain albums have received more attention than others. I make no claim to having written the definitive study; this is merely my journey through Todd Rundgren's formative years.

Hopefully, what emerges from these anecdotes, thoughts, and memories will be a widescreen picture of a true iconoclast who has made his own way in the world of recording and, in the process, amassed a vast trove of impressive audio documents.

"Wait another year," Rundgren once sang, "Utopia is here." And true enough, just when you think you know the real Todd Rundgren, another year has passed and he's changed again. In all likelihood, by the time you read this he will have morphed again into some new form or format. I have not pretended that I can pin him down like a bug in amber, but hopefully these stories will illuminate the road to Rundgren's future milestones, whether as an artist, producer, or some future job description not yet invented by the man himself.

May his dream go on forever.

Paul Myers
Berkeley, California.
November 2009.

1

Early Life And The Rise Of Nazz

Todd Harry Rundgren was born June 22 1948 in Upper Darby, Pennsylvania, near Philadelphia, and almost immediately became enamored with recorded sound via the meager album collection of his parents, Harry and Ruth, which consisted largely of show tunes and symphonic pieces. Harry had even built his own hi-fi system with his bare hands – a feat that surely made an impression on the young Todd. As a result, Todd, younger brother Robin, and sisters June and Lynette were granted early immersion into the symphonic language of Claude Debussy, Maurice Ravel, and Gustav Holst, the musical theater stylings of Richard Rodgers and Leonard Bernstein, and, significantly, the operettas of Gilbert & Sullivan.

By the time he was 16, Rundgren had grown as attracted to music and records as he was alienated from his domestic life and family. He shared a passion for music with his best friend, Randy Reed, whom he had met in the first grade. Fatefully, Reed possessed his own tape recorder.

"As a result," says Todd Rundgren today, "I became familiar with recording in the broader sense. The first trick we learned was that you could record something at slow speed and play it back at fast speed and suddenly you were The Chipmunks."

Rundgren and Reed had memorized and could sing "any song that Gilbert & Sullivan wrote. *H.M.S. Pinafore*, and stuff like that." He laughs, and starts to sing: "Hardly ever, hardly ever sick at sea ... What never? Well hardly ever!"

"By the time I was 16 or 17, Randy and I knew their entire libretto. It's all lost to me now, but we did it all mostly out of spite to show the teachers that we weren't stupid, or bad learners, we just knew what we wanted to learn. It was our way of saying, 'Oh yeah, you people think you're so damn smart, I'll show you smart! I can sing more words that you don't know the meaning of in the next two minutes!'"

According to Rundgren, both he and Reed were outcasts and considered themselves much smarter than everyone else in their age group. Reed also had what Rundgren refers to as "his own bachelor pad" where the two could "gag around" and record their ersatz spoken word radio programs, never broadcast, with titles such as 'Welcome To The Philadelphia Concourse.'

"Randy's parents had converted the basement into a whole room for him," says Rundgren. "That room became his lair but also my refuge away from home because I hated being at home so much."

While their initial recordings had been largely spoken-word affairs, that all changed when Rundgren became infatuated with the guitar-based music of The Beatles, The Rolling Stones, The Ventures, and The Yardbirds, not to mention the local 'Philly sound' of Gamble & Huff, The Delfonics, and The O'Jays. Music had been a logical avenue of expression for Rundgren since the age of eight, when he had taken some guitar lessons after a less-than-successful dalliance with the flute. He had started on his father's disused guitar, which he found hidden in the basement, but eventually broke the thing trying to tune it with a pair of pliers. Next, he acquired a cheap Japanese electric guitar, but no amplifier, but that was lost when the naïve youngster had lent it to a stranger whom he never saw again. By 17, Rundgren was ready to make his first steps on the path to musical expression when he and Reed put together a makeshift band they called Money.

"It was me, Randy, and Randy's younger brother," recalls Rundgren. "We always had trouble finding a drummer, and I didn't have a guitar at all any more so I always had to borrow one. We used Randy's tape recorder to record our meager performances. I remember one evening when the three of us went down to Lower Broad Street, where the Cameo Parkway Records offices and studios were. It was kind of Philadelphia's label, and it was the only label we were aware of. It was the golden era of the dance craze song and they all came out of the Cameo Parkway Studios."

Unaware that being white might be an impediment to attracting interest from a largely black music label, Rundgren and Reed, both only 17, walked in and presented themselves to the company. "We thought that we could just walk in and audition," Rundgren remembers, "like they'd take anybody. While they had a couple of token white artists, it was mostly all black artists who did songs about dances like Chubby Checker's 'The Twist,' Dee Dee Sharp's 'The Mashed Potato,' and 'The Watusi' by The Orlons. So when that didn't work out, we went to an arcade somewhere around Broad or Market Street, where they still had one of those Make-A-Record booths, and the three of us crammed into it and did a song. It sure would be great if we still had that disc, but God knows where it is now!"

Increasingly drawn to the urban music scene of downtown Philadelphia, and bored with life in the suburbs, Rundgren and Reed became frequent commuters. "When I was old enough to be independent," says Rundgren, "I just had this yen to constantly go into the city which, first of all, involved either hitch-hiking or taking the bus from Westbrook Park to 69th Street, the western border of

Philadelphia, where the terminus of the subway was. We'd ride on the El, which was elevated until it got to about 40th or something, and from the train, just as the El turned into the subway, you could see people lined up around the studio where they taped *American Bandstand.*"

By 1966, the 18-year-old Todd Rundgren, having more or less lived at Reed's house for the previous year, made the bold move to leave home and take a serious stab at being a professional musician. He packed a few belongings into an old typewriter case – "the only thing I had that resembled a suitcase" – and boarded a bus to Ocean City, on the New Jersey shore.

"It was something I had been determined to do for a number of years before I actually did it," says Rundgren. "I was just so relieved to get out of that environment and to be able to make my own decisions at that point that I really didn't care, at first, what happened at all. Everything that happened to me, after that, was kind of fortuitous and anybody who claims that they completely owned their success is full of crap. Being where I am now is as much a product of circumstances as my seizing the moment; if I'd seized the wrong moment, there might be no moment to seize at all. A lot of it was just dumb luck."

Rundgren had arranged to meet up with a local musician in Ocean City, but by the time he arrived, the man had been arrested, leaving Rundgren with no connections in a strange town. He wandered around the streets with no place to stay, eventually finding his way to an all-night diner, where he spent the night. "I remember thinking, 'Right, I'm going to live the dream now; I'm going to sit at a diner at 2am and drink coffee.' I had never drunk coffee before and it made me horribly sick. I didn't have any food and it just attacked my stomach like crazy and it made me really ill. I wandered around for a while until someone gave me a place to crash."

Rundgren met a drummer by the name of Joe DiCarlo, who gave him a place to stay and a tip about an upcoming concert, to take place in nearby New Hope, Pennsylvania, featuring The Byrds, The Shadows Of Knight, and a local band called Woody's Truck Stop. Rundgren didn't know the last band, but knew a lot about their lead guitarist, Alan Miller. Miller had gained national attention after *Time* magazine had written about his expulsion from school for having long hair. After the courts ruled that Miller, an 'A student,' could continue to attend school by telephone, he had become a hero to students everywhere.

"He had beaten the system," Rundgren recalls. "His excuse for why he had to have long hair was because he was the guitar player in a band, which was the same excuse I used all through high school. Only by this time, I was out of high school, anyway, so I didn't fucking care. I could grow my hair as long as I wanted."

Attending the New Hope show, Rundgren and DiCarlo were particularly impressed with Woody's Truck Stop and vowed to see them again. "They kind of tore it up," recalls Rundgren, "especially compared to some of the other bands. What they did was mostly blues and R&B covers, like maybe Sam & Dave's 'Hold On I'm Coming' or 'Said I Wasn't Gonna Tell Nobody,' but they were pretty cool."

Having learned that the band would be playing later that same weekend at the Artists' Hut, back in Philadelphia, Rundgren and DiCarlo vowed to attend the show and introduce themselves to the group. "The club was down on Walnut Street," recalls Rundgren, "in what would have been a basement apartment turned into a club that might have held about 80 people if it was totally packed. Woody's Truck Stop never had a full time drummer and seemed to have had trouble holding on to one. Joe was pretty aggressive and asked if he could jam with the band, so he got up and slayed them with this whole Buddy Rich thing. When they asked him to join the band, he told them, 'I'll join the band if you let my friend join the band too.' By then, I was able to play a convincing slide guitar, which nobody in the band presently did, so they agreed to let me in because it made the line-up of the band an exact duplicate of the Paul Butterfield band. Over the course of weeks, we became like the hottest thing there."

Rundgren admits that while he had very little stage experience, he faced the fear and did it anyway. This would later become one of his guiding principles in life. "There are certainly circumstances," Rundgren admits, "where it's kind of stupid not to be apprehensive about what's going on, but I eventually determined that fear was a useless emotion in most cases. My personal mantra is, 'It doesn't help to panic.' No matter what's happening, or how horrible it is, panicking will not make it better. You've just got to resign yourself to the best option possible."

Rundgren says that this combination of blind faith, confidence, and dumb luck was not something bred into him at home. "My parents had no qualms about saying that they thought aliens had left me," laughs Rundgren. "I remember watching *Father Knows Best* and *Ozzie & Harriet* and stuff like that on TV, and thinking, 'Why wasn't I born to them instead of these people?' I don't remember my parents saying, 'Yeah, go do that' very often. It was more, 'Don't do that.'"

Rundgren says he was advanced a little money from Woody's Truck Stop to pay down his first serious guitar, a used gold top Les Paul with 'soap bar' pickups, which he found in a pawnshop on Philadelphia's notorious South Street. "It was still a borderline neighborhood then," he says. "All pimp clothes, hock shops, and luncheonettes. I got the thing for $85. I don't think the guy in the store knew how much it was really worth."

With increased live work, Rundgren began to show real talent on the slide guitar, but as he became a sensation within the band, tensions developed between himself and bandleader Alan Miller. "People would come to see me," says Rundgren, "and I think he was also pissed off that I was considered 'cuter' in those days. We kind of became the most popular band in town and we had enough gigs to be making some money so that was enough at the time. I mean, we probably thought it would be great to make a record but we were doing mostly cover songs. How were we ever going to get to make a record from covering other people's B-sides?"

While Rundgren was impatient to record, he was also beginning to lose interest in the Truck Stop's trippy blues, particularly in contrast to the exciting new sounds he was hearing from The Beatles and The Who. When the Truck Stop announced their plans to decamp to the country and become more "like the Grateful Dead," Rundgren saw the writing on the wall. It was time to move on.

In his eight-month career with the Truck Stop, however, Rundgren was introduced to two significant contacts. One was Carson Van Osten, an art student who occasionally played bass for the band, and the other was Paul Fishkin, a fan of the band who had lent them money to buy equipment. Fishkin had been impressed with Rundgren's creative energy and musicality, and was among the first people to use the word "genius" to describe him. He would later play a pivotal role in getting that genius out to the world.

Resolved to leave, Rundgren stayed on with Woody's Truck Stop for a few high profile shows with Jefferson Airplane and Cream, as well as an unproductive demo session in which the band recorded a Rundgren/Miller composition entitled 'Why Is It Me?' (later reworked as Nazz's 'Lemming Song'). After one Woody's Truck Stop show, opening for Al Kooper's band, The Blues Project, at Philadelphia's Town Hall, Rundgren was gone, determined that his next band would record original songs and be signed to a major label.

"Getting a record deal became the Holy Grail," says Rundgren, "but it wasn't like we were thinking, 'Oh, I have all these ideas about what I want to do with records.' It was a means to an end. In the 60s, when I first became aware of recording, I really had no concept of what the experience of going into a studio to make a record would be like. You just knew that, with a hit record, you could radically expand the size of your audience. After I got out of high school, music was no longer just a pastime. I wanted to try and make some kind of a serious living out of this. A lot of it was not necessarily musical as much as visceral. The first time you see the Beatles in *A Hard Day's Night*, they're being chased down the street simply because they play a guitar. The math is not difficult to parse when you see that having a hit record equals all of your sexual frustrations being satisfied. So, in the end, it was also about getting laid and getting paid [laughs]. It wasn't until I was in Nazz that I did have that experience."

Founded in 1967, Nazz grew out of Rundgren's desire to be America's answer to The Beatles, combining their native Philly vocal harmonies with the 'flash' of trendy UK pop and the kick of heavier bands like The Who and The Yardbirds. "The late 60s stuff," says Rundgren, "like The Beatles after *Sgt Pepper*, but even the British Invasion just before it, had started the whole thing where anybody who could put four or five guys together could conceivably get signed. If they were cute enough, with some singable songs, that was pretty much all it took. It seemed like this giant boon to singing white kids."

Unsure of his own voice at this stage, Rundgren recruited Robert 'Stewkey' Antoni, from a local band called Elizabeth, as Nazz's lead singer. He also found drummer Thom Mooney, then playing with Munchkin, and tracked down bassist Carson Van Osten, who had earlier left Woody's Truck Stop to pursue a fine arts degree at Philadelphia College of Art.

Nazz spent far more time rehearsing, above Bartoff & Warfield's record store on Chestnut Street, than they did gigging. Aside from a few impressive gigs, such as opening for The Doors at Town Hall, Nazz kept a relatively low profile locally. When they did step out and play, padding their sets with covers like The Who's 'My Generation,' The Yardbirds' 'Nazz Are Blue,' or soul numbers like Smokey Robinson's 'Ooo Baby Baby,' the high volume of their performances would often get them thrown out of the coffee houses they had been booked into.

Rundgren was more concerned with a recording career, anyway, and happy to put the nascent Nazz into the incubator as they worked out their original repertoire. As he developed his own songs, though, he began to feel the strong influence of New York singer-songwriter Laura Nyro. "I really discovered Laura's music around that time," says Rundgren, "all the major seventh chords and variations on augmented and suspended chords, especially when I wrote on piano. Four-note chords just sounded better to me. But when I'm writing a song, I'm not thinking 'I want to sound like Laura Nyro.' At that point, I'm more struggling to find a way to sound like myself."

If Nazz were to be the American Beatles, they found their own Brian Epstein in promoter John Kurland. Kurland had been the publicist for The Mamas And The Papas and other important acts of the day, and saw the Nazz as potential teen sensations. On Labor Day, 1967, he and his assistant, Michael Friedman, took over the group's management and moved them all into a house in Great Neck, Long Island, to prepare them for a whirlwind recording career.

After recording four demo discs, some of them engineered by future Rundgren assistant engineer Chris Andersen, the band were finally signed, in 1968, by Atlantic subsidiary SGC (Screen Gems Columbia) and flown to Los Angeles to make their debut album at ID Sound, also known as Ivan David Sound, a shoebox-shaped studio on La Brea near Sunset. Rundgren was thrilled finally to get to make a record and came into the studio eager to learn how it was all done.

"I didn't know anything about production at that point," says Rundgren. "I had done demo sessions in studios but never really looked at the console, and thought I should know what all that stuff did. We had an English engineer [on the Nazz debut] named Chris Huston, who we'd met in New York, and he came out to LA with us."

The titular producer of the Nazz debut was one Bill Traut who, according to Rundgren, was not their first choice. "We had tried to get some other producers. I think we wanted an English producer, because we wanted it to sound like an English record. We wanted the guy who produced the John Mayall & The Bluesbreakers record, Mike Vernon, or maybe it was the engineer, Gus Dudgeon, who we really wanted. We didn't realize that, in a lot of cases, all a producer did was to make sure the session got finished. We were all about sound, and 'How did that record sound so good?' And that was probably the engineer! We should have been looking for an Eddie Kramer or someone like that, instead of a producer."

Having no luck finding an Englishman, they had settled on Traut, who had produced records by The Shadows Of Knight, The Count Five, and H.P. Lovecraft. While Rundgren had been impressed by some of these records, he found himself less impressed by the man himself. "He was this old fashioned kind of producer," says Rundgren, "the type who only made sure the sessions didn't run too long. That was all they were there for, you know? They were there to hire the musical contractor and collect the union forms. All he did was sit in the control room and read the trades while we were recording."

With Traut in the absent father role, Todd Rundgren seized the opportunity to step up and exert his own tastes on the recordings, learning production technique as he went along. "ID Sound," he recalls, "had one studio room and a little mixing room behind the studio. The producer just whipped through the mixes in a day or two, like he had some place to be, and then he was gone. So I got it into my head, 'Well, he's gone now, so why don't we just mix it again, more like the way we want it?' Our engineer didn't mind if we went and just started diddling around on the board, grabbing some knobs and pushing them up and down and things."

Set free on the console, Rundgren had his first experience with the world of frequency control. Always fascinated by technology and music, he delved deeper into the means of recording. "The consoles back then weren't super sophisticated," says Rundgren, "and they didn't have continuously variable parametric EQ. I had no idea what they actually did until I got that first-hand sort of feedback of turning the knob and hearing the sound change. I mean, I knew about tone controls on a hi-fi, or a guitar even, highs and lows, more or less, but that was it. The idea of discreet frequencies that you could boost and cut, and stuff like that, was new to me. It was pretty much trial and error."

After "messing about with equalizers" in the studio, Rundgren says he began to get a better idea about the relationship between certain instrumental combinations and their inherent sonic qualities. This seemingly insignificant insight would come to influence his entire future career as a producer.

By October of 1968 and the release of *Nazz,* mixed at Sigma Sound in Philadelphia and the Record Plant in New York, Rundgren had taken a stronger role in the band's overall sound. In addition to the songwriting, Rundgren brought much of the sonic character to tracks like the phase-shifted 'Open My Eyes' and the vibraphone-heavy Nazz original version of 'Hello It's Me' (with Antoni on lead vocal). He even took an early stab at string arranging on 'If That's The Way You Feel.' The producer in him had been awakened and, in a short self-written bio from the time, Rundgren confessed that his dream was to own a "huge recording studio on a mountain by the beaches of California, overlooking the Pacific Ocean."

Being blatant Anglophiles, Nazz and their managers felt that their next album should be recorded at the source: London. Unfortunately, after one brief session for a song called 'Christopher Columbus' at Trident Studios in Soho – chosen because The Beatles had recorded 'Hey Jude' and tracks from *The Beatles* there – sessions were abruptly suspended when the British Musician's Union indicated that their managers had wrongly booked their work permits as an instrumental group, a significantly different status from the vocal group they so clearly were.

"Trident was a brand new studio," says Rundgren, "and we were excited to be recording there but we only got one night before the union got wind that we were there. It was a totally fucked-up situation and, as a result, we never did get to finish the record and had to fly back to LA to finish the album at ID Sound. The only positive about the whole experience was that, while were there, we got to shop for new clothes on Carnaby Street, Liberty of London, and a bunch of other places."

When Nazz returned to Los Angeles, their managers introduced them to an engineer who would become a considerable accomplice to Rundgren in the coming years, James Lowe (also known as Thaddeus James Lowe). Like Rundgren, Lowe was a musician with a musical understanding of studio engineering. He had recently left his band, The Electric Prunes, whose single 'I Had Too Much To Dream Last Night' remains a landmark in psychedelic garage rock. Kurland and Friedman had also been guiding Lowe's independent production and engineering career, so an introduction was inevitable.

"Todd came over to ID Sound," says Lowe, "and we started talked about an album they wanted to do. I think Todd liked that I was working, at that time, with [LA arranging genius] Van Dyke Parks, so he probably went 'Oh all right, you must be okay then.' He had warned me ahead of time it was gonna be long hours and he wondered if I'd have any problems staying up late at night, which actually proved to be true; it proved to be a pretty long and extensive album project."

Lowe got on well with Rundgren and noticed that the guitarist had developed into the alpha dog of the Nazz, the producer in all but official title. "It's kind of hard to define the role of producer," says Lowe. "I mean, technically, Todd should have been credited as producer. Todd was strong enough that he could be the producer on it, and I had no problem with that."

While the band holed up in a hotel, golden goose Rundgren was sequestered, Brian Wilson style, in his own apartment across town. To top it off, many of Rundgren's newer piano-based compositions, on which he insisted on nudging out Stewkey to sing lead vocals, bore the undeniable influence of his new favorite,

Laura Nyro, for whom the other Nazz members had no such love. The inevitable rift came between the band and their prodigious leader.

"Todd was just very 'on it' in the studio," says Lowe. "He was kind of frustrated at times with the other guys because he was a step ahead of them, but then again, Todd was a step ahead of everybody. And he was just this East Coast Philly kid, with limitless energy. I recognized immediately he was very talented; he could play anything. He played the piano and some guitar leads that I think are blistering, but he could also pick up a saxophone and learn how to play it in ten minutes. Sometimes, he'd sort of have to talk the others into playing something, when I know he could have grabbed their instrument and done it himself. It was the same with the vocals."

As Rundgren delved deeper into the sonic architecture of music production, he actively sought to widen the palette of instrumentation with which he would paint the band's recordings. He assembled a glass harmonica out of wine glasses on the studio floor and took day trips to Studio Instrument Rentals, from whose warehouse he began to draw an exotic assortment of hired instruments. *Fungo Bat*, the working title for their intended double album, would either be the Nazz's masterpiece or their swansong, but either way, Rundgren was going to throw in everything bar the kitchen sink to make it a memorable listening experience.

Always interested in tape-speed experiments and reel flanging, Rundgren enjoyed a moment of mechanical happenstance while mixing a song written about Paul Fishkin, his friend from the Woody's Truck Stop days. 'Hang On Paul' featured an unintentional warbling effect caused by a glitch in the tape-speed controls during mixdown. Rundgren, however, grew to enjoy this psychedelic effect, so it stayed in.

As they had on the first album, Nazz took the LA session tapes back to the East Coast to add some orchestration and other overdubs. In addition to working out of Sigma Sound in their native Philadelphia, Rundgren and Lowe booked a memorable session at New York's Regent Sound where, according to Lowe, the 20-year-old boy wonder once again impressed him by scoring the charts all by himself, despite having had no formal training as an arranger.

"We were going to lay the strings and horn parts on 'A Beautiful Song' in New York," recalls Lowe, "and the night before we went in, I said, 'What are they gonna play?' Todd said, 'I don't know. I gotta go home and write it.' So I said, 'Have you ever done it before?' He said, 'No.' He told me he'd gotten this book on how to write string and horn arrangements, so he went back home and wrote all the parts out himself."

At the session, many of the players balked when they read the score, littered as it was with 'mistakes,' and broken rules. Lowe recalls that the murmuring stopped, however, when they played the piece as written. "All of a sudden they realized, 'Hey, this guy's a step ahead, man,'" says Lowe. "So it came out good for somebody who had never scored anything before. Todd just had no fear. He didn't have any limitations and he was looking to the right things for inspiration and stuff."

Rundgren may not have had any limitations of his own, but his plans for *Fungo Bat* to be released as a double album hit a severe roadblock when SGC decided, with the apparent endorsement of his bandmates, to pare it down to a single disc, released in May of 1969 as *Nazz Nazz*.

Rundgren was frustrated with Nazz, and Nazz were equally resentful of his dominance. The band limped forward until the fall when, prompted by the departure of Carson Van Osten, Rundgren himself left the band. Stewkey and Mooney continued to trade as Nazz for some time, but even they had packed it in by the time the remaining *Fungo Bat* tracks were released by SGC under the suitably uninspired title of *Nazz III*. As a parting shot, Rundgren's lead vocals on several tunes on the album had been removed and replaced with Stewkey. "They called me," says James Lowe, "and asked me if I would mix up their leftover stuff for *Nazz III*. I wouldn't accept the 'producer' credit, though; it was Todd's album."

Somewhat jaded, yet still only 21, Rundgren had already seen too much of band life. In the summer of 1969, after briefly considering chucking the whole business and becoming a computer programmer, he decided that, from that point forward, he would stay strictly behind the board, as a producer. Or so he thought. He moved to New York that summer to share an apartment with constant supporter Paul Fishkin. The two began to infiltrate the Greenwich Village club world, particularly Steve Paul's Scene, and Rundgren got to know a whole cast of Manhattan musicians and fashion designers.

Although he had severed ties with John Kurland, he was pleasantly surprised to get a call from Kurland's old assistant, Michael Friedman, who was now working in the New York offices of legendary folk-rock manager Albert Grossman. Friedman was offering Rundgren a staff engineer and producer job with Grossman's company. Friedman's invitation would radically alter the trajectory of Todd Rundgren's entire recording career.

Strictly Bearsville

At the invitation of Michael Friedman, Todd Rundgren found himself walking into the Manhattan offices of Albert Grossman, who also spent a great deal of his time in and around Woodstock, New York, running the careers of Bob Dylan, The Band, Peter Paul & Mary, Richie Havens, Gordon Lightfoot, The Paul Butterfield Blues Band, Ian & Sylvia, and Janis Joplin. Having made his name as a manager during the 60s, Grossman (who passed away in 1986) had recently built Bearsville Studios, near Woodstock, and had started a joint record company venture, Ampex Records, with the tape company of the same name. Eventually, Grossman's signings began to appear under the Bearsville Records imprint; by 1972, Bearsville had left the Ampex umbrella in favor of a long-term distribution deal with Warner Bros Records.

Grossman had dispatched Friedman to fill positions for the new studio and label, but according to Friedman himself, Grossman was iffy about letting the ex-Nazz singer loose in his rustic woodland artist colony. "Initially he didn't like Todd or think he was talented," Friedman told journalist Barney Hoskyns in 1998, "but Todd was with me and I basically presented him as a producer. Even at that point, he was brilliant in the studio."

In Bob Dylan's autobiographical *Chronicles: Volume One*, the songwriter compared Grossman's voice to "the booming of war drums," adding "he didn't talk so much as growl." Rundgren was thrilled to join the Albert Grossman Organization, although he still describes their partnership as a "curious" one. "Your relationship with Albert is never just good or bad," Rundgren says today, "it's always both. He was notorious in terms of ultimately screwing his artists over. When he represents you, he screws other people over on your behalf, but when things go bad between you and him then he'll screw you over. So to have him on my side was definitely an advantage at that time."

One of the first acts Rundgren brought to Ampex was a Philadelphia band called The American Dream, whose eponymous album, recorded in August 1969, was one of the first records made at New York's brand new Record Plant Studio. As 1970 began, Rundgren flew down to Nashville to produce an album for Ian & Sylvia Tyson's band, The Great Speckled Bird, at Charlie Tallent Studios. A country-rock affair, the album featured some fine players, including pedal steel player Buddy Cage, guitarist Amos Garrett, piano player David Briggs, bassist Norbert Putnam, and the Tysons themselves. "*Great Speckled Bird* was an interesting production for me," says Rundgren, "because of Cage and Amos and, being in Nashville, I believe the rhythm section had played with Elvis."

Significantly, the drummer on the dates was Norman 'N.D.' Smart II, who hit it off with Rundgren immediately. Rundgren knew of Smart because they had shared a manager, in John Kurland, and because Smart's band Barry & The Remains had opened shows for both The Beatles and Nazz. This was the first time, however, they had worked together, and the two would stay behind while the others were on a break and record what Rundgren refers to as "little ditties," such as a song called 'Duly,' which featured Smart on lead vocals. "We found," says Smart, "that we could get almost as much done on the lunch break as other people could get done all day."

Once the Great Speckled Bird album was finished, Rundgren pledged to keep Smart in mind as a drummer he'd like to work with again, said his goodbyes, and returned to Woodstock, only to discover that Smart was actually living there too. Meanwhile, back at his day job, Rundgren found himself in a new studio with all new equipment, and a new staff who were equally unfamiliar with the untested recording gear. In the kingdom of the blind, the one-eyed man is king, and Rundgren took full advantage of the chaos of the new enterprise. In short order, Rundgren was promoted to Bearsville's house engineer and was helming sessions for bluesmen Paul Butterfield and James Cotton.

"When I first became a record producer," says Rundgren, "I thought, 'That's it, I'm done performing.' So they sent me off with various old folk artists that they had who needed to be upgraded [laughs]: people like Ian & Sylvia, James Cotton, and other artists in Albert's stable. I did a couple of sessions with Levon Helm's girlfriend, Libby Titus, and Albert hooked me up with all his new artists, like Jesse Winchester, whom I had to fly to Canada to work with."

Jesse Winchester was an American singer-songwriter, evading the Vietnam draft by living in Toronto, where he had caught the ear of The Band's Robbie Robertson. "I kind of felt bad for the guy," says Robertson of Winchester. "He was just hiding out up there and hoping to not go to prison. But he was really good and had great songs. I wanted to help Jesse make a record, so I talked to Albert about it and told him that I'd have to go up to Canada to do it but I really don't know who to work with up there. At the time it was very important who engineered and, frankly, a lot of the other staff engineers couldn't really do anything with real character or a real vibe to it. Albert said, 'Well, we use this young kind of studio whiz guy by the name of Todd.' So I said, 'Hey, sounds good to me!'"

Robertson recalls playing some of Winchester's demos for Rundgren, to get him acquainted with the songs, and noting that he caught on quickly. "You could describe what you were imagining for a song," says Robertson, "in abstract or poetic kinds of terms, and Todd could translate those ideas readily. Probably because he was a musician first, before he was an engineer."

Rundgren, Robertson, and Levon Helm flew to Toronto's Eastern Sound studio to record *Jesse Winchester*, assisted by a supporting cast of Toronto musicians. "We just went up there and knocked this baby out," says Robertson, "did a little bit more stuff in the studio with it in New York and mixed it. We had a great time doing it, and it was a great experience overall."

Around this time, Bearsville had also kept Rundgren busy with varied projects including a live album with The Paul Butterfield Blues Band and a band called Jericho. Worked to the bone, he now considers this early experience not only a great time, but invaluable from a developmental standpoint. "It was right after the first Winchester album," says Rundgren, "that The Band asked me to engineer their *Stage Fright* sessions. I think *Jesse Winchester* was a kind of run-through for that, because I was pretty quick to get the sounds and they liked that. They hadn't had to worry much about that part at all."

According to Robertson, The Band had initially intended to record *Stage Fright,* their third album, in the form of a free concert staged at the Woodstock Playhouse for the local townspeople, whom they felt had been unduly disturbed during the previous summer's Woodstock Music & Arts Festival in nearby Bethel, New York. The town still harbored lingering resentment toward the rock musicians and hippies who had disturbed their formerly quiet artists' enclave, however. "We'd felt really bad about it," laughs Robertson, "so, as a gesture, we thought we could just rehearse some new material and put on this private concert for the townspeople. The town council said 'Thanks, but no thanks.' I think they thought that the show would just attract more Volkswagen buses like the year before."

Amending their plan, The Band remained at the Woodstock Playhouse, but without an audience. They set up on the Playhouse stage, as they would for an actual show, while Rundgren fashioned himself a makeshift control room area, just off stage, and monitored the music mainly through headphones. "You could perform with the curtain closed," says Robertson of the Playhouse's acoustics, "and it would give you this dry sound. But if you opened the curtain you got the sound of the whole house in there."

For the first time, The Band was without producer John Simon. While this appeared to give Rundgren a freer hand, Simon, says Robertson, felt threatened by Todd's presence. "I think John thought that Todd was now taking over his position," says Robertson, "but Todd just came aboard as an engineer, you know? He wasn't looking for anything else. The whole process got weird, though, when some of the other guys in The Band didn't exactly like Todd either. I know Rick [Danko] didn't like Todd, Richard [Manuel] didn't care, and Garth was just in his own world. As a result, the vibe took some getting used to."

Rundgren admits that his youthful impertinence was often at odds with the rudderless and leisurely pace enjoyed by The Band at that time. "They made all their decisions collectively," says Rundgren, "which made the records take forever, especially in the mixing part of it. They would actually come in somewhat rehearsed, but to get them all on the same page to play it seemed like an ordeal. You'd say, 'Where's so and so?' Nobody knows. You'd just wait for them to show up. With my [self-diagnosed] ADD, I just could not match my pace to their pace."

Robertson admits that, Rundgren or no Rundgren, a cloud was hanging over The Band at that time. "There was just a lot of distraction in the air," says Robertson, "and a lot of drug experimenting going on. There was also just the intensity of this being our third record. We'd all go in there and wait until the mood struck, and Todd grew impatient wondering what we were waiting for. But we didn't know either. Todd was kind of bratty, and it took him quite a while to try to comprehend Garth Hudson's approach to music-making. He was like, 'What's with this guy?' It wasn't boring, you know? You just had to go with the flow."

"Over the course of a day," Rundgren adds, "they might only play a dozen takes. Levon would sometimes fall asleep under a pile of curtains in the theater and nobody would be able to find him."

Robertson defends their relaxed approach as one of the main reasons they had opted to record outside of a conventional studio, "where the clock's always running. It was a different philosophy, but mainly, it was due to everybody being, you know, just leaning over the edge of life. It was tricky, but we did some good stuff too, so it was worth it."

Robertson recalls the day that the mounting tension between Helm and Rundgren reached a breaking point. Various accounts of this incident describe Helm going after Rundgren with a drumstick after Rundgren had unwisely referred to The Band's bearded and beloved keyboard player, Garth Hudson, as an old man.

"There *was* a chase," says Robertson, just short of confirming the entire story, "and Todd ran. I didn't expect that."

Rundgren concedes that, while he can't recall it, the story may well be true. "Well," he laughs, "Garth *did* look a little like Santa Claus. But the bigger problem, one that kept us from getting takes, was Garth's narcolepsy. Garth would just nod right off, you know? I was always wondering, 'Should we wake him? Should we let him sleep?'"

What saved Rundgren from being fired was his sole defender, Robbie Robertson, who championed the upstart kid despite his youthful lack of diplomacy. "He didn't play by the rulebook of sound engineers," says Robertson. "I don't think he even knew the rulebook. As a result, he would be more experimental and I, for one, was interested in finding somebody who was gonna *do something* sonically. So many of the sounds on *Stage Fright*, and on Jesse's album, were just printed [to tape] the way they were meant to sound in the final mix. That took a certain confidence, on Todd's part, to be able to say, 'Well that's the way it should sound.' Some of the guys would be cracking comments, like 'Well that kinda sounds like shit!' I think Todd was trying to figure out how to make it work, given the situation, working in a theater and not a conventional studio."

"Getting the basic takes done at that theater," Rundgren admits, "was something of a tedious ordeal. We would have recorded in the Bearsville Studio but for the fact that it wasn't really completed. After we finished the record, we took all the equipment from the sound truck and moved it into what was Bearsville Studio B."

The mood at the Woodstock Playhouse was temporarily enlivened by a visit from songwriter Bob Neuwirth, legendary associate of Bob Dylan and a mainstay of the Greenwich Village folksinger clique. Accompanying Neuwirth on the trip up from Manhattan was a shy young lady he'd recently met in a bookstore who had impressed him with her poetry. Her name was Patti Smith. "I have a little diary from 1970," Smith says today, "and it says that on June 6th, Bobby Neuwirth took me up to a recording session in Woodstock and that Todd was engineering. I don't think I'd ever been inside a recording studio before, so it was a great opportunity for me to see how it all worked. I think they were doing 'Medicine Man' ['W.S. Walcott Medicine Show']. Bobby had gone off to talk to the other musicians who were hanging out, so the only people who were working at the time were Todd and Robbie."

Smith was impressed with both Rundgren and Robertson, whom she described as focused individuals. "I like workers," says Smith, plainly. "I didn't smoke pot or anything at the time, and Todd, at least back then, wasn't interested in drugs either. I really liked watching him work and, over the course of the evening, we got to talking and discovered that we had a roots connection in common; my grandparents were from his hometown of Upper Darby, Pennsylvania. He was very sweet, with a beautiful face, and the two of us were sort of these misfit types; I wanna say 'wallflowers.' He just didn't fit in with any of the people there. He was his own person and although we were both sort of anti-social we talked with each other all night."

According to Robertson, Rundgren's greatest contribution to *Stage Fright* was his ability to capture The Band, in all their ragged glory, at a difficult time in their career. "Todd managed to get what I'd call a Polaroid sound," says Robertson. "He did a great job on 'The Shape I'm In,' and 'Stage Fright,' and then, toward the end of the record, we did 'Daniel and The Sacred Harp,' and 'W.S. Walcott Medicine Show' and they all turned out to be real highlights. When we recorded 'Strawberry Wine,' Levon and Richard were in pretty bad shape, you know, and even that's on the tape. The situation behind the scenes is in the sound as well; there are no disguises on this record."

Still, for all of Robertson's praise, The Band enlisted a better-known UK producer, Glyn Johns, to do a final mix of *Stage Fright*, in addition to Rundgren's. "I think Levon actually knew Glyn," says Robertson, "so it wasn't necessarily an act of aggression against Todd. Todd had done some early mixes in Woodstock and I think the consensus was that they were a little haphazard. It was agreed that the mixes needed to be done better, more professionally."

Rundgren lays some of the blame on Bearsville's untested control room, and the group's lack of consensus about how the record should sound. "We were mixing on these speakers that no one was really sure about," Rundgren recalls, "plus it was never as if there was someone who could say, 'Okay that's it.' In the end, they sent me over to England with all the master tapes. They booked Glyn Johns into some favorite place of his where he was comfortable working. I, on the other hand, was booked into this studio I had never been in before – it might have been Trident or something – and they had these Tannoy speakers, which I didn't like."

According to Rundgren, the two engineers would mix a reel each and then swap reels until each had mixed a completed version of the entire album. Rundgren then brought both sets of tapes back to The Band, who, naturally, failed to come to a consensus about either set.

"We ended up using some of Todd's mixes," says Robertson, "but the consensus was that Glyn had better captured the songs, so we used more of his mixes. But Todd had printed most of the sounds anyway, so the difference was minor, to me at least."

With *Stage Fright* worked out of his system, Rundgren confidently assumed his role as Bearsville's "boy wonder," in the words of Albert Grossman's widow, Sally, who recalled her impressions of him to writer Barney Hoskyns in 1998. "To be such a renaissance man as he was at the age of 21," Grossman said, "was very striking. We were spoiled, of course, because we were so used to brilliant people ... but he was like all of them, his talent was already full-blown."

Rundgren next attempted to produce Jesse Winchester's follow-up album, *Third Down 110 To Go*, but this time the magic vibe from Winchester's debut eluded them. *Third Down* would be shelved for two years, by which time Rundgren had worked his magic on *Taking Care Of Business*, an album by James Cotton's Blues Band, which was mostly recorded live off the floor at LA's ID Sound and reunited Rundgren with engineer James Lowe. The Cotton album featured a rotating cast of players, including keyboard player Mark Klingman, known to his friends as 'Moogy.' Klingman's band, The Glitter House, had dissolved around the same time as Nazz and he and Rundgren had met up while they were both jamming at Steve Paul's Scene. Klingman recalls flying out to Los Angeles to help him with personnel for the Cotton project.

"On drums," says Klingman, "I got Richie Hayward from Little Feat for a lot of it, but Norman Smart came out too. We had around five different guitar players, Todd played on a lot of it but we also had James's guitarist, Matt Murphy, Domenic Troiano, and our friends from out East, like Mike Bloomfield and Johnny Winter, who we all knew from Steve Paul's. I introduced Todd to Ralph Schuckett, a keyboard player, and he played accordion on one cut. Tom Cosgrove, who we got in for a later Todd session, sang on it, as did Cissy Houston."

"Edgar Winter even came in one night," says James Lowe, "he recorded some stuff, or at least he was part of the revolving cast who came by and jammed with everybody; I don't know if it got on the record. James was a good guy and he was interested in Todd. He realized that Todd was bright and he trusted him."

In addition to producing tracks for a Klingman solo album, Rundgren took one futile stab at producing Grossman's wildest act, Janis Joplin, who was, as it turned out, not long for the world. Rundgren flew out to Joplin's then home in Marin

County, north of San Francisco, to work with the troubled diva, but the sessions soon fell apart. Rundgren remembers that he considered Joplin too temperamental at that time and was also dismayed to find The Paul Butterfield Blues Band, contracted to back Joplin for the session, too hard to direct. He also felt constricted working in a union studio where he was not allowed, even as producer, to touch the board. The situation came to a head; Joplin fired Rundgren, completing what would be her final album, *Pearl*, with Doors producer Paul A. Rothchild. Rundgren says he lost no sleep over the firing, but learned a valuable lesson: It doesn't matter how big the artist is, if you're not going to enjoy the sessions, don't take it on.

Although Rundgren had foresworn his own music in favor of the producer's chair, those "little ditties" he'd made with Norman Smart back in Nashville had been more fun than he cared to admit. After a time, he approached Grossman about making an album of his own. Surprisingly, Grossman, with some urging from Paul Fishkin, agreed to let Rundgren make what would become his debut album as a solo artist, *Runt*.

"I don't think Albert kept that kind of distinction between star producer and star artist client," says Rundgren. "I was always problematic that way and it probably would have been worse for a different kind of manager than Albert, who was used to dealing with people who could be very self-directed, temperamental, or mercurial, like The Band, Bob Dylan, and Janis Joplin. And I wasn't concerned with satisfying record company demands. My attitude was, just make the record you make and then hope that the label can find a way to promote it. In fact," he laughs, "I kind of expected the label to just eat the loss!"

Nonetheless, Rundgren had structured a proposal that would insure Grossman's loss would, at least, be minimal. "I didn't get an actual advance for *Runt*," says Rundgren. "I just asked for a recording budget to pay the studio costs. The way I saw it, I was making pretty good money from the production work. In fact, I had no idea how much money I even had in the bank. If I needed cash, I would show up at the accountants and they would just give me hundreds or thousands of dollars," he laughs. "All I had to do was just do the work and the money would take care of itself."

A far more pressing issue for Rundgren was that of how to define his own sound as a solo artist. With Nazz he had established himself as a musician, songwriter, and producer, but who was Todd Rundgren the solo performer? "I could hold a melody well enough," he says, "and I'd sung on a bunch of songs for the second Nazz album, but it takes a different kind of stamina to be a lead singer, performing the whole song top to bottom. In a studio, I could stop the tape as many times as I needed to in order to catch a breath, so my principal concern was just staying in tune and I didn't have a great dynamic range. As a result, when I eventually recorded *Runt*, I was still imitating other singers and I had no particular voice of my own."

Rundgren admits he was a reluctant performer and notes that his expectations were radically different when he produced his own recordings, in comparison to those with other artists. "When I work on a production with somebody else," says Rundgren "I expect that they have most of the material written before they show up, so that when they get to the studio, it's time to perform. But when I'm the artist, it's essentially an interactive process and I use the studio, or whatever is passing for a studio – like my laptop, nowadays – to assist in creating a performance."

For Rundgren, it helps if one knows exactly what the role of a producer entails. "For me, the job is to figure out exactly what are the artist's shortcomings, in terms of making a record. If they don't have songs, or lyrics, I may have to write them for the artist and let them take credit for it," he laughs. "But when I do my own records, I don't think so much like a producer. I'm kind of just letting it happen."

Rundgren describes self-production as more of "an evolutionary process" and relates the process to different approaches in art and sculpture. "Working alone is for the most part, additive," he says, "like sculpting with clay. Working with a band is subtractive, like sculpting with stone, where you chisel away at everyone's ideas and pick out the good ones. When I'm composing, by myself, it's just my own sort of internal process. I'll start with something very rudimentary, a rhythm pattern or a bassline or something and, over time, that gets layered up and evolves into something more complete sounding. It's not strictly trial and error; I usually start out with some sort of overall feeling of where I want to go [but] I rarely have an idea of what the specific lyrics would be about, so I can't yet say, 'This is chorus, this is verse.' I'm just kind of wandering around in a musical area, waiting for whatever it is that I come up with to start coalescing and tell me where it's supposed to go."

For *Runt*, Rundgren elected to return to ID Sound, in LA, where he could once again work with James Lowe. As promised, he called on his Woodstock neighbor, Norman Smart, to come out and play the drums, but found that Smart had a prior engagement that precluded his involvement. While Rundgren's experience in Nazz had given him a taste for playing multiple instruments in the studio, his preference at this point was still to have a live bass player and drummer cutting the basic tracks with him. His recent days jamming at Steve Paul's Scene had introduced him to the brothers Hunt and Tony Sales, a drummer and bass player respectively, the teenage sons of iconic American TV host Soupy Sales. Although they were based in Hollywood, they had spent their summers getting to know the New York music scene where, Tony Sales recalls, they first met Rundgren.

"I hadn't really heard Nazz," says Sales, "so I didn't know who Todd was, I was more steeped in Cream, Hendrix, and all those people. When we got to the Scene, everybody was there, members of Zeppelin, Janis, Van Morrison; it was just ludicrous! Hunt and me had been waiting to get a chance to jam, when someone eventually said, 'Okay guys, you can get up with Todd now.' We got up with him and started jamming out some improvisational stuff, some bluesy Cream kinda stuff, just thrashing around, and it sounded great."

As it happened, the Sales brothers were due to head home to Hollywood for school in September. They exchanged phone numbers with Rundgren and vowed to keep in touch. "I was about 17," says Tony Sales, "and Hunt was only 14 and, you know, we didn't go to school much, but we came back out of legal necessity. Then, about two weeks later Todd called us and said he was coming out to LA and did we want to do this album with him. We said sure."

"I figured," says Rundgren, matter-of-factly, "that since I'd jammed with Hunt and Tony and they were the only people I knew out there, I'd get them to do the basic tracks with me. They hadn't done much actual recording, and I recall that Hunt, who was only 14, was a little unsteady, time-wise, back then. They were so used to jamming, so the challenge was to kind of pare everything down and start hearing things in terms of song structures as opposed to twelve-bar jams."

Arriving in Los Angeles, Rundgren took an apartment, rounded up the skeleton crew of Lowe and the Sales brothers, and loaded into ID Sound, still unsure what songs he would actually record. Tony Sales recalls frequent visits from Rundgren's then girlfriend, Miss Christine [Christine Frka], from the notorious Frank Zappa endorsed "groupie group," the GTOs, or Girls Together Outrageously. "Miss Christine brought up Miss Pamela, Pamela Miller," says Sales, "who later became Pamela Des Barres, and I starting having a thing with her. I mean, she had a thing with *everybody*. She wrote about all of this in her book, *I'm With The Band*."

According to James Lowe, however, hard work, not socializing, was the dominant mode of the day. "Hunt and Tony were in with a different crowd of people," says Lowe, "and Todd was from the East and just knew fewer people out here. So it could be social, to keep everybody feeling loose, but we really put it to it and got a really intense feeling from everybody. I hear it in those tracks still, everybody just having a good time."

While the Nazz recordings at ID had been done strictly eight-track, Rundgren recalls being excited about having a Stephens 16-track machine for the *Runt* sessions. "It was a very rare unit," says Rundgren, "with no pinch rollers on it. Instead, it had this thing that was all done with tension and tape contact with a spindle that essentially would determine the speed by adjusting tape and the tension in the motors. Working in 16 tracks meant that the bass would always have its own track and we could splurge and dedicate as many as five channels for drums. There wasn't a lot of noodling around, it was either guitar or piano on the basic tracks."

James Lowe says that Rundgren was keen on discrete close miking on every drum in the kit, a technique that he says was not yet the norm in 1970. "Most folks," says Lowe, "were doing your basic overhead right and left splash miking. The beauty [of close miking] was that you could take one of the tom toms and put it through a limiter and squash it and stretch the sound a little bit and those kinds of things to make it sound different. We used to do that particularly with the snare drum, to create a lot of different sounds with it, after the fact. We'd end up with six or seven tracks of just the drums, which we would submix down."

An easy camaraderie developed between Lowe and Rundgren, which Lowe feels was based on the fact that they both thought as much like musicians as engineers. "I looked at engineering differently from a union engineer at a big company or something," says Lowe. "So we were able to actually create something rather than going by standards. One thing that characterizes pretty much all of the work that I did with Todd is that everything is EQ'ed really top-endy. I'd take it places and people would say 'What's wrong with this record?' because it had so much sparkle to it. Well, in those days, with analog tape, you'd take your final mixes to mastering and you'd always lose a noticeable amount of presence in the transfer to disc. Then, after transmission to the radio it got even more muted and rounded out. So, in Todd's mind, he could compensate for that by making everything bright and sparkly. I guess if there was probably any area that we were a little remiss in, it was that we didn't put a lot of bottom end in. We'd do a bass track, but it wasn't a real fat sound because it just didn't go with everything being so bright and sparkly."

Lowe also says that the small room at ID Sound presented a few necessary limitations on the recordings, such as how many people could fit in the room. "I'd say you could probably fit about 15 musicians in there, tops," he recalls. "Plus, it was right on La Brea, so every time trucks went by, the control room would shake."

Lowe also recalls Rundgren seeming less frustrated than he had been during the Nazz sessions. "I didn't see the same things going on with him that he'd had with the Nazz members," says Lowe. "He didn't seem to have to work Hunt and Tony so much; all you'd have to do was light the fuse and they were gone. Of course, sometimes they would go into the wrong area," he laughs, "but you could always bring 'em back. Thing is, if somebody doesn't light the fuse in the first place, you can never get it going. I think what I saw in those sessions was Todd being more able to really lead a group. If you go back and listen to it, it's very sophisticated material, especially for a guy so young."

According to Tony Sales, the team would cut an average of two or three basic tracks a day, recording over out-takes to save tape. He was excited by the raw energy of Rundgren's material. "I remember cutting 'Devil's Bite' and 'Broke Down And Busted,'" says Sales, "and thinking, 'Fuckin' that's it, I'm into this!' All that bluesy stuff, I loved his guitar playing, and it was just so different from any of the other stuff I had been hearing. He was also doing some great, Laura Nyro-like, things on the piano. And ID was such a cool little studio, with a really old tile floor and old machines from the late 50s or early 60s with big knobs on 'em. We'd go in, Todd would run through the song once or twice, and we'd throw our own shit in there too. There's some great feel music on there; real peaks and valleys."

According to Lowe, Rundgren quickly proved himself adept at building up copious layers of his own background vocals. "We would do those right in the control room," recalls Lowe. "We'd drag a Neumann U-87, or a 67, in there – a real discrete microphone and just perfect for Todd at the time – and hang it over the console. Todd would sit and do background vocals, sometimes singing so soft you would think nothing would come out of it, but then you'd combine all four tracks and the playback would be these glorious harmonies. Years later, I ran into Kenny Rogers in the studio and, hearing that I'd done those records with Todd, he said 'That guy's the best background vocalist I ever heard in my life, man.'"

'We Gotta Get You A Woman,' yet another song inspired by Rundgren's friend Paul Fishkin, had lyrics loosely based on the pair's "post hanging days" in Greenwich Village. It would become Rundgren's first solo hit single. After the piano, bass, and drums had been recorded for the song, Lowe watched in amazement as Rundgren personally added all the harmonies, percussion, handclaps, and guitars. "When we'd tracked it," says Lowe, "it was just three guys playing instruments and there's no vocal on it yet. So I had no idea what this was going to turn into. Then, after the magic had been added, it really sounded like a hit single. The last line just sent me out: 'And when we're through with you, we'll get me one too.' What a way to end it! I remember thinking, 'If this ain't a hit, what is?'"

Rundgren's penchant for layering his own voice resulted in one of his earliest experiments, 'There Are No Words,' a Beach Boys-like precursor to the sort of vocal-only excursions Rundgren would eventually get into on his *A Cappella* album, 15 years later.

While *Runt* features a smash-cut medley comprised of 'Baby Let's Swing,' 'The Last Thing You Said,' and 'Don't Tie My Hands,' Sales recalls that any of the three, plus a tragically lost fourth song, would have been standouts on their own. "I loved the Motown-ish vibe on 'Don't Tie My Hands,'" says Sales. "It was really cookin.' I didn't really know why he didn't use that whole song. 'Baby Let's Swing' could have been great on its own too, but what's really sad is that we did another song that got destroyed. We had just finished this track and, instead of pushing the stop button, Todd must have pushed the reverse and forward button at the same time and the tape snagged and snapped and got all tangled up. It was a sad moment. Everybody just looked at Todd and tears came to his eyes. It was like his painting had been destroyed, you know? We never attempted to cut that track again because we'd already spent a lot of time on it, so [we thought] let's move on."

After finishing most of the album in Los Angeles, Rundgren returned to New York's Record Plant, with Jack Adams engineering, to record three more songs that would end up on *Runt*. A frenetic and Zappa-like workout entitled 'I'm In The Clique' featured a horn section and an ace New York session crew, including Moogy Klingman on electric piano. "Todd had brought along the bass player, Johnny Miller," says Klingman, "who is now a top bass player in New York and the top contractor of musicians for Broadway. I was thrilled, though, because he had also hired this drummer, Bobby Moses, who had been playing with my idol, Keith Jarrett, at the time."

Surprisingly, given the *Stage Fright* struggles, Rundgren managed to retain Levon Helm and Rick Danko to play on 'Once Burned,' a song which, Rundgren readily acknowledges, owed much to The Band's own signature sound. "I was imitating Richard Manuel on that song," admits Rundgren. "So why not get Levon and Rick to play on it? Early on, as I say, I had no idea what I was supposed to sound like, so I sounded a little different on every song."

Also in New York, Rundgren recorded the album's sweeping finale, 'Birthday Carol,' an epic work of wide-ranging dynamics, from soft folk song to boogie workout and even an orchestral flourish. It was the kind of big finish that Rundgren had been so proud of on 'A Beautiful Song,' from his Nazz days. The rhythm section for the date consisted of bassist Don Ferris, drummer Mickey Brook, and guitarist Don Lee Van Winkle.

Impressed with the range and variety of the final results, plus a lot of belief from Paul Fishkin, Ampex/Bearsville agreed to release the *Runt* album. Advance pressings featured 'Say No More,' which was eventually removed after much deliberation, as was an early version of 'Hope I'm Around,' which Rundgren would try again on his next album. While at least three versions of *Runt* were released, the most well known edition was issued in May 1970. 'We Gotta Get You A Woman' was released as the single and became a reasonable hit on radio, largely due to the hard work and belief of Fishkin, who had, after all, inspired the song in the first place. Fishkin had begged Grossman to finance a nationwide American radio station tour on which he and Rundgren would cross an unsuspecting nation, preaching the gospel of Todd. Fishkin's gambit worked and the single eventually crawled to Number 20 on the pop charts. "If 'We Gotta Get You A Woman' had never been a hit," says Rundgren, "I don't really know what would have happened. Hits sometimes give you a certain advantage but the way you apply it can be completely different."

In Rundgren's case, he applied his newfound visibility to an ill-considered *Runt* touring group (with Klingman and the Sales brothers) before returning to LA to plan out his next solo album, *Runt: The Ballad Of Todd Rundgren*. Yet, even as he was doing so, Miss Christine began to tell him about a group of Los Angeles Anglophiles he should check out, called Halfnelson. Intrigued by their quirky glam-rock demos, Rundgren would not only summon Grossman to LA to sign them, he would insist on personally producing what would become the debut album by Sparks.

3

Sparks

As Todd Rundgren prepared to record his second solo album, he found himself increasingly at home in sunny Los Angeles and socializing with Miss Christine of the GTOs, who constantly urged him to get his head out of his headphones and frequent the local music scene. She had been particularly eager to turn Rundgren on to the music of a pair of UCLA fine arts students, the brothers Ron and Russell Mael, trading at the time as Halfnelson. For the past year, the Maels had been writing and recording their quirky, original songs at the home of their guitarist and resident recording enthusiast, Earle Mankey. These recordings showcased Russell's preening falsetto vocals, Ron's minimalist keyboard arrangements, and Mankey's sinewy guitar work atop a makeshift percussion bed comprised of lampshades, ashtrays, and cardboard-box drums.

"We were doing what we thought, even at that time, were pretty clever recordings," says Russell Mael. "But we were basically just a 'recording' band as opposed to a 'live' band that went out to play at clubs and hone their skills in front of a live audience. That's kind of the key to what became our first album. We've always gone at things thinking that the recording is the most important thing. You can always work backward and figure out, 'Well, how do you perform that?'"

Mankey had been enamored of home recording since the sixth grade, when his guitarist father, a fan of Les Paul's experiments with overdubbing, had brought home the family's first National tape recorder. "It was a quarter-inch tape machine," Mankey recalls, "so you only had two tracks in one direction and two tracks in the other direction. But if you modified it, you could do four-track recording, which nobody was doing at home in those days. I started to learn all of these Les Paul tricks, like vari-speeded guitar, which was handy if you couldn't really play a part well enough."

Russell Mael says the three took great pride in what he calls their "primitive and basic" early experiments in sound. "We'd all be in there," says Mael, "hitting pots and pans and playing things slowed down and sped up, even voices. All these studio gimmicks on a student's budget! We felt that our budgetary constraints gave our recordings more character."

As imaginative as their recordings were, the band had failed to garner interest from a major label until Miss Christine fatefully whispered their name into her boyfriend's ear. While the band sounded decidedly "strange" to those ears, their quirky recording techniques and British influences were imbued with a good deal more character than most of what Rundgren had typically heard coming out of LA.

"They had clearly invested a lot of work in their demos," says Rundgren, "but it was also obvious to me that they didn't play live a lot. It was truly a product of the interaction between them and whatever limited recording gear they had available to them."

Russell Mael admits he knew very little about Todd Rundgren's work, yet based on the British influence running through the Nazz records, he sensed that the Philly producer would be sympathetic to their tastes. "Image-wise," says Mael, "Nazz looked more like they were from England than Philadelphia, so we thought Todd might be responsive to what we were doing. When he said he wanted to do an album, we were shocked; it was the beginning of our whole career, really."

Albert Grossman was flown out from New York to catch the band's live set, which presented a minor problem in that the band didn't play live very much. "We used to rehearse," says Mankey, "in this factory that made bunk beds for dogs. Whenever we had to play live for a record company, we'd just invite them to this controlled environment and make it feel like they were coming to an official club."

Halfnelson turned the dog bed factory into the world's most exclusive nightclub, its only table reserved for Mr Rundgren, Mr Grossman, and their guests. "This whole elaborate thing," laughs Rundgren, "was set up just for us. They put out some chairs and Russell, all glammed up, sat out front at a little table, handing out tickets and selling candy bars and stuff like that. Ron, with his little moustache, looked a little like Hitler. Well, he had more hair than Hitler, so he was a little more Chaplinesque than Hitleresque, and did this thing where he'd be completely expressionless."

"Russell called the venue the Doggie Factory," recalls early Sparks drummer Harley Feinstein, "and we had done maybe 20 or 30 of these shows already. We would always do other really intricate decorations. It was really pretty goofy."

"We did a little bit of lighting," says Mankey, "and we had Russell's toy cash register out front, just like at a movie theater."

"I remember we stayed up until three in the morning, one night," adds Feinstein, "making this little parade float, a papier-mâché cruise liner, inside of which Russell would sing 'Slowboat,' while someone pushed him around."

According to Rundgren, the showcase clinched the deal for the band, and Grossman was so impressed he signed Halfnelson to a recording and management deal and let Rundgren produce their debut. In anticipation of the sessions, the band visited Rundgren at his LA apartment. Mankey recalls being particularly impressed with Rundgren's home gear. "Albert had set him up with that 16-track Stephens tape recorder," says Mankey, "and a WEM mixer and PA system, right there in this apartment. I thought it was really cool that he could record his material at home, just like we had been doing. The difference was, of course, he had a 16-track and we had my kludged-together four-track."

They also paid a visit to ID Sound; ostensibly to get to know the room and to meet Rundgren's engineer James Lowe. "Todd told us that James was the Electric Prunes guy," says Mankey, "and that was okay with us then. We didn't even care if he was a good engineer, although he was; we just liked The Electric Prunes."

Mankey says that the band also thought of Rundgren, with his long, streaked, and colored hair, as something of a glam mentor. "He had just come back from London," says Mankey, "and knew things about glam and English rock star clothing and style, which was something we were all kind of interested in. Todd had come back with authentic English suits and clothes we just couldn't get in the shops in Beverly Hills."

By the time they began recording at ID Sound, Earle Mankey's bassist brother James had joined Feinstein in the rhythm section as Rundgren carefully pored over Halfnelson's demos to see which happy accidents and one-time tape effects could be preserved and/or replicated in a real studio. 'Saccharin And The War' and 'Roger' would be built more or less around these initial tapes, while Rundgren would attempt to recreate or better the rest in a proper studio. 'High C' – said to be Ron Mael's personal favorite – was among the first tracked. (A Bearsville bio sheet from the era also mentions two more unreleased songs, allegedly recorded during the sessions: 'Do The Factory,' also known as 'The Factory,' and 'Spider Run.')

Lowe recalls that Rundgren clearly enjoyed the band's sound and made no effort to change the band's direction. "Todd," Lowe recalls, "always used to say, 'If you've got your shit together, you can come in here with us.' He respected that it was your record and he wasn't going to interfere if you had a strong idea and knew what you wanted to do. What we did do, on a song like 'Roger,' though, was to lay some of the original four-track onto Todd's 16-track master and add more vocals and percussion to it. There was a little bit of signal loss dubbing it down, but in the end, 'Roger' holds up just as well as any other cut we recorded directly to the 16-track."

"'Roger' was so outside," says Rundgren, "I thought, 'Nobody's doing this,' which is exactly why I had to do it! They had all these bizarre sounds in there, and Russell singing falsetto, 'Roger! Roger!' There were sped-up and arpeggiated guitars and pots and pans and all kinds of cutlery clanking. There was no point in trying to rebuild that track, it was already there in a sense. Our final version wasn't exactly like the band's initial tape, but it wasn't like some tortuous re-arrangement of it either."

On 'Simple Ballet,' Halfnelson took advantage of having a better studio, and more tracks, to create something they couldn't achieve at home; multiple layers of grand piano. "I don't even think Ron would know how many pianos were on that tape by the time we were done," says Russell Mael. "We had recorded our home demos in Earle's apartment and there definitely weren't any grand pianos hanging around there."

Mankey, who would later become an accomplished producer in his own right, says that he and the Maels learned a lot about the studio from watching Rundgren. "We'd never really had serious experience in a real studio," says Mankey, "and Todd actually brought a slew of fresh sounds to the record. For example, he had found this little synthesizer in England, called a Stylophone, which had a small role in our record."

One of the album's better-known songs, 'Wonder Girl,' features a simple shuffle rhythm that was a direct result product, says Feinstein, of interaction with the studio technology. "I was trying all these different drum grooves when Todd came up with the idea to just play this really basic two-and-four drum beat. Then he turned on the tape echo delay and I would jam to it in my headphones, kind of playing this echo-shuffle."

Other solutions required no technology at all, such as the "wallet on the snare" trick Rundgren employed on 'Big Bands.' "He wanted to have one snare sound during the verse," says Feinstein, "and another snare sound during the chorus. So, while I was out in the booth tracking it, Todd would take out his wallet and place it on the snare head to dampen it, and then take it off where he wanted the snare to ring out more."

Feinstein also recalls that Rundgren's in-the-booth advice had a life-altering effect upon his approach to drumming. "One time," says Feinstein, "I was playing something sort of fancy on the hi-hat with my right hand and Todd just stopped me. He said, 'Why don't you just keep a solid 1, 2, 3, 4, eighth-note beat on the hi-hat and do all the variation with your bass drum or on the snare.' He was absolutely right and that little bit of advice actually altered the way I played drums."

Early on, Russell Mael says he had become enamored with double and triple-tracking his lead vocals. "I honestly can't remember who was responsible for it," says Mael, "I've just always liked doubling my voice and to have the kind of stereo split on things. It's like John Lennon and the way he used that slap-echo effect; I totally understand that whole way of doing things. I feel that, this way, it just takes on this extra-recorded quality."

There was also a more practical purpose behind the multi-tracking. "Ron's lyrics and melodies tend to be really fast," declares the singer, "and he crams a lot of words into a sentence. Sometimes he'll even have a line with overlapping parts. Frankly, it's just really hard to sing each long line and then get to the next line, so we'd have another track of me coming in singing the next round. A good example of this was on Earle's song, 'Biology 2,' where my vocal fades out on one side then fades in on the other side and you can actually hear me sing 'I ran out of breath!'"

With a lot of hard work going into seemingly simple sounds, Mankey recalls a few tense debates and "a kind of us versus them" negativity flaring up from the band, at times, toward Rundgren. "Todd became more humanized as went along," says Mankey, "and sometimes we'd run up against him if we wanted to do another take but he wouldn't let us. Our way of fighting back was to start making fun of Todd's idiosyncrasies, but he actually took it well, and even made us laugh too. He did this thing with a Neumann windscreen where he folded the bottom of the thing over on itself so it looked like a Charlie Chaplin hat."

"It was always more fun than not," insists Mael. "Todd would take two drumsticks and stick one up each nostril so that he looked like a walrus. The thing is, we had no other reference points for how you're supposed to act in a studio or anything," he laughs. "We had stern discussions but it was always positive, and I don't recall any strife or animosity. Ron and I have made 20 albums since then, and I can tell you it doesn't always work that way."

"Besides the walrus thing," says Lowe, "I remember Todd standing there with a vibra-slap and squeaking it during 'Saccharine And The War.' You could hear this little squeaking going on in the background and everyone's laughing. It was a crazy way to do a record, you know? But Todd was always outside himself. There was no fear or trepidation about picking up anything or fooling around in the studio. We took the tops off of tape rolls and put the machine on high speed and let the tape go all over the control room; crazy stuff, but it kept it loose and fresh."

Feinstein recalls that at one point Rundgren even requested more of the hilarious antics he'd witnessed at the Doggie Bed Factory showcase. "Todd reminded us," says Feinstein, "about how, when we had done 'Simple Ballet,' I actually played a part of the song off-stage. We were trying to get kind of a mystical, far off sound for the cymbals on that song, so I would go into this sort of echoey bathroom in the neighboring unit and play my part on the cymbal. At ID Sound, Todd would ask us, 'Why don't you guys do that wacky stuff any more? Harley, go into the other room or something.'"

Bearsville initially released the album as *Halfnelson*, but then Grossman and his team proposed that the album, and the band, be renamed *Sparks*. "As far as I know," says Russell Mael, "everybody at Bearsville was really happy with the record, creatively, but it wasn't selling. Albert thought *Halfnelson* was maybe too oblique and esoteric sounding. He and Todd thought that Ron and I were really 'funny guys,' and Albert said we reminded him of the Marx Brothers, which we didn't totally get. He said, 'I know, what if you called yourselves The Sparks Brothers?' We just cringed a bit and said, 'Oooh, no.' Then we said, 'Well, what about just Sparks?' It was innocuous enough as a band name, and had no significance after the first five minutes that you heard it. Everybody agreed and that was that. Later on we were told that, in England, 'sparks' is a nickname for an electrician or lighting guy, so a lot people get confused over there."

Rundgren says he always thought the name Halfnelson suited their music more. "It was more off-the-wall," says Rundgren, "but either way, the record was a curiosity but had no real commercial success. It would take them a few years, and probably a few tours, to start connecting with a broader audience."

'Wonder Girl,' backed with a slightly sped-up edit of '(No More) Mr Nice Guys,' did actually become an effective calling card for Sparks on American radio. The single rose to Number 92 on the *Cashbox* chart (apparently reaching Number One in Montgomery, Alabama). Then, on July 29 1972, America got its first look at the band as they mimed the single on Dick Clark's *American Bandstand* television program.

"The whole time we were making the record," says James Lowe, "I had thought 'Wonder Girl,' or maybe 'Fa La Fa Lee,' was going to be a huge hit, but I was wrong. I guess their lyrics were a bit too radical for the time."

Today, Earle Mankey credits Rundgren for lessons he has since applied to his own production work. "Todd was just very pragmatic about recording bands," says Mankey. "He showed me that production is ultimately a very nuts-and-bolts thing. It's about walking a line between having the band think that you're not doing anything or having them think that you're trying to push them around. I think a good producer, like Todd, merely fills in what's missing."

Mankey also notes that, beyond the studio experience, Rundgren gave the band an entrée into other aspects of the music business. "Up until then," Mankey admits, "I probably didn't realize how much just being on the scene and hanging out, and all of that, is important to the promotion of a band, so Todd really helped us out that way too. And when *The Ballad Of Todd Rundgren* came out, Todd used a lot of Ron Mael's photographs, from a film Russell had done at UCLA, inside the packaging. In the photograph for 'Boat On The Charles,' I'm the guy in the rowboat. That's my little six degrees of separation!"

Not everyone fared so well. After the Sparks album was done, Miss Christine left Rundgren for Russell Mael, before eventually falling victim to her other dalliance, heroin. While neither gentleman opts to discuss that sad business today, Russell Mael, claiming to speak for his typically silent brother Ron, says the Sparks brothers choose to dwell on the good times and remain indebted to Rundgren for giving them a kind of Lamaze birth into the world of recorded sound.

"When we had to revisit all of our albums," Mael recalls, "for our 21-night stand in London [May 16 through June 11 of 2008, at the Carling Academy, Islington] we played the first album from start to end and we were really happy with the way it sounded. There's nothing there that really sounds 'of an era' because it didn't exactly sound 'of an era' at the time. It may sound corny, but if it hadn't been for Todd, there might not have been a Sparks, so we owe him the whole thing. It's actually kind of sad and strange that our paths haven't crossed at all in 40 years. There are a few people in our past that you would really like to say nasty things about but we don't have anything nasty to say about Todd. So if you see him, say 'Hi' and send him our warmest regards."

Long Nights On Astral Drive

After the unexpected chart success of 'We Gotta Get You A Woman,' Todd Rundgren's profile as both an artist and a producer had been raised substantially, effecting radical changes within him and around him. Notably, as he began to work on his second solo recording, the previously drug-free Rundgren had begun to regularly alter his mind with marijuana. "Up until I was in my early twenties," he says, "I was a complete teetotaler. I didn't take any kind of drugs or drink or anything. In fact, I had found the behavior of my peers, while they were high, to be somewhat questionable."

But shortly after the release of *Runt*, Rundgren had visited his childhood friend, Randy Reed, by then a student at Jefferson Medical College in Philadelphia, who had already been smoking pot for some time. One night in his student apartment, Reed offered Rundgren a hit of his joint. "I thought, 'Okay, me and Randy do everything together anyway, so he won't make a jerk out of himself.' So I smoked my first joint. As far as the way that drugs affect me, it was entertaining, I suppose, but it also gave me a whole different sensibility about time and space and order. That, in turn, had a big effect on the songwriting for *The Ballad Of Todd Rundgren.*

"Smoking the pot helped me to hear my brain better, to objectivize my own thought-processes and, in a way, internalize them. I started to write more about stuff that I knew about, instead of just coming up with any old lyrics to go along with my musical ideas. I felt that pot helped me really to focus in terms of songwriting, which seems ironic. Most people would think the pot would make you more scatterbrained, but for somebody who's already scatterbrained, it had somewhat the opposite effect."

While chemical alteration would, over his next albums, become his modus operandi, Rundgren insists that his subsequent excursions into pharmacology were more purposeful experimentation than mere escapism. "The initial purpose was that I might have felt that I'd gotten to a sort of mental cul-de-sac and needed a different way to see things. Sometimes, you can fall into that trap of seeing the world as having limited possibilities. And in order to get out of that trap, it's good to reboot, in a sense, and change the ground rules."

The Ballad Of Todd Rundgren was a more coherent set of songs, due in equal parts to his chemical adjustments and to the fact that, true to the title, most of the songs were ballads, and composed on piano. While still touched by Laura Nyro's templates, Rundgren was now less willing than he had been on his first record to merely emulate his influences. "I had made it over that initial hump," he says, "of realizing, 'Okay, if you're gonna sing, take it seriously and try and sing with your own voice.' I took to writing material that was a little bit more appropriate for me, although I still hadn't developed any real strength as a singer yet."

Musically, Rundgren considered it a new high-water mark, in terms of composing on the piano. "I'm self-taught on the piano," he says, "and have continually limited technique. I approached it more as a compositional tool and was not really interested in becoming a super-proficient player. A lot of what one might call my 'distinctive voicings' on the piano have more to do with the way my hands fall on the keyboard. I don't get into a lot of arpeggios because I was more interested in finding the changes that worked for the song with the minimum amount of embellishment."

According to James Lowe, once more assisting at ID Sound, Rundgren's new stylistic consistency was also the result of his considered self-evaluation of the *Runt* album. "Listening back," says Lowe, "you naturally pick out something that irritated you about it and say 'I'm never doing that again.'"

Musically, Rundgren had very clear ideas for the basic structures and chord patterns for *Ballad*. "Once I had the basic structure and changes of a song, I could go in and track it. I always write the lyrics after the tracks have been recorded, which is sometimes bothersome for the people who have to play on it, because they have no idea whether they're going to be interfering with something I'm going to be singing. They just have to take my word that what they played works."

Being more aware of his strengths and limitations as a singer helped him compose the songs. He recalls that the basic tracks were "knocked out" very quickly. "This was the first record where all my basic tracks were recorded in one place, although we went back to Bearsville to do a lot of the backing vocals."

As with *Runt*, Rundgren insisted on interacting with a live rhythm section for the basic tracks. Tony Sales returned to play the bass for most of the record, and Rundgren was thrilled to discover that the timing was finally right to bring in drummer N.D. Smart. "I'd see him around Woodstock," Smart recalls, "and then, sometime near Christmas, he asked me if I wanted to go to California. I said 'Hell yeah,' because it's cold back East, you know? He offered to fly me out, with room and board, and he said he'd pay me well. That's one thing about Todd, he always paid well."

While working on the record, Smart and his girlfriend stayed with Rundgren at his rented house at 2501 Astral Drive, near Nichols Canyon in Hollywood. "There was a white grand piano on a white rug," Smart remembers, "and he had these metal grasshopper sculptures. At one point there was this gallows thing he'd had built in there too. I don't know why he did that, I think it's because somebody had said, 'We're gonna give you enough money to hang yourself.'"

Smart and Rundgren would rise each day at around 10am and head down to Sunset Boulevard for breakfast before a full day at ID Sound. "Todd drove like a maniac down that hill to Sunset each morning," says Smart. "It was terrifying. After breakfast, we'd go make records until about six or seven at night. He'd show me a tune, and then I'd sit in the drum booth and start messing with my parts. He let me come up with parts, but if there was something he specifically wanted that I wasn't doing he'd tell me. He was pretty diplomatic about it, though. We'd do about two a day; once we got a take he was happy with, we'd move on."

"N.D. was a real strong drummer," says Lowe. "The drums were so loud in the room when he was playing. I think that was important to Todd; he saw that if you didn't get the beat down on the basic track, the mistake just got exacerbated as you started laying overdubs and you couldn't correct it later."

Smart remembers cutting the opening track, 'Long Flowing Robe.' "Todd was on the clavinet, and he'd told me to imagine what was gonna be there and he kind of sang a [wordless] scratch vocal for me. He explained that he wanted me to play more aggressively, and to do those harsh tom shots on the turnaround. That wasn't my style, and later, people couldn't believe that it was me on the record."

Tony Sales recalls that, in contrast to the atmosphere on the first *Runt* album, the sessions appeared more purpose-driven, a little smokier, but steeped in what he calls "romantic melancholia. By this time, I knew Todd a little better, and I had noticed that he was having some romantic trouble. There were people smoking dope, but everybody was doing that at the time. It was still a fairly low-threshold vibe, you know? Todd always knew what he wanted for the songs but, of course, anything can happen when you get into the studio, and it often did."

Acknowledging a Robbie Robertson influence on his guitar part for 'Bleeding,' Rundgren admits to absorbing minor influences from all of his production clients over the years but insists that his goal is to blend them seamlessly into his own music. "It's just a natural consequence," says Rundgren, "of being in somebody else's musical milieu for a while. There will be something that you're working on that would get stuck in your head like any other song. Sometimes you pick up a lot and convey very little, and sometimes you convey a lot and pick up a little, so it's not always equitable, I suppose. There are some acts that I could probably say with some certitude that we may have given each other very little to take away from the whole experience."

Smart recalls Rundgren taking command of the studio like no musician he had witnessed before. "I never followed so closely what engineers did," says Smart, "the way Todd could. He was one of the very first in our era, just as Buddy Holly or Les Paul had been in their eras. Todd also realized, pretty early on, that the producer didn't really do shit, and that it was the engineer who had all the controls!"

Lowe adds that Rundgren could "see it all in his head," a talent which called to his mind another bright light of LA recording, Van Dyke Parks. "Van Dyke would work for three hours on a song," says Lowe, "recording a blurb here, and a squirt there, and a squiggle, a harmonica honk here, and you'd have no idea where it was going. Then, suddenly, he'd put one track on it that pulled everything together. Todd was a lot like that, so what might sound dissonant at first, would actually fit right in once the thing was complete."

While Smart and Sales comprised the rhythm section for most of the album, Tony's brother Hunt Sales plays the drums on 'Parole' and provides a conga part on 'Boat On The Charles.' Rounding out the album, drummer John Guerin, from Tom Scott's LA Express, and bassist Jerry Scheff, from Elvis Presley's legendary TCB band, backed Rundgren on the plaintive soft-shoe ballads 'Be Nice To Me' and 'Hope I'm Around,' which he had left to one side during the first album sessions. With the LA tracking complete, Rundgren took the tapes back to Bearsville Studios to add additional voices and perform the final mix. Lowe recalls these vocal sessions and the careful pre-planning Rundgren had put into his track assignments from the first days at ID Sound.

"When you've got somebody who is recording all the overdubs himself," says Lowe, "he's got to have a sense of where he's going with it and Todd always did. He'd sing all the high voices, or whatever, then we'd submix that group. Then we'd do the other section or grouping and mix those down to another group. We'd have these submix sessions where we'd just ping-pong things to open up other tracks. Some of the vocal stuff he would go back and do himself at Bearsville, and do that thing where he'd just sit in the control room with the overhung microphone."

Released on June 24 1971, *Runt: The Ballad Of Todd Rundgren* is considered by many to be one of the great singer-songwriter albums of its era. While Rundgren would soon eschew such easy categorizations, he now says that the album was important for him as he struggled to find his sound, lyrically and vocally. "On my first record, songwriting was just a whim and the material was purposefully eclectic because I had no particular direction, just a lot of ideas that I wanted to get off my chest. But by the time I got to the second record, I started being more deliberate, facing up to the possibility that this might become successful and I'd have to go out and perform it."

While 'Be Nice To Me' and 'A Long Time, A Long Way To Go' were released as singles, neither repeated the chart success of 'We Gotta Get You A Woman.' Critically, reaction was mixed, with arguably the most significant rave review coming from Rundgren's new friend in New York, Patti Smith, who was financing her own poetry by writing poetic record reviews for rock periodicals like *Creem* and *Rolling Stone.*

"Like Mozart," Smith raved in the August 19 1971 issue of *Rolling Stone*, "Todd Rundgren never wanted to be born; his mother labored hard to put him here and he's fought hard to sign his musical autograph in the progressive pages of rock & roll ... 'The Ballad Of Denny And Jean' and 'Wailing Wall' are more personal and float in more fears than all the children in the world ..."

"I was an advocate for him," Smith says today. "First of all because he was so interesting. He was always slightly outside, and ahead – I mean, sometimes he would even baffle me – but he was also accessible and I could tell when people were influenced by him and lifted from him."

It was around this time that Rundgren picked up a significant guitar, the psychedelically painted Gibson SG originally owned by Eric Clapton, who had played it on a variety of Cream recordings, including 'Sunshine Of Your Love.' The custom paint job came courtesy of Simon Posthuma and Marijke Koger, the legendary London-based Dutch artists collectively known as The Fool. As the story goes, Clapton had initially given the guitar to George Harrison, who then passed it on to Apple recording artist Jackie Lomax. Lomax sold the guitar to Rundgren, its condition by then as unfortunate as the circumstances under which the sale transpired.

"Jackie was up around Woodstock," Rundgren recalls, "and he showed me this guitar, which I recognized immediately, but it was in terrible shape and totally unplayable. He said he needed some money so he said he'd take $500 for it, and there was talk that he might buy it back from me when his finances were in better shape. In the meantime, I fixed it up a little and played it all the time. After a few years, he hadn't come back for it, so I invested in a major restoration of it."

Rundgren nicknamed the guitar 'Sunny,' in tribute to the Cream hit on which it had appeared. It became a common sight at Rundgren's live shows over the next decade and a half. In 2000, after 'The Fool' (as the guitar is widely known) had been relegated to a Sacramento storage warehouse for some years, Rundgren auctioned it off through Sotheby's. It allegedly fetched $150,000, although Rundgren, who currently plays a replica model, refuses to comment on the sale or the price. (Unconfirmed reports allege that the unnamed buyer immediately resold the guitar for $500,000.)

To promote the *Ballad* album, Rundgren enlisted Moogy Klingman to form a touring Runt band that featured guitarist and singer Tommy Cosgrove, bassist Stu Woods, and N.D. Smart, once again, on drums. The band lived and rehearsed with Rundgren at his Astral Drive home but, apart from a few live radio broadcasts, the album wasn't taking off and gigs for Runt were few and far between. The tour was quickly abbreviated.

In his defence, Rundgren points out that *The Ballad Of Todd Rundgren* "fell through the cracks" in the wake of Grossman's break with Ampex and prior to the signing of Bearsville's new distribution deal with Warner Bros. Nonetheless, the album had allowed Rundgren to further extend his range as an artist and performer while experimenting with recording techniques he could later use as a producer.

In the fall of 1971, Rundgren was offered the chance to produce, or at least finish, the third album by Badfinger, the seminal power-pop group who had been discovered by The Beatles and signed to Apple Records. While his newly honed production skills would certainly be put to good use, he would be walking into a troubled production already a year in progress. *Straight Up*, as the record would become known, had already been attempted once – with Beatle engineer Geoff Emerick producing – before George Harrison himself stepped in.

That summer, however, after tracking only four or five songs for the record, Harrison had received an urgent call from his sitar mentor, Ravi Shankar, in distress over the famine in the South Asian nation of Bangladesh. Moved first to tears, then to action, Harrison and Shankar immediately ceased all other activities and hastily arranged a groundbreaking charity concert, to be held August 1 at Madison Square Garden, with guests including Bob Dylan, Ringo Starr, Eric Clapton, Leon Russell, and Billy Preston. While he invited Badfinger to join him at the show, Harrison had surprised the group by abruptly walking away from their album project altogether. Apple's US label manager, Al Steckler, in desperate need of a fill-in producer who could work fast, on budget, and on schedule, was told about Todd Rundgren. Within days, Albert Grossman had negotiated a large sum for Rundgren's services, thanks in no small part to his own managerial clout. Before starting the project, however, Rundgren met with Harrison at Apple Studios to discuss it.

"George told me that he just had no time for the project," says Rundgren, "but he told me that we could use, or not use, anything that he'd done with Badfinger. He didn't really care at that point, it was out of his hands. That was the only time I ever met him and just about the only exchange we ever had."

By September 26, Rundgren was seated behind the board at London's Air Studios, presiding over the recording of 'Baby Blue,' written by Badfinger guitarist Pete Ham. "When I got there," Rundgren recalls, "they had about ten songs they'd done with Geoff Emerick in the can, as well as a few songs that George had started. But they also had another four or five songs lying around that they hadn't recorded yet. One of those was 'Baby Blue.'"

While Rundgren was partial to some of the leftover songs from the Harrison session, he says he was appalled by the drum sounds on them. Having established a new drum sound for the tracks he cut from scratch, Rundgren took the radical step of insisting that drummer Mike Gibbins go in and meticulously re-record all his drum parts over the master tapes.

"The drums on the Harrison tracks just sounded too flat and weird," says Rundgren. "I think it was this thing that Ringo had been doing, maybe around *The White Album*, where they put towels over everything. Ironically enough, they never did that on the ones Geoff Emerick had recorded. I guess Emerick wasn't as hung up on that sound as The Beatles were. We just opened up some new tracks, pushed the original drums way back, and brought the new drums way up."

In the end, Rundgren says, only "around two or three" of the Harrison masters were used, but among them was another Pete Ham song, 'Day After Day.' Like 'Baby Blue,' it was a mid-tempo rocker, this time featuring Leon Russell's elegant piano and a slide guitar duet routinely credited to Harrison and Ham. Rundgren, however, disputes this prevailing idea as nothing but "an urban myth based on the fact that Harrison had been involved with it. I don't think it was George," he insists, "because I saw them play it. I'm pretty sure one of the guys in the band,

Pete or Joey, played it. We made some alterations to pretty much everything that I got from those Harrison tapes. There was re-singing of lead vocals and additional background vocals, too, so almost nothing was left from the original song. In addition, we used maybe four of Geoff Emerick's original tracks, but probably made some alterations on those, too."

Badfinger guitarist Joey Molland, today the only surviving original member of Badfinger, contradicted Rundgren's memory of events and actually praised Harrison's work on the track, at Rundgren's expense, in an interview with Gary Katz. "Pete and I were working the parts out," Molland told Katz, "and [George] came over and said, 'Listen, would you mind if I played slide on this? I'd really like to play.' And, of course, I said, 'Well, yeah, sure, go ahead.' [George] was great, anyway, to work with in the studio – brilliant arrangements and the sounds that he was pulling out of the board ... Todd, on the other hand, was a star – an ego that preceded him, you know – just outrageous and just rude and obnoxious. And it was really a horrible experience for me."

"It was my job," Rundgren insists today. "I had been hired to fly in and cobble this thing together in just under two weeks. They'd been trying to get this album done for over a year by the time I got involved. We did whatever we needed to do in order to tie it all together."

Rundgren flexed his burgeoning production chops on the album opener, 'Take It All,' which features his preferred loose snare drum sound and a keyboard-heavy mix including a Hammond organ, suggestive of Garth Hudson, and a suitably 'Fab' compressed piano, underscored by Ham's dry and startlingly McCartneyesque lead vocal. Throughout the record, Rundgren had the band lay in multi-part harmony vocal sections, in lieu of the orchestral overdubs Harrison had originally planned, feeling that they were more personal-sounding and, frankly, cheaper and quicker to record.

One impressive feat of studio re-construction was the artificial bridge Rundgren built between Tom Evans's 'Money' (which Rundgren had re-cut) and Joey Molland's 'Flying' (from the Emerick sessions). Rundgren wanted the two songs to segue together, but found they were in disparate keys, so he simply slowed down the tape on Evans's song while speeding up Molland's track, giving Molland's voice, in the process, a slightly trippy 'chipmunk' quality.

In Dan Matovina's in-depth biography, *Without You: The Tragic Story Of Badfinger*, Molland shared his general complaints about what he felt were strong-arm tactics by Rundgren, whom he felt had misrepresented the band's rockier side by selecting only mid-tempo songs for *Straight Up*. Yet in the same volume, drummer Mike Gibbins praised Rundgren's drum sounds. "Todd was the fastest, zippiest producer we ever had," he told Matovina, "He came into one studio and told the engineer to take the day off, even the tape operator. The guy was a wizard behind the board. I was really impressed."

After a month of London studio-hopping, from Air to Morgan Studios with stops at Command Studios, Rundgren did some rough mixes back at Morgan before flying with the tapes back to New York's Bell Sound for the final mix.

When the *Straight Up* album was released, on November 15, Rundgren was miffed, and remains so, that after Harrison had "washed his hands of it," Apple had given the ex-Beatle the full producer's credit for the single, 'Day After Day.'

"I was sort of annoyed about it," admits Rundgren, "because I could have left it off the record altogether if I'd felt like it, and my version didn't sound much like what he had done. And Geoff Emerick also received no credit for the songs that he contributed to the record, which of course had also undergone all these alterations. It just didn't strike me as kosher. Later, I realized that it may or may not have been something purposeful, just some by-product of a general Beatle hubris. You don't contradict a Beatle. Anyway, it wasn't as if we had some formal redress, although 'Day After Day' was also a big hit, so I was probably due some royalties there."

While Rundgren had fulfilled his obligations, producing a hit album with two worldwide smash singles, the experience had soured Badfinger on Rundgren. They did attempt to record with Rundgren again, at Apple Studios the following January (two tracks of which materialized on their 1973 album, *Ass*), but the sessions were called off after a contract dispute. Ham (who would tragically take his own life in April of 1974) was still upset with Rundgren in a 1972 interview with *Phonograph Record*'s Mark Leviton.

"First off," Ham grumbled, "he wanted four times the money he deserved. He even wanted credit for the things George had already produced. It was ridiculous. And his ideas restricted the band's own ideas and creativity. He certainly won't be producing our next LP."

Leaving Badfinger behind him, Todd Rundgren headed back in Los Angeles, ready to take another shot at his own recordings. Engineer James Lowe once again assisted Rundgren as he began work on what would be his first double album, *Something/Anything?*

"After the two *Runt* albums," says Lowe, "Todd seemed to be formulating just who he wanted to be, his public persona. Albert had told him he could be the new Elvis if he wanted to. He just had to come up with the right stuff. So I think Todd started seeing himself in a more serious light, as somebody who could be a lead performer, rather than trying to hide behind shenanigans like putting a noose around your neck and stuff."

If pot had helped Rundgren find a sense of order in his music, new chemicals were about to change him yet again. He had recently been introduced to the focused speediness of Ritalin, a drug that would have a profound effect on the already over-achieving musician and producer. "By the time I had got to *Something/Anything?*" says Rundgren, "my songwriting process had become almost too second-nature. I was writing songs formulaically, almost without thinking, knocking out a song, reflexively, in about 20 minutes. Songs like 'I Saw The Light' or 'Marlene' just came out of me in one piece, in a very short time. Of course, it's not a really complex song or anything, and the lyrics were fairly inane. It wasn't that the songs were necessarily insincere, but I kept drawing off the same source material; this one failed high school relationship. Well, by then, a lot had happened to me since that I wasn't writing about."

As Rundgren began turning out these songs, still planning a single album release, it became obvious that he had almost two albums worth of usable material. Having only a short two or three week window in which to record it all, he realized he'd have to work longer hours to get it all tracked. Additionally, Rundgren installed a Scully eight-track tape machine, mixing board, and some synthesizers into the living room of his Nichols Canyon home so he could continue recording, at night, after leaving the studio proper. This, he says, is where the Ritalin came in handy.

"Ritalin allowed me to completely focus on the process," says Rundgren. "I could work for hours and wouldn't know the time had passed. Funny, it doesn't have that effect any more, but back then it enabled me to really bore down and work late into the night. I'd record all day and night, but somehow get normal sleeping hours in. My sessions didn't start until like one in the afternoon, so I'd go until maybe five, and then I'd go home, have dinner, then start working at eight or nine at night and finish at three or four in the morning, as depicted on the photo on the cover. Then I'd crash for a bit, get up at noon, have some breakfast and go to ID Sound to record again."

For the first time on any of his albums, Rundgren finally felt confident enough to track most of the bass, drums, voices – everything – all by himself. As liberating as the situation was, Rundgren recalls that building tracks from the drums up presented certain challenges. "Doing the drums was the logical place to start," he says. "It always starts with the rhythm. Early on, I tried to play to a click-track, but I wasn't very experienced, so it was always difficult for me to stay locked to it. I gave up on that idea and, in a certain sense, my drum tracks sounded a little more natural as a result."

Rundgren describes a curious process, whereby he would sit alone in the drum booth and predict the appropriate changes, smashes, or pushes for the songs, without any guide track. "I just found it easy to imagine a song in my head and simply play to that. I might hum the melody quietly to myself, although I rarely if ever had the lyrics written before tracking. I was still using an engineer for that album, so if I screwed up a part, or got lost, James could conceivably do a rolling punch-in with me playing along. Sometimes the tempo would be mildly different, but not in a perceptible way."

Rundgren proved to be his own best sideman. His drum parts retained some of Keith Moon's studied sloppiness, while his bass overdubs avoided the typically busy approach of most guitarists who try to play bass. And then there were his signature mass-overdubbed vocal sections. "Todd is actually best," says Meat Loaf's composer Jim Steinman, "when he does all the background vocals himself. Having one voice, stacked up, produces a totally different feeling than three voices. And if it's a great voice, like Todd's, it somehow seems more thrilling to me."

James Lowe still recalls how inspiring he found it to witness Rundgren's blossoming creativity, both as a producer and artist. "A lot of people were making stuff that didn't matter," says Lowe, "but Todd was actually coming from the heart. I'd see him write the lyrics or sit down and figure something out, and he wasn't just trying to write a hit, he was letting out what was inside of him. It was pretty amazing."

The range of songs and sounds Rundgren explored at home, and back at he studio, was extremely broad. 'I Went To The Mirror' was an open invitation to blow the listeners' minds using no drug stronger than stereo imaging, while on the other end of the spectrum, 'Song Of The Viking,' dedicated to his ongoing champion Patti Smith, was the first of what would be a recurring tendency toward comical music-hall numbers inspired by his childhood fascination with Gilbert & Sullivan.

"I had a lot of musical freedom," Rundgren recalls, "but I was still using other people's tools. This was the first time I had actually done any serious recording of my own, alone. Especially all the stuff I did back at Astral Drive. The great advantage of the home set-up was that, if I felt like just knocking off for half an hour or something, or just to switch the noise off and sit and contemplate what was going on, I wouldn't be wasting anybody else's time. It took time, for example, to program my little Putney [EMS VCS3] synthesizer. You had to plug all these pins into this little matrix, and before you could play anything musically, you had to let it warm up or it would drift out of tune. Then you'd just have to hope that it'd stay in tune for the duration. So, I remember sitting there, alone, with my Putney, a little keyboard and my guitar, working on some of the little things like 'One More Day,' 'I Went To The Mirror,' and 'Breathless,' where I used one of those slobber-box [talk-box] things."

In addition to programming a few synthesizer sounds for 'Little Red Lights,' one of Rundgren's more memorable evenings' work at 'Runt Recorders' was the spoken word 'Intro,' which opened side two (on disc one of the vinyl release), wherein Rundgren humorously demonstrated a variety of ill-advised "sounds of the studio."

Lowe recalls Rundgren debuting the piece over the big speakers at ID Sound. "I just cracked up," he says. "It was hilarious, with all the punch-ins, the hiss and drop-outs and stuff. You have to realize this was the first time they'd let us idiots run loose in the studio. Usually you had to have a union guy or somebody there going 'Don't push the board level over this much,' you know? This was a new era that had sort of begun around 1968, when you could actually take control of the studio and mash or mutilate all this equipment as much as you wanted. It was actually more fun to misuse a piece of gear than to use it correctly."

Having compiled enough self-recorded material for three sides, Rundgren felt he had "pretty nearly exhausted" the do-it-yourself approach. "I had an album and a half," he says, "and while I could have continued to do more, I thought I'd like to just do something a little bit more fun, and somewhat less formal."

Initially, Rundgren had hoped to book an LA studio, pack it full of live musicians and track something live off the floor, but just as he was finishing up in Los Angeles a seismic event occurred beneath his feet.

"I had only rented that Nichols Canyon house for a year," says Rundgren, "but in early 1972 there was an earthquake. It was the first I'd ever been in and I hated it. I had finished the recording at the house and we'd taken that photograph which went on the inside of *Something/Anything?* After we took that picture, I went to bed and the earthquake happened five hours later. Fortunately, I had already booked a flight out to New York that day, so I just drove around, frantically, until it was time for me to leave. I think my tapes had been sent already, or I might have been carrying them, I wasn't thinking about it at the time. I was thinking about the fucking earthquake. It really messed with my head for a good long time and was of the reasons I decided not to stay in California. The other being that you had to drive to do anything in LA and I was used to New York, where you can walk everywhere."

Safely back on the terra firma of pedestrian-friendly New York, Rundgren booked himself into The Record Plant, on a Sunday, for a marathon 'live in the studio' session. Once again, Rundgren contracted Moogy Klingman to pack the studio with the best players he could find on short notice. "Moogy would play organ on the sessions," says Rundgren, "because I was playing the piano on that day. We did three songs in a row, over one 16-hour session; it was a busy day."

Klingman got the call from Rundgren on a Friday night. "He needed to get a full band by Sunday morning," Klingman recalls. "He wanted horns, singers, everything, so I made a ton of phone calls. I got Rick Derringer on guitar, but he couldn't come for the first song, so I also called a guitarist friend I knew from high school, Robbie Kogale. Stu Woods played the bass but also couldn't make it for the first song, so I got my friend John Siegler. We had John Siomos on drums, and I brought in a great horn section – Michael Brecker, Randy Brecker, and Barry Rogers – and any singers I could find."

Klingman's singers included Richard Corey, Cecelia Norfleet, Dennis Cooley, Hope Ruff and Vicki Sue Robinson (who later recorded the disco hit 'Turn The Beat Around'). The three songs recorded that day were 'Dust In The Wind,' a Klingman composition, plus two original Rundgren selections: 'You Left Me Sore,' a light-hearted paean to sexual transmitted diseases, and a radically updated arrangement of his Nazz tune, 'Hello It's Me.'

"I was hearing the song in my head a different way," says Rundgren, "more up-tempo with a different feel, so I thought I'd give it a try with this new arrangement. It was the first song I ever wrote, so I thought why the hell not. Maybe I could finally get it out of my system, all these songs about some fucking girl who dumped me in high school."

This new recording of 'Hello It's Me' would become Rundgren's major-league calling-card and, for better or worse, the song most commonly associated with him. He says that, given the caliber of the musicians assembled, he gave them all carte blanche to wail as they pleased on the session.

"Despite whatever else made 'Hello It's Me' a hit," says Rundgren, "it was all live and we didn't slave over it, you know? There were no charts written out, people were faking what they were playing, and all that horn business at the end was just an impromptu thing that the horn players just started playing. The singers just started repeating, 'Think of me' on their own, I didn't tell them to do that."

According to Rundgren, after having done it all himself in California, the New York sessions came as something of a relief. "That was the point of it," he says, "to be kind of informal, in a way. Throughout the various phases of what I've done, I've always placed an emphasis on being able to actually perform it, even in the studio. If I'm doing it myself, obviously, I can't play everything at once, but if I'm working with a band or doing a production with somebody else, I'm always encouraging people to try and do it as live as possible."

"Todd would be singing and playing," says Klingman, "and still trying to engineer. He'd show people their parts and then go back and forth to the booth to get the sounds and levels right. He had [Dan Turbeville] in there working for him, but everyone knew it was Todd's concept. I remember that, for putting the band together, I was paid triple time in contractor's fees because it was a Sunday. I got a check for $2,200, for one day's work. That was a lot of money back then."

Two additional tracks, 'Piss Aaron' and 'Some Folks Is Even Whiter Than Me,' were recorded back at Bearsville Studios with engineer Nick Jameson. Woodstock regular Jim Colegrove recalls his lone session as bassist on 'Piss Aaron.' "Todd wanted a line-up of Great Speckled Bird members," he says. "So they had Amos Garrett on guitar, Billy Mundi on drums, Ben Keith on pedal steel, me on bass. Todd played electric piano. At the beginning of the song you hear Todd describing what he's looking for in the track and then you can hear Amos reply, 'Ah, my meat.'"

"I played piano on 'Some Folks,'" says Klingman, "and we had Billy Mundi on the drums again, plus members of the Paul Butterfield band, without Butterfield, of course."

The remaining song on the album, 'Slut,' was a raucous leftover from the ID Sound sessions with James Lowe. It featured Hunt and Tony Sales, with guitarist

Rick Vito, piano player Charlie Schoning, the tenor saxophones of Jim Horn and John Kelson, plus backing vocals from future *Battlestar Galactica* and *Miami Vice* star Edward James Olmos. Remaining in LA after Rundgren's departure, Lowe says he was grateful to have played a key role in Todd Rundgren's recorded history up to that point. "He's a very, very bright guy," says Lowe, "and the records we made together were worthwhile. And that's a great thing to stand next to. It really is."

Something/Anything? was released in February of 1972. It climbed to Number 29 on the *Billboard* album charts but took a full three years to reach RIAA Gold Award status. Still, the record dropped three notable singles: 'Hello It's Me' (Number Five on *Billboard*), 'I Saw The Light' (Number 16), and the Nazz-like, proto-power pop anthem 'Couldn't I Just Tell You' (Number 93).

In addition to displaying prodigious production chops, Rundgren was increasingly tagged as the rock singer/songwriter of the day, most commonly as the male counterpart to Carole King, an easy categorization that didn't sit well with him. "I think there was an expectation," he says, "that I would continue to pursue that role. With all due respect to Carole, I took no comfort in merely being labeled a 'singer/songwriter.' It wasn't what I was hoping to create as a musical legacy for myself. So, after *Something/Anything?* had been such a big success, I saw it as a chance to take stock of what I wanted to do next, change a few things and redefine myself. I wasn't really aware, at that time, that I'd make such a radical shift – in every way – for what would become my next record, *A Wizard, A True Star*."

5

A Wizard, A True Star

"Ignore Me," a smiling, dynamite-wielding Todd Rundgren dared listeners in the Bearsville print ad for *Something/Anything?* But in 1972, ignoring Rundgren was not a growth industry. To the critics and the rock audience at large, the unprecedented and unexpected success of Rundgren's double album had heralded his arrival as both a major artist and a tech-savvy self-producer. While there were detractors, who had found it overstuffed, overindulgent, and unfocused, most rock writers gushed over Rundgren as the rightful 70s heir to the throne of 60s studio mavens such as Brian Wilson or The Beatles. But a funny thing happened on the way to what young John Lennon once called "the toppermost of the poppermost." Todd Rundgren got bored. After a disappointing Runt tour, including an underwhelming debut at LA's Troubadour, supported by N.D. Smart's mime-rock band, The Hello People, Rundgren returned to New York City with change on his mind. The runt was in a rut.

"I became aware," says Rundgren, "that I was doing things out of habit, writing short pop tunes, recycling the same methods at all the same places. After listening to it over and over, *Something/Anything?* had started to lose its cachet for me. I felt like I'd been musically lazy, like I wasn't expanding or incorporating anything new into the music. I tend to think it's more valuable when an artist, myself or some other artist whom I admire, does something that they haven't done before. I don't like formulas, and I'm personally incapable of following them, anyway."

Once again living in New York, in an East 13th Street brownstone apartment with Bebe Buell, a beautiful young model from Virginia whom he had met in April, the only thing Rundgren knew for sure about his next album was that it would be "more eclectic and more experimental," if only because he had recently been introduced to the technicolor world of psychedelic drugs.

"Actually the very first psychedelic I took, I didn't like very much," Rundgren admits. "It was DMT (Dimethyltryptamine) which produces this 15-minute, but really severe, hallucinogenic trip. You smoke it, and it was extremely fast and intense, but it tasted like melted plastic bags. As a result, I soon became fascinated with the whole idea of psychedelic drugs, and started doing mescaline, psilocybin, mushrooms, and things like that. I never took acid, to my knowledge, but I imagine it would have been similar to some of the other experiences I'd had."

As he approached the making of *A Wizard, A True Star*, the sound and structure of Rundgren's music would be further informed by his new, post-hallucinogenic, state. "I became more aware," he says, "of what music and sound were like in my internal environment, and how different that was from the music I had been making. My new challenge was to try to map, as directly as I could, the various kinds of chaotic musical element in my head."

It wasn't strictly about songs, either, as Rundgren recalls actively pursuing noises and sound effects that often blurred the line between music and total abstraction. "There were sounds that make you think of things," he says, "like frickin' dogs fighting, laughter, or song fragments that don't complete themselves. All these little musical instrumental bits that essentially are supposed to create some sort of imagery without the benefit of lyrics. It was very ADD, actually, and I wouldn't dwell on whether a musical idea was complete or not. In that way, it sort of resembled the arc of a psychedelic experience."

Before he could begin, Rundgren first needed to build his own studio in order to facilitate these ongoing explorations into musical innerspace. "It was really important to me," he says, "to create a new work environment where I wouldn't be a slave to the clock or the gear that they had at a given studio."

Enter, once again, Moogy Klingman, who had been renting a loft in an industrial building on 24th Street near Eighth Avenue, where he lived and rehearsed with his own band, Moogy & The Rhythm Kings. "The guy who lived there before me," says Klingman, "had actually built a tiny studio in the front area of the loft, and the back half was the living area. It wasn't very elaborate, though; the guy had just put up a wall with the glass and a separate control room area. The space was great for me, because nobody else lived in this building, so we were able to play all night. Todd used to come up and jam with us sometimes."

Rundgren says he had been planning to invest some of the royalties generated by the hit singles from *Something/Anything?* into his own studio when Klingman came to him with a proposition. "Moogy said, 'If you get the equipment, I'll provide the space and we'll make a studio.' I said, 'Okay, that sounds fine.' And that's how we started Secret Sound. The very first session we did there was for *A Wizard, A True Star.*"

"This was just as 'Hello It's Me' was getting into the Top Ten," says Klingman, "and I had also gotten a $10,000 advance from Capitol Records for my second album, *Moogy II*, which Todd co-produced with me. I dumped that money into building Secret Sound. We converted the entire place to Todd's exacting standards. He really liked to do little electronics projects, so he decided to wire up the studio all by himself. He spent about two or three months wiring away while his single was Number One. Frankly, he should have been out on tour, following up on the chart success."

"It was pretty much like in the old *Little Rascals* movies," laughs Rundgren. "We didn't know about wiring up a studio or how to build walls, but we just kind of did it. We built a little drum booth and a control room, nailing all the two-by-fours ourselves. I built the console myself. And this was during my whole psychedelic period, so I was taking peyote buttons and wiring the studio at the same time. It was a lot of repetitive work, wiring and schematics, so it made it more interesting. Still, I'm a little surprised it all worked."

"Todd brought in sets of vibes, organs, other keyboards, all this equipment," Klingman recalls. "Fairchild equalizers, some Dolby stuff, as well as his Stephens 16-track machine. It was breaking down all the time and this guy, John Stephens, was the only guy who knew how to fix it. We'd have to call him long distance in England. That studio was barely held together with band-aids and bubble gum."

"The whole reason I built Secret Sound," Rundgren admits, "was to explore sound. I originally designed it to be a four-channel, quadraphonic studio, what was then surround sound. But we didn't have much call for quad projects, so every once in a while we would do something in quad, just for fun. I have to say that, in some sense, *A Wizard, A True Star* was kind of rushed through because the studio wasn't finished. Often, we'd have to wire something together, get the song tracked, then unwire it again, and a lot of it seemed sort of ad hoc."

According to Rundgren, he was still wiring the console seconds before recording 'Sometimes I Don't Know What To Feel,' but Klingman disagrees, recalling that the first song recorded was the album opener, 'International Feel.' "Todd was in the room by himself," he says, "and he said, 'Hey Moogy, I'm gonna start recording now.' Then, he laid down the bass part to 'International Feel,' and just started adding on to it with these very noisy synthesizer growls. The more overdubs he did, the more it started to sound like something."

Rundgren says that he intended the album to follow a kind of flight plan, starting from a chaotic opening before flowing seamlessly from track to track with no breaks other than the necessary limitations of side one and side two, inherent to the vinyl album. Side one opened and closed with two entirely different recordings of 'International Feel.' The first version was with all instruments played by Rundgren alone, whereas the second, 'La Feel Internacionale,' was a full-band remake with Moogy & The Rhythm Kings, including John Siomos on drums, Ralph Schuckett on keyboards, and John Siegler on bass.

Rundgren says that, while he had planned most of the album's segues, certain others were the product of happenstance. "Obviously, the segue between 'International Feel' and the second track, 'Never Never Land,' with Moogy playing the piano part [and Rick Derringer on pedal steel guitar], is somehow constructed, because of all the overlapping echoes and such; but for the most part I had some vague idea what the running order was."

As the listener wades through the latter part of the record, Rundgren's design called for the vibe to "settle down into recognizable forms," including a medley of his favorite soul tunes, among them Curtis Mayfield's 'I'm So Proud,' Smokey Robinson's 'Ooh Baby Baby,' and The Delfonics' 'La La Means I Love You,' topped of by a mildly sarcastic take on The Capitols' 1966 dance craze hit, 'Cool Jerk,' rendered Zappa-esque by a 7/4 time signature.

Saxophone star David Sanborn was part of a horn section that included Barry Rogers and Mike and Randy Brecker. Sanborn, who had first met Rundgren back in Woodstock as a member of The Paul Butterfield Blues Band (and had played on the *Taking Care Of Business* session in LA), described his part in *Wizard* to Doug Ford, host of the popular RundgrenRadio podcast, in January 2009.

"He was the first guy that I knew of who really used the studio as an instrument," Sanborn said, adding that Rundgren would allow the players to "screw around with the stuff and discover parts ... but Todd was always very much in control about the direction of the music ... we felt like we were active participants in the creation of that music."

Rundgren insists that, while the so-called soul medley may have appeared "somewhat incongruous," at first, it was all part of the hallucinogenic storyline of the record as a whole. "It's like opening up a hole in your memory, and suddenly these memories – soul records you loved, say – start leaking out from who knows where. That's another aspect of psychedelic drugs sometimes, hearing and seeing things that would be familiar to you if you weren't so psychedelic. You suddenly see them differently and they convey a different meaning."

Rundgren's proximity to Moogy & The Rhythm Kings, whom he used throughout the band tracks for *Wizard*, was both advantageous and convenient. "Moogy and I were useful for each other at the time," says Rundgren. "He was a good piano player who liked to jam with everybody and therefore knew lots of players. He was kind of like a walking Rolodex. Moogy did a lot of session work, whereas I was not a session musician. I would sometimes jam at Steve Paul's Scene, but I wasn't a big socializer and I didn't hang. Moogy, though, would go out to all the clubs and he knew people like Buzzy Linhart and Bette Midler and all the people on our first Secret Sound sessions."

"We were up in Moogy's rehearsing every day," says John Siegler. "We'd all show up around four or five o'clock and we'd play until around 11pm. Then everybody would go out to dinner, and maybe out to The Scene to jam, or to a gig at Reno Sweeney's. That was our routine. So when Todd needed guys to play on his record, we were already there. It was like a club, Secret Sound was our clubhouse, and suddenly Todd was the leader of the club."

According to Siegler, an average day in the clubhouse involved Rundgren coming in with a piece of music, written on piano or guitar, which the band would learn, by ear, making their own notes and charts if needed. "Todd's piano style is very left-hand bass, right-hand choppy chords," says Siegler, "so sometimes the bass would be clearly indicated. Todd never ever sang on a session, though, so you never knew what the melody was. Todd may have had a sense of one, but we rarely heard it while we did the basic tracks. We rarely even knew what the title of the song was at that point."

'Just Another Onionhead,' the next in Rundgren's emerging line of comic numbers (see 'Song Of The Viking' on *Something/Anything?*) smash-cuts into the outré vaudeville of 'Dada Dali,' Rundgren's Bonzo Dog Band-like tribute to Salvador Dali, sung over a wildly re-imagined version of the 20s Al Jolson standard, 'Toot, Toot, Tootsie.'

Klingman recalls an odd moment from the tracking session. "Todd wanted us to play all wrong notes, so we did. He's up there singing 'Da Da Dali, Goodbye' like Jolson, and we're playing all these weird dissonant notes when, out of the blue, Albert Grossman walks in to watch the session. All these musicians are playing all wrong notes, and Todd's running back and forth to the control room and singing like Jolson; but Albert didn't miss a beat. He didn't say, 'What the hell are you doing Todd? You should be working on a follow up to "Hello It's Me,"' or anything like that. He just kept silent and nodded like everything was fine."

"I have to say," Rundgren adds, "that Albert, in as much as he was simultaneously my manager and the owner of Bearsville Records, was surprisingly receptive to the whole thing."

Siegler recalls being encouraged to bring "whatever we wanted" to the music, and has particularly fond memories of tracking 'Sometimes I Don't Know What To Feel,' which once again included the Brecker Brothers horn section. "That's one of my favorite Todd songs," says Siegler. "I remember he just sat down and played that on piano and we learned the chords. Everyone was hearing these great chord changes, reacting and coming up with parts that complemented what he was doing. Later, when the track was done, I heard the melody and the lyrics for the first time and it was just amazing."

Siegler also witnessed the flowering of Rundgren's musical theater side on tracks like 'Never Never Land.' "He still needed Moogy to play that for him," Siegler remembers, "he couldn't play it on the piano, but it totally fitted what he was doing. When someone's a real talent with great originality, like Todd, it's usually a product of what he grew up with. I hear a lot of Ravel in Todd, and Gilbert & Sullivan, and it sometimes leaks through. He's so musically intelligent he couldn't help but be influenced by all that stuff."

Keyboardist Ralph Schuckett concurs with Siegler, recalling that Rundgren often spoke of Ravel as his favorite classical composer at the time. "He surely couldn't help but be informed by a man who many considered one of the best orchestrators of all time. He likely got some of those chords, like a G chord with a C in the bass, from listening to all those impressionistic composers like Ravel or Debussy."

Schuckett notes, however, that Rundgren's own unique voicings would themselves influence a generation of later pop acts in the 70s and 80s, from Barry White to Prince. "Nobody [in pop] was doing that stuff before Todd," Schuckett insists, "and I listened to everybody, you know?"

One element that Schuckett felt he and Klingman had brought to Rundgren's music was their shared passion for jazz and funk. "I pretty much split all the keyboard parts, half and half, with Moogy on *A Wizard, A True Star*. We were both keyboard fanatics who had pretty good chops, so we would figure out all these interlocking funky parts. I don't think Todd really listened to much funk, so we were kind of showing him that stuff."

Rundgren spent the next month recording *A Wizard, A True Star,* often by himself or with the band, depending on the track. "Todd was the sole engineer," says Klingman, "he would go in the control room and set levels and come out and we would play and then he would run back in and adjust the levels. It was astonishing to watch, but that's how he liked to work."

The album closes with a song that has since become something of a Rundgren concert anthem and fan-favorite, 'Just One Victory,' the basic tracks for which had been started well before the *Wizard* sessions, and before Secret Sound was even built. "That song," Rundgren declares, "was always meant to have an anthemic quality. I had actually recorded it on an eight-track machine at Advantage Studios and never finished it. In fact, I'm not exactly sure how, but I bounced it up to the 16-track machine at Secret Sound, later on. It was just a leftover, based on a jam that I had done with a bunch of musicians including a bass player with whom I only played a couple of times ['Buffalo' Bill Gelber] and Johnny Siomos on the drums. I just showed them these simple, repeating parts and we did it. It was all thrown up so fast that nobody noticed that the tape machine was running at 7½ips instead of 15ips, so I had to do some fixing, later on, to get it sounding better. Since the track was kind of peculiar to itself, I later realized that it seemed to fit into the mixed-bag approach to *Wizard*. After, of course, the song took on a life of its own and has since become something of an expected concert closer. People get pissed if we don't do it."

With all his eclectic fragments laid out on pieces of tape before him, Rundgren went about the arduous task of editing it all together – from cosmic to comic, and funny to funky – until he had two sides of continuous music with few breaks. "I was conscious that there was this shape to *A Wizard, A True Star*," he says, looking back. "Obviously I didn't adhere strictly to the story arc, but still there's a sense that while it may veer or loop-de-loop in some places, it's going to return to it eventually. It's like something interesting happens here, something adds tension here, then another peak at the end, then a resolution, and so on. There was a lot of consternation from the record label, actually, because I had decided there wouldn't be any singles on it. I intended it to be taken as a whole, because all these songs are either too long or too short, or about something weird!"

To further complicate matters, *A Wizard, A True Star* was released just as late-starter single 'Hello It's Me' was finally nudging its way into the upper reaches of the American hit parade. Assessing the album in 1998, Bearsville Records' label boss, Rundgren's old friend Paul Fishkin, explained their "bad luck with timing" to *Mojo*'s Barney Hoskyns.

"Todd was off on his psychedelic adventure," Fishkin told Hoskyns, "and then a year later 'Hello' becomes a hit. At which point we're up against Todd in a completely different mindspace ..."

Rundgren recalls that while Fishkin and the Bearsville front office fretted over the missed opportunity to "make me the new Elvis," Grossman continued to actively support his artistic statement, right down to its unique (and costly) packaging design. "Albert was actually the one who came up with the idea of putting the little [Patti Smith] band-aid poem ['Star Fever'] inside, as well as the die-cut postcard that said 'If you send this card in we'll put your name on the *next* record.' Those were all his marketing ideas. Albert didn't seem to have the same aversion that ultimately the critics and some other people had to it."

In the end, Rundgren swears he had no special agenda behind the album. "It was fairly early in my psychedelic explorations, so everything at that point is just pretty colors and this world of new discoveries. *A Wizard, A True Star* is just like a baby trying to get back to an un-imprinted point where all of this input doesn't necessarily have a preconceived meaning. I left it up to the listener to place it somewhere or rank it, evaluate it, remember it, forget it, whatever."

While Bearsville braced for *Wizard*'s March 1973 release, Rundgren put together a touring band, often referred to as Utopia Mark I, comprised of upstart rhythm section Hunt and Tony Sales, a Floridian keyboard player named Dave Mason (not to be confused with the guitarist from Traffic), and a French synthesizer specialist named Jean-Yves 'M Frog' Labat. Journalist Ron Ross described some of the technological advances promised on the upcoming Utopia tour in a March 1973 feature for *Phonograph Record.*

"Each of the Utopians' instruments will plug into *the module*," Ross wrote, "and headsets will keep them in communication with Jean-Yves. A large art deco Theremin will hang behind the band, which they can play at will by intercepting the space between its two globes. Todd will play a double-neck 'flying W' lead guitar, with six and 12-string necks, while Tony's guitar is unique in having six-string guitar and four-string bass. The Electronic Music Studio [EMS], an English synthesizer manufacturer and designer, has devised a new sound for Todd's guitar, the 'Popeye Mutilator.' Like fuzz tone or wah-wah it is completely at its master's control, one more step toward the guitar's evolution as the most useful sexual tool since KY jelly."

By most accounts, however, Utopia's subsequent mid-April tour was an ambitious failure. A rare overreach by Rundgren, the show was taken off the road by the first week of May. "It was pretty funny," says Tony Sales, recalling the mayhem of the two-week fiasco. "I remember Jean-Yves was pretty spaced out, playing his synthesizers in that geodesic dome while Hunt was eight feet in the air. He was getting a one second delay on the music up there. At the time, *Ziggy Stardust* was really huge, so I think Todd was trying to get in on the whole glam, space-rock thing. We all had different colored hair: Todd was three-colors, Jean-Yves was lime green, mine was pink, and Hunt had his skunk hairdo, with a tail and that whole thing. Norma Kamali had designed these crazy looking black spandex stage outfits with these silver glitter wings on them and, at one point, we even had these space helmets converted from welders' helmets. Our guitars were decorated too, so when we came on, the whole thing must have looked pretty good under all the lights."

As he had sung in 'International Feel,' Rundgren would have to "wait another year" to launch a reinvented and notably improved Utopia. In the meantime, he bought time and generated income by continuing to take on outside production work. In addition to *Mother's Pride*, a mostly-forgotten album by all-female rock group Fanny, Rundgren was about to preside over two of the most notable rock albums of 1973: The New York Dolls' self-titled debut and Grand Funk Railroad's commercial breakthrough, *We're An American Band*.

6

New York Dolls

"The New York Dolls," wrote the young Morrissey in his 1981 book about the group, "were the first real sign that the 60s were over. Their unmatched vulgarity dichotomised feelings of extravagant devotion or vile detestation. It was impossible to look upon the Dolls as adequately midstream, just as it was impossible to ignore them."

The industry may not have known what to make of them, but The New York Dolls' impact on a generation of kids, particularly in Britain, was nothing short of revolutionary. Their 1973 debut, produced by Todd Rundgren, struck such a chord with Morrissey that he was not only moved to form his own influential group, The Smiths, with Johnny Marr, but would eventually convince the surviving Dolls to reunite for the 2004 Meltdown Festival in London.

But first, let's go all the way back to New York's Endicott Hotel where, on December 24 1971, the original New York Dolls – David Johansen (also known as David Jo Hansen), lead guitarist Johnny Thunders, bass player Arthur 'Killer' Kane, guitarist Sylvain Sylvain, and his childhood pal, original drummer Billy Murcia – made their debut.

"We were all these young club kids," says Sylvain Sylvain, squinting from the distance of 2009. "We were not part of the 60s. We'd all heard our own callings and came to New York to become stars and to show our wares. The Dolls was only supposed to last a few weeks, you know? We just said 'Hey, maybe this will get us some chicks.' That seemed like a good enough reason."

Sylvain and Murcia had originally planned to go into the clothing business, via their Woodstock-based company, Truth And Soul Sweaters, but as the 70s began, they were back in New York City and working out of a Lexington Avenue 'hippie boutique' called Different Drummer.

"This guy, Johnny Thunders, used to come in and shop there all the time," says Sylvain. "The place was across the street from a toy repair shop called the New York Dolls Hospital, which is still around today. I always used to say to Billy and Johnny, 'Man wouldn't that be a great name for a band, someday.' They'd say, 'What, New York Dolls Hospital?' I'd go, 'No, just The New York Dolls.'"

Johnny Thunders had tried his hand at little league baseball and dealing drugs before picking up the electric guitar. His uniquely sloppy way with a slashed power chord seemed tailor-made to accompany singer David Johansen's swaggering stage manner and the two would eventually draw endless comparisons to the Stones' Jagger and Richards. The New York Dolls were ragged and unpolished but something about them seemed to work, and they soon touched off a kind of downtown glam-rock rebellion.

At the end of October 1972, the Dolls flew to England to open for The Faces (and The Pink Fairies) at the Empire Pool, Wembley (now Wembley Arena), to great critical interest. But while partying in the UK, drummer Murcia suffocated in a bathtub after ingesting a lethal combination of drugs and alcohol. Shaken, but driven to succeed, the band had replaced him with Jerry Nolan by the year's end, as managers Marty Thau, Steve Leber, and David Krebs continued, in vain, to secure them a recording contract.

Back at home, New York's hottest cult band packed out Max's Kansas City and improvised venues like the Mercer Arts Center. The Dolls were determined, as Sylvain recalls, to fake it until they could make it. "We had to make ourselves *feel* famous," says Sylvain, "before we could actually become famous. We acted like we were already rock stars. Arthur even called his bass 'Excalibur' after King Arthur. It was crazy."

By late 1972, on the heels of 'I Saw The Light,' Todd Rundgren was a genuine rock star. When he socialized at the Scene or Max's, Rundgren's long, green, purple and yellow streaked hair was his calling card, earning him almost as many second looks as his model girlfriend, Bebe Buell. "Bebe brought Todd by to see us play [at Max's]," says Sylvain, "but it wasn't like he was there with a mind to produce the band; he was probably just like everybody else who was brought there by their girlfriends."

At the time, Rundgren's own tastes were leaning increasingly toward the progressive rock stylings of Frank Zappa, Yes, and John McLaughlin's Mahavishnu Orchestra. As such, he says he found the Dolls' act more comedic than musical. "There was definitely a sense of humor about it," Rundgren recalls, "and part of it was also that there was kind of a limit to how seriously you were supposed to take yourself. And I guess that was what kept you from playing too good," he laughs. "It was provocative, but only in the sense that The Rolling Stones were provocative when they would get dressed up in drag. Johnny Thunders wasn't much of a guitar player, but he had that attitude, and the way he looked became highly influential later on. The irony is there that were other raw and sloppy bands in New York, at the time, but those bands were truly unable to play their instruments. By contrast, The New York Dolls came off as competent."

Rundgren also recalls being intrigued by the stage antics of the band's front man, David Johansen. "David had a lot of charisma," says Rundgren, "I mean, there were other lead singers around at the time, but they were either hideous or unable to carry a tune. A lot of it was the legacy of The Velvet Underground, but whereas The Velvet Underground had real musicians like John Cale in the group, the Dolls weren't out to expand any musical horizons."

Rundgren also noted the band's penchant for Brill Building pop and happy-go-lucky rock and roll. "The Dolls were actually from Long Island," says Rundgren, "so there was a distinctly different sensibility from the urban New York thing. Their musical influences were things like The Shangri-Las, and the subject matter of their songs, as punky as they were, usually had a lot to do with the same old boy-girl thing but in a much more inebriated way."

Sylvain recalls that the crucible of fan reaction had already forged most of the material that would later comprise their debut album: "Songs like 'Personality Crisis' or 'Trash' or our version of Bo Diddley's 'Pills' had been tested by the kids who came to see us. To them, these songs were hits before we even recorded them. Our song 'Frankenstein' was a big hit in our live show, but even before we got to make a record of it, Edgar Winter came out with his own song called 'Frankenstein.' Now, his thing didn't sound at all like ours, but I'm sure he stole our title. That's why we decided to call our song 'Frankenstein (Original)' on that first album."

Acclaimed *Rolling Stone* journalist Bud Scoppa was then publicity director at Mercury Records, and recalls the first time he and Mercury A&R man Paul Nelson saw the band in their natural habitat, with a roomful of excited fans, at the Mercer Arts Center. "At first," Scoppa recalls, "they appeared to me to be a cartoon version of The Rolling Stones. They were funny but I didn't think they were very good, so I split after the first set. Paul stuck around for the second set, though, and after the show he called me and said, 'You should have stayed. I think they're really special.' Then, after that, I fell in love with them anyway."

In March 1973, The New York Dolls, barely out of their teens, signed a two-album deal with Mercury Records. "When we got that deal," notes Sylvain, "some of our parents had to sign for us because we were too young."

Scoppa recalls Mercury's search for a producer who could exploit the band's sound on record in a manner that would best capitalize on the buzz among local fans and critics. He also recalls the first time he and Nelson took the band to Chicago to attend a board meeting at Mercury's head office. "There were some funny times," says Scoppa. "I'll never forget these incredibly straight record executives on one side and David just putting his head in his arms and dozing off, right there in the Mercury conference room."

Johansen was awakened just as Rundgren's name was being floated to produce them. "We just thought, 'Todd? Of course!' He was right under our noses. We were kind of persona non grata, at the time, with most producers. They were afraid of us, I don't know why, but Todd wasn't. We all liked him from Max's and the Scene and we dug the Nazz. Todd was cool and he was a producer."

"It was more a matter of who was available," Sylvain adds, "and who'll take the money we're offering so we can get it out as soon as possible. It wasn't a long list. Todd was in New York and seemed like he could handle the pace."

Mercury booked Rundgren and the band into the Record Plant Studios, despite Rundgren's concerns that it was, to his ears, "the worst sounding studio in the city at that time. There was pressure to finish the record and get it out on time, so we took the only studio available. As it turned out, most of our problems had nothing to do with the recording itself. There were critical expectations, more for the band than me, because the Dolls were critics' darlings and the press had kind of adopted them. Plus, there were lots of extra people around, socializing, which made it hard to concentrate."

Although Sylvain acknowledges the floating party atmosphere, he adds that Rundgren sometimes brought Buell and their dog, Puppet, to the sessions. "He used to put his Chihuahua up on top of this expensive Neve or something console," says Sylvain. "This thing probably cost like a million dollars."

David Johansen, who openly admits that his own memories of the events are often colored by things he's read about them since, recalls a "festive atmosphere" throughout the sessions. "As I recall, it was like the 1920s, with palm tree décor and stuff. Well that's how I remember it, anyway."

Bud Scoppa, on the other hand, says he never witnessed any true craziness at the Record Plant, at least not during his admittedly early visits of an afternoon. "I just remember seeing Todd behind the board in the control room wearing lots of shiny clothes, but he wasn't really involved with any of the funny stuff around them. He just got the job done. There certainly was not an entourage, but things might have gotten a little nuttier as the night wore on. But frankly, I never saw any drugs around until later on, after the album came out."

Johansen agrees that Rundgren, as the band's designated driver, steered the album to completion with the steady hand of a pilot. "It seemed like we were all on this big dirigible and Todd and [engineer] Jack Douglas, and whoever else was making this record with us, were up where they steer the thing. All we wanted to do was get good beats, tempos, and sounds, so we left a lot of that to Todd. It was just about going in and banging out songs and when we enough good takes, we started fixing them up a little bit. To be honest, we probably didn't say that many words to each other while making that album."

One afternoon, Scoppa witnessed an amusing exchange between Rundgren and Kane. "We were in the control room with Todd and the engineer when the band started a take, but something wasn't sounding right. Todd got on the talkback mic right away and said 'Hold it, hold it!' Then he goes out into the room and walks up to Arthur's bass cabinet and plugs in the cord. He said, 'Yeah, that's all you needed. Okay let's try it again!' It was sort of an encapsulation, I thought, of his attitude toward the band. Todd was such a 'musician' while they were just getting by on attitude and energy. But as disdainful as he appeared to be at some points, he got the job done really well."

Sylvain says he never felt like Rundgren talked down to the band: "I think he was actually quite taken that we obviously derived our talent from the streets. We may not have been professionally trained, but we could still write three minutes worth of magic. He probably played with other well-seasoned players who may have graduated from Julliard or worked the orchestra pit, but could they write a damn good fucking tune? Todd knew we were writing tunes for our generation."

Sylvain adds that while Rundgren was "basically hands off," he wasn't afraid to step in and be the producer if it meant getting a better take. "There were a few times where Jerry just couldn't keep the beat, so Todd joined him in the isolation booth with a drumstick and would whack out the beats on a cowbell, sort of a live click-track, for Jerry in his cans."

Tony Glover, writing in *Rolling Stone* magazine in 1973, described a lead-vocal session for 'Personality Crisis,' in which Johansen, having presumably been coached beforehand by Rundgren to go wild on the microphone, sauntered back into the control booth, earnestly inquiring, "Was that ludicrous enough?"

"A lot of David's vocals," Rundgren recalls, "sounded like some guy who's just drunk and screaming. But in other ways it was kind of articulate because of his propensity to incorporate certain cultural references into the music. 'Personality Crisis' was a great example of that."

Sylvain Sylvain has a surprisingly clear memory of the gear used on the album, especially when one considers that it has been almost four decades since they made it. He also explains the real reason why the Dolls chose their iconic Gibson Les Paul Junior guitars. "They only cost around $200 to $300, whereas Les Paul Customs or Black Beauties cost like $900 or $1,000. Later, people called us geniuses for picking up the Junior, but we were broke and could never fucking afford a Custom. We called them 'automatic guitars' because you didn't have to fuck around with like ten knobs or three pick-ups or this and that. There's no master volumes or three-way switches."

Besides the occasional Fender Twin Reverb amp, The New York Dolls' main amplification setup involved running the output of a 100 watt Marshall Plexi head into the speaker cabinets of a Fender Dual Showman. "Plexis were all Marshall made back then," says Sylvain, "and we'd only use the Showman because it was the biggest cabinet Fender made, so we married those two together."

As legend has it, Johnny Thunders and Todd Rundgren did not share any great mutual admiration, with Thunders famously carping to a journalist that Rundgren "fucked up the mix" on the Dolls' debut. Johansen, however, can't really recall witnessing any open hostility between the guitarist and producer in the studio. "John used to mouth off to everybody," he insists, "it was kind of a defense mechanism, but usually he was kidding. I don't think Johnny had any special dislike of Todd, though."

Bud Scoppa likewise never saw any conflict between Rundgren and Thunders. "Johnny Thunders was kind of a knucklehead," laughs Scoppa. "I remember he used to run around in these high-heeled sneakers, actual Converse All-Stars with high heels. But he didn't seem to me to be a terribly intense guy; he just seemed to be having fun at that point. We'd take them all to the automat next door and they'd be really happy to just get some free food."

Scoppa says he could see where Rundgren's work ethic might have clashed with the band's freewheeling lifestyle, however. "Todd's professionalism probably forced them to maintain a certain schedule. He doesn't put up with bullshit. I mean, those guys rarely started their live sets before midnight, so who knows? Todd was very much in charge in the studio, however, and I got the impression that everybody was looking to him."

Of the few instrumental ornaments added to the band's live sound, Buddy Bowser added a raunchy, freeform saxophone to 'Lonely Planet Boy', while

Johansen overdubbed some distant extra vocal sounds by singing into overdriven guitar pickups. The singer also added some bluesy harmonica to 'Pills' and an Asian gong to 'Vietnamese Baby.' Rundgren was encouraged to add some piano flourishes to 'Personality Crisis' and 'Private World,' synthesizers to 'Frankenstein' and 'Vietnamese Baby,' and was part of the background vocal wash on 'Trash.'

"I actually played the first rhythm piano on 'Personality Crisis' on the studio's Yamaha grand," Sylvain insists. "Then Todd came in and [added] all those Jerry Lee Lewis swishes. For 'Frankenstein,' I remember him getting those weird sounds from this beautiful old Moog synthesizer he brought in. He said it was a model that only he and The Beatles had."

Although Rundgren attempted to keep the band away from the mixing session, as he would do with most of his clients over the coming years, he warily recalls the Dolls insisting on being present, even though they clearly seemed, to him, bored and distracted. Rundgren now admits that, as a result of being rushed and second-guessed by the band, the mix quality suffered as a whole.

"In many ways the album got away from them," admits Rundgren. "I don't think I'm the first producer who ever wanted to ban a band from the mixing sessions. It's too easy for it to become a free-for-all, with every musician only hearing their own part and not the whole. They all had other places to be, so rather than split, they rushed the thing and if that wasn't enough they took it to the crappy mastering lab that Mercury had put them in."

Today, Johansen praises Rundgren for enduring their frantic energies and getting what he feels was a great-sounding record. "As far as I'm concerned," says Johansen, "one of Todd greatest strengths as a producer is his EQ, just the way he makes what comes out of the amps or your mouth or the drums sound. I like it a lot. It makes you feel like you're in a room and there's a band playing. He could take this *mishigas* [craziness] of us playing and then he could go off, listen to each instrument, and EQ them in such a way that they all sound really enriched, I think."

"A lot of producers would try to make you seem perfect," adds Sylvain, "instead of presenting you the way you are. They'd have you doing your track over and over or else they'd 'fix it in the mix.' But that's about the producer's execution not the musician's, and it kind of takes away a little bit as far as I'm concerned. Todd made it sound exactly like a band on a stage. He put Johnny Thunders on the right side and me on the left side. You know, the kids have talked about that for years. That thing that became The Ramones and The Sex Pistols and that whole punk thing."

"Introducing The New York Dolls: A Band You're Gonna Like, Whether You Like It Or Not" read the Mercury Records ad slogan announcing the release of *New York Dolls* in August 1973. The album sleeve bore an iconic Toshi photograph of the band in drag, crowding onto a long couch like a group of transvestite wallflowers at a particularly dull social event. Yet the music inside was anything but.

Reviewer Nick Kent had this to say about it the August 25 1973 issue of Britain's *New Musical Express*: "The New York Dolls are trash, they play rock'n'roll like sluts and they've just released a record that can proudly stand beside Iggy & The Stooges' stupendous *Raw Power* as the only album so far to fully define just exactly where 1970s rock should be coming from ... Todd Rundgren has worked miracles cooling out his often impetuous whiz-kid overkill to present a vivid document ... on vinyl."

Trouser Press founder/editor Ira Robbins called the album a "seminal slab of early-70s punkitude" and praised the Dolls' "raunchy and sloppy brand of untogether brilliance," concluding that Rundgren had "captured the raucous noise, note for note."

When the Dolls returned to the UK to appear on *The Old Grey Whistle Test* in November of 1973, young British fans, such as 13-year-old Steven Morrissey of Manchester, were as roused by the sexy glamour of the band as they were appalled by the blasé reaction of a clearly underwhelmed 'Whispering' Bob Harris, who legendarily dismissed their sound as "Mock Rock."

"Some bands grab you and they never let you go," Morrissey later told filmmaker Greg Whiteley in the Arthur Kane documentary, *New York Doll*. "No matter what they do, they can never let you down ... The Dolls were that for me."

The album's status as a forerunner to the punk-rock explosion is amusing to Rundgren on several levels, but mainly because he never felt like the band was punk-rock at all. "The irony is that I wound up producing the seminal punk album, but I was never really thought of as a punk producer, and I never got called by punk acts. They probably thought I was too expensive for what they were going for. But the Dolls didn't really consider themselves punk. Now, perhaps Johnny Thunders identified with it, later, but back when I was working with them, they weren't about defying convention in the way that these more hardcore punk acts were politicized. There was nothing political about The New York Dolls."

Grand Funk
We're An
American Band

Grand Funk Railroad, later Grand Funk, were always a divisive band among critics and fans alike. The band was formed in 1968 by guitarist Mark Farner and drummer Don Brewer from Terry Knight & The Pack. They added bass player Mel Schacher and assumed the name Grand Funk Railroad, a playful tribute to the regional Grand Trunk Western Railroad, which ran through their home state of Michigan. Retaining Knight as their manager and career visionary, Grand Funk Railroad had become, by 1971, a stadium-filling act with a string of gold albums to their name. But they had also earned the dubious distinction of being the band that critics loved to hate.

Despite moving large quantities of their first five studio albums, and selling out all 55,000 tickets for a 1971 gig at New York's Shea Stadium within 72 hours, the power trio remained hungry for artistic credibility. Shortly after releasing their 1971 album, *E Pluribus Funk*, the band parted with Knight, setting off a blaze of legal hassles that would take years to extinguish. After promoting tour manager Andy Cavaliere to full manager, and adding keyboard player Craig Frost, they released their self-produced *Phoenix* in 1972. Respect, however, was still not forthcoming, as über-critic Lester Bangs made clear in the pages of *Rolling Stone*: "[*Phoenix*] mostly sounds just about as thin as its predecessors and the material is ... just about as plodding as we've come to expect ..."

Clearly, Grand Funk could never win with the critics. Or could they? Cavaliere and the band were determined to find a way to continue selling millions while commanding at least a modicum of respect. And with *Phoenix* selling more slowly than their previous releases, they needed a plan fast. A scheduled promotional appearance on the ABC TV music program *In Concert* introduced them to one of the show's directors, photographer Lynn Goldsmith.

"*Phoenix* had only sold around 400,000 units," Goldsmith remembers, "where they were used to selling more like a million. I didn't think that Andy, who had been a great road manager, understood larger creative concepts the way I did, so I told him I'd work for him for nothing, but when Grand Funk had a Number One single, I'd [become] a full management partner. He said, 'They've never had a hit single!' I said, 'Trust me, they'll have a Number One, but you'll have to follow everything that I say.' He agreed."

Don Brewer recalls the atmosphere within the Grand Funk camp as they regrouped back at The Swamp, Mark Farner's converted barn and rehearsal studio in Parshallville, about 25 miles outside of Flint, Michigan. "We had been through this whole lawsuit deal with our former manager. He was suing us – and every promoter in every city we were playing in – over the use of our name. We'd been a big hit on FM radio with seven-minute album cuts like 'Closer To Home' and 'Inside Looking Out,' but by 1972, FM had become the new AM radio, so now you had to have three-minute hit songs with commercial appeal."

During the Phoenix tour, Brewer had been humming a little tune based on a list of observations he'd made from his drum stool, the tour bus, and various hotel rooms. Opening act Freddie King, floating poker games, and a celebrated groupie named Connie were all elements in the swirling road reality of a hard-working American band. Unconsciously, Brewer had begun composing the song that would enable Goldsmith and Cavaliere to enact their master plan.

"Up to then," says Brewer, "Mark had been doing most of the writing. But we were really searching for a hit single for Grand Funk, you know? So now, I was starting to jot down ideas too. I remember this line just came into my head, 'We're coming to your town, we'll help you party it down.' Which is exactly what I saw us doing."

Mark Farner added a few musical flourishes of his own as the band huddled in the Swamp and hammered out a workable arrangement for Brewer's tune. "I added that little *diddle-iddle dah* turnaround lick on the guitar," he says, "and kind of suggested ideas for the drum intro, like the cowbell. I said, 'Man, this would be a great intro with the cowbell up-front like in Mountain's 'Mississippi Queen' or the Stones' 'Honky Tonk Women.' I said if we just start this thing with a cowbell it's gonna be a smash hit."

Farner, of course, would be proven right and 'We're An American Band' would eventually become the tip of the spear for Goldsmith and Cavaliere's chart offensive. "At the time," says Goldsmith, "English bands were all the fashion. So to stand out, it seemed logical to have this song that proudly declared that they were an American band."

Goldsmith didn't have to look very far afield for a producer who could polish the song into the number one they craved. She was based in New York, and already friendly with one of the hottest producers in the city, Todd Rundgren. "I had been writing songs with [Rundgren associate] Ralph Schuckett," Goldsmith explains, "and sometimes we'd record them over at Secret Sound, with Todd at the board. So I just told Andy, 'We'll get my friend Todd to produce it.'"

"Lynn was totally gung-ho about Todd producing us," Don Brewer recalls.

"We had looked around at some other producers, but listening to some of Todd's stuff, we just thought, 'This is the guy.' Between the lawsuits and needing to get on singles radio, it was sink or swim time."

The commercial success of 'Hello It's Me' and Badfinger's 'Baby Blue' had proven that Rundgren could deliver hits, if he felt like it. Yet on the critical acceptance front, he had credibility-by-association with The New York Dolls and his own latest solo album, *A Wizard, A True Star,* had cemented his reputation as a creative dynamo. Goldsmith imagined that the headline "Todd Rundgren To Produce Grand Funk" might just wrest the band some respect in the trade papers, so she set up a meeting with him one afternoon at Secret Sound, to discuss the project.

"They were essentially trying to recast the band as a kind of post-Grand Funk," Rundgren recalls. "Up to then, they'd enjoyed a lot of notoriety but it hadn't given them a lot of credibility. Terry Knight had insisted on producing their records, only he seemingly didn't know anything about producing. I suppose Lynn figured that, if they wanted to enact some sort of transformation on the band, I was as transformative a producer as anybody."

Goldsmith wasn't sure if a musician of Rundgren's caliber would be interested in such a meat-and-potatoes Midwestern rock group, so opted instead to make him an offer that was as financially appealing as possible. "I told him, 'We'll pay you a lot, it'll take you ten days tops.' We had booked Criteria Studios in Miami; we'd fly him down there and get the record done while enjoying the sunshine."

Albert Grossman seized the moment to secure a $50,000 advance from Capitol for the Grand Funk sessions, a record amount for 1973, effectively making Rundgren the highest-paid producer in the world at the time. For Grand Funk, it was a considerable investment, but one they were willing to make. Rundgren admits that the he took advantage of the "overvaluation" of the record producer's role in the 70s.

"Magazines started recognizing producers in articles," says Rundgren, "and I was getting 'Producer Of The Year' Awards from *Creem* and stuff. The industry was just starting to recognize that the person in the control room, usually a man at the time, could have a qualitative effect on the final product. More importantly, people at least believed this to be true. I mean, George Martin has a great reputation, but he also produced a lot of acts after The Beatles, none of them anywhere near as big. Well, certain people at that time believed certain things about *me*, and for a string of projects I did during the 70s it was potentially true, too!" he laughs. "Everything that I got involved with enjoyed a degree of success or attention it wouldn't have gotten otherwise."

At the end of May 1973, Rundgren signed his fat deal and prepared to fly out to Michigan to meet the four-piece Grand Funk on their home turf. His only previous exposure to them had been as a loose, improvisational power trio. "At that point," he admits, "I really knew nothing about them except their reputation. When I'd seen them live, I'd found the music a little too dependent on just jamming and stuff. To put it nicely, they weren't exactly Cream. In fact, being a trio was about all they had in common with Cream. So I was curious to see if being a quartet, with keyboards, might change things."

Meanwhile, in anticipation of Rundgren's visit to Flint, Farner says that he and his bandmates saved up ideas and questions to ask him when he arrived. "We were looking forward to seeing how Todd might react to being out there at the Swamp."

Like the alien stepping out of the space capsule in *The Day The Earth Stood Still,* Todd Rundgren set his platform-heeled boots down on the streets of Flint, Michigan, looking roughly 110 per cent more glam than anyone else in the blue-collar town. Don Brewer, who billeted Rundgren at his apartment during the stay, recalls heads turning as band and producer patronized Flint's local eating establishments. "There's Todd, with the long, tri-colored hair," laughs Brewer, "and me with this big Afro. Flint, back then, was not a real progressive town, probably still isn't. There were a lot of redneck factory workers who didn't like long hair in the first place, let alone the crazy clothes Todd liked to wear."

As soon as Rundgren entered the Swamp, he was relieved to find that the band were "funny and friendly Midwestern journeyman musicians who weren't prima donnas about their music. They had all come up working with guys like Bob Seger and playing endless rounds of covers. Michigan was the kind of place where you get your chops together and check your attitude at the door."

Rundgren was equally thrilled to discover that the band had started to become a bit more serious about writing actual songs, as opposed to jam-session riffs. "And they weren't as crappy as everybody had said they were," he says, laughing. "They generally seemed to be making sure we wouldn't be wasting anyone's time when we got to the studio."

While Rundgren had a few arrangement tips, he says the pre-production sessions at the Swamp were more about direction than dictation: "What I tried to do was guide them in a certain path but not be too specific. I'd say, 'Those songs there, that's the direction we want to go in,' things like that."

Rundgren says he also spent a little extra time with guitarist Mark Farner to help him develop a wider tonal palette for the recordings. "Mark is obviously a serviceable enough guitar player," he says, "but he seemed to favor this really *squanky* guitar tone, which I tried to get him away from." Farner says, "Having a great guitar player like Todd there just pushed me to be better, to measure up to him, you know? That's what peers do; iron sharpens iron."

Rundgren was also eager to expand the role of newest member, Craig Frost, by employing more keyboards in Grand Funk's overall sound. "They had evolved," he recalls, "which was better for me because you don't necessarily have to depend so much on doing it all with one guitar."

Satisfied that Grand Funk were as ready as they'd ever be to enter the studio, Rundgren flew home to New York City before reconvening with the band in mid June, down in Miami. "Criteria wasn't my choice," says Rundgren, "and I was ambivalent about it. I would have preferred Secret Sound, but there were certain projects where it just wasn't apropos to do it there. Still, if they wanted Criteria, Criteria it was. And I think they were all happy to be staying [at The Playboy Plaza Hotel in Miami] where they could hang out on the beach before the session. It was all pretty easy-going."

Criteria's fabled Studio C was renowned as the birthplace of hits by James Brown and Aretha Franklin, and it was a favorite of the legendary Tom Dowd, who had produced Derek & The Dominos' *Layla And Other Assorted Love Songs* there. Hallowed ground or not, Farner says he was just excited about his band heading into new and unfamiliar territory. "I tend to think that anything new might inspire me to write a new song or riff. Stuff like that can be the magic it takes to get that feel or sparkle on a record. If you take the feel out of a song you got like 20 per cent of the song left. And luckily for us, Todd is all about feel."

With only ten days booked, Rundgren and the band laid down an impressive two to three basic tracks each day. Their first two days of recording, June 12 and 13, turned out to be miraculously rewarding for all concerned. "The very first day," Rundgren recalls, "we recorded about three basic tracks including the one for 'American Band.' Took us half the day to set up and get sounds and then we went right into cutting it. We had to move fast – they had already established a release date for it."

Cavaliere and Goldsmith had briefed Rundgren on the importance of the 'We're An American Band' single in their overall launch strategy for the album and, for that matter, Grand Funk's career. "It all hinged on that first single being a big hit, ahead of the album," says Rundgren. "So we finished overdubs on it on the second day, and mixed it and mastered it right there – they had a mastering lathe at Criteria – and sent it off to be duplicated and shipped."

With its thunderous drum intro, Don Brewer's earthy, raucous lead vocal, and just the right amount of cowbell, Rundgren's production was exactly what the team had hoped for. While he had felt unsure about mixing such an important single on an unfamiliar console – on only his second day ever inside Criteria – Rundgren says he "just got lucky" with it: "It just happened to sound good enough on the radio that people would want to play it. Maybe if I had had some greater familiarity with that studio, it might have sounded different than it did."

One week later, while the band was still recording the album, 'We're An American Band' entered the singles chart in the Top 20. "Everything had been timed to the day," Rundgren laughs. "In those days, you could ship platinum based on a million pre-orders, so the week after we cut it, Capitol had already gotten the promos out to the radio stations and shipped enough pre-orders to retail to get it into the Top 10. It was just stupefying, and I had never seen anything like it, and it hasn't happened to me since."

Mark Farner recalls the thrill of watching their single enter the charts while they were still making the *American Band* album. "It was like wind in our sails. Now we knew that people were actually waiting for the record."

While Farner had previously been the 'voice' of Grand Funk, Don Brewer's lead vocal was yet another signifier of the band's new direction. Farner, however, credits Rundgren's ingenuity in coaxing the formerly shy drummer out from behind his kit. "I always felt that Don had wanted to be upfront and sing," says Farner, "but he'd been stuck behind the drums. But now, he was writing songs and this was a way for him to be known as a singer. And the boy can sing, you know? So Todd just managed to get Donnie to a place where he was confident with his voice."

Rundgren recorded Brewer's voice with a distinctive room echo, generated from a favorite piece of gear at the time, called a Cooper Time Cube. "In those days," says Rundgren, "we didn't have digital devices to create that sort of room delay, so we used this little Cooper box, which was about the size of a suitcase, with a really long piece of plastic tubing all rolled up inside it. I had one in back at Secret Sound and they had one at Criteria. Aside from the psycho-acoustic effect, it was a cheap way of essentially doubling the voice, and it just helped the voice stand out in the track."

"It really did," confirms Brewer. "He'd put that thing on everything so you'd get this big, husky sound, right up in my headphones. I'd be singing with the effect right on my voice, and I believe he printed it to tape, so I already knew it sounded pretty cool."

According to Rundgren, having Brewer on lead vocal allowed the record-buying public to rediscover Grand Funk "with new ears. Don had more of a straight-ahead rock voice than Mark, and that ended up being more radio-friendly. To some, Don's voice, and all the keyboards, probably made them sound like a new band."

Craig Frost recalls Rundgren emphasizing his rhythm work on the keyboards. "I'd use the Clavinet the way you'd use a rhythm guitar," says Frost. "I played the riff on 'We're An American Band' on the Clavinet, matched up tight with Mark's guitar line. In most Grand Funk songs, I had my left hand on the Clavinet and my right hand on the Hammond B3 organ or maybe the Wurlitzer electric piano, but never a Rhodes."

Frost took notably few solos, and saw his role as a rhythmic link between Farner's guitar, Brewer's beat, and Mel Schacher's bass. "Rhythm is just where I seem to shine," says Frost, "and I remember Todd really liked some of my little things, like the pumping Hammond on 'American Band.' And sometimes he had a few ideas of his own, and they were usually very good ideas!"

One of Rundgren's better ideas was urging the keyboard player to step out and take a solo on 'Black Licorice.' "I came up with this little thing on the organ," says Frost, "and it was probably one of the best solos I've ever done. I think if I tried to play it today, it would be harder for me so I must have been pretty good back then!"

Rundgren saw hard-working Americana emerging as a dominant theme on the album, and was intrigued by a song called 'Working On The Railroad,' which conflated the blue-collar rail workers of the American rust belt with the long hard slog of an American band named after a railroad line. To hammer this point home, literally, Rundgren sent the band out into Criteria's live area to bang on various pieces of metal over the song, which became known as simply 'The Railroad.'

"We wanted to relate to the back-breaking American laborer," says Farner, "and in many ways, it was one of those classic working man's songs. Conceptually,

Todd shared our vision for the song, with the sound of striking down railroad ties, this hard working guy, beating this metal down."

Farner and Brewer's 'Walk Like A Man,' tipped as the second single, was not destined to reach the dizzy heights of the title track, but Farner says that the band were pleased enough with the song that it later became a Grand Funk concert staple. "I was just jamming those chord changes," recalls Farner, "and Donnie liked what I was playing and said 'Hey, man you got any lyrics to that?' He came back with these real rock'n'roll lyrics about strutting like 'a cock until I'm 99.'"

Near the end of their week-and-a-half run at Criteria Studios, Rundgren set about mixing the full album. By this time, he says, he was a lot more comfortable with the console. "The single was very punchy and in your face, but I think that the rest of the mixes on the record are better. By the time we got to the end of record, I had a little bit better sense of what the studio sounded like."

Farner and Brewer both recall watching, in amazement, as Rundgren performed these final mixes. "I just loved his whole approach to mixing the drums," says Brewer. "It was just the coolest thing I'd ever experienced. Todd threw the rulebook out the window; he'd printed everything much hotter to tape than most engineers, who'd always warn you that you're not supposed to push the recording levels too much into the red. Todd ignored all that, and had all this crosstalk and other sounds bleeding through the 16-track tapes. But it sounded great, so who cares whether that's technically the right thing to do or not. If it sounds good, do it."

According to Farner, Rundgren played the mixing board like an instrument. "He knows what he's after, so he's very fast, because doesn't have to think about it too much. He showed me that, rather than boost a frequency to hear it better, you could actually get rid of the other frequencies that were in the way. He'd zero in on certain frequencies then say, 'Aha, that's the one I wanna pull right there!'"

With the single already on its way to Number One, Lynn Goldsmith and Andy Cavaliere, now co-managers of Grand Funk, filmed a ten-minute promotional film for 'We're An American Band,' a kind of long-form precursor to today's rock video, featuring the band jamming up at the Swamp, polishing their cars, and riding motorcycles over Farner's land. Goldsmith's packaging concept for *We're An American Band* – a simple reflective gold cover with a disc stamped on 'gold vinyl' – would become a legend in music marketing. "Of course I was thinking about The Beatles," Goldsmith explains, "they had no band picture on the cover of *The White*

Album. So we did the same but with a simple gold cover, and shipped the album on gold vinyl. We also shot a naked picture of the band, which we put inside the sleeve, but not on the cover. People would have to buy the album to see it, and we also wouldn't have any problems with retail stores."

After the soaring success of the title track, the next single, 'Walk Like A Man,' climbed to a respectable Number 19 on the *Billboard* Singles Chart. The album climbed for weeks, threatening to top the charts before hitting Number Two and then slowing down.

"*We're An American Band* took many by surprise," wrote the late Greg Shaw in a 1974 feature for *Phonograph Record*. "The title song itself was astonishingly good, one of those rare anthems that come once in a lifetime for most groups ... If nothing else, 1973 established that Grand Funk were as much a singles band as a live act ... their acceptance of Rundgren indicated Grand Funk's awareness of pop, of glitter even ..."

To this day, Brewer feels that 'We're An American Band' is "an amazing single. It stills sounds so fresh today, doesn't it? When I hear it on the radio I go, 'God, it really sounds like a hit record, you know?'"

Having risen from the ashes of *Phoenix*, the band was now hotter than ever as they returned to the Swamp to plot their next move. What could they possibly do for an encore? While Goldsmith, Cavaliere, and the members of a reinvigorated Grand Funk sorted that out, Todd Rundgren was already back at Secret Sound, eager to resume his psychedelic wanderings and sketching the blueprints for a new, more expansive, Utopia.

8

An Elpee's Worth Of Toons

A WIZARD, A TRUE STAR

Having aborted the ill-fated Utopia Mark I at the beginning of May 1973, Todd Rundgren had reverted to his increasingly lucrative alternative career as a record producer. By July, he was back in New York City, continuing his research with psychedelics and imagining his next solo album. His 1972 single, 'Hello It's Me,' had continued to linger in the chart even after the March release of his new album, *A Wizard, A True Star*, which contained no singles. To the subtle dismay of Bearsville Records, Rundgren had not shown any inclination to capitalize on 'Hello It's Me' and had floundered with his touring bands. Back at Moogy Klingman's loft on West 24th Street, Rundgren thought about his next move and turned once more to Klingman's crew, who congregated there nightly.

"I ended up co-opting some of Moogy's guys to do a lot of things where I needed a band," says Rundgren. "I'd already worked with Ralph Schuckett and John Siegler, but the drummer, John Siomos, was lured away by Peter Frampton's Camel, and went on to phenomenal success with *Frampton Comes Alive*, so Moogy brought us Kevin Ellman on the drums."

Ellman had studied jazz drumming at Berklee College of Music, and while he had comfortable gigs with Bette Midler, Buzzy Linhart, and Barry Manilow, he was looking for a challenge. "Todd's music had a lot of variety," says Ellman, "plus I knew John and Ralph, so when Todd needed a drummer I was happy to take the gig."

Klingman had employed Ellman on various recording sessions and he seemed to work well with Rundgren's new music. "Todd liked him," says Klingman, "so he started to do some sessions and TV shows and we started to do shows here and there as 'Todd Rundgren.' It was a while before we formally called it Utopia."

Meanwhile, in July and August, Rundgren padded around Secret Sound, laying down the initial tracks that would become his next album, *Todd*. While his earlier psychedelic explorations had taken him all over the map on *Wizard*, he had by now developed something approaching a personal cosmology. For Rundgren, hallucinogenics were not about mere escapism; he needed his trips to take him somewhere.

"Sure, it's great just to see the pretty colors and stuff like that," he says, "but the reason why these explorations have a kind of sacramental significance in all these cultures is because you're supposed to frickin' learn something from it, you know? You're supposed to retain something about what is not normally seen, like when these South-American tribes use these exotic roots that they blow up their noses and hallucinate for three days. They don't think of these as party drugs; they're religious sacraments and are supposed to make a contribution to your spiritual life."

Rundgren's inner explorations led him – logically, one might say – into a self-study of religion and spirituality. He had never been especially religious, nor was he much of a reader, yet for the first time in his life he was devouring every spiritual or religious text he could find in the bookstores of Lower Manhattan. "I was reflecting and reprocessing all the input I was experiencing," he says. "I started to have a greater curiosity about where that psychedelic experience fits into not just my own personal history but the larger history of people's quest for meaning. So I started accumulating all of these books, from Madame Blavatsky to Rudolf Steiner, from Krishnamurti to everything else. It became a sort of hobby; when I would go out on the road there would be a little occult bookstore in every town, and I would go in and find these old one-of-a-kind dusty volumes. Of course each of these books is fervent that you should believe absolutely everything it says, regardless of the fact that it may contradict whatever you find in the next book. But I wondered if there was some small grain of reality or truth in each one of those things, that would perhaps give you an overview of the overall truth."

Working alone, with more synthesizers than ever as well as his usual guitar, pianos, and whatever else he had at hand (including spoons), Rundgren began making short, personal instrumental pieces, like 'The Spark Of Life,' 'Drunken Blue Rooster,' 'Sidewalk Café,' 'In And Out The Chakras We Go (Formerly Shaft Goes To Outer Space),' and 'How About A Little Fanfare?' As with *Wizard*, Rundgren used these electronically enhanced pieces to form musical transitions between his more traditional songs. 'Fanfare,' for instance, segued neatly into 'I Think You Know,' the first vocal song on the record.

"By this time," says Rundgren, "my psychedelic adventures were more a part of a spiritual quest to have a greater understanding about the nature of things. As a result, *Todd* is naturally more orderly, but it also dealt with alternative concepts such as empathy to the point of telepathy. So, on 'I Think You Know,' it's also saying, 'I think at the same moment that you know,' which is the formula for telepathy."

Rundgren's Gilbert & Sullivan roots show in 'Elpee's Worth Of Tunes,' a comic slice of musical theater, heavy on sound effects, with lyrics that bemoan the futility of trying to make a living and "change the world" in the petty-crime scene that the music business so often resembles. Increasingly, Rundgren was finding that light comedy was a handy way to couch serious themes. "In a sense it's all sort of funny to me and, as a result, it comes out as a serious record with a few comedy moments. I give you a little breather, and then it's back to the heavy stuff again. I sometimes regret that I can't do a comedy record with a few serious moments. You know, if one were to take a closer examination of all my lyrics, the humor is actually more universally distributed than it first appears, even in the context of a so-called serious song. The ultimate punchline would be, you know, to stand in front of your Creator, at the end, and ask, 'What was this, just a fucking joke?' and he says, 'Yes.'"

'A Dream Goes On Forever,' a holdover from the songs written for *Wizard*, was a wistful ballad with a flanged clavinet, beat-box rhythm and synthesizer flourishes. While many Rundgren fans welcomed it as a return to the sweeter sounds of *Something/Anything?* the man himself is less fond of the "sappy little song," saying it was the sort he could write, in those days, in his sleep. "I recognized that people like those sorts of tunes, and I have a facility for writing them. People relate to them, but, as with other songs on *Todd*, like 'Useless Begging' and 'Izzat Love,' I usually have to break it to them that, while the songs are sincere in that the emotion in them may be inspired by real events, they're not about a specific thing or person. I compare it to acting. You can tell a bad actor from a good actor; they can move you. My job is to perform the songs convincingly, even if it's not actually about me."

Aware of his own limited keyboard abilities, Rundgren enlisted Klingman to play a variety of classical-sounding keyboards on his somewhat straight recital of the Lord Chancellor's 'Nightmare Song,' from *Iolanthe* by W.S. Gilbert and Arthur Sullivan. "Gilbert & Sullivan had a long-lasting effect on me, musically. When we were teenagers, Randy [Reed] and I could suddenly break into [sings] 'When you're lying awake with a dismal headache, and repose is taboo'd by anxiety … de-dah, de-dah.' So when we cut it for *Todd,* Moogy played it from the original scores, and it was a lot of sheet music to get through. There's always an element of musical theater in my work, and I often think I would enjoy, and possibly do well in, a Broadway or theater context."

Two full band tracks, 'The Last Ride' and 'Don't You Ever Learn,' showcase Rundgren's dexterity, mixing Philadelphia soul with progressive rock, washed in a reverb-heavy mix suggestive of late-period Marvin Gaye. Rundgren recalls consciously exploring "cavernous spaces," courtesy of a new toy, a brand new reverb unit. "By then, I was getting more comfortable with my studio," he admits. "I seem to recall we had a new console and we were getting other bits of equipment in there all the time. I was, both unconsciously and deliberately, messing around with tape delays a little bit more, using all these new tools to create a sense of locality in the sound. Something that would sound cool on headphones – although it wasn't done with that kind of 'stereo demo record' sensibility!"

In addition to having Klingman on piano and Schuckett on organ, Rundgren was joined on 'The Last Ride' by bassist 'Buffalo' Bill Gelber, who had previously played on *Wizard*'s 'Just One Victory,' and drummer Wells Kelly, from the group Orleans. Rundgren processed his Clapton SG through an EMS pitch-to-voltage converter in order to attain his uniquely shrieking guitar tone. "The EMS box had both direct and oscillator outputs," he recalls, "which we would sometimes mix together and then process even further."

Another standout moment on the recording was the soprano saxophone solo by former New York sessioner Peter Ponzol (incorrectly spelled 'Ponzel' on the liner notes). Rundgren had met Ponzol while producing Buzzy Linhart's album, *Buzzy*. "Todd asked me to come up to Secret Sound," the saxophonist recalls, "and I ended up playing two solos over the track and Todd combined parts of both together. There was a lot of talk amongst players about that album since my dear late friend, Mike Brecker, also played on some tracks ['Sons Of 1984'], and yet I ended up with the solo. NYC was an exciting place in the 70s, and Todd's studio was a great place to hang out. Many great late-night jam sessions were held there, with an often interesting mix of jazz and rock players."

Kevin Ellman recalls going up to Secret Sound for his first formal *Todd* session. "We were recording 'Don't You Ever Learn,'" says Ellman, "and I remember being impressed that this wasn't just some makeshift space they'd thrown together, it was a very professional and nicely put-together studio. They didn't have a floor-to-ceiling drum booth, just this drum area enclosed by five foot high baffles, but it worked, and we spent a lot of time in there, working on the sound."

Over the course of the two-month recording window, Ellman would impress Rundgren with his drum technique on subsequent sessions for 'Everybody's Going To Heaven / King Kong Reggae,' and 'Heavy Metal Kids.' While session bassist John Miller was also impressive on these sessions, Rundgren says he had noticed a special chemistry between Ellman and bass player John Siegler when they tracked 'Number 1 Lowest Common Denominator.'

"These guys were bringing an almost 'fusion jazz' sensibility that was not entirely familiar to me," says Rundgren. "Now everyone wanted to play aggressive combinations of rhythm & blues, rock, funk, and jazz, all mushed together. John Siegler was on this cutting-edge Larry Graham kind of jazz funk thing, and he contributed some very curious basslines and stuff that I wouldn't have thought to do. He played well with Kevin, and it takes a rhythm section that pretty much knows where they're at, so that everyone else, regardless how far off the map they stray, can take some assurance that somebody knows what they're doing."

The culmination of this was in a live recording session at an afternoon concert held on August 25 1973 at Wollman Rink in New York's Central Park. For the special 1pm matinee, Rundgren set out to capture a few songs on tape, particularly the anthemic 'Sons Of 1984.' He booked the Brecker brothers, Hall & Oates, and a solid backing ensemble comprised of Klingman, Schuckett, Ellman, and Siegler.

"We played a little mini concert," Siegler recalls. "I think we played 'Black Maria,' 'I Saw The Light,' and 'Hello It's Me,' followed by 'Sons Of 1984,' which was the whole point of the show. I remember that besides Daryl and John we had my friend Googie [Coppola, from Siegler's other band, Air] there singing."

To capture a sing-along section in 'Sons Of 1984,' Rundgren and his crew had strung up some microphones in the Central Park trees. "The plan," says Rundgren, "was to overdub other audiences in different cities, singing the same section."

"He overdubbed another crowd from a show in San Francisco," Siegler recalls. "Todd was always thinking conceptually, you know? He just said, 'We'll just put two cities together and split it down the middle [of the stereo spectrum].'"

"You are the chosen ones," Rundgren sings on 'Sons Of 1984.' He had finally chosen Schuckett, Klingman, Siegler, and Ellman to be the new Utopia. According to Schuckett, Rundgren's delay in adopting them may have come down to a matter of visual style. "Moogy would always pump him, like, 'When are we gonna be on the tour, when are we gonna be a band?' Todd would just say, 'Well, we'll see, we'll see, I'm not sure yet.' He was always very concerned with the visual aspect of his show, and those Sales guys were really hot looking and dressed real trendy. I don't know if he ever articulated it, but there was a general feeling that the guys who played on his records, we didn't look much like rock stars. We weren't exactly bad looking, but comparatively, we were just a bunch of nerdy Jewish guys with curly hair."

To remedy this, and to indulge his desire for more theatrical presentation,

Rundgren insisted that the band wear the platform boots, glittery outfits, and face makeup that had become an integral part of his stage look. Adding to the visual flair, he had also welcomed back green-haired synthesizer player Jean-Yves 'M Frog' Labat. "Frog's role in the band," says Rundgren, "was to process other people, mostly my guitar, through the synthesizer modules. He'd control the pitch-to-voltage conversion on the guitar so it didn't wobble around too much, and he'd make essentially a few goofy noises here and there. It was similar, I guess, to what Eno would have been doing in Roxy Music; a flashy, interesting guy who makes noises but doesn't really know how to play like the others."

"He was an interesting visual effect," says Klingman, "I think of him the way you'd have a dancer on stage. Todd put all of these knobs and dials in front of him, and he had his green hair and it would move around. Still, he was a friend of Todd's and Todd liked having him around, so there you go."

"I don't even think Todd, on the stage, could really hear what Frog was doing," says Schuckett. "The sound guy [John Holbrook] would decide what he wanted to use in the mix; if it sounded like Frog's stuff was really happening, he'd mix that in. If it wasn't, they'd just take Todd's regular guitar sound, which was great anyway."

"I always really liked Jean-Yves," says Siegler, "he was a really cool guy but he was just out of our league, as far as musicianship. Todd basically set up all of his synthesizers, anyway, and Jean-Yves just turned them on. But [while] Ralph, Moogy, Kevin, and I were kind of like a brotherhood, Frog was just an adjunct of Utopia. He was never on a studio session we did. Todd did all the synth stuff himself."

Throughout November and December, the new Utopia played material from *A Wizard, A True Star* and *Something/Anything?* following an opening set by Rundgren, alone at the piano, often with taped backing tracks. "Then the guys would come on," says Rundgren, "and we'd do a full band set. On 'Never Never Land,' I'd go out with a magic fairy wand that had an explosive charge in the end of it that I would shoot off at a critical moment. Every once in a while I would accidentally shoot myself with it and, one night, I actually burned a hole in my stage costume [laughs]."

On December 7 1973, Rundgren famously confused American television audiences, his label representative, and some of his bandmates, by performing 'Hello It's Me,' on NBC television's *The Midnight Special*, sitting at a piano wearing pasted-on peacock feathers and full glam eye makeup. Bearsville's Paul Fishkin later complained to journalist Barney Hoskyns that Rundgren had looked "like a fucking drag queen," while performing what was supposed to be a Top 40 soft-rock ballad. Backstage, preparing to go out for their second number, 'Black Maria,' Schuckett recalls apprehension amongst the band-members. "I remember Moogy saying 'What the hell is he doing?' I'm sure he alienated a bunch of people, but Todd just didn't care. He gets bored easily, doesn't like to repeat himself and likes to make waves. I actually admire and respect that in him because that's what an artist does."

With Bearsville aghast over the mixed messages that the TV appearance had sent the nation, the incident did nothing to alleviate the problems Rundgren was having regarding the imminent release of his now-completed *Todd* album. It was promised in pre-release catalogues as a single album with a December 1973 release date, but Rundgren's prolific summer at Secret Sound had produced a double-album's worth of tunes. Artistically, this was nothing new – *Something/Anything?* had been a commercially viable double set – but in late 1973, a global oil crisis had caused the record industry to think twice about how much (oil-based) vinyl it was using.

Bearsville and its parent company, Warner Bros, eventually consented to a two-disc package, albeit with two platters stuffed tightly into one cardboard sleeve, but pushed the release date to late February 1974. As Christmas approached, Utopia came off the road and Rundgren proposed that they take advantage of the caliber of their musicianship to collaborate on a real team effort in the coming year. "The very first concepts that I had of Utopia," he says, "were more along the lines of an English progressive rock band, but more free form. I think of progressive rock as having a certain element of structure. It would get a little flabby sometimes in performance but for the most part it would be fairly strict arrangements, probably of some complexity; the whole approach would be like an orchestra, or a big band, or something like that, not necessarily a hard bop jazz jamming band."

In January of 1974, as he awaited the release of *Todd* and a subsequent March tour with Utopia, Rundgren got another call from Lynn Goldsmith. Grand Funk was once again looking to have Rundgren guide them to chart gold. This time, however, the band had decided to heed Rundgren's earlier advice that they should try to record their next album in their natural habitat, The Swamp studio in rural Parshallville, Michigan. "We put some new equipment in," says Mark Farner, "which brought it up to world-class standards for that time. Todd also brought some of his own effects, keyboards, and pre-amps and stuff. We wanted to have all the comforts of home around us to make it a very secure, solid-feeling record."

Rundgren recalls heading back to Parshallville to work on the record, which was already titled *Shinin' On,* just as *American Band* had started to ebb on the charts. "I always think it's better to record in your own space," says Rundgren, "because you can do it on any freakin' schedule you want. It was probably worse for me [at the Swamp] because I was out in the middle of Farmland, USA."

While Rundgren would elect to take the Swamp tapes back to Secret Sound for final mix and other treatments, he had no major issues with tracking there. "It was fine, and since we all knew each other from the first record, everything went fairly quickly this time anyway."

As friendly as the sessions were, both Don Brewer and Farner attest to a gloomy mood hanging over the proceedings. "I think after *American Band*'s success," says Brewer, "certain personalities were changing within the band as well as outside the band."

"There was just this heavy feeling in the air," adds Farner. "I think it got captured on a song we cut called 'Destitute And Losing.' Actually, it had such an ominous feel that we left it off originally and it got shoved onto a B-Side at the time. But it has since appeared on a compilation and as a bonus track on the *Shinin' On* CD."

Goldsmith says that she also noticed darker, heavier material drifting out of The Swamp, and unbeknownst to the band, took Rundgren aside and advised him to keep his ear out for more upbeat material. "I told Todd that they were a party band. I said, 'Remember to get them to do something fun.'"

Some of the fun came during the song 'Carry Me Through,' on which Farner and Rundgren trade lead guitar solos. "We wanted Todd to put as much of himself into the project as he felt he could," says Brewer, "and there were just so many elements of his own style coming through at the time, as you can hear from some of his keyboard ideas on 'Carry Me Through.'"

The title song, 'Shinin' On,' was tipped to be the first single, and was also something of a showcase for Frost's deft work on the Hammond organ. "Todd showed me how to get this really percussive B3 sound," says Frost. "It really had a pop to it. He said he was using this piece of gear that was actually broken. That broken box just happened to make a lame organ sound fabulous."

'Shinin' On' was not, however, the big obvious hit the band were looking for, and bluesy numbers like 'Mr Pretty Boy' or the Band-like 'To Get Back In' weren't going to land them back on the charts. Mindful of Goldsmith's pre-production advice to get the band to lighten up, Rundgren's cocked his ear for something fun to balance the album's heaviness.

Don Brewer recalls the moment, toward the end of the sessions, when Rundgren and the band found it. "We usually broke for dinner around six o'clock each evening," recalls Brewer, "and then we'd come back to work at like seven o'clock. On this one night, Mark came back in from dinner just singing this song."

"I just walked in the studio door," Farner recalls, "singing 'Everybody's doin' a brand new dance now!' Craig and Donnie were standing there, so they started singing the background part, 'Come on baby, do the loco-motion.' It just seemed kind of funny at first, you know? Grand Funk doing 'The Loco-motion,' that would be so *stupid*."

It didn't sound stupid to Rundgren, who heard the commotion and came out of the control room with a broad smile. He strongly suggested that the Little Eva classic might just be the fun single they'd been looking for. "I think I also found it conceptually perverse," laughs Rundgren, "that they had been known as the Railroad and here there were singing 'The Loco-motion.' I really thought we had to do this, so we went straight to work on it and they essentially let me do what I wanted to do with it."

Rundgren cast the song in a sing-along mode, suggestive of The Beach Boys' 'Barbara Ann,' albeit in a heavier style befitting Grand Funk. "Todd made it sound like there was this big party going on," Brewer recalls, "with everybody singing, clanging ashtrays together, and having a good time. This being Todd, of course, it still had that big overblown rock feel."

With Brewer's lead vocals and a fair chunk of the entire mix once again pushed hard through the trusty Cooper Time Cube, Rundgren joined in with the band on the rowdy, call-and-response choruses. "We had everybody standing around a microphone," says Brewer, "and Todd's singing all that real ultra-high falsetto stuff. Those backgrounds were doubled and doubled again you know, just stacked and stacked as many as you can get."

To underpin the rhythm section, Rundgren asked Frost to create a synthesizer patch on his brand new Mini-Moog that was meant to resemble a baritone saxophone. "I had just gotten this Mini-Moog," says Frost, "and I didn't know diddly about it. I could barely turn the damn thing on, you know? So Todd just walks over and grabs the controls and says 'Okay, here!' That sound kind of made the song, in some ways, because it added this growly bass that really leapt out of the speakers at home. But of course, when it was time for Farner to play the guitar solo, Todd came up with that sweeping, swooping sound for him."

The erratic guitar solo on 'The Loco-motion' was the product both of Farner's prowess on the guitar and Rundgren's facility with a tape-delay unit. "A lot of people think that wild sound was done later, in the mix," Farner explains, "but the whole thing was done live as I played it. My friend Jim Fackert, from [electronics company] Littlites, had rewired my old Echoplex tape delay and the machine had this little slide head on the tape loop. So when I was about to do the solo, Todd grabbed that knob and said 'Okay, let's do it.' As I was playing, Todd would be fucking around with that slide, shoving it to one end, then bringing it back down so it sounded like the guitar was eating itself."

It was another landmark day of recording for Grand Funk, and their last with Rundgren. 'The Loco-motion' was released in February. True to the Goldsmith plan, it followed 'We're An American Band' to Number One on the Billboard Charts. Grand Funk's *Shinin' On* album followed a month later, and spent weeks on the album charts, climbing to Number Five. "Working with Todd," says Mark Farner, "was absolutely necessary to our survival at that point. Who knows what would have happened had we not hooked up with Todd, who finally brought us sonic satisfaction. Some people in this music business only care about the business and forget the music. But for people like us and Todd, it's all about the love, brother."

After two successful albums with Rundgren, Grand Funk moved on and did their next album with producer Jimmy Ienner. "The funny thing was," says Goldsmith, "I always thought Jimmy's production on the first single, 'Some Kind Of Wonderful,' sounded like a complete rip-off of what Todd had done on 'The Loco-motion.'"

Having delivered on his promise to bring both commerciality and artistic credibility to Grand Funk, Rundgren was rightly proud as he watched the boys from Flint recede in his rearview mirror. "The critics had to reappraise them," he says. "They hadn't realized that they had this much actual musicality in them. I think being taken seriously as artists went to their heads a little, because a couple of albums after we did *Shinin' On,* they thought, 'Well, that worked, let's get Frank Zappa!'" he laughs.

As *Shinin' On* hit the racks, in March 1974, Todd Rundgren and the new Utopia were already on tour supporting the *Todd* album. In contrast to Arthur Wood's florid and surrealistic painting that had adorned *A Wizard, A True Star*, *Todd* offered a stark color headshot of an exhausted-looking Rundgren, his matted, multi-color hair framing a smugly smiling face. And, true to Albert Grossman's promise, the *Todd* sleeve contained a poster bearing the names of all who had dutifully returned their postcards from the *Wizard* album.

Former XTC guitarist Dave Gregory recalls listening in awe as the BBC's Bob Harris played 'The Last Ride' on his *Sounds Of The Seventies* radio program. Shortly afterward, Gregory discovered the *Todd* album in full and became a fan. "I loved the maverick spirit of the guy," says Gregory. "He'd just start with the drums and keep over-dubbing himself until there was something he couldn't play, at which point he'd bring in a specialist. He was talented enough to stick a finger up to the industry and say 'This is my record – take it or leave it.'"

In May 1973, after returning from his first truly successful three-month tour with the new and improved Utopia, Rundgren planted himself behind the mixing desk at Secret Sound to follow through with some of the production offers that had come his way. These included albums for his friend N.D. Smart's band, The Hello People, ex-Rascal Felix Cavaliere and his Philly friends, who had likewise moved to New York, and Daryl Hall & John Oates.

Hall & Oates
War Babies

In 1967, Daryl Hall, singer for The Temptones, and John Oates, from The Masters, met in a service elevator behind West Philadelphia's Adelphi Ballroom. They were both fleeing for their lives after a local 'Battle Of The Bands' had suddenly turned into an actual gunfight. Within a year, they had left their respective groups and began writing songs together as Hall & Oates. By 1972, they had been discovered by manager Tommy Mottola, who secured them a recording deal with Ahmet Ertegun's prestigious Atlantic Records label, home to so many of the great soul artists who had inspired them.

Despite having Atlantic's star producer Arif Mardin on board for their 1972 debut, *Whole Oats*, the act had yet to establish what would become their trademark 'rock'n'soul' sound. While their self-produced 1973 follow-up, *Abandoned Luncheonette*, faired slightly better, the single 'She's Gone' would not become a smash hit until 1976, by which time Atlantic had dropped them from the label.

Depending on who you ask, Hall & Oates's hasty departure from Atlantic was in part a consequence of their decision to hire Todd Rundgren to produce *War Babies*, their third and final album for the label. The product of two weeks of intense artistic collaboration, commencing on June 19 1974 at Secret Sound, *War Babies* was a progressive soul detour for the young Philly duo. Unfortunately, it was not the hit-laden commercial success that Atlantic had hoped for.

"So what?" Rundgren replies. "I didn't care what the label wanted. We weren't even pondering what they wanted, or their expectations, which I suppose was the issue. In those days, it was supposed to be the era of freedom for the artist, and I think Hall & Oates took advantage of that. The label had other things in mind."

At the time of the album, Rundgren adds, Hall & Oates had yet to be "locked into" the slick soul-pop sound that would later become their calling card. "So, in one sense, they were merely continuing as they had before, but with greater conviction. Still, after *War Babies* flopped commercially, it stung them so badly that for a long time I don't think even Daryl wanted to take credit for his own contribution to the record. To some degree he wanted the label hype to be the story, that being that it was my influence that caused them to make such a patently noncommercial record."

In June of 2009, precisely 35 years after he and John Oates entered Secret Sound, Daryl Hall appears to have re-appraised *War Babies*. "To me," Hall says, "*War Babies* was sort of the first Daryl Hall solo album. John and I had grown up together and I'd been working with him for a few years already but always with the basic premise that we were separate entities who happened to be working together. When we did *Whole Oats*, it was the typical 'first album' in that it was just a lot of the songs we'd written before the album, which were already a few years old. Then we did *Abandoned Luncheonette,* and that to me was the quintessential Daryl and John album."

John Oates, for his part, disputes Hall's characterization of *War Babies* as a solo work. "I don't know what he's talking about. We were looking for a partner [in Rundgren] to help add a different dimension to the two previous albums we had done on Atlantic, which were very 'singer/songwriter' and 'acoustic' in style. Todd's greatest assets [as a producer] are his unique personality and his guitar playing."

Hall adds that, while Philadelphia had brought the duo together in the pursuit of the blue-eyed soul groove, their subsequent relocation to New York City had also fostered the first divisions between them. "John and I had slightly different reactions to New York. I'm the kind of musician who is influenced by environmental sounds as much as music, and the whole kinetic environment, the aural milieu, of New York at the time was strikingly different from the sound of Philadelphia. I was really into things like John Cage and all that other avant-garde stuff; but more than anything, I was really into just the sound of the city, which really jarred me. It's hard for me to overemphasize that. Subsequently, my new songs were much more kinetic and sort of disturbing. That feeling and those songs were the genesis of *War Babies*."

Oates's sole solo composition, 'Can't Stop The Music (He Played It Much Too Long),' which opens the album, was his personal reaction to life on the road, insomnia, and he says, "being a bit compulsive mentally." But there was no doubt, he adds, that "the music was our expression of the chaos of the city that we were finally immersed in."

As Hall began composing songs like 'Better Watch Your Back,' '70s Scenario,' and a moody piano number called 'Screaming Through December,' the duo began to realize that they would require a neutral third party to produce them. "Not only was Todd a Philly guy and around the same age as us," Hall recalls, "he had moved to New York just a year or two before we had, so we knew he 'got it.' He had no reservations and his mind just knows no limits."

The duo were duly impressed with the range of Rundgren's *Something/Anything?* and particularly noted Rundgren's 'soul medley' from *A Wizard, A True Star*. They had also sung at Wollman Rink with Rundgren's Utopia ensemble, which he felt displayed a passing similarity to his then favorite progressive group, King Crimson. "We sat down at my apartment and just talked about music," says Hall. "I think I played him a couple of ideas and he said, 'Okay, yeah. Sure, let's go! Let's do it,' you know? We certainly didn't overthink it. The next thing I remember, we were up in Secret Sound."

Rundgren says that the *War Babies* experience was unique both for Hall & Oates and for his newly upgraded Secret Sound studio. "Not only is it unlike any other Hall & Oates album, before or since," says Rundgren, "I don't know that they had ever attempted to do a 'concept record,' before. I think part of the concept was maybe just assuming this posture that they were not necessarily going to do what was always expected from them. It was also one of the first [outside projects] that we ever did at Secret Sound. In fact, in some respects, we tamed the kind of sounds I'd been getting into [on *Todd* and *Wizard*] a bit for Hall & Oates."

Hall agrees that the stylistic extremes of *War Babies* were necessary for Hall & Oates to shake up early preconceptions of what the duo was about. "We wanted to cut loose from what we called the gingerbread eaters," says Hall, "the people who had seen us doing acoustic stuff in the folk clubs, who thought that we were just these nice safe, folkie guys. Certain people in our initial fan base got violently upset about that album. We lost a lot of them, but I think that the fans we gained later, who carried us across, realized that we were innovators. I think that has characterized our creative direction ever since then."

The drummer in the Hall & Oates band, at the time, was 21-year old John G. Wilcox, more commonly known as 'Willie.' "I remember them writing some of the songs for *War Babies* in various hotel rooms during the Abandoned Luncheonette tour," he recalls. "I'd have this little Remo practice-pad kit, and Daryl and John had their acoustic guitars or a Wurlitzer piano and we'd just run through 'Is It A Star?' or something. *War Babies* was the first record I had ever made in my whole life, and my introduction to Todd. The rhythm section for that record was me and John Siegler, Utopia's bass player, and I thought we played well together."

"I guess they didn't have a regular bass player at the time," recalls Siegler, "so Todd asked me to come in. In many ways, it was just another day at work, but I clicked well with John and Daryl, locked in with Willie, and they turned out to be great sessions."

While regular Hall & Oates guitarist Richie Cerniglia played the solo on 'Is It A Star?' the bulk of the album's instrumentation came from a core unit of Hall,

Oates, Siegler, Wilcox, and Rundgren himself, who Hall says played the majority of the guitars on the record. "That was perfect for us," says Hall, "because Todd was always exploring. He would slow the tape down and play the solo, then speed it up again. You know, all kinds of tricks like that. Whatever works."

"I think Todd may have even come up with Richie's guitar parts," says Wilcox. "So all through the album you'll hear Todd's signature guitar sound. Daryl and John were accomplished songwriters who were pretty hands-on when it came to their songs, but I think they really soaked up the Todd vibe on that one."

"I would play Todd a basic song and we would just run with it," Hall recalls. "I remember I just started playing 'Better Watch Your Back' on the mandolin, and Todd was at the board with his guitar, so we started jamming it out together and everybody just started playing along."

Rundgren says that, guitars and sonic textures aside, his main influence was in the areas of vocal phrasing and song arrangement, largely because the new songs hadn't been 'road tested.' "Up until that particular record," he adds, "they had always thought of their harmonies in terms of the two of them, like The Righteous Brothers. On this album, we began to work with some deeper, three-part harmonies, and got them thinking more in terms of a section thing as opposed to just a lead vocal and one other guy."

Rundgren admits that it was "pretty easy" to coax lead vocals out of an "incredible singer" such as Hall. "I never had to call him out for being flat, I mean, he's already gonna know when he's flat, so we'd just go again."

Much has been made, over the years, of the similarities in the vocal styles of Daryl Hall and Todd Rundgren. While both singers acknowledge their shared Philadelphia roots, each has his own take on the situation. "I wouldn't necessarily assume that we influence each other that much," Rundgren insists. "We're both still trying to emulate our common influences, the great soul singers who, in our minds, are better singers than either of us."

"I'm sure I influenced Todd," Hall declares, laughing only slightly at the assertion. "I was always more regionally identified than he was. Up to then, he'd always run away from Philadelphia; the Nazz had been looking to England or various other places. I think he rediscovered his Thom Bell, Philly thing through me, and suddenly realized he also had that music in his head."

Utopia's Ralph Schuckett confirms a change in Rundgren's singing style after the *War Babies* sessions. "On our tour before that, he never could quite cut it as a live singer, for whatever reason. But after he finished [*War Babies*], Todd was suddenly a great soulful singer. Later that year, when we cut the first Utopia album, it was really noticeable. Todd has this ability to learn something through osmosis, and I think Daryl's whole thing just rubbed off on him."

In addition to their shared Philly roots, Hall says that he and Oates – and Rundgren – were all deeply into the visual and musical edge of David Bowie at the time. "Bowie's influence was all-pervasive in our lives back then," he says. "You couldn't get away from it. Todd even had it going on, although we weren't out to copy Bowie's music; we just appropriated the attitude."

According to Rundgren, a lot of work went into 'War Baby Son Of Zorro,' which he considered the album's "centerpiece." He recalls: "That song was important to Daryl, and it was intended to elucidate at least what the title of the record was about. It was the theme song, as it were, just as The Beatles had done with the song 'Sgt Pepper.'"

John Oates adds that 'War Baby Son Of Zorro' was the duo's attempt to create a musical collage of their shared memories of childhood in 50s Cold-War America, as illustrated on the cover by artist Peter Palombi. Rundgren remembers Hall's concerns about the song's chaotic structure: "It had some interesting harmonic elements in it, but when we first were running through it, we weren't exactly sure if they sounded right. There was no intention, at all, of making anything resembling a pop song; this was high-concept music at this point."

Hall laughs when recalling the aural atmosphere on the track, which included everything from glockenspiels to synthesizers and other processed sounds, and even featured a credit to a 'television solo' and "all kinds of crazy things like that! We were like curious musicians going crazy in a music shop, using traditional or strange 'found instruments' in unusual ways. Then, we'd add all that phasing and Todd's big reverbs to create this chaotic atmosphere. One unique thing to Todd's records in those days was the EQ he put on everything. It's all really trebly and it adds to that kind of jittery, kinetic kind of sound."

As much as he felt responsible for the musical direction, Hall says he actively encouraged Rundgren to exert his sizeable influence on the work. "Otherwise we could have just produced it ourselves. I was a big fan of his chaotic Utopia thing, and some of Todd's more epic stuff, like 'International Feel.' You can hear it in the episodic arrangement [of 'War Baby']. I think the song was probably subconsciously influenced by that."

The soulful, shuffling 'Is It A Star?' marked the introduction of a low-tech beatbox into Hall & Oates's musical mix, a technique that they would later use to platinum effect on 'I Can't Go For That.'

"I can't even remember the name of that [beatbox]," says Hall. "It was just an early, early drum machine that Todd had. I think it only had two beats on it, so we put some echoes on it to give it that shuffle. I think it was the first time I ever used a beatbox on a record, and I used them a lot after that."

Rundgren did not, as one might expect, play the keyboards on *War Babies*. According to Hall, most of the synthesizers on the album were performed and programmed by Don York, one of the premier session players of the day. "Don was an early synthesizer guy who had played on a well known Maxwell House coffee jingle at the time. He was the synthesizer star of New York."

The album closes with a Hall & Oates co-write called 'Johnny Gore And The C Eaters,' whose title, John Oates reveals, was inspired by a midnight drive through Georgia while on tour. "I noticed a marquee in a small town while heading toward Alabama," says Oates. "It read 'Tonight: Live, Johnny Gore And The C Eaters.' I was intrigued and wrote it down in my journal. A few days later, on that very same road, on the way back through that town, I saw the other side of the marquee, which read: 'Tonight: Live, Johnny Gore And The *Cheaters*,' so it was just that the H was missing on one side of the sign. [But] the rest of the lyric was really about our band and the insanity of being on the road for the first time."

As for their overall approach on the album, Hall offers the words "fun" and "dark," meaning they took a serious approach to progressive music without taking themselves too seriously. "It's a funny thing," says Hall. "You know, years later I did the same thing with Robert Fripp. To me, the sort of exploratory, artsy kind of thing doesn't have to be so deadly serious. I like to inject a mischievous element to things."

The sessions were completed on July 4, and after months of hemming and hawing in the Atlantic Records boardroom, Hall & Oates's declaration of independence was released to commercial indifference on November 12 1974. Max Bell, writing in *New Musical Express* on November 23 1974, praised Rundgren's production for its New York "punch," which he preferred to what he called the "ersatz stodge perpetuated by the Philly Sound." He added that Rundgren's "control panel work [was] invariably the best around, whether it's upbeat rhythm or straight ahead melody, both of which the album has in abundance."

Today, Todd Rundgren defends the artistic detour Hall & Oates took on his watch, but understands why Atlantic Records "freaked out" when he delivered the album. "Up until that record," he says, "Hall & Oates had only had one single, 'She's Gone' from *Abandoned Luncheonette*. So they were probably thinking, as they are wont to do, maybe they could do 'She's Still Gone,' or 'When You Comin' Home,' etc [laughs]. But the lack thereof was probably the reason they got dropped immediately after we turned the album in. The impression you got from the label was that it was a bad record, which was not true; but everyone came away from the experience with this idea that we had really fucked up bad. All we had done was to essentially thwart the label's expectations."

As history showed, Hall & Oates went on to bigger and better things and a career of accomplishments, from having a string of platinum singles and albums to recording with their beloved Temptations at the hallowed Apollo Theatre in Harlem. It was with no small irony, however, that in 1998 the album that had gotten Hall & Oates dumped from Atlantic Records was among the 50 titles re-released by the label as part of its 50th anniversary celebrations. Included was a liner note from none other than Ahmet Ertegun, who noted that it was one of the "great moments in the history of the label."

"*War Babies* absolutely shook up the direction of Hall & Oates," says Daryl Hall. "Todd completely changed us, and to this day we remain friends. I think that he and I are very much in the same musical camp. We've always had an experimental side but people know us for the hits."

"*War Babies*," says John Oates, in retrospect, "filled in the musical gap between the first two albums we made. Having done that, we established a lifelong relationship with Todd, and when I look back on that recording it was by far our most adventurous and experimental project."

"I think there was this sense at the label that I was supposed to steer them into something a little more commercial, a little more like *Something/Anything?*" says Rundgren, in conclusion. "When that didn't happen, I was thrown under the bus by their manager at the time and blamed for all of it. I don't blame Daryl and John for going along with the story at the time. Getting dropped from a label is a scary thing; you'll be panicked for a while. But they did okay in the end, you know?"

Midtown Madness; Getting Busy At Secret Sound

Throughout most of 1974, Todd Rundgren's midtown Manhattan studio, Secret Sound, was rarely dark. As co-owner Moogy Klingman – by then a full member of the revamped and rebranded Utopia – recalls a revolving cast of bands came and went during the year. Rundgren had mixed Grand Funk's *Shinin' On* there, and cut albums for Fanny and Felix Cavaliere (former singer of The Rascals), as well as *The Handsome Devils*, an album by The Hello People, the mime rock band featuring his old friend Norman Smart.

"[Hello People] were a good little band," says Klingman, who played on some of the record and had one of his songs covered by the band. "They all sang well and they would do this mime thing on stage. Todd used them on some things and later on they joined us on his Back To The Bars tour."

Smart recalls frequently "hanging out" at Secret Sound with Rundgren, regardless of whether or not he was producing his band. "We also did another [album] with Todd, called *Bricks*. But by then, of course, we were already longtime friends. We were very theatrical musically, besides just the mime makeup, and did a lot of a cappella singing and jazz-influenced rock. Todd would pick up odd things from Hello People, and Hello People would pick up things from Todd. Although, when Todd synthesizes something it becomes his own, and then even he doesn't even know where it came from."

The *Felix Cavaliere* album temporarily returned Rundgren to the role of Bearsville house producer, although his actual task on the record was to cobble together something coherent from a series of uncompleted recordings he had not overseen. "[Cavaliere] had started it for another label that lost interest," Rundgren told Brett Milano in the liner notes for a 1992 Rhino compilation, "and I was sort of the boy wonder troubleshooter at Bearsville. We hit it off because we liked the same kind of music. Being from Philly, I'd always had a certain amount of obligatory R&B in my repertoire."

In the same spirit of utility that brought Utopia bassist John Siegler to Hall & Oates's sessions for *War Babies*, Rundgren put Siegler and Utopia drummer Kevin Ellman to work replacing both the bass and drums on the existing Cavaliere masters. "Don't ask me why," says Siegler, "but I guess the recording of the original rhythm section didn't sound good. It was logical to get us to play on it because all this was going on at Secret Sound all the time. Whatever piece of music was going that day, we did it; for better or for worse. The Hello People and the Brecker Brothers are on it too."

As for the Fanny album, *Mother's Pride*, keyboardist Nickey Barclay described the sessions to the *New Musical Express*'s Charles Shaar Murray in June 1973 as "comic opera." "He [Rundgren] comes in with a false nose and glasses," Barclay told Murray, "[running] into the studio cracking a whip and doing Richard Perry imitations. Todd played [a] cauliflower on 'Solid Gold.' We had a lot of raw vegetables with us in the studio, and he came out at the end of the take, put his head inside the piano, and crunched as it faded. At the time it was exactly what we wanted and needed."

Cauliflower madness aside, Rundgren's most outré recording project of the year was the debut album by the newly assembled Todd Rundgren's Utopia. "Initially, we put my name above it for obvious commercial reasons," says Rundgren. "I mean, besides the fact that I had put the band together, nobody knew what the Utopia brand was, at that point. So if the band was going to get any attention at all, it had to include a more familiar brand – my name."

Regardless of having his name out front, Rundgren was happy to share the musical responsibilities with his fellow Utopians. Utopia's three-keyboard approach afforded him a chance to stretch out on guitar and concentrate on his 'chops.' As he began to delegate certain compositional elements to the group as a whole, Rundgren noted a curious shift toward jazz-rock. "It became apparent," he says, "that the music that was starting to catch everybody's attention was John McLaughlin's Mahavishnu Orchestra and that whole fusion thing, which kind of came to characterize our music at that point. It seemed like most of the musicians felt this heavy R&B influence, this sort of 'free-jazz' experience [laughs]."

Rundgren appeared to have left the world of short piano ballads behind, at least for now, but even on top of this complex music he was still singing catchy melodies. "It was elucidating for me," he recalls, "working with players who had other techniques, or ways of hearing things, that weren't strictly linear. We used to get very 'out there,' sometimes, get into Zappa-esque kinds of things. Utopia had a high propensity to get into that kind of thing because of the Mahavishnu Orchestra influence, at first, but what it turned out to be, in actual application, was a fairly concise kind of progressive rock, verse/chorus type of thing with endless jams in between some of these sections. Obviously it made more sense in a concert setting, so the studio records were more concise, 30-minute versions of what we ultimately wound up doing live."

Throughout the early months of 1974, Todd Rundgren's Utopia composed and recorded the selections that would appear on their debut album. Rundgren recalls that the band's flexible and informal schedule was attributable to the fact that he and Klingman owned the studio. "We could get together whenever we wanted," he says. "For the most part, our routine was to go out in the evenings and do stuff, to Max's or some other musical venue, and then next afternoon we'd show up at Secret Sound and work out something and probably record it. It was like 'Hey, anybody got anything?' Somebody would have just a little idea they'd been working on, or somebody else would have a whole song, and we'd figure out if one part could fit into the middle of another."

According to John Siegler, Rundgren had built, in Utopia, "a playground for himself, where he could explore his musical ideas and go wherever he needed to," to which Kevin Ellman adds, "While it was definitely *Todd Rundgren's* Utopia, it wasn't just the Todd Rundgren Show, either."

Their all-hands approach culminated in the 30-minute opus 'The Ikon,' which, Rundgren recalls, presented unique organizational challenges. "The hardest part was figuring out how these fragments were supposed to segue together [when] each of them had some internal things that were challenging enough to play. Once we'd learned them, we could start thinking about how they went into a larger context."

"All those musical pieces were recorded separately," Klingman says. "It was five or six different pieces we had developed by jamming. I had this piece called 'The Conquering Of The West,' then Ralph and John started writing material for it. Eventually Todd named the whole thing 'The Ikon.'"

"Todd would always add all the words," says John Siegler, "so he'd come up with the titles, too. I recall him explaining his idea for 'The Ikon' as his sort of conceptual Utopian community."

"There's probably another half hour or 40 minutes that never made it to the album," remembers Ralph Schuckett. "I don't think the rest of us were even in the studio with him when he edited it, but then he presented it to us and we proceeded to rehearse it for the tour."

"There wasn't a whole lot of actual jamming on the final record," says Rundgren, "but in concert, that 30-minute piece was like an hour and a half. By the time all the keyboard players and I had our turns soloing, the songs would start to seem just endless!"

Klingman and Siegler worked up the music for the ten-minute long 'Freak Parade,' over which Rundgren added his Zappa-like call to all the freaks among us to "get off the sidewalk" and join in the parade. "It was extremely clever stuff," says Klingman, "and he had encouraged us to write some weird, wild music. So I had some musical ideas and John wrote the middle section, which is the funky section that has the vocals over it. Todd helped us arrange the pieces, and then he put the vocals by himself."

"When we came back and heard Todd's vocals and words," says Siegler, "I just couldn't believe how great they were. At that point, Utopia was a real band. Anyone who had music they could think of could bring it in. Todd was totally up for it."

Ralph Schuckett categorizes the band at this time as a benevolent dictatorship: "Todd had really good judgment, though, so I'm not complaining. It's just that you couldn't really call it democratic because he had the final word. But he'd let the band record our compositions, which was generous of him both artistically and monetarily."

According to all of the members of this Utopia, music aside, there existed a clear social division between them and Rundgren. "He didn't eat the same food as us," says Siegler, "and he had Bebe with him on the road, so he wasn't chasing chicks the way we were. I think we fulfilled that need that he had for good musicians. He was happy to work with us and we could literally play anything he could think of."

"Most of the communication between us was musical," adds Ellman, "not verbal. There was no grand intellectual discussion about it. Right after we played, Todd and Bebe would disappear."

'Utopia Theme,' originally written by Rundgren and Dave Mason for the first Utopia, had been reworked on the 1973 tour as a fourteen-and-a-half minute showcase for the new line-up. In contrast to the highly edited 'Ikon' sessions, Utopia had nailed the 'Utopia Theme' in one single live performance at Atlanta's Fox Theatre, the previous November.

"We tried recording for three nights in a row," says Kevin Ellman. "The first two nights, there were mistakes, and that's a long tune not to make a mistake. Then, on the third night we played it, our last night recording, we got it. I remember hitting the final note and we all looked around asking each other 'Did you make a mistake? I didn't. No, me neither.' That was our last chance, so it was great to get it down."

According to Rundgren, besides his own loud and highly processed guitar, the added sounds of three keyboard players and the occasional cello from Siegler called for certain roles to emerge within the band. Ellman also notes that the sonic soup required a particular sense of discipline from himself and Siegler. "Like a lot of early soul rhythm sections," says Ellman, "John and I always locked the bass and the bass drum to an identical beat, no matter what else was going on above it. I'd drop little 'place holders' to count out the pattern. I'd call these 'Helen Keller' fills. As in, you'd have to be blind, deaf, and dumb not to understand what's coming next."

Rundgren's concession to a single on the album was the four-minute metallic anthem 'Freedom Fighters.' While it was hardly the kind of single Bearsville could work at commercial radio, the multi-part vocals on the song's chorus suggest, in hindsight, the sort of shorter, pop-infused material that would come to characterize the later incarnations of Utopia.

Released on November 9 1974, *Todd Rundgren's Utopia* drew enthusiastic notices from some while further confounding others. For some it was a case of too much musical information, and the pomp and circumstance of the music frightened off fans of Rundgren's earlier pop material. Musicians such as Rush mega-drummer Neil Peart (a confessed fan of Kevin Ellman's drumming) attended many of their multiple dates that year, as did David Bowie, whose attendance at Utopia's Carnegie Hall debut in the spring bestowed an air of credibility on the enterprise.

Throughout the first year of Utopia, however, the 'Rhythm Kings' contingent had been grumbling about the odd man out of the group, their green-haired French synthesist Jean-Yves Labat. Ralph Schuckett says that while Labat had attended a lot of the recording sessions for the first Utopia album, he was never quite sure what his role was.

"I mean, he'd made that solo album, *M. Frog,* on Bearsville," says Schuckett, "which was all electronic synthesizer that was sequenced. Bearsville probably released 50 copies and it sold three. The stuff he'd do with Todd's guitar, I mean, they have all these guitar boxes today that can do it, although, to be fair, at the time there weren't many boxes other than fuzz tones or phase shifters."

"I think," says Rundgren, "some of the guys took a little bit of umbrage because his setup was so complicated that it seemed like an imbalance of energy was going into what sounded like a bunch of noise to them. So Jean-Yves left. He had other things to do anyway. We actually worked together again, on another album of his, a few years later."

According to Roger Powell, who would replace Labat, Rundgren and his management had been quietly seeking a possible replacement – Japanese electronic composer Isao Tomita's name was even briefly considered – at least as far back as June, when Powell received a mysterious invitation from the Grossman organization to come down from Boston to attend Rundgren's June 22 birthday show, with Utopia and The Hello People, at New York's Wollman Rink.

In addition to having composed and released his own electronic album, 1973's *Cosmic Furnace,* Powell was working at the time for synthesizer pioneer Robert Moog, following a three-year stint with the Arp synthesizer company, where he'd had a hand in designing, among other things, the Arp 2600. Recalling the scene at Wollman Rink, Powell says, "I wasn't even clear why I'd been invited, and I'd never actually heard the band at that point, so I went down to check it out. Later, I heard that the synthesizer guy was gonna be leaving, but they didn't give me any details about it. It was really hectic backstage, everyone was there to celebrate with Todd, so I left and went back home to Boston. The next day, I got a phone call that explained more clearly why they were replacing the synthesizer player and that my name had come up as a possible replacement."

Two weeks later, Powell flew to Utopia's show at the Olympic Island Festival in Toronto to give them a closer look. This time, Powell paid special attention to what Labat was doing and later learned of certain tensions that had arisen in the band. "Jean-Yves had this whole bank of these EMS VCS3 'Putney' synthesizers," says Powell, "like four of them bolted together. I talked to Todd and the guys after the show and discovered that one of the issues was that Jean-Yves had been processing everyone else's sounds, in addition to Todd's guitar. This, of course, didn't go over well with the keyboard players who didn't really want their sounds touched."

By October, and throughout the beginning of 1975, Powell was on the road with Utopia, working out new live material for the group and assisting Rundgren with the synthesizers for studio tracks that would comprise part of his next solo album, *Initiation*. "When Roger joined," says Rundgren, "Utopia's live thing got even more complicated because Roger could actually play."

"For the first year," says Powell, "I mostly made noises. Ralph and Moogy were monster players, so they just wanted someone to make neat synth noises and, of course, avoid processing anybody else's sounds [laughs]."

Back at Bearsville Studios, Powell and Rundgren began to work on the sprawling synthesizer epic, 'A Treatise On Cosmic Fire,' that would dominate a whole side of the vinyl release of *Initiation*. Lyrically, the entire album was another conceptual exploration, this time Rundgren's ruminations on the evolution of consciousness. Musically, however, an overlap was beginning to show between Utopia and Rundgren's solo material. Feeling that he had exhausted his approach to writing lyrics for the time being, Rundgren was anxious to explore the instrumental realm.

"This was especially true," says Rundgren, "on the second side, where Roger and I were mucking about with the synthesizers. I don't think I had yet done any movie or TV soundtracks at that point, so instrumental exploration seemed highly desirable to me. Ever since *A Wizard, A True Star*, I had gotten into this habitual problem of recording more than could fit on a record. *Initiation* was the same deal, almost 30 minutes a side, but I was hearing things in somewhat different form, at that point, than what the vinyl could accommodate."

"The 'Treatise On Cosmic Fire' was this really long and thorny electronic landscape," says Powell, "and a lot of that material is really me and Todd holed up in the Bearsville Studio with my Moog and as many synthesizers as we could assemble together at once. We'd just let them kind of go crazy and get it all on tape. Then, Todd took it back to Secret Sound and kind of whittled it all down, as it were, to a mere 36 minutes."

The 'pop songs' side opens with 'Real Man,' a relatively straightforward, prog-soul anthem and the only song featuring the entire 'Rhythm Kings' line-up of Utopia (that is, no Roger Powell.) Prior to the other sessions for *Initiation*, Siegler, Schuckett, Klingman, and Ellman had laid down the basic track at Secret Sound, and Rundgren, as usual, engineered and added everything else later. "It's curious," recalls Rundgren, "I had 'Real Man' before I had fully conceptualized the rest of the record. When we were recording that song, I wasn't actually thinking, 'OK, now I'm starting an album.' The album, in some ways, evolved out of it."

Deceptively hooky, 'Real Man' was as complex as any Utopian workout behind the Philly sheen. "Sure," says Rundgren, "it had that Gamble and Huff tom-tom thing and all the percussion, but at the same time I was doing something harmonically uncommon. Many of the changes were not the most obvious, and had a certain amount of emotional ambiguity to them. I'm always using suspensions and minor sevenths and major sevenths and diminished whatevers – I don't know the names of these chords half the time."

'Born To Synthesize,' a nearly a cappella vocal meditation, features a healthy amount of textural noise with vocals filtered through Roger Powell's Moog and other synths. Powell says that these early synthesizer sessions, his first with Rundgren, were a great way to get to know each other, and he discovered they had much in common. "We were both, obviously, really into technology," says Powell, "but later on, when I got to expand my keyboard role and start to compose for Utopia, I discovered that we shared a similar harmonic approach and we both used dissonances, extended voice and unusual chords."

Rundgren says that the musical information on 'Born To Synthesize' was meant to create a sonic atmosphere, disarm the listener, and confound their expectations; something that he was now doing regularly, with each new album. "There's a little sound," says Rundgren, "that goes on in the background throughout the whole thing. [I'm] messing around with the delay time and feedback on the vocal delays to keep changing the size of the space arbitrarily. One minute, it sounds like you're in a big space, then suddenly you're in a tiny space. All this is happening in real time, though. You're not thinking, 'Oh wow, I'm in a weird space now!' This, once again, was inspired by the way psychoactive drugs work. [I was trying to] reinforce that [notion] that things go back to being the way they were before you had started applying all your automatic filters to them to determine what their meanings were."

After such unmitigated trippiness, Rundgren felt the need to follow up with something more upbeat, so he cranked up his guitar for 'The Death Of Rock And Roll.' Lyrically, the song seemed to underscore his growing disaffection with the rock establishment and the journalists who fed and bled it. The musical track, recorded at Media Sound with Jack Malken engineering, was prototypical Rundgren rock, with a scorching lead guitar panning speaker to speaker and a cameo appearance by his old friend from the Scene, Rick Derringer, on bass. Ralph Schuckett plays a barely audible clavinet, while Kevin Ellman, in his last studio appearance with Rundgren, was teamed with another drummer, Willie Wilcox from the Hall & Oates band, making his first. "It was right after we made *War Babies*,' says Wilcox, who would join Utopia by summer's end, "and I loved doing the double drums thing with Kevin. It was a wild session."

"That double-drummer thing," says Rundgren, "was something I had wanted to try out for some time, so I did it for a few of those live sessions for that album."

Many of the themes on *Initiation* (as well as the lyrics for what became Utopia's 'The Seven Rays') were directly inspired by the writings of Alice A. Bailey, whose many volumes Rundgren had devoured in his spirituality studies. Among these were *Rays And The Initiations: A Treatise On The Seven Rays* and, logically, *A*

Treatise On Cosmic Fire. Rundgren insists that he found the latter too opaque to finish, but overall Bailey's New Age themes suited his curiosity at the time. Similarly, his reading had partially informed the humorous tone of 'Eastern Intrigue,' which appeared to deflate the self-seriousness of organized religion, asking the musical question, "Will the real god please stand up?"

"There's jokes there," Rundgren admits, "but I don't have that kind of Bill Maher hostility toward religion. I could say that I'm open to the possibility that I could be anything, but my own belief is that all I can do is try and behave myself. I specifically don't believe that I need to beg somebody's forgiveness in order to get into heaven afterward, if there even is such a thing."

Back at Secret Sound, once again assisted by Jack Malken, Rundgren brought back bass player John Miller to play on 'Eastern Intrigue,' this time pairing him with drummer Roy Markowitz (the drummer from Don McLean's landmark hit 'American Pie,') along with percussionists Lee Pastora and Barbara Burton. Rundgren played most of the other instruments himself, including all of the synthesizers and a Coral electric sitar for atmosphere, while Roger Powell was credited with "nose flute." The title song, 'Initiation,' was also cut at Media Sound (with Malken assisting), with drummers Bernard Purdie and Rick Marotta, and Lee Pastora joining on conga drum.

"The double drummer thing," says Rundgren, "was still appealing to me so on 'Initiation,' I thought, let's get two really good drummers like Marotta and Purdie and have them play together. In fact, I think all the *Initiation* tracks with the two drummer thing were only done at Media Sound, because we didn't have enough equipment back at Secret Sound to record two full sets of drums at the same time." Utopia's Siegler and Powell added bass and synthesizer respectively, while jazz guitarist Bob Rose and saxophone star David Sanborn lent some atmosphere to the track. "[Todd] said, 'Just play,'" Sanborn told RundgrenRadio host Doug Ford in 2009. "There weren't many takes. Todd didn't want it to get too calculated, and whatever else he wanted for that track, he didn't want that."

On the side closer, 'Fair Warning,' Rundgren appeared to be pushing back against all expectations – musical, commercial, social or otherwise – in the same manner as he had on 'The Death Of Rock And Roll.' "I know that you've been wondering if I'm the same man inside," he sings, adding "I gave you fair warning I could never be tied down ... the world doesn't own me."

The basic track on 'Fair Warning,' also recorded at Media Sound, paired drummers Barry Lazarowitz (Leonard Cohen) and Chris Parker (Joe Beck, Bonnie Raitt), along with Klingman on organ and members of Edgar Winter's White Trash; Winter playing a standout saxophone solo alongside bandmates Dan Hartman on bass and Rick Derringer on guitar.

'Fair Warning' ends with a brief reprise of 'Real Man,' which lends the first side of *Initiation* an artificial continuity not unlike the manner in which 'International Feel' opened and closed side one of *Wizard*. Factor in the side-long 'A Treatise On Cosmic Fire,' and *Initiation*, clocking in at 67:34, was one of the longest vinyl albums yet produced. According to many listeners, Ralph Schuckett among them, the sheer amount of music compromised the disc's overall sound quality.

"The sound really gets degraded closer to the end of the record," says Schuckett. "I remember, people would say 'But Todd, the sound quality's going down' and he'd go 'Eh, the sound quality's not important. It's rock'n'roll,' you know?'"

"I was always making more music than vinyl albums could hold," laughs Rundgren. "To that end, later on, CDs seemed a little more natural for me, in the same way that an hour-long TV show seems about right. Of course I would eventually fill those up too."

Heading into the summer of 1975, Rundgren's growing disdain for the social demands of New York City life had resulted in he and Buell leaving their three-story Manhattan brownstone for a woodland sanctuary in upstate New York. After his relationship with Albert Grossman had cooled somewhat, Rundgren's day-to-day management was now being handled by Susan Lee at the Grossman Organization, who advised him that it would be wise to reinvest a portion of his prodigious production income into real estate. And what better place to build his next home and studio, Rundgren thought, than the Woodstock area, where it had all began?

"It was funny," says Rundgren, "at one point, I had so much money that I pretty much had to buy a house. It was stupid to have all this money and not invest it in something. So that's when I bought the house on Mink Hollow Road in Lake Hill, New York."

Recalling the history of the Mink Hollow Road location, high up in the woods, near the foot of the Catskill Mountains, Roger Powell says, "The property had originally been purchased by this architect, who was going to build a big house on it. But the first thing he did was build this little wooden A-frame house, so that he had a place to live while he was building a fancier house, a little further up the hill. When Todd bought the property, he moved into the fancier house and eventually converted the smaller wood house into his studio."

As he began to draft plans for what would become Utopia Sound, Rundgren also had some band business to deal with. Coinciding with the release of *Initiation*, on June 14, there would be another tour with Utopia, only this time Kevin Ellman would not be part of it. "By the time we got to the second Utopia record," says Rundgren, "Willie Wilcox had become the drummer. Kevin had decided that, as much as he was into music, he was going to leave it all behind to manage Beefsteak Charlie's for his dad, Larry Ellman, who owned the Cattleman's Restaurants, a relatively upscale steak chain."

"I had gotten married," says Ellman, "and I didn't want to travel anymore. I always loved the playing, but I didn't really enjoy being on the road in a band."

John 'Willie' Wilcox grew up studying jazz greats like Count Basie, Duke Ellington, and Max Roach and even, as a young student, got to sit in with Gene Krupa's band at a restaurant owned by Miles Davis's producer Teo Macero. Yet, after attending both the Berklee and Manhattan schools of music, his professional career had begun with Hall & Oates. After Ellman's departure, Utopia's John Siegler had remembered Wilcox from the *War Babies* sessions and suggested him to Rundgren. "John had liked the way we locked in," says Wilcox, "and it was John who wanted me to be in Utopia. I never actually spoke to Todd about it. All of a sudden, I'm in this rented airport hanger in Poughkeepsie, New York, with a full stage setup, rehearsing intensely, two or three hours every day, to get these complex songs down."

The Initiation tour kicked off in Ohio on July 4, with Wilcox joining Rundgren, Schuckett, Klingman, Siegler, and Powell as they played material culled mainly from Rundgren's most recent solo albums, plus a couple of compositions by Leonard Bernstein and Jeff Lynne, and some new Utopia material. While Ellman's flash may have previously impressed the percussionistas in the crowd, Siegler says he found it easier to groove with Wilcox's humbler feel. "Somebody had to hold the thing together," laughs Siegler, "because it could be in danger of flying off into space."

Toward the end of August, these shows would be recorded for inclusion on the second official Utopia release: *Another Live*. John Siegler recalls the theatricality of a Utopia live show at this time, which led to them recording the new album in concert rather than in the studio: "Even without the costumes and the makeup, the overall arc of a Todd Rundgren concert went from beginning to end, in a vague kind of way. There are all these actual show tunes like 'Something's Coming' from *West Side Story* and 'Never Never Land' or 'Lord Chancellor's Nightmare Song.' So, by the time we got to 'The Ikon,' we're playing 45 minutes of what was, in Todd's mind, a little theater piece. More conceptual things, like 'The Seven Rays,' were Todd's vision, lyrically, of each guy in the band at the time. Each had a color and a different type of person they were, like a scientist, a writer, a thinker ..."

Siegler says that songs like 'The Seven Rays,' and Rundgren's entire approach to the *Another Live* compositions, were an extension of the leader's desire for Utopia to be more inclusive. They became the basis for the band's increasingly collaborative methods. "Todd brought in 'The Wheel,'" he adds, "I collaborated with him on the music for 'Seven Rays,' and Ralph came in with the music for 'Another Life,' and then Todd would go off and think up stuff to sing on it."

Roger Powell recalls bringing in some music he had composed prior to joining the band, which he had originally titled 'The Emerald Tablet Of Hermes Trismegistus.' "Todd liked it," Powell recalls, "so we adapted it for Utopia performance, only Todd always thought the full name was too much of a tongue-twister, so it became 'Mr Triscuits.'"

"Siegler and I had our things in there and even Roger, the new guy, had something," says Schuckett. "Moogy also brought in some things, but even though we recorded them, Todd didn't include any of those tunes in his final cut; he didn't think they fitted. I think Moogy's always been a little resentful of that."

"I had a couple of big songs," says Klingman. "One was called 'Night In New Orleans Suite' and that was like three songs with musical interludes that told a musical story. Then I had this other thing called 'Where There's A Will There's A Way,' which was like a classical piano concerto with some vocal sections. Everyone else had tunes on *Another Live* but me, which didn't seem fair since I was one of the organizers in the band."

Another Live was released on November 15, featuring live performances largely culled from the band's August 25 homecoming gig at Wollman Rink in Central Park. Side one was all of the remaining Utopia collaborations, while side two, after Powell's 'Intro/ Mr Triscuits,' consisted of Bernstein and Sondheim's 'Something's Coming,' Rundgren's 'Heavy Metal Kids,' Jeff Lynne's 'Do Ya' (allegedly a response to The Move's cover of Nazz's 'Open My Eyes'), topped off with what had become Rundgren's closing anthem, 'Just One Victory.'

As *Another Live* hit the stores, just two weeks before Utopia's European tour was scheduled to commence in Birmingham, England, Ralph Schuckett announced his decision to leave the group. "You know fame and money wasn't our main motivation," says Schuckett. "We were music guys all the way, but as long as we were playing with this famous guy, we wanted to have hit songs, T-shirts, and merchandise and make a lot of money. Todd didn't see the band that way."

As Schuckett was leaving, Klingman, miffed over his snubbing on *Another Live*, also felt it was time to leave Utopia and concentrate on studio work. "It was really a successful group," says Klingman, "and we were amazingly successful, playing to thousands of people, getting multiple encores and stuff like that. But Todd was talking about how he wanted to move his studio upstate and I was gonna stay in the city with Secret Sound which was now open to outside clients. I had been working with Bette Midler, producing *Songs For The New Depression*."

"Ralph had a lot of session and jingle type work lined up in New York at the time," says Rundgren, "and I could see how that seemed like a better situation for him. So after Moogy pulled out, that left four of us."

The sudden exodus of keyboard players, two weeks before a European tour, put increased pressure on Roger Powell to cover a lot of sonic ground. "I had classical training," says Powell, "and had played jazz, classical, and avant-garde things. Trouble was, when I first joined the band, Ralph and Moogy had pretty much covered all of the organ and piano, so I hadn't played those parts. They actually said, 'We haven't heard you play keyboards, all you've done is make noises.' So they made me audition for the job."

When Powell passed the audition, it marked the end of the first era and the beginning of a new four-piece era for Utopia, the band that some at Bearsville still dismissed as 'Rundgren's folly.' With so much to rearrange and rehearse for the tour, Rundgren wasn't confident that the four-piece band would be able to tackle the elaborate backing vocal parts in time for Europe, so he padded the band with three of the best backing singers in the business at the time, David Lasley, Arnold McCuller, and the soul legend Luther Vandross, fresh off his recent work backing David Bowie on *Young Americans*.

Touring into 1976, arriving back in America as the country celebrated its 200th birthday, Rundgren began to take stock of the ten years he had now been in the music business. As he wrote and recorded a few new ideas for his next official solo album, selected sounds and songs of 1966 came flooding back to him.

11

Rock The Catskills; Building Utopia Sound

Beginning in Birmingham, England, Utopia's 1975–76 Winter tour made stops in Scotland, Belgium, Denmark, The Netherlands, and France before a brief detour back to the Liverpool Empire to tape *The Old Grey Whistle Test* for the BBC. From there, it was back home for a week off, before finishing the year with concerts across an America already giddy with anticipation for its upcoming 1976 Bicentennial celebrations.

Drummer Willie Wilcox noticed a new economy in the group's playing as the current Utopia – himself, Rundgren, Siegler, Powell and the three hired male backing singers – adjusted to their new format. "The larger band," says Wilcox, "had everything happening all at once. But when it was just bass, drums, guitar, and keyboards, we just kind of took our positions. All of a sudden, Todd's guitar had to cover a lot more ground, harmonically and sonically, as did Roger on piano, organ, and synthesizers."

"When Roger came in," Siegler adds, "he was a revelation. Here was somebody who really knew synthesizers but who could really play keyboards as well."

Rundgren was still on the road with Utopia when he announced his plans to use the band on his next solo album, which would be recorded in various studios at certain cities on the tour. "Todd had a commitment," says Siegler, "and the record company wanted a new 'Todd Rundgren' record out in the spring, so whenever we had days off, we went into studios and recorded some tracks that would later come out on *Faithful*."

Rundgren approached *Faithful*, his seventh solo album, differently than he had his other records to date. For one thing, the whole first side would be comprised of cover versions of songs he had been listening to back in 1966, the year he'd turned pro. But unlike David Bowie, who had put together a similar set of covers, *Pin Ups*, a couple of years earlier, Rundgren eschewed stylistic reinterpretations of the material, opting instead for six detailed sonic pastiches, each faithfully recreating the sound and style of the original recordings.

"It was my tenth anniversary in the music business," says Rundgren. "I had graduated from high school in 1966, and joined Woody's Truck Stop that year, so I picked out the songs you would have heard anywhere you went ten years earlier, in boutiques, on the radio, or just coming out of people's doorways. It was my little tribute to an era that was already ten years gone."

Perhaps the giveaway was his choice of opening track, 'Happenings Ten Years Time Ago.' Originally recorded by The Yardbirds, the song sets the stage for a six-song stroll down memory lane, via Carnaby Street, with stops at The Beach Boys, Dylan, Hendrix and two Beatles songs, both by Lennon.

For side two, Rundgren composed six original songs that he felt reflected, to varying degrees, the influence of his 60s record collection. "Those songs," he says, "weren't meant to literally map one-to-one onto any of those other particular songs [on the covers side]: it was just more like, 'That was then, this is now.'"

According to Rundgren, *Faithful* was recorded in a piecemeal fashion, picking up tracks in different locations as the tour progressed. While he says he has forgotten where most of them were recorded, he seems to recall cutting some initial tracks at Rampart Studios in London, an old stomping ground of The Who.

"We did 'Happenings Ten Years Time Ago' in that session," says Rundgren, "and, I think, 'Love Of The Common Man' as well. Then I know some of it was done in the Bearsville Studios, and we may have even done some at Secret Sound."

The relative lack of complexity of the new Rundgren originals was out of step with his more complex recent work. "Take a dive from your ivory tower, we'll catch you," he sings in 'Love Of The Common Man,' and while the material seems to indicate a desire to get back to his post-hanging days in Manhattan or the poppier, romantic themes of *Something/Anything?*, Rundgren insists he was now approaching them in a more intellectualized way: "At a certain point I started realizing that I had been writing a lot about relationships and 'love,' purely out of habit, because that's just what songwriters wrote about. But in most cases, love songs aren't really about love, they're about possessiveness or sexual attraction or some other thing.

"At some point, I made a conscious decision that I was no longer going to just reflexively put the word 'love' in my songs in a thoughtless kind of way. I suppose the ultimate of that was 'The Verb "To Love,"' which is actually getting into an almost self-referential lyric-writer's dilemma. I cut way down on my use of that, and cut out almost altogether what some people would call romantic – what I might call sycophantic – songs, essentially about the mating ritual. So if I wasn't going to write about that, I had to seek out all other kinds of subject matter to write about."

Musically speaking, John Siegler recalls the decidedly uncomplicated approach extending to the recording process as well. "We'd walk into some studio – me, Willie, and Roger – and Todd would just pick up a guitar and say 'Here it is guys, let's do it,' and it would be one of the simpler songs, like, 'Love Of The Common Man,'

'Cliché,' or 'The Verb "To Love,"' one of my favorite things I ever did with Todd."

While three decades and millions of miles have blurred specificity of location, most of the players involved recall recording 'Rain' in Cleveland, most likely around November 3 1975. "We just went into these places," Siegler recalls, "and listened to all of those old records and then did our best to imitate them."

Roger Powell, uncharacteristally, played the rhythm guitar on their remake of Jimi Hendrix's 'If Six Was Nine.' Recorded at Secret Sound, it was likely one of the last sessions Rundgren held there. "The guitar part was so dead simple," says Powell, laughing slightly. "Just *du-nuh, du nuh*, you know? Todd used to go back and forth between New York and Woodstock around then, so we did a bit of stuff in the city. But pretty soon after this, he would have gotten all of his equipment out of Secret Sound."

Considering its creator had grown up listening to Philadelphia soul, *Faithful's* covers, Hendrix aside, were surprisingly preoccupied with the more Caucasian-oriented sounds Rundgren had heard on the radio in the mid 60s. "Well, I didn't feel at that point that I was in the same category as Daryl Hall," says Rundgren, "in that I could, or should, exploit all my R&B roots. Yes, there was other music on the radio at the time that I certainly could have done in tribute but, if you look back, I had already done a lot of tributes back when I was living it. Woody's Truck Stop was covering Sam & Dave and Albert King, and later I did the soul medley on *Wizard*. So by *Faithful* I was looking to do stuff I hadn't done before."

Back at Bearsville Studios, Rundgren and his musicians tackled two of the record's most startlingly accurate pastiches, The Beatles' 'Strawberry Fields Forever,' and The Beach Boys' 'Good Vibrations.' But as dramatic as these recreations were, Rundgren insists he was never out to duplicate them to the letter. Yet, while he made almost no attempt to cop Hendrix's vocal style on 'If Six Was Nine,' he does offer a flat-out impression of Albert Grossman's former client, Bob Dylan, on 'Most Likely You Go Your Way (And I'll Go Mine).'

"To a certain extent," Rundgren admits, "we wanted them to sound similar, even though we may have had to use a different technique to achieve the final product. For instance, we never hired cello players to come in on 'Good Vibrations.' We faked that sound up with my Putney synthesizers, while 'Strawberry Fields' was similarly cobbled together with spit and rubber bands."

Roger Powell says that part of his day jobs at both the Moog and Arp synthesizer companies had involved "extracting and mimicking" acoustic sounds on their products, a skill he found useful on *Faithful*. "It was like this little puzzle. We had to try to get these all sounds on my synthesizers. I had developed a talent for duplicating sounds by ear, like the Mellotron-ish type things on 'Strawberry Fields.' We didn't have any Mellotrons, and besides, what fun would it have been if we had? On the original 'Good Vibrations,' the Beach Boys had used this keyboard-operated Theremin developed by Raymond Scott, a colleague of Bob Moog. But for our version, I emulated the sound on a Mini-Moog, using the portamento control and the modulation wheel."

Powell recalls cranking up a distorted Clavinet to match Rundgren's raw guitar on 'Black And White.' "I loved using the Clavinet quite a bit around then," he says, "but they were so fragile. It has a very honking, sort of guitar-like sound, but my only complaint was that you couldn't bend the notes the way Todd could on a guitar."

In a brief return to studio self-accompaniment, Rundgren recorded the calypso-tinged 'When I Pray' entirely on his own at Bearsville Studios, where he also layered all of his lead and backing vocals for the entire album. Powell's synthesizer strings fill out a song that John Siegler believes to be one of Rundgren's finest Philly soul ballads, 'The Verb "To Love,"' which was recorded at SugarHill Studios, in Houston, Texas, some time around the band's November 19 1975 appearance there. "It's a classic," says Siegler. "I mean, nobody else in the world would ever write a song like that. I remember Todd was trying to get us to play it so slowly that we could barely breathe. It wasn't that we were necessarily rushing it, but Todd just really wanted the song to be very, very, very slow. It was really hard to play it as slow as he needed it."

Utopia's live sound engineer, John Holbrook, assisted Rundgren at most of the *Faithful* studio sessions on the road, and remembers the Houston session well. "That album was really the first studio assisting job I did with Todd. When we cut that track at SugarHill Studios, I remember it was meant to be a big deal that we were at the same studio where Freddy Fender had recorded 'Before The Next Teardrop Falls.'"

Faithful concludes with a Canned Heat-styled shuffle rocker called 'Boogies (Hamburger Hell),' in which Rundgren, a strict vegetarian at the time, warns, "I know where you're going, I can tell / Don't go looking for me down in Hamburger Hell." He follows that with the kind of careening guitar solo he'd excelled at during the reign of the six-piece, prog-rock Utopia.

In the end, Rundgren says that purpose of the *Faithful* album was to have a little upbeat sonic party for the fans who had stuck with him, faithfully, through all of his more way-out adventures in sound. Additionally, he thought, "it might be fun to listen to. Half of it was about making these copy versions, which was this study in sort of 'rock classicism.' I had been a keen student of the studio, so I was very detailed about that aspect of it. It wasn't like I was trying to make some bigger statement beyond the fact that I was sort of A/B-ing my musical influences. That was enough of a 'concept' for the album."

Shortly after *Faithful* was finished, the Rundgren, Siegler, Powell, and Wilcox line-up went back into Bearsville to record another entire album's worth of instrumental disco tracks, which made up the infamous 'lost' album, *Disco Jets.*

A completely tongue-in-cheek exercise, ostensibly designed to exploit the US bicentennial year and the concurrent trends of CB radio, *Star Wars*, and disco, *Disco Jets* had begun after Rundgren had painstakingly rearranged the theme from *Star Trek*, one of his favorite TV shows, which had also debuted in 1966. In no time at all, he and the band had cooked up nine more instrumentals, including 'Space War,' a reworking of a Utopia live jam formerly known as 'Bassball,' and 'Cosmic Convoy,' a futuristic answer song to the then current CB-radio-inspired novelty hit 'Convoy,' by one-hit wonder C.W. McCall. Rundgren and his compatriots also exploited the bicentennial with a star-spangled 'Spirit Of '76.'

Roger Powell recalls one long weekend spent "cranking out" *Disco Jets* as a lark. "It was a disco spoof, but it was a hoot to record and I remember laughing so hard I cried."

Musically as interesting as anything Utopia ever did, with memorable soloing from Rundgren and Powell, *Disco Jets* languished in the Bearsville vaults and remains officially unreleased, although the tracks were included on the Japanese compilation *Todd Rundgren: Demos And Lost Albums (Todd Archive Series Vol. 4)*. "It was not one of our stellar moments," Siegler concludes.

Two dramatic shifts occurred immediately before the release of *Faithful.* First, immediately following the *Disco Jets* session, John Siegler left the band, citing tour fatigue and the feeling that he'd done all he could do with the band. The three remaining members began auditioning replacements immediately, but after six or seven candidates Rundgren abruptly stopped the process and went on vacation, informing the others that he intended to get Tony Sales back upon his return.

Early in 1976, Rundgren's domestic life was in flux and, with the band on hold, he seized the moment to take a breather from the prolific writing, recording, and touring treadmill he had been on since 1972. He packed some things, bought a Pan-Am Airlines 'Around-The-World' ticket and went on a kind of 'walkabout.'

"I'd felt the need to explore all of this stuff that I'd been reading about," says Rundgren, "from Indian mystics to Turkish dervishes. I got off at Istanbul and then just made it up from there. With the Pan Am ticket, as long as I flew in an eastern direction, I could stop anywhere I wanted. So I went to Iran, Afghanistan, India, Nepal, Sri Lanka, Bali, Thailand, Japan, and Hawaii. I was gone for two months. Prior to this, I'd been to Europe a lot, of course, but never to these exotic locales."

Rundgren had expected to find enlightenment in these places, but as he rode his moped past scenes of poverty and misplaced worship in India, he only grew more bewildered: "At the temples, there'd be all of these poor Indian people who had mutilated themselves in order to get sympathy, waiting outside. Inside, it was all Western people dressed up like Indians and rich Indians dressed up as Western people. I went to see Sathya Sai Baba, just outside of Bangalore. We waited for hours and hours until he finally came out, walked around and took a bunch of envelopes full of money. He sat on a chair for a little while, did a couple of spurts of vibhuti [sacred ash used in Hindu worship], and walked back into his house to do private audiences with rich people. It was strange and ironic."

While Rundgren was gone, Powell and Wilcox, not particularly keen to re-enlist Tony Sales, had kept the search alive for a bass player. It was then that Powell received a hot tip from his friend, composer Michael Kamen. "I was house-sitting for Todd at the time," says Powell, "and Michael called and said I should meet this bass player kid, by the name of Kasim Sulton, who was playing with Cherry Vanilla. We had him come up to Woodstock to audition and he was, of course, fabulous. At first, he wasn't quite the bass player that John Siegler was, but he was a really good singer and we thought he might breathe some new life into the songs. Willie and I just thought he was perfect."

As Sulton recalls, Rundgren was not entirely sold on him. "The audition was in April of 1976, and I had just turned 21 the previous December. When Todd came back from India, they told him that they had found somebody that they wanted him to hear and he was not happy about it. He thought I was just too young and inexperienced, and he wanted Tony back in the band. As I understand it, Roger and Willie told Todd that if he had to have Tony back in the band, he'd have to get another keyboard player and drummer."

Faced with a mutiny, Rundgren reluctantly agreed to the demands of Powell and Wilcox, and Kasim Sulton was now a full member of Utopia, even if Rundgren barely spoke to him for the first year.

Faithful was released in May, with little fanfare, no tour, and no advertising thanks to a 'silent' promotional strategy, as revealed by Bearsville's Paul Fishkin in a *Creem* magazine interview that year. "Musically, this is one of the most consistent, accessible records Todd has ever made," Fishkin told *Creem*, "so we're doing something unique on another level: we will not be advertising nationally initially."

Phonograph Record's Ben Edmonds embraced the album, and his April review was entitled "*Faithful*: The Todd Rundgren You've Been Waiting For." But while 'Good Vibrations' was played in high rotation on American radio, and 'Love Of The Common Man' was released as a late single, the silent treatment and lack of a tour resulted in flat sales for the album.

In late May and through the first half of June, prior to a two-month tour in the early summer of 1976, Utopia were eager to record a new album. But first the band would be called upon to help Rundgren with his latest outside production client, the celebrated English guitarist Steve Hillage, who had recently left Daevid Allen's Gong for a solo career. Rundgren explains how this, the first outside production he had done in the new Utopia Sound Studios, in Lake Hill near Woodstock, New York, became a kind of template for the way he would come to work on projects there over the next decade and a half.

"Ever since I began producing other artists at Secret Sound," Rundgren explains, "we had never kept track of studio hours. We figured we would roll it into a larger production advance, which ultimately resulted in a cost saving to the label on most projects. By 1976, I had opened Utopia Sound and shortly thereafter my neighbor died and his wife offered to sell me their house. This enabled me to offer housing as well as a studio and now the up-front advance became even more comprehensive. The label got an all-in budget they could live with and, depending on how efficiently the recording process went, I could make more or less than my normal production advance."

Hillage had self-produced his initial solo offering, *Fish Rising* in 1975, but was now interested in having objective yet sympathetic ears for his next record. Having been impressed with Rundgren's own musical approach, including his recent work with Utopia, Hillage was delighted when his Virgin Records A&R man, Simon Draper, called to tell him that Rundgren was both amenable to working with him and available to take it on.

"I wanted an album that would present my take on the musico-spiritual values that had been our philosophical currency in Gong," says Hillage, adding that he hoped to achieve what he called a "second-wave take on psychedelia."

After an overseas phone call, a formality so Hillage could "check that we were on the same wavelength," a deal was struck. Soon after, Hillage and his partner Miquette Giraudy were walking the grounds of Rundgren's Lake Hill home, ready to create Hillage's album, *L*. "Todd's guest house," says Hillage, "was set in a large garden in the woods. We rented a car and went for regular drives around the area and into Bearsville and Woodstock. It was a very beautiful area. On the whole, working there was really productive."

While respecting Hillage's artistry, Rundgren says he found the Englishman to be curiously eccentric. "He was this slightly dotty, peculiar, idiosyncratic guy," says Rundgren, with seeming affection. "He came from this very hippie sort of Hawkwind and Gong world, and these bands would jam for six hours straight. I think he probably felt, based on some of the records I had done, that we might have been kindred spirits. What he couldn't have realized is that I am a more skeptical and sarcastic person than sometimes is fully represented in my records. Or maybe he was ignoring that part."

Hillage says he was eager to get Rundgren's "stamp on the record" and, having no band of his own at the time, was both "thrilled and honored" when Rundgren offered Utopia as his accompanists for the sessions. "We had seen Utopia live in the UK, the previous year, with John Wilcox and Roger Powell, but not Kasim. I had also noted Roger's involvement in the synthesizers on Todd's *Initiation* album. It was a buzz to play all [my] tracks live in the studio with [Utopia]."

In return, Rundgren recalls that, as eccentric as he and Utopia found Hillage, they likewise found him to be focused and concise about his music while remaining "a hoot" to play with. "He liked to kind of stretch out and jam," says Rundgren, "but he knew what he wanted to accomplish and was pretty clearheaded about where he was going musically. He had all these other kinds of odd tools that he used and this whole self-invented terminology he would use. He had what looked like an old piece of silverware, like a knife handle, and he would kind of slide it up and down the guitar. He called this 'glissing,' but he also had this whole little language of his own for all these little personal techniques."

"Steve was a wonderful guy," recalls Kasim Sulton "so nice and kind and polite but kooky too. He and Miquette together were a trip."

"Miquette was much taller than Steve," says Rundgren, "but she had this little tiny voice and would always say, 'That's so *biz-aaah*,' in this thick French accent. Everything was 'biz-aaah' to her, but they were both kind of bizarre to us, too."

"Miquette has an amazing vibe," says Hillage. "She's my partner, co-writer, and co-conspirator. She is also a synthesizer player, but she didn't do so much on the *L* record, as Roger was handling most of the electronics. Her presence is certainly felt on the record; she did quite a few vocals and was very much involved with 'Lunar Musick Suite' and in the choice of tracks such as [Donovan's] 'Hurdy Gurdy Man,' [Uma Nanda and Kesar Singh Nariula's] 'Om Nama Shivaya' and [George Harrison's] 'It's All Too Much.'"

Rundgren was amused that Hillage opted to do a Beatles tune, and a Harrison song at that, but was happy that it was at least one of the more 'obscure' numbers in the Beatles songbook. "I recall that what I really got into about the original," says Rundgren, "was the keyboard sound. It was just some overblown Farfisa organ, but it sounded to me like a calliope, or something, going through a Marshall amp."

Hillage recalls that he and Giraudy arranged most of the music before the sessions, but concedes that Rundgren naturally influenced these final arrangements, most notably in the area of sonic design. Hillage was particularly fond of Rundgren's brand new, pre-release model Eventide Harmonizer, and even put the entire drum mix through it on 'It's All Too Much.'

According to engineer John Holbrook, who assisted on the three-week long sessions, *L* was also a great initiation for Utopia Sound's gear. "Todd had just moved his Stephens 16-track machine up from Secret Sound," says Holbrook, "and I think he still had that home-built console, although he later replaced it with a Neotek board and a rack of Soundcraftsmen graphic equalizers, one for each track."

Holbrook, no doubt drawing upon his own background as an employee of the British synthesizer company EMS, was left alone with Hillage to "cook up the ambiences" for the album. "Todd didn't have a lot of patience for working out sounds," he says, "so he was quite happy to leave us out there for days together, overdubbing all kinds of great stuff. Steve was, and still is, a unique and amazing player and he did things with guitar ambiences that I'd never heard before."

In addition to guests such as Sonja Malkine, who played a 15th-century hurdy-gurdy on the Donovan tune, and tabla player Larry Karush, Hillage invited jazz great Don Cherry to add trumpet, Tibetan temple bells, tambura, and voice.

"Don Cherry was an old friend of Daevid Allen," says Hillage. "We heard he was in New York and thought it would be great to ask him to come up and play on our album. His pocket trumpet solo on 'Lunar Musick Suite' is pure genius. He also added some nice touches on some of the other tracks. It was pretty surreal being there in upstate New York country with Todd and Don Cherry; a really inspiring event."

Rundgren says he was also amused by Hillage's insistence on only recording songs during certain phases of the moon, as they did on 'Lunar Musick Suite,' or turning the bed to face a certain way. "Steve was very pre-Feng Shui," laughs Rundgren, "and just very mystical. He had a whole regime of little New Age things he would do. They would go down by the stream that ran by the studio and take off all their clothes, and he would play and she'd do yoga."

While acknowledging a few stubborn clashes with Rundgren, over arrangements and other matters, Hillage is adamant that, when it was all done, he'd gotten exactly what he had wanted from his producer. "One particularly amazing arrangement thing Todd did," Hillage recalls, "was to completely restructure 'Lunar Musick Suite' at the final mastering in New York City, by some really radical edits. We were most surprised, but blown away, by the result."

After Rundgren had finished the mixes and handed the finished *L* album to Hillage and Virgin Records, he assumed that, as fun as it had been to make, nothing was likely to come of the record. "But it got just incredible rave reviews in England," he says, "and was by far the biggest record he ever had and made him a star for years after. We never worked with him again, ironically enough, but I've heard he became a producer and 'mixologist' at one point, doing all these sort of hip-hop records."

On June 18, Utopia headed back on the road, in Utica, New York, with Sulton now a full member. Over the course of the next two months, Utopia's four-voice blend became a strong aspect of their live sound. "Kas and Todd clearly had the stronger lead voices," says Roger Powell, "and while I was never really comfortable singing at all, especially lead, I found that I could harmonize and pull off a pretty good falsetto; our four voices stacked together really well for the type of music we were making. And, to be fair, we had a really good live engineer, Chris Andersen, who put it all through these Eventide Harmonizers."

"The most challenging thing for me in that band was the actual playing," says Sulton. "The singing was secondary. The material was extremely complicated, and things like 'Initiation,' which I think was one of my audition pieces, had tons of key changes, time changes and odd riffs."

By late summer, back from their first tour with Sulton, the band could at last get down to recording the next Utopia release, *Ra*, named after the ancient Egyptian god of the sun who was believed to command the sky, the earth, and the underworld. To Roger Powell, the Egyptian mythology themes in some of the *Ra* material struck a chord with those on his own pre-Utopia solo album, *Cosmic Furnace*.

"It was purely coincidental," says Powell, "that Todd had been getting into mysticism at roughly the same time as I had. I think that was another reason we kind of hit it off at the time. My solo album had featured all this elitist crap about Hermes Trismegistus, but of course Todd had this platform for exposing all this stuff and getting it out there to a wider audience."

Even before they had recorded a note for the *Ra* album, plans were under way for a massive stage set for the tour, which would not be until the following January, and Rundgren's designated manager at the Grossman Organization, Susan Lee, had been consulting on stage designs with a tour coordinator named Eric Gardner, from Panacea Entertainment Company. A minor controversy arose when the supposedly equal partners in Utopia were informed that a large portion of their recording advance had been pre-allocated toward the staging costs.

"I remember the four of us were at some dinner party thing at Todd's house," says Sulton, "and Albert Grossman was there with some other people. Todd was discussing this whole Middle Eastern concept, including a huge pyramid and a giant Sphinx head behind the band, with paws on either side of the stage. They wanted to do this special effects thing, centered on the four elements of the earth, and we were going to build a whole musical concept around the stage design."

Sulton says that he was fine with the large scale planning until he realized that roughly 95 per cent of the record budget would be spend on the sets "without anybody's consent, just because that's what Todd wanted to do. In our defense, I seem to recall that we all just said, 'Yeah sure, sounds like a great idea, let's do it,' but even if I had I opened my mouth up, I would have been laughed out of the room. Todd just did what he pleased."

Willie Wilcox adds that, while it may have added entertainment value to the ticket price, he was on the fence about it, from a business standpoint. "We were supposed to share band income four ways, so I wasn't really on board with it. For one thing, the pyramid was so big it precluded us from playing in certain smaller venues because it was too tall, so we'd end up in larger places where we shouldn't be playing. The Ra tour dates were based around where the stage could fit, and where we could pack in enough people to pay for it. We had to drag around three tractor trailers and 20 crew, just to set it up and manage it."

In addition to the stage set, Rundgren commissioned Florida-based luthier John Veleno, who had previously built guitars for Grand Funk's Mark Farner and the Climax Blues Band's Peter Haycock, to build two all-aluminum guitars for him, in the shape of an Ankh, the ancient Egyptian hieroglyphic sun symbol denoting eternal life. "Those Ankh guitars," says Rundgren, "and Kasim's [Ankh] bass, sounded great, and were reportedly the last guitars Veleno ever built."

Over much of 1976, Panacea Entertainment had also been making a transition from tour co-ordination to artist management, and late that summer, although Lee and Grossman were still officially managing Utopia, Gardner had gotten the band added to the bill for the third annual Knebworth Festival, held on August 21 1976 in Hertfordshire, England. Playing before a crowd of 400,000 revelers, Utopia appeared alongside headliners The Rolling Stones as well as Lynyrd Skynyrd, Hot Tuna, and 10cc.

When not on the road, Utopia were back at Bearsville Studios or Utopia Sound, happy to finally rip through new songs, many of which they had been performing since June, including 'Communion With The Sun,' 'Jealousy,' 'Hiroshima,' and an extended "electrified fairytale" entitled 'Singring And The Glass Guitar.'

Kasim Sulton recalls the group dynamic being especially democratic as they prepared the new material: "Todd had told us all that he wanted Utopia to be a democratic, four-piece band with equal participation from each of us, and everybody making the decisions. I remember sitting down and coming up with little bits and pieces, like 'Eternal Love,' which I completed with Roger. And there were parts of 'Glass Guitar' where Todd probably had about three quarters of an idea of how it was going to go and, from there, everybody just put their own bits and pieces in to complete it."

While most of the tracks were recorded in either Rundgren's studio or the larger Bearsville facility, with John Holbrook and assistant engineer Tom Mark, 'Communion With The Sun' and 'Jealousy' were recorded in the nearby Turtle Creek Barn, on mobile recording equipment owned and operated by the legendary Yes producer, Eddie Offord. Holbrook recalls how those sessions came about.

"Eddie had taken up a two year residency in the Barn," Holbrook remembers, "down the hill from the Bearsville studio, and he cut a lot of records down there. Eddie had this quirky setup that he'd brought over with him from England, and he put all this recording gear, the mixing board and everything, right out in the middle of the Barn, where the bands would play. No control room. He had these huge JBL speakers, which he used for playback, but the band would hear them as they were playing. Since he was set up, more or less permanently, in the Barn, Todd and the guys must have thought, 'Let's go in and see what we can do with Eddie.'"

Lending some classical weight and pomp to the album, 'Communion With The Sun' opens with a synthesized excerpt from Bernard Herrmann's 'Overture: Mountaintop And Sunrise.' But the most progressive rock-inspired piece on *Ra* was the epic, and episodic, 'Singring And The Glass Guitar,' featuring a *Monty Python*-esque spoken word introduction by a pixie-voiced Scotsman, portrayed by Holbrook.

"I'm really not sure why I ended up being the fake Scottish narrator," laughs Holbrook, an Englishman. "Todd had written out the text and I suppose I picked up the sheet and started reading it in a silly fake Scottish accent. Todd just said, 'Great, let's do that, but why don't we speed it up?' So we adjusted the vari-speed control and 'chipmunked' it, you know? I think I may have been inspired by the old Goon shows on British radio. I couldn't have got through more than a few sentences without breaking up laughing, so there were probably a lot of edits involved to get rid of all the laughter."

As promised, this third version of Utopia really was far more democratic than earlier incarnations, and Kasim Sulton recalls basking in the feeling that he could "play anything" he wanted as Rundgren and the entire band collaborated on the theatrically Beatlesque 'Magic Dragon Theatre.'

"I was given pretty much free range," recalls Sulton. "I first felt it during the Steve Hillage sessions, and it was true of most of what we did with Todd. I mean, if there was something specific he wanted to hear, he might ask us to play this note or play that riff, but otherwise I think he trusted everybody around him musically."

Roger Powell, whose nimble trumpet work adorns 'Magic Dragon Theatre,' recalls that, while everyone could weigh in on every musical decision, Rundgren asked that they observe one golden rule. "You couldn't just shoot an idea down," says Powell, "unless you had an idea to propose in its place. You couldn't just say 'I think that that chorus stinks,' you had to make a positive suggestion about how to change it."

Willie Wilcox, who got to play guitar on 'Jealousy,' which he co-wrote with Rundgren, noted the band's slow evolution away from progressive rock to something more concise and potentially more commercial. "It was starting to lean more toward rock-pop," says Wilcox, "and I don't know if *Ra* could still be considered progressive, by comparison, but we were becoming a regular band. Todd's presence was always very strong in that band, but so were the individual personalities of the four members. We were starting to share more of the whole thing."

Powell believes that the only reason Utopia had a recording career at all, at this point, was down to Rundgren's steadfast will for it to exist. Powell and the others felt, rightly or wrongly, that Bearsville would have preferred it if Utopia had "just gone away."

"But Todd's contract," says Powell, "called for a certain number of albums over a certain number of years, so he decided that every other album would be a solo album and every next one a Utopia album. Todd was still the most prolific writer among us and, in some cases, he would just write the whole damn song because it just occurred to him in like 30 seconds. But what I clearly remember from this whole period was just getting together at a session, and each guy would throw stuff into the project and pick up on it or add parts to it."

With the album in the can, and plans finalized for the January 1977 Ra tour to coincide with its release, another major shift was about to occur in Rundgren's career. On the eve of the December 1976 Japanese tour, which Eric Gardner had arranged for the group, Susan Lee had resigned and Rundgren, while still signed to Bearsville, was no longer a managerial client of the Grossman Organization.

"The night before Utopia was leaving for Tokyo," says Eric Gardner, "Susan called me up and informed me that she was no longer managing Todd, and asked if I would accompany Utopia on the Japanese tour. So I met Todd and the band at the airport the next morning, and we flew to Tokyo together."

By tour's end, and the dawn of 1977, Eric Gardner would become the full manager of both Todd Rundgren and Utopia. The coming year would be filled with more triumphs, more heartaches, and more forks in the road. But first, Rundgren would attend to one of his most celebrated detours, the making and breaking of Jim Steinman's gothic rock epic, Meat Loaf's *Bat Out Of Hell.*

Meat Loaf
Bat Out Of Hell

On the surface, Todd Rundgren's most commercially successful production appears to bear few of his sonic signatures. Yet *Bat Out Of Hell*, a Wagnerian rock song cycle imagined by piano-pounding composer Jim Steinman and belted out by the gargantuan voice of a hefty singer known as Meat Loaf, remains one of Rundgren's best-known works from the golden age of studio rock productions.

Look closer, however, and it makes perfect sense that, given his childhood love of musical theater and the resultant Gilbert & Sullivan and Bernstein compositions on his own albums, Todd Rundgren was the ideal man for the job. It seems unlikely that *Bat Out Of Hell* would have existed in its final form without him.

In fact, when discussing the record's epic struggle to be born, the word 'unlikely' often springs to mind. Consider the odds: a Broadway brat, with a penchant for opera, writes one of the biggest rock albums of the 70s, with a 300-pound singer/actor cast as the romantic lead. A name producer and futuristic rock pioneer agreeing to do the album 'on spec,' deferring his fee until the album finds a label, even after everyone else has rejected it. And yet, all these unlikely things – and more – actually happened. As a result, the battle for *Bat Out Of Hell* was a gothic melodrama packed with heartbreak, struggle, negotiation and, finally, a big finish. Come to think of it, it was not unlike a Jim Steinman song.

Steinman's career had begun in 1969 at Amherst College, near Boston, where his student project, a three-hour epic rock musical entitled *The Dream Engine,* had caught the attention of the New York Shakespeare Festival's legendary impresario Joseph Papp, who offered to produce the work.

Looking back, Steinman says he considers the early work his own *Citizen Kane*, "in the sense that it's always gonna be the best thing I'll ever do. It almost caused riots; some people were shocked and I just know that I'll never equal it. Still, I couldn't have written *Bat Out Of Hell* if I hadn't done *Dream Engine*."

The buzz had earned Steinman a publishing deal with Chappell Music and a tiny writing office near Broadway where he continued to fashion songs that straddled the line between his two earliest influences. "Opera and rock'n'roll," Steinman explains, "were both very heightened and larger than life. As a boy, I would constantly go from Wagner to Little Richard."

After writing the musical *More Than You Deserve* in 1973, Steinman met a transplanted Texan who had come to New York via the Los Angeles cast of *Hair*. Marvin Lee Aday, known simply as Meat Loaf, was already a veteran of numerous off-Broadway productions, including *The Rocky Horror Show,* in which he originated the role of "Eddie," which he would later reprise for Jim Sharman's film adaptation, *The Rocky Horror Picture Show.*

When Meat Loaf was cast in the touring production of *The National Lampoon Show*, Steinman signed on as its musical director. Prior to this, Steinman had been pitching a stage musical adaptation of Peter Pan, called *Neverland*, but after meeting Meat Loaf he began to feel that some of the songs, such as 'Heaven Can Wait' and 'Formation Of The Pack' (later known as 'All Revved Up With No Place To Go'), might form the basis of a conventional rock album built around the size large singer. By February 1976, after a depressingly short run in *Rockabye Hamlet*, Meat Loaf took a break from the stage so that he and Steinman could dedicate their full energies to getting the album realized.

By this time, however, Bruce Springsteen had released his breakthrough album, *Born To Run*, to widespread critical and commercial acclaim. It would be almost two years before *Bat Out Of Hell* reached the stores, by which time many rock critics assumed that Steinman was merely imitating Springsteen, an accusation that still clearly rankles with Meat Loaf. "Jimmy had written the songs for *Bat Out Of Hell* well before *Born To Run*," he insists. "Yes, it's true that Jimmy did actually go to see Bruce at The Bottom Line, back in 1975, but he'd already written the majority of the *Bat* songs by then. I love Bruce, and I've probably got every one of his records, but that 'Springsteen clone' tag came from *Rolling Stone*, who apparently went out of their way to put a negative spin on *Bat Out Of Hell* when it finally came out."

As Meat Loaf remembers it, Steinman called him from a pay phone, immediately after Springsteen's 8:30pm set, and begged him to catch the 11:30pm set. "Jimmy," Meat Loaf recalls, "said, 'You gotta get down here. He's kinda doing what we do!' That night, after seeing Max Weinberg and Roy Bittan play with Bruce, Jimmy knew that they would be the perfect musicians to complement our stuff."

"I was so impressed with what Bruce was doing, period," says Steinman, "but I could see how it related to what I was writing. Although to be fair, Springsteen's songs were like graphic realism, Scorsese's *Mean Streets,* whereas mine were more like Fellini's *Juliet Of The Spirits*, wild color and sort of phantasmagorical."

Springsteen's success did, however, provide Steinman with a template for how his larger-than-life musical ideas could be mass-marketed. Emboldened, he and

Meat Loaf set about pitching the *Bat* material to recording executives in a string of intimate, live auditions. While Steinman attacked the piano, Meat Loaf, accompanied by singer Ellen Foley, his girlfriend at the time, and male vocalist Rory Dodd, staged an impassioned, theatrical spectacle for, they claim, "every label in New York," but failed to find a buyer.

"We were turned down," laughs Steinman, "by people who had only vague ideas of some day in the future having a record company. Clive Davis had just started Arista Records and he told Meat Loaf he couldn't sing and told me I couldn't write. He said, 'You have a 300-pound guy named Meat Loaf, singing these operatic love songs, very theatrical.' Then he points at me, 'Meanwhile, this guy is banging the shit out the piano with his fingers bleeding. I don't know what the fuck this is all about, let alone what radio station is ever going to play it.' Of course, every time I see Clive, these days, he goes, 'Isn't it great that I was one of the first believers.'"

Eventually, the team got a bite from Tomato Records, a small, RCA-distributed label, and moved on to the search for a producer. After several big names of the day had passed on the project, including Bob Ezrin and Jimmy Ienner, Steinman received a call from Moogy Klingman, who had left Utopia the year before and was looking for acts to produce.

"After I'd done the Bette Midler album," says Klingman, "I wanted to do more of that kind of work. I thought Meat Loaf was the greatest thing I'd ever heard and I wanted to produce them. When I told them I had played with Todd, they said, 'Oh? We love Todd Rundgren. If you can get Todd involved in the project we'll do the album with the both of you.' So we set up a meeting so they could sing their songs for Todd."

Steinman recalls Rundgren sitting, wordlessly, through a private audition at the Nola Rehearsal Rooms, just off Broadway. "Then, at the end, he just stood up and said, 'So what's the big problem? We just record it and that's it.'"

"Todd was sitting there, laughing," adds Ellen Foley, "he just thought it was hilarious but he really did save the whole project."

While acknowledging the unmistakable Springsteen similarities, Rundgren says it was the humor that set Steinman's music apart from what he saw as the earnest melodrama of The Boss: "Jim's songs were just so comically over-the-top that I didn't see it as a rip-off; it seemed more like a parody."

"He was the only person," adds Meat Loaf, "who ever walked into the room and just got it. He immediately started discussing the songs with Jim. Once we had Todd on board, I decided that this was going to happen, come Hell or high water. I just became the most tenacious person on the face of the earth."

In November, as a two-week period of pre-production and rehearsals got under way in the accountants offices at Bearsville Studios, conflicting assumptions about the supposed Rundgren/Klingman co-production came to an awkward head.

"Moogy had brought Meat Loaf to me under this sort of arrangement," Rundgren recalls, "assuming he would get half the production fees and royalties. The problem being that he didn't tell them that. They thought they were just getting an introduction to me."

"We just figured it should just be Todd," says Steinman. "Todd was very cool, and he always impressed me as being larger than life, like a cartoon character. Which to me is a good thing. It's like it's one step above being a human."

"So we got up there," continues Rundgren, "and Steinman and Meat Loaf came to me and said, 'You know, we don't need Moogy for anything here, could you arrange for him to go? I say, 'If you want him to go, he'll go, and that will leave me as the sole producer of the record.'"

Klingman graciously dropped out, leaving Rundgren to continue working with the musicians he and Steinman had selected for the sessions. Among them were two members of Bruce Springsteen's E Street Band, drummer Max Weinberg and piano player Roy Bittan. Rundgren insists that it was Steinman's idea to hire them, adding that he wasn't entirely sure if Weinberg, as impressive as he was with Springsteen, was necessarily the right drummer for the *Bat* material.

"I think [Jim and Meat Loaf] wanted Roy and Max to make it more E Street," Rundgren says, "and Max had that tendency to speed up and slow down, which was great for the E Street band; it was a big part of what they did."

"I thought Roy was the best pianist I had ever seen in my life," says Steinman. "And for the kind of music I do, he's without parallel. I was very impressed with Max too. I loved the fact that, even when Max was rehearsing 'Bat Out Of Hell,' it would speed up. Max's emotionalism was my favorite thing about his playing. It was like a classical rubato, where the conductor controls the flow."

While Rundgren would himself play all the guitars, he also brought in all the current members of Utopia, drummer Willie Wilcox, bass player Kasim Sulton, and keyboard player Roger Powell, plus his old friend Edgar Winter to play the occasional saxophone. Sulton recalls that he was sharing a house with Powell in the nearby town of West Hurley, when Rundgren called him early one morning to see if he could come over to play bass on a record.

"I asked him what the name of the artist was," says Sulton, "and he said 'Uh, Meat Loaf.' I laughed and said, 'All right Todd, stop kidding around and tell me, for real, what the artist's name is.' He got a little pissed off at me and said 'Look, if you wanna play on the record, just show up at the studio at one o'clock.' When I got there, they performed most of the album for us and, when they were done, we all kind of looked at each other, and I thought, 'This is a comedy record. We'll have a blast doing it, and we'll never hear it again.' It was just so camp and so out of the mainstream, but also kind of fell right into Todd's niche. He's the kind of guy who would think, 'Why would I want to do an album that anybody could do? I want to do an album that no one can do.'"

Rundgren recalls bringing his full range of skills to bear in order to get the record completed. "I was not only producing, but I'd be jumping back and forth between playing the guitar, engineering, arranging, conducting the band, and addressing all the challenges of making the record itself."

"But that's where Todd's brilliance came in," says Sulton. "He just had this sixth sense about how to put these songs together and make them work with a band. Before we even set foot in the studio to roll tape, we had pretty much rehearsed everything up in that accountant's office."

Rundgren and Steinman insist that the intense rehearsals were a necessity, as they wanted to record, as much as possible, live off the studio floor with minimal overdubs. According to Ellen Foley, they likened the preparations to those of a Broadway show before opening night. "Even though we'd lived with this material for a long time," she says, "we all sort of felt like we only had one shot at capturing these live performances."

The production suffered another setback when Tomato Records, which had been kept out of the loop thus far, discovered that Rundgren had been contracted as the producer and threatened to pull the plug on *Bat* unless he was fired. "Tomato Records hated Todd," Steinman admits, "and wouldn't accept him as a producer because they'd hated the Hall & Oates album, *War Babies*. I loved that record though, so we tried to hold out and finish the record before they shut us down."

According to Meat Loaf, he and Steinman had managed to avoid a confrontation until the fifth week of production. "Around then, we started sending tracks down to RCA, and they flipped out, saying, 'We told you we didn't approve of Todd Rundgren.' It kind of came to a dead stop but by then it was Christmas time and we were gonna stop anyway."

Midway through the entire process, but with no label for the project, Rundgren says he had no choice but to intervene. "I remember thinking, 'What the fuck, you mean we're going to have to send all these people home?' So I went to Albert and said, 'Let us complete the record and Bearsville Records can have first crack at it. And if not, I'll just have to compensate you when we find somebody to distribute the record.' I could have just said to everybody, 'Go home, Meat Loaf quit his label.' But I thought there was no reason why Bearsville shouldn't have this record, you know? I mean we're doing it in Bearsville Studios, so they can absorb studio costs themselves."

"Todd took it on," says Steinman, "and basically paid for the record, through Bearsville. It was kind of a leap of faith, which is really amazing when you think about it. It was very nice, considering he probably thought the record was a big joke. At least, we could start recording again."

Rundgren recalls that, after sorting out the business matter, the sessions were knocked out in relatively short order. "It went about as quickly as I usually like to record things," he recalls. "With all the rehearsal, we were primed to get all basic instrumental tracks done in about two weeks."

Steinman was particularly impressed with Rundgren's speed in dialing in the right sounds. He noted his ability to give him an approximation of Phil Spector's classic rock and roll sound on 'You Took The Words Right Out Of My Mouth (Hot Summer Night).' "That was amazing," says Steinman, still in awe. "Todd didn't even blink, he just said 'OK' and started pushing a few little buttons, and suddenly he had this Spectorian Wall Of Sound. And when we did the vocals, he captured the Spector sound there too, with those snarly 'Na, na, nas.' I had written that riff in the original tune, but when he added those backup vocals I thought they were very Todd in their phrasing."

Willie Wilcox recalls reluctantly wresting the drum chair from Weinberg on 'All Revved Up With No Place To Go,' 'For Crying Out Loud,' and the downtempo ballad 'Two Out Of Three Ain't Bad.' He insists it was no reflection on the E Street drummer's skills.

"Different drummers," says Wilcox, "just have different feels. No better or worse. For a lot of drummers, the most difficult thing to do is to play slow, but I was really accustomed to playing slow tempos. Actually, for me, the only challenge on that track was that we had no guide vocal, so we really had to trust that we knew the structure."

Kasim Sulton confirms that, while he considers Weinberg "a great, great rock drummer," he just wasn't suited to Rundgren's needs for 'Two Out Of Three Ain't Bad.' "Actually," says Sulton, "before we put Willie in, we went and got another great drummer, Andy Newmark, into the studio, but he couldn't play it slow enough either. Finally, they just brought in Willie, who seemed to be able to play it to Todd and Jim's liking."

Wilcox admits that, for him, 'All Revved Up With No Place To Go' was by far the most challenging song of the sessions. "We were cutting it with a full orchestra of about 30 people," he remembers, "totally live. Even Meat Loaf was singing live. For some reason, I showed up to the session with just one pair of drumsticks and, during the run-through, I broke a stick and had to turn ask the percussionist for a drumstick. As a result, I played the track with two unmatched sticks, so it was lucky that we got it on the first take."

Since backing vocals play such a vital role in the overall sound of *Bat Out Of Hell*, it is surprising to learn that Meat Loaf was initially reluctant to allow any other voices on the album, except for his duet with Ellen Foley on 'Paradise By The Dashboard Light.' "Probably because of my ego," he admits, "but I didn't want somebody covering up my vocals. The whole time, I was fighting Jimmy and Todd tooth and nail on that."

According to Rundgren, a great deal of time was dedicated to tracking Meat Loaf's lead vocals. "I don't know if it was his inexperience," says Rundgren, candidly, "but at that point, Meat Loaf had a tendency to stray out of tune in the studio, so the vocals took a bit longer. Meat and Jim were very specific about what they needed, emotionally, but we got it eventually."

At Foley's insistence, she and Meat Loaf performed their erotically charged duet face-to-face, to preserve the emotional authenticity of the piece. "I had Meat come out into the room with me so I could sing it at him," Foley explains. "I'd never been on a record before, so the whole idea of everybody being separated was alien to me. I remember Steinman and I raving at Todd that 'this should really sound like *West Side Story*,' and he'd be rolling his eyes at us, like 'Okay, okay, shut up and do it already!'"

Foley delivered an impressively impassioned solo but recalls feeling decidedly less confident as an ensemble singer, never having sung background before, particularly under the watchful eye of Todd Rundgren, whom she describes as a "master vocal arranger."

"I don't think Rory [Dodd] had ever sung background before, either," admits Foley, "so it took us a little while to do it. While Todd was incredibly genial about it, he was very precise about voicing. He was like 'If you don't get it, I'm gonna do all these voices myself!' Of course, he could have done it all, in his sleep."

A much-discussed moment on the track 'Bat Out Of Hell' was the revving motorcycle engine sound that Rundgren produced using nothing but his overdriven Stratocaster and a Marshall 2x12 amplifier. "There was a lot going on [on the track] already," says Steinman, "and I'll never forget Todd asking me, 'Is that enough? Are we done?' I said, 'Todd, you promised me there would be motorcycles.' I got sort of childish, nagging him like a five-year old asking for ice cream. So he just gave me that sarcastic Todd look, and said, 'Ooh, I forgot, I promised you motorcycles.'"

In lieu of field recordings of actual motorcycles, Rundgren went out into Bearsville's live area with his guitar and began methodically adjusting the amplifier dials before cueing an assistant engineer to roll tape. Steinman describes what happened next as a "miraculous moment" to witness. "When it comes to the right moment," he remembers, "Todd revs up his motorcycle guitar sound, with the 'Vroom, vroom' revving and idling sounds. He yells over to me, as the tape's still rolling, 'Did you want a wheelie?' I said 'Sure.' You can actually hear the motorcycle do a wheelie and then the big crash, all of it, on guitar. Todd was like a magician to me!"

Rundgren could be an impatient magician at times, however, and both Steinman and Meat Loaf recall being taken aback by his steadfast refusal to coddle their fragile egos. "After a take," Steinman says, "he might say, 'Was that excessive enough for you, oh King of Bombast?' Overall, though, the sarcasm didn't bother me too much because I felt that Todd just had the greatest musical instinct in the world. Like, when we were listening back to the bed tracks of 'Two Out Of Three Ain't Bad,' before we did the backup vocals, he said 'Okay, lets go try to salvage this wreckage.' But when we did add in the backup vocals, they really did glue everything together, so it could be said that we really did 'salvage the wreckage.'"

"To listen to Todd and Jim banter," says Ellen Foley, "was like watching a tennis game, two really great minds, they were very funny together. There was a lot of witty repartee."

"And when he did give any praise," Steinman adds, "it was usually withering, which really affected Meat Loaf sometimes."

"Todd can be very condescending," says Meat Loaf, thinking back. "I saw it with the way he gave Jimmy his motorcycle, really sarcastic. You know, I love him but he's really an ornery old cuss sometimes."

Steinman says that, from his vantage point, Meat Loaf took the sarcasm harder than he did. "I think he felt a little left out. One time, while we were rehearsing, Meat Loaf sort of sauntered over to Todd and said 'Maybe, on this part, we could do like a Motown thing, you know?' Todd just shook his head and said, 'No, it doesn't fit Motown, Meat. Now go back, have a seat and let us finish this record.'"

"That whole record," says Sulton, "Meat really didn't open his mouth other than when he was supposed to sing. He really was relegated to the corner for most of that record."

After the basic tracks were down, Roger Powell added some synthesizer parts back at Utopia Sound. "It was mainly just me and Todd," says Powell, "but sometimes Jim and Meat dropped by. I recall using my own custom-made Powell Probe on 'Two Out Of Three Ain't Bad,' and there's one place, in fact, where the Probe gets pushed way up in the mix and it sounds like a sliding steel guitar. I also used another of my own designs, the Databoy digital synthesizer, along with my Minimoog, a Korg Poly-800, a Sequential Circuits Prophet 5 and an RMI Keyboard Computer, which had a really thick piercing sound that worked especially well against Todd's wall of guitar. It's funny, I only got paid $250 for the session, but I did end up getting a Gold record from it."

After non-starts, false starts and big finishes, the *Bat Out Of Hell* project appeared to finally be ready for release to an unsuspecting world. According to Steinman, trouble returned after Rundgren's first attempt at a final mix at Utopia Sound. "Todd's little tiny studio," says Steinman, "was more like a big outhouse, really. I must say the one bad thing about Todd is that he has a short attention span and, as a rule, you don't want to let him mix the record. For one thing, he originally mixed the whole album in one night, and then he handed it to us and said, 'Go down to Sterling Sound and tell Greg Calbi to make it sound good.'"

When they took the tapes back to Steinman's apartment to have a listen, the two men were devastated by what they heard. "It was the most depressing thing of my life," says Steinman, "Up to then, I had heard everything sounding so huge and now it's mixed down to two tracks and it sounded tiny, the whole thing was so compressed and fucked up that Meat Loaf and I actually cried. This was like the last thing that Job was hit with by God. After all we'd done to get this thing made, the producer did a great job, but now the final mix sounds terrible."

Steinman recalls driving back up to Woodstock, in mid-July, to beg Rundgren to remix the album. "We didn't just wanna throw Todd overboard, so we went up to tell him it didn't sound right. Todd says, 'Uh, well no one ever likes mixes at first. I'll see if I can do anything; it's probably just the EQ.'"

"I don't like to do lots of mixes," Rundgren adds, "but that always happens if the act gets involved in the mix. I think there was a period of endless remixing after the first mix."

Everyone agreed that they wouldn't touch Rundgren's Phil Spector styled mix for 'You Took The Words Right Out Of My Mouth (Hot Summer Night),' which had so impressed Steinman during the tracking. "It was actually mixed pretty much at the same time we recorded it," says Steinman. "Todd had made all of the settings as we went. The song was about five minutes long, so that's about how long it took to mix it. Later, when we remixed the album, we tried different people remixing that song, but no one could even come close to Todd's version. That was the only mix I felt that way about."

Next, Steinman took the tapes to producer Jimmy Iovine, a logical choice, as he was the man who had mixed Bruce Springsteen's *Born To Run*. While Iovine's mix came back lean and spare, Steinman recalls that there was just one problem with it.

"Everything sounded 'big' again," says Steinman, "so we were relieved, at first. But then I realized that it was because Iovine had left out all the background vocals. Now, for me, the backing vocals were an important part of the orchestration, almost as critical as lead vocals, so that just wouldn't do."

After checking the master tapes to make sure all the vocal parts hadn't been erased, Steinman next approached engineer John Jensen at the Power Station in New York. "Jensen and I basically mixed the whole album," says Steinman, "except for Todd's mix of 'Hot Summer Night' and Iovine's mix of 'Two Out Of Three Ain't Bad.' Incidentally, you'll notice Iovine's mix is pretty much voice and piano, although it does have the background vocals."

Mixes completed, Bearsville Records waived their option to release it on the label, opting instead to offer it to their parent company, Warner Bros, who requested a private showcase with the act before deciding to take it. After flying the principal performers to Los Angeles for a humiliating live audition, Warner Bros also passed on the record.

While Rundgren had bankrolled the budget for the album, purported to be anywhere from $100,000 to $150,000, he agreed to wait it out until Steinman could sell it to another label. "Bearsville had underwritten the project and charged it back to me," says Rundgren, "with the option of absorbing the record and then paying me an advance when they found a label. But it took them months to find somebody to even distribute it."

"I didn't know what we were going to do," Steinman recalls, "but Meat Loaf's manager, David Sonenberg, said, 'I'll think of something.' Then, we were thrown a lifesaver when David got a call from Steve Popovich, who had his own label called Cleveland International."

Steve Popovich had been a celebrated A&R man at Epic Records and had been rewarded with his own boutique label, an imprint of CBS/Epic. "He was brilliant," says Steinman. "Practically anything that made a difference at Epic Records in those days was his signing."

"I think," offers Ellen Foley, "that when Popovich came in, seeing Todd's name on the project probably lent the record the validity it needed for him to release it."

According to Steinman, Popovich wanted to release *Bat Out Of Hell* before he'd even heard the end of a single song. "Steve calls up Sonenberg," Steinman recalls "and says, 'I don't know how I got this, but I have this demo on my desk. So Sonenberg asks Popovich, 'Did you listen to it?' He said, 'I only heard the first song, it's called 'Hot Summer Night.'"

According to Gary Marmorstein's book, *The Label: The Story Of Columbia Records*, it was E Street Band guitarist Steven Van Zandt who had first tipped off Popovich about 'You Took The Words Right Out Of My Mouth (Hot Summer Night),' telling him that it had "the best intro in the history of pop music."

"Popovich told Sonenberg," Steinman recalls, "that he didn't even have to listen to the whole song. He told him, 'I'm ready to buy it based on the intro.' Eventually, of course, he listened to the rest and he became a fanatic believer. He loved it."

Cleveland International finally released *Bat Out Of Hell* on October 21 1977. Ironically, the record was now being distributed by Epic Records, one of the first labels to have initially passed on the project. The irony wasn't lost on Steinman. "Epic was the perfect name for that record," says Steinman. "Of course, everyone at Epic still hated it, but the Cleveland deal got it into the family, sideways. I'll never forget what Popovich taught me. He said, 'Having 10,000 people at a big company working their asses off for you is not as important as having one person alone who believes to the death in you.' I still believe that."

Since most of the CBS executives in America had, at one point or another, already passed on the *Bat Out Of Hell* project, enthusiasm was initially muted among CBS/Epic promotion teams around the country. A surprise break came months after its release. A promotional film of Meat Loaf performing 'Paradise By The Dashboard Light' with Foley's tour replacement, Karla De Vito, lip-synching Foley's parts, found its way onto the UK television program *The Old Grey Whistle Test*, introduced by a frankly uncertain Bob Harris. Suddenly, this most American of musical offerings was finding some love in Europe. "It actually broke in England, Germany, Australia, Canada," says Steinman, "and everywhere else, before America."

By all accounts a 'grower' at retail, and a hit or miss proposition with the critics of the day, *Bat Out Of Hell* went on to sell more than 40 million units worldwide, is consistently among the top ten best sellers of all time, and regularly appears on lists of greatest albums of all time, alongside such heavyweights as *Thriller* by Michael Jackson and *Rumours* by Fleetwood Mac.

Rundgren admits he was generally surprised when the album finally took off, months after release. "I had never figured that it would actually be a hit," he recalls, "although, by the time we were done with it, I think I was reasonably happy, musically, with what we'd done. It was just another album that had as much chance as any record of becoming 'commercial.' But Popovich refused to let the record die. Cleveland worked it for a year in America before they had a hit record."

Overall, Steinman's musical memories of *Bat Out Of Hell*, and of Todd Rundgren, are fond ones. "I don't use the word 'genius' much," says Steinman, "but Todd definitely deserves that title. I don't care if he says a good word to me, ever. I never stopped looking at him with awe and appreciation. He was the savior of this record and I'd work with him again. And I did have him come in to work with me a couple of years later, on *Bad For Good,* which was supposed to be Meat Loaf's second album before Meat Loaf lost his voice. And I hired Todd to do backgrounds on the Celine Dion hit 'It's All Coming Back To Me Now.' The way I look at it, anyone who's a visionary doesn't always have to be a nice guy. It's just that there are so many aspects of Todd; but I tell you, he's someone I really love."

Meat Loaf, who appears to have gotten over Rundgren's ribbing in the studio, now praises Rundgren as both an underrated guitar player and songwriter: "I don't know why Todd Rundgren isn't one of the biggest acts in the world."

Before he leaves, Jim Steinman offers a parting story from the night he and Meat Loaf drove up to Lake Hill to approach Rundgren about doing the remix. "We were listening to stuff from the record," Steinman recalls, "and then, around 10pm, we took a break and Todd wanted to show me this new *Star Trek* video game he was thrilled about. He turns it on and there's this huge, abhorrent sound like something blew up. Then everything went dark. Todd tinkered around a little with a flashlight in his hand, and the lights flickered on for a second before they stayed out for good. Around midnight, Meat Loaf and I told Todd that we'd better be getting back to the city and we left him there, still tinkering. All the way home, on our two-hour drive back from Woodstock, Meat and I had been talking so obsessively about how we'd definitely need to do a remix that we hadn't noticed, until we were on the West Side Highway in Manhattan, that there were absolutely no lights on anywhere in the city."

The date was July 13 1977, and Steinman had driven into the infamous New York blackout of that summer, when the East Coast from New York to Philadelphia went dark for three and a half days. "I had never seen New York like that," says Steinman, "and it freaked me out. Later, I heard that they were able to pinpoint that the incident had started at 10:17pm, exactly when Todd had blown out his video game. Now, you'll never convince me that Todd didn't cause the blackout. So, I'll never forget that summer of 1977. Elvis died, Son Of Sam was terrorizing Manhattan, the Yankees won the World Series, Todd caused the East Coast blackout and, to top it all off, *Bat Out Of Hell* finally got released."

Studio Hermit

By all accounts, 1977 was a tumultuous year in Todd Rundgren's personal life. His relationship with Bebe Buell had deteriorated to the point of ongoing estrangement, no doubt complicated by her open, on-off affair with Aerosmith lead singer Steven Tyler, whose child she had been carrying since the previous October. Shortly before the birth of daughter Liv, on July 1, Rundgren and Buell had taken an unsuccessful stab at stabilizing their home life, if only for the imminent arrival of the child. And yet, by September, Buell and her infant daughter were moving out, while a new woman, Karen Darvin, was about to move in. While Rundgren knew there was "a distinct possibility" that he was not the biological father of the child, he had made the decision to act as her spiritual father. The unpleasant details of these family struggles are better left to the tabloids but suffice it to say that Rundgren's year of domestic upheaval has an impact on our story, if only because the emotional turbulence would surface, albeit cryptically, on his 1978 solo album, *Hermit Of Mink Hollow*.

But first, Rundgren had to get through 1977, a year when his career had actually never looked brighter. After months of false starts and near misses, the Meat Loaf project *Bat Out Of Hell* was finally finished and would soon become his most successful artist production ever. His current Utopia line-up, now featuring Kasim Sulton, Roger Powell, and Willie Wilcox, was the most democratic yet, and found Rundgren sharing the songwriting burden and band decisions equally among the four players. The band's most recent album, *Ra*, was released in January, as Utopia set off on one of their most successful tours to date, taking their elaborate, Egyptian-themed pyramid stage set and Rundgren's custom Ankh guitars to more 60 cities and playing into the middle of May.

Back in Lake Hill, Utopia Sound was officially up and running, with the leftover gear from Secret Sound constantly being added to by Utopia's live sound engineer, Chris Andersen. He would soon leave the road to assist Rundgren with the outside production clients solicited by his new manager, Eric Gardner.

In 2009, Chris Andersen recalled the layout of the studio, and rattled off a list of some of the key equipment that would play a central role in Rundgren's recording in the coming years. "I was Todd's nuts-and-bolts guy," says Andersen. "I did all the grunt work of getting the bands there, getting them all set up, ordering the tape, aligning the machines, and making sure everything worked. That allowed to Todd to be more creative."

Andersen says that Rundgren initially transplanted his ROR console, custom-built for Secret Sound by Ted Rothstein, along with eight stereo Soundcraftsmen ten-band graphic equalizers. Originally, Rundgren had also retained his old faithful Stephens 16-track recorder, before upgrading to an Ampex MM1200 24-track machine, "which weighed about 800 pounds."

"We brought in a Neotek console, with 28 inputs," says Andersen, "and later replaced the Ampex machine with an Otari MTR 90. Even though the Neotek board had its own EQs, Todd still wanted the Soundcraftsmen racks. I noticed that Todd would put so much EQ on things that he was clipping the output without even realizing it, so I had one of our engineers, George Cowan, design a circuit with a gain control on the input and a gain control on the output so Todd could see when the input or output was clipping. We had a bunch of dbx noise-reduction units so he could record at 15ips, instead of 30ips, and save tape. He liked to save tape."

For mixdowns, Rundgren had Andersen find a Studer B67, quarter-inch, two-track machine and two Dolby SR units. "When I first started working for him," says Andersen, "Todd was mixing on a pair of Klipsch Heresy speakers that he had hung up in there. But he said they were never loud enough for him, so I had a custom set of monitors built for him by EAW (Eastern Acoustic Works), powered by either Crown DC 300A or Phase Linear 700 amplifiers. They were big monitors; I think they had a 15-inch bass speaker and a horn and a tweeter in them. He never liked to use smaller speakers, always resisted listening back on Auratones or anything. I wanted to give him a set of Yamaha NS-10s, which were all the rage at the time. Everybody was using them, and Bob Clearmountain had made them very popular. But Todd really didn't like them."

A cursory listen to any of Rundgren's recordings from the time reveals a penchant for outboard processing gear, in particular compressors and limiters. "He had brought four of his favorite Urei 1176 limiters up from Secret Sound," says Andersen, "and later, I found him an 1178 stereo model, which he used as the final program compressor on everything. For Todd, no mix was complete until every compressor in the room was used. Pretty much every single sound would also have some kind of dynamics control effect on it. He also had a bunch of dbx 160s in the room and a Urei Filter Set, which we rarely used."

While Rundgren stocked a variety of flangers, phasers, de-essers, and delay units, including a $16,000 Lexicon 224L reverb unit, Andersen says the most valued piece of gear at Utopia Sound was arguably his Eventide H910 Harmonizer, which was new at the time. "He loved that thing," says Andersen, "it was responsible for a lot of the Utopia [band] sound, especially on vocals. It was like pouring sugar on the vocals, it had a little bit of pitch shift in it, and an inherent 30 millisecond delay that you couldn't get rid of."

Andersen recalls that control room in Utopia Sound was built upstairs in what had been an open-walled sleeping loft, at the top of a ladder staircase. "There was a full bed to the left of the console," says Andersen, "which Todd would often lie on, during sessions, and read computer magazines."

Since the high angle from the control room initially prohibited seeing down into the performance area or vocal booth, a large angled mirror was installed, high above the live room, to facilitate visual contact. "If you looked across from the control room loft, eight or twelve feet off the ground, all you could see was the other wall," Andersen recalls. "So we hung this big mylar mirror, on about a 45 degree angle, near the opposite wall."

Underneath the control room was a bathroom and a kitchenette, and Andersen set up an area to store Rundgren's two-inch production master tapes, as well as a "cramped maintenance shop," where he could perform any repairs or cable soldering as needed.

Immediately after coming off the road on the Ra tour, Rundgren and the other members of Utopia regrouped to work on their next band album, *Oops! Wrong Planet*. Assisting Rundgren was an apprentice engineer named Mike Young. "His parents were from the Woodstock area," says Bearsville engineer John Holbrook, "and he was really keen to get into recording and production, so somehow he ended up at Utopia Sound. I think Todd basically tolerated him being his assistant, but he mainly stayed out of the way."

While Andersen remained Utopia's live engineer, in the coming years he would assist Rundgren on most Utopia studio recordings and outside productions. As he recalls it, most of the Utopia records were made the same way. "The guys would come in and get about one or two instrumental tracks done a day and then quit early. Later, after the band was gone, Todd would spend time in the studio writing all the melodies and lyrics. Then, he would do all the guide-vocal parts, even if it was a Kasim, Willie, or Roger lead vocal; and then, the next day, the guys would have to re-cut the part exactly to his specifications.

"Todd had a very clear vision, which was kind of fantastic," he continues. "Any deviation, in terms of phrasing or interpretation, was not tolerated. But you know, even though Todd did end up putting most of the work in, they really ran

Utopia as a democracy. He wanted it to be a band, not just Todd and his sidemen." According to Kasim Sulton, each member of Utopia was responsible for bringing in song fragments, which they called "musical modules."

"Then," says Sulton, "we would just put the puzzle together, after the fact. It was like; this one would work well with that one, that one would work well with the next one. We might change keys, or write a little bridge, to make certain things fit with other things."

Sulton cites the apocalyptic and episodic 'Marriage Of Heaven And Hell,' from *Oops! Wrong Planet*, as a perfect example of their modular composing process. "Todd is a Beatles fan," laughs Sulton, "whether he admits it or not, and 'Marriage' was our attempt at writing a kind of 'A Day In The Life.' So, where the first part of the song is this raucous, rock'n'roll thing, it breaks into this completely other type of piece that I had written for the middle."

Rundgren concedes that once Utopia was up and running, he began living what he calls a musical "double life" with a constant need for new material. "I believed there was a value in collaboration," he says. "Even while there was also a great deal of self-discovery involved in making my solo records, where there were no compromises, and I could just do what I felt like and didn't have to discuss it with anyone else in the band. Inversely, if you don't hand over some of the musical responsibility to somebody else, every once in a while, you face the possibility of exhausting yourself and running into a musical cul-de-sac."

Rundgren says there was always a clear distinction between his solo albums and his collaborative work with Utopia. "My own albums tended to be about songs and songwriting," says Rundgren, "and not as much about musical flourishes or lots of wild guitar. There might be some succinct solos in there, but for the most part I'd save my flashy stuff for Utopia, where I could solo my frickin' brains out. In the context of my own music, there are not enough of those guitar solos to really develop your chops. As time went on, actually, I was playing less and less guitar in the context of my solo albums."

According to Sulton, it would have been naïve to assume that a celebrated songwriter and trusted producer such as Rundgren would be a mere equal in the partnership, and adds that there was always an unspoken understanding about who was Utopia's creative director and overseer. "Todd has the ability to kind of switch back and forth," he says, "and turn one faucet on and another one off. Todd's Utopia things were always more concept-oriented, and there was always a theme or back-story to them. At that point, he was extremely prolific, doing a solo record every 18 months and a Utopia record every nine months. So there was a lot of material getting thrown around. Todd always managed to come up with at least four or five completed songs for each Utopia record before we started."

Willie Wilcox recalls that, as the band evolved from its original six-piece progressive rock incarnation to the period immediately after the Ra tour, Utopia become stronger as it began to more accurately reflect the individual personalities of all four members. "Todd's presence was always very strong," he says, "but the four members began to share more and more responsibilities for our musical direction and all our collective goals, creatively and economically. Although, as far as the management was concerned, Todd's solo direction was always their main focus, so Utopia could never could ever just be a 'real' band."

Sulton recalls that eventually the group dynamic extended into a situation where Rundgren would collaborate on working out the background vocals for *Oops* and subsequent Utopia albums. "We'd have a song arranged," says Sulton, "and three or four of us would sort of sing around the microphones and work out the background parts together. But then, once we had an idea of what the notes were, we'd multi-track these takes of everybody singing the same note through the entire song. If it was a three part harmony, we'd all sing the low part from top to bottom, and then we'd go back and together sing the middle part, and then we'd sing the high part, so you'd usually have three background singers on each part, totaling nine voices singing backgrounds. And then, sometimes we would even double track that!"

The overriding concept for *Oops! Wrong Planet* is best exemplified by the apocalyptic sci-fi themes on the song 'Trapped,' where Sulton's preening lead vocals on the verses were complemented by a shrieking Rundgren vocal on the choruses, but also on funkier numbers like 'Abandon City,' which also featured a jazzy trumpet solo from Powell, the song's composer. Rundgren's knack for great pop is also in evidence, from the anthemic rock of 'Love In Action' to the soul-searching ballad, 'Love Is The Answer.'

"There were about four songs that Todd had recorded before we started recording together," says Sulton. "'Trapped' and 'Love In Action' were definitely all Todd, and while he wrote 'Gangrene,' he had Willie sing the lead." In the end, *Oops! Wrong Planet* was the sound of a band, "settling into each other."

"I was finally being accepted into the fold," he recalls, "and figured I wasn't going anywhere for a while. It's funny that the biggest song on that record was 'Love Is The Answer,' but not until it was covered by England Dan and John Ford Coley. I think that with our first two records you can see the direction that Todd wanted the band to go in, because prior to this there was no other lead vocalist on Utopia records, and they were all mostly Todd songs. On this album, though, 'Crazy Lady Blue' was Willie's music and Todd wrote the lyrics. Roger had written 'Windows,' which he later did again on one of his solo records, *Air Pocket*. I wrote the 'The Martyr' with Todd. Then there'd be things like 'My Angel,' which Roger wrote the music for, and Todd the words, but then they got me to sing it."

According to Chris Andersen, however, regardless of whether or not the band were comfortable with each other, nobody in Utopia seemed overly fond of spending extended periods of time together in the studio. "They really didn't 'like' recording," says Andersen. "They cut all the basic tracks live to get them done faster. The catchphrase was 'What time tomorrow?' You couldn't get them out of there fast enough."

Sulton says they frequently found themselves rushing to get the recordings over with, and recalls a "scary moment" during the *Oops!* sessions, when a hasty Rundgren accidentally dropped a reel of 24-track tape, bending it slightly. "We thought we were going to lose the entire reel's worth of work," he laughs. "Luckily, we didn't, but we still couldn't wait to get the record finished."

Bearsville released *Oops! Wrong Planet* in late September 1977, at roughly the same time Buell and baby Liv were leaving the house on Mink Hollow Road. And while Rundgren was now free to pursue his next significant relationship, with actress/dancer Karen 'Bean' Darvin, it was nonetheless, in Sulton's words, "an ugly, ugly, time for TR."

While the stark, unadorned images of the band on the packaging for *Oops!* indicated a shift from the Egyptian pomp of *Ra*, the complexity of the music inside was still a far cry from the trendier punk and new wave sounds of artists like the Sex Pistols or Talking Heads, which had distracted most of the rock critics of 1977. A little printed message on the jacket implored the listener to "Use Your Head, Use Your Heart, Save Yourself." Over the following months and years, Rundgren would employ every part of the first two in a diligent effort to enact the third.

Utopia played out the remaining months of 1977 with a two-month tour of America that began October 14 in Columbus, Ohio, and included one date with Cheap Trick in Long Island, New York. As a fresh coat of snow covered the

Catskill Mountains, Rundgren returned to his home and studio to contemplate his life and get on with his work. As he explored his inner self, he would begin to record what many believe to be one of his most focused and accessible solo works: *Hermit Of Mink Hollow.*

Interviewed some 11 years later by journalist Paul Lester for the liner notes to the 1999 Sanctuary/Castle re-release of *Hermit*, Rundgren was candid about his domestic issues at the time of the album. He said that while he knew there was a distinct possibility that Liv wasn't his biological daughter, someone had to assume the father role, so he did. "At the same time," he said, "I had the full realization that I could not live with Bebe ... so I became essentially a figurehead father ... Liv grew up with Bebe's cousins in Maine."

In discussions for this book, Rundgren preferred to steer clear of the subject but did, however, elaborate on an added motivation for becoming the child's "figurehead" father. "My dad had been about eight years old when his dad was gone. So he had no idea how to relate to his own children ... and I hated him, growing up. I didn't understand that he was deprived of any sort of education on how to be a father. So I grew up thinking that I would break that cycle. I'd never want to make any child feel the way he made me feel."

Alone in the house on Mink Hollow Road, Rundgren was faced with the requisite time and isolation to put his years of New Age study to practical use. "When I had first moved to Woodstock," he says, "I still kept the three-story loft on Horatio Street, in Manhattan. I didn't feel the confidence, initially, to just give up on the city. But after I discovered that I didn't want to cohabit any longer with Bebe, in any sense of the word, I eventually let go of the city place. A fortunate by-product of being so out of everything all the time and always being the odd man out ... is that you have plenty of time for self-examination.

"I spent a lot of time wondering why my life was the way it was. How would I like it to actually be? What do I have to do to get it that way? What changes do I have to enact in myself if I'm ever going to change the way things are? It was almost like when a tribal elder in some culture says 'You have to go out there to this far desert by yourself and take this drug, and just be stuck with yourself for awhile. And if you can survive being stuck with yourself then you can live with the rest of us.'"

Hermit Of Mink Hollow was the inevitable title for an album of songs inspired by such a period of deep introspection, especially since this was the first time, since the all-nighters on Astral Drive in Hollywood, that Rundgren was responsible for every sound on the record, including the admittedly rudimentary saxophone solos. And while engineer Mike Young would come around, now and again, to check on his progress and tidy up, Rundgren's life at the time was that of a "studio hermit," sequestered in his own private sound cave.

"I could wake up at three in the morning with an idea," he recalls, "and go down and just start working on it. Even when we had Secret Sound, I wasn't living there, so by the time I got all the way up to 24th Street, I would have forgotten what I was thinking to record. *Mink Hollow* was probably the most ideal situation that I'd ever had, in terms of percolating musical ideas and stuff. I was in this insular little 24-hour-a-day think tank. I wouldn't be disturbed and wouldn't see any people for days at a time. Until I finally got into that completely solitary environment, I hadn't been aware just how much social interaction had affected my overall creativity. For years, after that, the only way that I could write was to go into this sort of isolation. Prior to that, I had been able to sort of interleave it with my normal existence."

Rundgren says that his only concept behind the sound of *Hermit,* if there was one at all, was to showcase both his piano-based compositions and his increasingly strengthened vocal abilities. He admits that since the start of his singing career he had been singing incorrectly, as untrained rock singers often will, but had become unsatisfied with the results. Now, after much retraining, he was singing from his diaphragm and, as a result, his voice was not only stronger but also noticeably lower. "At that point," he says, "I had done enough records and fronted Utopia long enough that I felt fairly confident as a singer; and by the time I got to *Hermit Of Mink Hollow* this confidence somehow informed the songwriting, because I could sing nearly anything I could think up."

He adds that, going into *Hermit*, he was composing fewer songs on guitar, and piano was now his signature compositional instrument, particularly on his solo albums: "In the Nazz, I wrote it all on guitar. But from around *Ballad* on, I was already focusing more on the piano; and by *Something/Anything?* piano became the foundation of every song. I'd be on TV shows, seated at the piano, at the same time I was thinking, 'Jeez, I should be playing more guitar!'"

According to Rundgren, the most difficult part about recording alone was getting from the performance floor to the loft control room and back again. "Engineering it all yourself makes it all a bit more tedious," he says. "I would have to run up and down the stairs to start and stop the tape machine, every time. There was no remote way to punch in, so if I screwed up a basic drum track, I would have to stop and pick it up from where I was and then actually go and do a tape edit in order to construct a proper drum track to overdub everything else onto. That was more or less a persistent problem throughout the record.

"In some instances, I might go two-thirds of the way through a piano part and then screw it up, so I'd just open up another track and pick it up from where the mistake was and 'comp' them all together afterward. It would take me, probably, 20 or 30 seconds to get down the ladder to the piano. I would run a lot of pre-roll, and then, of course, cut it out later. After that album, actually, I had a remote switch made, but the cable wasn't long enough to reach all the way to the piano, so I still had to run back and forth.

To conserve blank tape, Rundgren would cram as many takes as possible onto one reel. And he rarely saved out-takes, opting to record over them. "So in the end," he recalls, "I'd wind up with all these things on one reel, one after the other, with paper leader in between. Plus, I was incredibly paranoid about letting the machine just rewind itself in case it accidentally went over a previous take. So, for my own piece of mind, I would always go all the way up the stairs and check the tape myself."

Rundgren says that, for him, it all starts with a rhythm, and most of the tracks on *Hermit* began with him sitting behind the drum kit. "I might have done the piano part for a song like 'Bag Lady' first, since there's not really a lot of drums in that. Although it's just as conceivable that I first sat there at the drums and counted the whole song out on the hi-hat. I mostly counted everything out in my head, and I imagine if you soloed the overhead mics, you might possibly hear a little bit of humming now and then. I really didn't have a lot of range on other instruments, other than guitar, so I can only play the drums the way I play the drums. The hard part of doing the drums alone like that is that the further you get [in the track], the higher the stakes are and the more critical a fuck-up becomes. That said, there's a palpable sense of accomplishment when you've actually gotten through an entire drum take without fucking it up really bad. Sure, there are little things, like speeding up or getting ahead or behind the beat, but that's the 'organicity' of it, you know?"

To a minor extent, Rundgren says he adopted different personas to suit the 'players' of the instrumental overdubs. "I suppose I could probably be 'funky guy' on the bass for something like 'You Cried Wolf,' but maybe more McCartneyesque on something like 'Determination,' where I do some of that squiggly McCartney 'Paperback Writer' stuff in the outro."

The bright sounding guitar on 'Determination' was a personal favorite of Rundgren's at the time. Made by Alembic, the custom-built guitar had active electronics and a piezoelectric pickup in the bridge, which Rundgren says gave it "that super-crystalline sound. I used that guitar on a lot of stuff in that era."

For Rundgren, the easiest part of any solo project was the arranging and recording of the background vocals. By 1978, he had multi-tracked his own voice countless times over many albums and, since he was singing better than ever on *Hermit*, his 'grouped' vocals remain a stunning example of a master at work. "It usually starts with a melody," says Rundgren, "unless you've got some sort of signature line that needs to be in harmony. In terms of arranging melodies, The Beatles and The Beach Boys were highly educational. You know, back in the ninth or tenth grade at Upper Darby High School, the only extracurricular activity that I was ever seriously involved in was chorus. That was the only time I was ever excited to get up early and go to school. I learned a lot about choral singing and got a lot of pointers from the music teacher about what was, and wasn't, proper. So, as I sang the parts [on *Hermit* and other albums], I was applying these same disciplines, which is why the parts seem to lock together so well."

While much of the music for the songs had been formulated before the actual sessions, Rundgren says that he often "cooked up" a track as he recorded it. "Just like I had on every record since *Something/Anything?*" he says, "I wouldn't get around to seriously writing the lyrics until the music track was finished. I would have an idea for the sound or the arrangement of a song but only a vague idea what it would be about and possibly no lyrics at all until it would be time to sing it. Then I'd start singing along with the track, trying to find melodies to go along with it, and eventually words would start coming."

Once again, Rundgren credits marijuana as an invaluable way of bypassing his own intellect in the lyrics and getting to the heart of the matter. "It's not that I couldn't write lyrics without it," Rundgren insists, "but the whole process of writing lyrics became far more automatic. Otherwise, if you think too hard about it, the results are usually not especially satisfying. It sometimes gets telegraphed in the lyrics, you know, that this was something too clever by half, perhaps."

Among the albums in Rundgren's discography, *Hermit Of Mink Hollow* has often been compared to other seemingly confessional works such as Joni Mitchell's

Blue or Bob Dylan's *Blood On The Tracks*. But while songs like 'Too Far Gone,' 'Hurting For You' and 'Lucky Guy' display the emotional candour of a man with his heart strung across the keys of his Story & Clark baby grand, Rundgren insists they aren't purely autobiographical. "I wouldn't make that close a connection to my real life," he cautions. "Like 'Too Far Gone' wasn't directly about me leaving home as teenager. Like most of my songs, they're only biographical to the point that other people can identify with them."

While generally critical of confessional songwriters whose only goal, he says, is to "draw attention to themselves," Rundgren admits to a degree of self-therapy in his own lyrics. "A lot of it is me objectivizing thoughts that are in my head, so I have an opportunity to evaluate where I'm at in relationship to the world. Then, I can see my thoughts and go, 'Hmm, that's a blindness in me,' or 'Wow, that's a revelation about the dynamics of something that I never realized before!' I hope to get something out of it, first and foremost, before anyone else does. I've come to believe, however, that if I do that successfully, by some extension other people will also get the point. Whatever it is. Once I've externalized these thoughts, and ordered them, the listener can internalize it and imprint them onto their own thoughts. Luckily, I've gone to the trouble to do that for them!"

In addition to the upbeat and global-minded 'All The Children Sing,' *Hermit* had comic relief in the sonically literal 'Onomatopoeia,' which was the latest in a long line of Rundgren music-hall numbers that included 'Just Another Onionhead' from *Wizard* and 'An Elpee's Worth Of Toons' from *Todd*. On the darker end of the spectrum, Rundgren took a stark look at the world outside himself on songs like 'Bread' and the Nyro-esque 'Bag Lady.' While these songs comprised his most socially conscious material to date, critics and casual listeners tended to focus on the so-called 'breakup songs,' particularly the US Top 30 hit, 'Can We Still Be Friends,' which many believed to be a direct reference to his break from Buell. Once again, Rundgren rejects the idea that the song was confessional, and credits the smoke and mirrors of Tin Pan Alley songcraft for the song's appeal.

"Most songwriting is done to a presumed formula," he insists. "Ostensibly, the songs tend to be about people being madly and sincerely in love all the time or the alternative to that, being heartbroken, sad, or angry. Most songwriters simply decide which of those emotions they want to cover; then it's just a matter of finding some lyrical twist on it. That's why I hate country music, there's this calculated fakeness to it, and most of the songs are completely derivative except for an occasional clever rhyme. It's always about being drunk, 'heart broke,' or 'an A-*murr*-ican.'"

Hermit closes with the Utopia-style sonic mayhem of 'Out Of Control,' followed by a soothing, reverb-drenched lullaby, 'Fade Away,' in which Rundgren, his voice seemingly filled with resignation, admits, 'I've forgotten more than I remember / Sometimes I want to hide myself away.' As he says, the song was merely an amplification of a core emotion in the service of a song. More likely, however, his true emotional state on *Hermit* could be summed up in the message of the Nazz-like guitar-rocker 'Determination.' "Three days in the rain / And I ain't had no sleep," he sings, "But I won't break down now / I got a promise to keep."

In May, *Hermit Of Mink Hollow*, its sleeve adorned with a simple, blue-tinted video screen image of Rundgren alone in his garden, was released to the general approval of critics and fans alike, many of whom applauded his seeming return to the role of ivory-tinkling balladeer. In lieu of a nominal Hermit tour, Rundgren, at the urging of Bearsville's Paul Fishkin, consented to an ersatz 'Greatest Hits' tour, accompanied by many of the musicians he'd played with over the past 13 years. Certain of these shows would be recorded for the two-disc live retrospective set, *Back To The Bars*. The notion of releasing a double-live album had apparently been bolstered by the phenomenal success of other double-live hits packages of the day, such as Peter Frampton's *Frampton Comes Alive*, Bob Seger's *Live Bullets*, and the landmark *Kiss Alive*.

The album was culled from a week of shows at The Bottom Line, New York, from May 10 to 14, a May 17 to 23 residency at The Roxy, Los Angeles, and an additional August 23 date at Cleveland's Agora Ballroom. Musicians featured include early Utopians John Siegler, Moogy Klingman, and Ralph Schuckett; current members Willie Wilcox, Kasim Sulton, and Roger Powell; Norman Smart, Greg Geddes, Bobby Sedita, and Larry Tasse from The Hello People; and featured guests Daryl Hall, John Oates, Stevie Nicks, Spencer Davis, and Rick Derringer.

According to Sulton, Utopia toured well into the coming year in support of *Back To The Bars*, taking strategic breaks every two months to allow Rundgren to work on album productions, often with Utopia as his studio band. That summer, Rundgren found a few days to co-produce an album with and for Rick Derringer, *Guitars And Women*. While Derringer dominated the sessions, Rundgren was largely responsible for pre-production, backing vocal arrangements, repertoire assistance, and the final mix.

Also that year, somewhat incredibly, Rundgren laid the foundations for his Utopia Video venture. Rundgren had been dabbling in video as early as a 1974 Utopia tour. By 1978, his record production fees, from projects like Grand Funk and Meat Loaf, had netted him enough capital to seriously invest in television production equipment. "Almost everything that I made from *Bat Out Of Hell* went into building Utopia Video," he says. "Having my own studio gave me an opportunity to do videos that were a little more on the experimental side, like my visualization of Holst's *The Planets* for an RCA Laserdisc."

In the fall, Rundgren had started working on the album *Remote Control* for San Francisco art-rock collective The Tubes. He accompanied the band to their date at the Knebworth Festival in England on September 9 1978, where they appeared on a bill with Frank Zappa, Peter Gabriel, The Boomtown Rats, Rockpile, and Wilko Johnson's Solid Senders. Rundgren even joined The Tubes on stage for their encore medley of The Who's 'Baba O'Riley' and 'The Kids Are Alright.'

The Tubes – comprised of singers Fee Waybill and Re Styles, synthesizer player Michael Cotten, keyboard player Vince Welnick, guitarists Bill Spooner and Roger Steen, bassist Rick Anderson, and drummer Prairie Prince – defied easy categorization. Combining the satirical bite and musicality of Frank Zappa with the camp theatricality of Alice Cooper, the eight-piece ensemble had a flair for onstage spectacle. In concert, the sight of Waybill, in character as rock star 'Quay Lewd' and being trampled by an oversize amplifier stack, was key to appreciating 'White Punks On Dope,' from the band's 1975 debut. Unfortunately, the band's conceptual brilliance was matched only by their lack of commercial acceptance. Factor in the costs of their highly costumed and choreographed touring show, and The Tubes found themselves at a crucial juncture in their recording career. They found a sympathetic ear in Todd Rundgren, a musician with a fondness for ensemble arranging, hooky choruses, and elaborate staging. "After Todd came up and played with us," recalls Tubes keyboardist Michael Cotten, "we all went back to Knebworth Castle to discuss doing the album when we got home. Todd had, by then, heard some of our demos and was telling us which songs he loved and stuff."

Cotten, The Tubes' resident conceptualist, recalls that he and drummer Prince had begun planning the album early that year, working with primitive sequencers and early electronic drums in a basement in Northern California. "Prairie and I were just crazy about this new sequencing technology," he says. "So every night we went to the basement and made up little dance grooves with sequencer stuff and drums. A lot of it ended up being the backbone of the songs on *Remote Control.* Although it was pretty rough, Todd, being a good producer, knew how to turn this coal into diamonds."

Recorded at Music Annex Studios in Menlo Park, California, *Remote Control* is dominated by Rundgren's presence. According to the producer, his expanded involvement in the record was largely a product of necessity. "When I work on a production with somebody," he says, "my expectation is that they will have all the material written before they show up. I'd rather spend my time evaluating the material and not necessarily involved in the writing process. As a producer, one is making suggestions all the time about how to best frame the material, but in the end, I can't make them do anything they don't want to; it's their record. My job is to look at it and try to figure out 'What's missing here?' And if I have to, I will fill that in. If they don't have lyrics, or a bridge, or a chorus, I'll write them."

Rundgren and the band collaborated on a thematic concept for the album, a subject close to the producer's heart at time: the all-encompassing, hypnotic effects of television culture. To achieve this, Fee Waybill concocted a story line about one man's fetishistic desire to enter, carnally or otherwise, the seductive world of his television. Michael Cotten's front cover concept depicted a baby suckling on the teat of a space-age mini-TV, while the back cover depicted the members of The Tubes as guests on the actual set of *The Hollywood Squares,* a popular American television game show of the era.

"Todd suggested we make a concept album," laughs Cotten, "although the idea of something like a 'rock opera' was just absurd and ludicrous to us all. On the other hand, it was so silly that it was irresistible, so we agreed to do it. All the songs were already written but we reworked the lyrics to fit this 'television' concept. I'm sure we were kind of unconsciously doing a little bit of a *Tommy* thing; that's the prototypical concept album."

Cotten points out that, whereas The Who's protagonist was born deaf, dumb, and blind, Waybill's character is rendered 'virtually' deaf dumb and blind by his copious exposure to television culture. As the children of the first television age, The Tubes related deeply to the subtext of the theme. "We're the TV babies," laughs Cotten, "so why not make a story about the TV baby? This gave us a reason to focus all the songs and then Fee put this storyline together to hang them on."

Musically, *Remote Control* immediately hooks in the listener with three big songs in a row. A short buzzing synth pattern trips off 'Turn Me On,' an urgent introductory anthem that leads into a catchy Rundgren/Tubes co-write called 'TV Is King.' Calming down slightly, the band wades ever so gently into new wave territory on 'Prime Time,' featuring a seductive Re Styles purring Deborah Harry-like over a groove suggestive of Talking Heads. 'Love's A Mystery (I Don't Understand),' a Rundgren co-write, was an over-the-top, radio-ready love ballad, roughly in the same ballpark as Utopia's 'Love Is The Answer.' On *Remote Control's* big finale, 'Telecide,' Waybill's protagonist announces his inevitable plan to commit suicide, fittingly, on live television.

"I used to know him, he seemed like a regular guy," deadpanned Re Styles in the song, sounding like a bystander interviewed for the six o'clock news as the Tubes plowed ahead to a punk-rock finish. Then, after a brief instrumental reprise of 'Love's A Mystery,' *Remote Control* fades out, like the dot on your screen at the end of a broadcast day.

As with many of Rundgren's productions of the day, the producer's own voice is heard prominently in the ensemble background vocal parts. Cotten credits Rundgren, and The Tubes' late keyboardist Vince Welnick, for the arrangements. "Todd and Vince worked well together," says Cotten, "because Vince was so good at breaking out harmonies and structure for the chordal and vocal parts; but there's no question it was always Todd style in the vocals. He would direct the vocal phrasing and say 'Sing it like this,' and they would just trust him and sing it, you know? Fee was such a shape-shifter, so if Todd suggested a vocal phrasing he could do it, happily. He wasn't dictatorial about it and everyone was into it. And, I mean 'Love's A Mystery' was such a grandiose power ballad thing, we were just going, 'God, can we do this? This is so lush, it's crazy.'"

Bud Scoppa, who had gotten to know The Tubes while working for A&M records, and had also witnessed Rundgren's 1973 sessions with The New York Dolls, recalls dropping by at the *Remote Control* sessions. "Fee was the genius in the band," he says, "and seeing him and Todd together was a real meeting of two minds. I'd never seen The Tubes so together in the studio and I think maybe Todd was responsible for bringing out their innate professionalism. Todd just seemed truly comfortable with the guys. Mike always had his shit together and, even in their worst days, never lost it; and I suppose Todd must have loved Prairie the most of all, because he's used him on all kinds of things since. You could tell that the Tubes loved Todd's stuff too, and you could see how much they had in common."

Having finished the tracking for the Tubes project, Rundgren was already moving on to his next project, a Patti Smith Group album (discussed in depth in the next chapter). Miraculously, he also found time to produce the second album by the Tom Robinson Band, *TRB2*, which came about after Rundgren had met Robinson after a show in Toronto. The sessions, at London's Pye Studios, had been timed to coincide with Rundgren's weeklong residency at the Venue Club in December 1978. "I was going to be there anyway," Rundgren recalls, "I believe it was with some of the guys in Utopia and we'd do the Robinson sessions in the daytime and the gig at night. I didn't do the Venue show every night, but that was the reason why I was there."

Kasim Sulton recalls the whole team staying a rented house in London's Mayfair district. "Tom was a great guy," says Sulton, "and his guitar player, Danny [Kustow], was a really nice guy too. Todd asked me if I wanted to come in and sing backgrounds with him on two or three songs and I had fun doing it. I believe Tom was one of the few people who had an entirely pleasant experience doing a record with Todd. He managed to squeeze that whole album out of this short time, but he was always like that; it took him maybe two weeks to do a record, top to bottom, in those days."

One song on the *TRB2* album, 'Bully For You,' was co-written by Robinson and Peter Gabriel, and both had joined Rundgren on stage at one of the Venue shows. According to Rundgren, he and Gabriel had initially met in 1976, when the ex-Genesis front man was seeking guidance and a producer for his first solo album. "Peter came up to Bearsville Studios," Rundgren recalls, "and we discussed me doing his record. I still remember sitting with him in the studio while he played some of the new songs for me. He was a very quiet, shy guy, and it seemed like he was in this transitional space and not super confident about where he was going with everything. I think he was looking for me to give him something 'certain' to hang on to, but I didn't know what exactly it was he should do at that point. I think he eventually got Bob Ezrin. Later, at sporadic intervals throughout his career, he would call me and we'd talk about the possibility of doing something, but it just never seemed to happen, for whatever reason. So he and I have a certain kind of connection; we know each other by sight."

Rundgren wasn't entirely surprised, then, when Gabriel had showed up to the Venue, as Robinson's guest, and the two joined him around the piano for an impromptu version of 'Hello It's Me.' "They were both wearing these big long overcoats," he says, laughing, "which made them look like [the man on the cover of Jethro Tull's] *Aqualung* or something like that. That was fun. It's one of my more vivid memories of the whole time of those sessions."

Rundgren acknowledges that the bridge section in 'Bully For You' bears a remarkable likeness to his own music, but says he had nothing to do with the writing of that song. "I think I had some idea how it should sound," he says, "and what kind of instrumentation we should use, but those kinds of chords were something Peter would also have done, and I guess there was some musical overlap in what we were both doing."

Rundgren mixed the *TRB2* album over Christmas, back at Bearsville Studios, during a break from the Patti Smith album. When it was released the following year, the record was praised by only a few critics, such as Simon Frith in *Creem*, who wrote that Rundgren had provided the band with "a much richer sound than they've had before." Most TRB fans, and many UK critics, savaged the album. According to Rundgren, *TRB2* was so "slagged off" that EMI aborted their promotional campaign before it had even begun. "Most of the critics saved their worst shots for me," he says, "blaming me because the album wasn't what they had hoped it would be. Only, I was there, and I can tell you I didn't have to twist anyone's arms on those sessions. We all had fun making it."

Outside of the studio that year, Todd Rundgren had also staged the world's first interactive television concert, beamed over the Warner/QUBE system, and also the first live nationally broadcast stereo radio concert, transmitted, by microwave, across 40 North America cities. Before leaving 1978, however, Rundgren had reunited with an artist he'd first met at the dawn of his engineering and producing career. By this time, his poet and critic friend Patti Smith had blossomed into a critically acclaimed recording artist in her own right. Now Smith had asked Rundgren to preside over what she presumed would be her final recording: *Wave*.

Patti Smith Group
Wave

By November 1978, much had changed for both Patti Smith and Todd Rundgren since their first meeting, during The Band's *Stage Fright* sessions at Woodstock Playhouse, in 1970. Back then, Smith had only just arrived on the New York arts scene and was living with fellow artist Robert Mapplethorpe at the Chelsea Hotel, reading and performing every now and then at the St Mark's Place Poetry Project and networking with singer-songwriter Bob Neuwirth and playwright Sam Shepard. Her friend Todd, one of her earliest artistic supporters, was often in the audience for her shows.

"I was fascinated with the intensity of her performance," Rundgren says today. "She would go off into these improvisations and it was just incredibly intense, for a single person, the way that she captured the audience and took them through all these various facets of her personality."

Almost 40 years later, in the back room of a favorite Greenwich Village café, Smith recalls the times, and Rundgren, with great affection. "I was working in a bookstore," she says, "writing poems and just starting to perform them. Within my poetry readings, I would talk a lot and tell funny stories from my childhood or Bible stories or the Classic Comics versions of my favorite books or *Little Lulu* episodes. I think Todd appreciated the most esoteric of humour."

Indeed, Smith admits that, at the time, she felt that a future in comedy seemed might be one of many avenues open to her. "I really loved Johnny Carson and I told Todd my secret dream, which was to someday take over from Johnny on *The Tonight Show*. Todd actually said he had some connections and he tried to get me on *Rowan & Martin's Laugh-In!* He really saw me as a comedienne, but I didn't have any specific ambition. Todd would come in and out of my life and we were great friends. I remember when he wrote 'Be Nice To Me,' he let me hear it on a cassette before it came out and I was so excited to have this privilege. Sometimes he'd come and visit me and we'd buy a Carvel ice cream cake and eat the whole thing together. He was out of town a lot, but if I had a reading or I had any little performance, he always came out."

Heeding Bob Neuwirth's advice to get into songwriting, Smith began tailoring her poetry into lyrics, some of which found their way into the songs of her friend Allen Lanier for his band, Blue Öyster Cult. All the while, Smith remained a fierce advocate for Rundgren's music via her moonlighting role as a rock critic.

"When I had various records come out," Rundgren recalls, "she would not only make those kinds of contributions, like the little band-aid poem [included in the package for *A Wizard, A True Star*], but she wrote these glowing record reviews, too. So she was hugely helpful to me."

Shortly after forming an initial duo with guitarist Lenny Kaye, in 1974, Smith launched The Patti Smith Group, adding keyboardist Richard Sohl, guitarist/bassist Ivan Kral, and drummer Jay Dee Daugherty from cult New York band The Mumps. Legendary music mogul Clive Davis signed the group to Arista Records the following year and, over the course of three albums, Smith's Rimbaud-inspired, post-beatnik, literate punk-rock put her, and New York City, on the rock map while forever redefining the image of what a female rock star should look like.

Watching from afar, Rundgren had remained a fan of Smith's "power and charisma," but secretly lamented that, as she became more of a conventional rock singer, he missed the subtlety and intimacy of her initial one-woman shows. Still, he says, it was probably inevitable that she would form a rock band.

"I mean, everyone was doing that at the time," sighs Rundgren, "but it was kind of a shame. As I recall, in that whole New York proto-punk period, there weren't a whole lot of bands fronted by women who could hold their own, like Patti could. Blondie were definitely not selling the same thing that The Patti Smith Group was selling. So, I followed her band career, as a fan, but through all the records she did in the 70s there had never been any discussion of me producing them."

But in 1978, a few months after The Patti Smith Group released their third album, *Easter*, featuring their breakthrough single, 'Because The Night,' Smith reached out to her old friend Todd. Her life had been radically transformed as much by rock success as by her blossoming romance with Fred 'Sonic' Smith, a guitarist best known for his work with seminal Detroit group, The MC5. *Easter*, says Patti, had been a very "physical" record inspired by the power of her new relationship.

"I'd met Fred," she says, "and felt very empowered by having this 'fella' in my life. I'd written 'Because The Night,' with Bruce Springsteen, but my lyrics were for Fred. I was feeling a lot of bravado [on *Easter*], with songs like 'Rock N Roll Nigger' and '25th Floor,' which I also wrote for Fred."

Lenny Kaye recalls that, in the wake of their hit single, The Patti Smith Group went back to touring with a vengeance and, having done three albums, felt a shared vitality as they contemplated their fourth album. "By a band's third album," says Kaye, "if they even get to that, they're usually fairly confident about how make a record. We had grown a lot as a band on *Easter*, so we were pretty unified when it came time to make the next record."

What few knew at the time was that The Patti Smith Group's fourth album would also be their last. In private, Smith had resolved to sacrifice her hard won career successes by moving to Detroit to "withdraw with Fred." She says that the album's intended title, *Wave*, held significance to her on many levels, not the least of which was the simple act of waving goodbye. Having come full circle, she felt it only right to finally bring in her friend from the early days, now a successful producer in his own right, to collaborate on the group's swansong.

Rundgren admits to feeling at the time the combined pressures of commercial and personal expectations placed upon him to make good for Patti, who had asked him not to share her secret decision to leave it all behind. "It was years after the heat of that punk scene," Rundgren remembers. "All the bands had gone their separate ways. The Dolls had already broken up, and The Patti Smith Group had three albums out and had finally gotten a Top 40 hit. Patti said she was retiring from the music business to raise a family with Fred in Detroit. She didn't tell the band any of this, however, and she didn't want me to tell the band. So I was in a kind of a difficult position."

"Lenny didn't even know," says Smith, "I think I told Todd, because I could've counted on him to keep it close. He wasn't the sort to bring it up or be provocative or to throw something like that out there sarcastically."

According to Rundgren, Smith was also living "between her two worlds," emotionally and physically, at the time. "She was half here, half there," Rundgren recalls, "and going back to Detroit whenever there was a break. Fred had become an unspoken collaborator on the record, even though he was never there, physically. She played him all the songs as we cut them, and Fred would vet the mixes along with her, and she'd incorporate his criticisms with her own thoughts. If Patti had some dissatisfaction with something, it usually was because Fred was not enthused with it. This was a little bit surprising to me, as she had always been so sure of what she was doing. I think that if you knew that she had one foot out the door already, it would explain some things about the record."

Nearing the US Thanksgiving holiday, in November, The Patti Smith Group traveled from New York City to Woodstock, to record at Bearsville Studios. The sessions would drag through the winter months, on and off, into February 1979. "Some of the band," Rundgren recalls, "were living at the apartments in Bearsville and some would get put up at this other place at Turtle Creek. I'm not sure they had ever done this kind of remote, wood-shedding type of thing before, so being out of their urban element may have been a factor in terms of making this record."

"It was very freezing," recalls Ivan Kral, "and since we were all used to living in Manhattan it was definitely weird to be suddenly out in the woods."

"We'd never made a record outside the city," adds Kaye, "but it seemed like a good move forward. We'd had a very public year and I don't think we thought it was a bad idea to go away for a few weeks and make a record. Todd was really familiar with Bearsville and he only lived down the street."

"It was nice, because there were no distractions," adds Jay Dee Daugherty, "but it was also a little tough because there were no distractions! It was really beautiful up there, though; there was snow all around and fog on your breath when you'd go out."

"We were in this very challenging, rustic setting," says Smith. "There were heavy snows and we were eating bean soup or stews or whatever Richard Sohl was making, short of going out and shooting squirrel, you know?"

Daugherty recalls driving up to Woodstock a day early, at Smith's request, to get drum sounds. "Sometimes it takes a relatively long time in the studio to put all the mics in the right places and get a good drum sound," Daugherty laughs. "I got up there and set up my Sonor kit, but we were done in like 20 minutes. Todd knew it was going to be a rock record so he just knew where to place [the microphones]. It was the quickest setup I'd ever done, in fact. I remember thinking, 'Oh oh, this guy's going too fast, it can't be right.' But then, you'd listen back and it was amazing."

According to Rundgren, the band's material was "still in flux" when he heard it, with many songs yet to be arranged and Smith still writing lyrics in the studio. Daugherty confirms that they were the least prepared they had ever been, but notes that it seemed like the players and their producer felt comfortable enough which other to proceed confidently. Smith recalls that Sohl, her classically trained keyboard player, seemed uncharacteristically intimidated in Rundgren's presence, however.

"Richard was the youngest among us," says Smith, "but I felt he had the most confidence of anybody in the band. But working with Todd was the first time I ever saw him a little in awe of somebody. He would often ask Todd his opinion about what he should play and then he'd play it. I say this, really, in tribute to

Todd because usually Richard wasn't easily told what to do, but there was this level of trust there."

Smith says that, although she shared a special bond with Rundgren, he never played favorites with the musicians in the room. "He didn't take me aside and cut me off from the band," says Smith. "So many producers will try to triangulate, or they have some drummer who's always better than your guy or something. But I wanted people to know that, if they bought a record that was supposed to the Patti Smith Group, then that's what they heard."

Daugherty says that the sessions went pretty quickly, owing largely to Rundgren's fast pace in the studio and his familiarity with the Bearsville console. "Patti needed to go back to Detroit," adds Daugherty, "so we worked pretty efficiently and cut all the basic tracks live, doing about one track a day or something like that."

Wave opens with 'Frederick,' Smith's head-over-heels paean to new partner. Smith says the song came to her while strolling on a beach, and recalls having no specific ideas for what the recording should sound like, only that it be "so happy and accessible that everybody would want to dance." Rundgren responded with an upbeat arrangement packed with multi-part background vocals, layered by Smith herself.

"I have no ear for harmonies," says Smith. "I can sing but, especially at that time in my life, I was more of a 'performance singer' and I didn't have that much training. Todd's task was to help me widen my horizons, and he got me singing all these layered harmony parts. It was hell for me, because I don't hear harmonies, and feel silly doing falsetto. I couldn't imagine how these voices would translate, because I don't have the aural vision that Todd has. He built 'Frederick' as if it was a cake, with the layers and the icing and all of that, you know?"

Kaye says it was "amazing" to witness Smith and Rundgren in the control room adding the background parts. "Todd just said, 'Sing here, then sing here, sing here,'" says Kaye, "until he'd created this whole four or five-part harmony section. It's quite remarkable to hear it, even now. Todd has always had this incredible grasp of abstruse harmony."

Kaye says the bassline he played on 'Frederick' came from Rundgren's suggestions for a "circular" pattern, "without any starting or stopping to it." Smith says that, as a result, the song turns "like a disco ball."

"I didn't want it to be a disco song," says Smith, smiling at the thought, "but like those glittering balls, I just wanted the song to radiate joy because it was really a song about me starting a new life with the person that I loved. And I think that in suggesting the bassline and the way he arranged the vocals, he did a beautiful job."

Rundgren was confident that 'Frederick' seemed the best candidate for the single from *Wave*, owing largely to its similarity to 'Because The Night.' He remains convinced, however, that 'Frederick' was a better song.

"I always thought 'Because The Night' was just a song," Rundgren admits, "whereas 'Frederick' was about real feelings for a real person. It was unlike anything else on *Wave* and it was a needle-threading exercise to get the balance right, because there was something very 'little girlish' about it."

"Patti obviously felt really strongly about 'Frederick' and wanted the world to hear it," adds Daugherty. "I think that was probably why she got Todd to give it those trademark Todd background vocal sections. She was like, 'Okay, Todd's the hit maker, let's do it.'"

Kaye says that, counter to alternative rock wisdom, one should never apologize for having a hit single adding that he and Smith were out to find a hit single on every album they made. "A hit single," says Kaye, "doesn't necessarily change the integrity and the commitment you make to the song. I remember I had a cassette of it in my car, coming back from the first mixing session, and I remember crossing the George Washington Bridge and heading down West Side Highway, thinking, 'Man, this is gonna sound great over the radio.'"

According to Rundgren, 'Dancing Barefoot,' co-written by Smith and Ivan Kral, was more representative of the core Patti Smith Group sound. Kral had brought an instrumental demo recording to the group after it was decided that *Wave* needed just one more song. "Ivan gave me a cassette with the riff on acoustic guitar," Smith remembers. "I liked the riff, but I took it to Lenny who was the one in our group who could take ideas and give them structure."

Daugherty recalls being pleased when, just before they were tracking the song, Rundgren walked in and picked up the bass to play it himself: "I'm not knocking Lenny nor Ivan, who normally played the bass in our band, but neither of them were really bass players. Todd's groove matched perfectly with our sort of minimalist approach, so it felt great when it was being put down."

Rundgren says he can't recall what possessed him to jump in on bass, but chalks it up to his overall philosophy about doing whatever was needed to get the record finished.

"So much of the material was not really rehearsed when we came in," Rundgren remembers, "and it was a very germinal idea that we were still working out, so it would have been organic for me to just play bass on it. Also, I think there was a kind of openness about roles in the Patti Smith Group. There was none of this 'I'm the bass player' or 'I'm the lead guitarist' stuff. Particularly not from Lenny, who was kind of like Colin Powell in that all this turmoil may be going on around him, and sometimes he may not 100 per cent agree with the policy, but he's always doing his best to 'make it happen.' So if I had to become bass player on the song, so be it."

"I remember that he had a great, fat bass sound," says Kaye, "which really provided a lot of pulse of that particular record." Kaye was also happy with Rundgren's other ideas for 'Dancing Barefoot.' "There's some really interesting tones in the acoustic guitar that opens up the track," he says, "but I also loved certain things he came up with, like instead of having a guitar solo, he had Richard do a synthesizer lead."

Rundgren also hooked up a Syndrum electronic drum synthesizer for Daugherty to play on the song. "It was one of those early drum pads," Daugherty says, laughing, "the kind you'd hear on early disco records. I play it on the backbeat, with the snare hits, on the choruses. Thank God you can't really hear it!"

Rundgren once again asked Smith to layer her own voice for the backing vocals on 'Dancing Barefoot.' "It was just me and Todd in the control room," she recalls, "and he gave me a microphone and I had to sing high-pitched, like a mouse or something, 'I'm dancing bare-foot!' I was nearly in tears, because I always tended to gravitate toward the lead vocal. Todd would sing a part for me, and then I would just forget it and start singing the lead melody. If it was hell for me, it must have been triple hell for him. But he really needed to have this 'sound.' In hindsight, it would have been a lot easier to get a nice girl singer in who could actually do it. Still, he got it out of me and, in the end, I was quite proud of it."

Wave also features the group's energetic cover version of The Byrds' 'So You Want To Be A Rock'n'Roll Star,' yet only those close to Smith at the time knew the subtext behind it. As the sessions were continuing in Woodstock, Smith had received unsettling news about her road manager and brother Todd Smith, who had been injured terribly in a violent altercation at New York City nightspot Hurrah's. These events would come to inspire the rage, venom, and righteous anger fairly dripping from the recording.

"My beloved brother had gone into a bar with his girlfriend," Smith explains, "and this other guy had started taunting him. Now, my brother was a very gentle guy but no wimp, you know? So he told the guy to be respectful to his girlfriend, but then the guy, who turned out to be Sid Vicious, took a beer bottle, broke it and shoved it in my brother's face."

Vicious was hauled off to jail, while Todd Smith was taken to local hospital. "He almost lost his eye," Smith recalls. "He called me up and said, 'I want you to know, in case this ends up in the papers, that I'm alright. I also want you to know that I did a very unpopular thing. I pressed charges [against Vicious], because when he looked at my face I saw a guy crying, screaming for help. I think that if he isn't put behind bars, or in a hospital, he's gonna kill himself.' Apparently people were yelling at my brother, 'You put Sid Vicious in jail!' Like it's their 'hero' in jail. But then, after Sid's mother bailed him out, he was dead, something like a day or two later."

Kaye recalls the incident happening at a "crazy time" for the New York punk scene, when its core vitality and energy had turned destructive. "When Sid Vicious broke that fucking glass in Todd [Smith]'s face," Kaye begins, still moved by the event, "we just saw this music scene, which we had been very much a part of, move into this kind of self-destruction. It was very symbolic to us and created a lot of the energy of that song."

At the insistence of her ailing brother, Patti Smith reluctantly finished the record rather than join him in the city. She credits Rundgren's empathy for allowing the song to have a special "fierceness," and for letting her add some extremely meaningful feedback guitar to the track. "I think I'm really good at feedback," she says, "and after all, I married Fred 'Sonic' Smith, who gave me a lot of feedback tips. Todd turned me way up in the mix, so you really hear it. Todd knew I was still pretty angry over what happened to my brother, and he rose to where I needed him to be and took it all extremely seriously."

Smith also channeled her rage into the improvised dialogue in the middle section. "I sort of merged these two characters," she says. "my brother and Sid Vicious, into one being or one experience. So that's where I got the 'broken glass' line – the bottle that Sid cut him with – and 'recognize my face' – my brother's face. 'Hey you, come 'ere, look up,' or 'Hey you, come 'ere, come on.' It's the confrontation. 'Recognize my face. They call me broken glass, that's because of the way I play my instrument ...' So they are both embedded in the song ... and now they are both gone."

Having survived his injuries, Todd Smith died in 1994, of heart failure. Smith describes 'Rock'n'Roll Star' as the emotional peak of the *Wave* album, and recalls Rundgren being "very quiet" and respectful while tracking it. "None of these things were discussed at the time," she says, "and I wouldn't want to take the magic out of things by breaking it all down. Todd and I had gone through a lot in our friendship together and had remained extremely close. We were 'peers,' accepting fully of each other."

Smith remembers Kral bringing in some "strong, simply structured, but dark and sarcastic" music for the song, 'Revenge,' to which she added some particularly angry lyrics. "Lyrically, it's from a very strong female point of view," says Smith. "It's sort of my song 'encoding' anybody that fucked with me; especially all males who had messed with me. It was like, 'Fuck you!' because I had Fred and nobody could touch me now."

Kaye says it was Rundgren's idea for the track to feature twin guitar solos: "Instead of either me or Ivan taking the solo, Todd asked us both to play on it. So we have this little strange guitar duel."

While the *Wave* sessions continued, Rundgren was frequently darting back and forth between the Bearsville Studios and the burgeoning Utopia Video Studio next door, attending to wiring or other technological issues. "Todd was really ahead of the video curve," Kaye recalls. "I remember he was creating sets to use in these video productions. Still, there was an engineer, all the sounds were there, so why not let the band make a record? This was our fourth record, so we knew what we were looking for and how to find it."

"Todd was both there and not there," says Kral. "I felt that he was distracted by his new love for video production. His studio was divided, half was video equipment."

"I think that part of the reason Patti picked him to do the album in the first place," says Daugherty, "was that he could set us up in a very professional way and also give us the freedom to do whatever we wanted. On some tracks, we would just start recording and he'd wave through the glass and leave to work in his video studio for a while. Then, he'd pop back in, later, to see how it was going and, at crucial moments, he'd shepherd us through the process. It was an interesting combination of 'hands on' and 'hands off' and everybody was really comfortable with that."

Kaye recalls that the arrangement particularly suited the band on the experimental numbers like 'Wave' or 'Seven Ways Of Going,' where the band didn't especially need, or want, Rundgren to hold their hands. "So instead of sitting there through two days of takes," says Kaye, "he'd come in at the end and ask us which one we liked and then ask us if there was anything we needed to add to it. I think that's more respectful to the artist, he didn't need to direct us so he just skated down the hill on the ice [to the video studio] when he wasn't needed."

Smith recalls feeling that her own perfectionism tested Rundgren's patience while they were trying to record 'Seven Ways Of Going.' "I had a vision that sort of had to come out 'mystically' because I didn't know how to do it, technically. I kept thinking 'the next one will be better, and the next one.' I would only know the right take when I heard it. Todd got a little impatient. He didn't split hairs like I did, and he said, 'I'm leaving. You figure it out, because they all sound very similar to me and I can't tell which one is the right one.'"

"Yet it still only took us a couple of days to track," adds Daugherty. "Actually, I think we spent a couple of days getting a take on it and then there was one track that the engineer, George Carnell, accidentally erased [laughs]. We had to go back and record it again! To be fair, though, George was very upset about it."

Kaye remarks that sessions were "very healthy," owing in no small part to the clean Catskill Mountain air and the fact that he and Sohl had both recently quit smoking. But Daugherty and Kral recall a failed experiment with psychedelic mushroom tea that was intended to open the band up when they were stuck on 'Seven Ways.'

"We were probably trying to have some sort of 'shamanistic' experience," laughs Daugherty, "but we failed to achieve lift-off. You know, somehow we got this reputation for drug use, but there wasn't really a lot of drug use in that band. There was, though, this division in the band between people who liked pot and people who liked other substances, so we all harmoniously agreed to ingest some kind of psychedelic substance."

"We would especially never indulge in the studio," says Kral. "We'd be too afraid that we were going to screw up the track. But after we'd spent a whole day on a basic track for 'Seven Ways,' Patti was still not happy with it the following day. She was urging us to push ourselves. Finally, this tea shows up out of nowhere. Me and Jay Dee just looked at each other, horrified, and Patti said, 'You guys are gonna drink it, same as everyone else.' Believe me, Jay Dee and I were straighter than ever after that; nothing at all happened."

According to Smith, the title track, 'Wave,' was a reference to the waving hand of a recently deceased Pope whom she had adored, but she also allows that it might have been a symbolic wave goodbye to her old life, her band and potentially her fans. "My pope had died," Smith recalls. "I'm not Catholic, but I loved Pope John Paul I. He was just such a pastoral, beautiful man and he had died so quickly. I really believed that he would have been a revolutionary Pope, had he lived."

Smith admits that her grief at losing a leader of such great promise was not unlike what many Americans had felt after the 1968 assassination of Robert F. Kennedy, who had also died before having the chance to forge the change he had always advocated. "I felt the same kind of sorrow in losing somebody," Smith remembers, "having them snapped out from one's hands. So I wanted to do a piece for him and I really wanted to build this piece from the bottom up."

Unsure where he fit in and trusting that Smith could sort it out, Rundgren handed her the metaphorical and physical keys to the studio, leaving her with one of the Bearsville house engineers while he flew to Chicago to play a rescheduled New Year's Eve show at the Uptown Theatre on January 5 1979. "It was the first time that I'd been alone in the studio and given complete control," says Smith. "So I just built the song from the piano up. Then, I asked each of my musicians to come in, late at night, and each person did something which I had specifically asked them to do."

Kral was asked to play the cello, while Sohl programmed his Moog synthesizer to simulate the hissing sound of an ocean wave. "It was really sweet," Kaye remembers, "when Richard got that wave sound and Patti was able to kind of use it to stroll upon the beach with, so to speak."

Smith mixed the track herself, with the engineer, and feels that the finished track sits well alongside Rundgren's mixes. "Todd trusted me and gave me complete freedom to do it alone," she says. "He told me he was really happy with my mix."

For 'Broken Flag,' Smith had written a simple poem over which she and Kaye created what she calls a "goodbye song." "Todd grasped it, immediately," she says, "since I'd told him about my plans. The children [in the song] were marching on to Algiers, singing, 'We'll be gone, but they'll go on. And on and on.' Todd arranged the vocals, and everybody sang on it, even Todd. He built up this extremely 'anthemic' ending, which was his specialty."

Kaye brought out his brand new autoharp for 'Hymn,' a song which provided a rather sweet corollary to the dark and nasty snarl of 'Revenge.' "I wrote this sweet melody," says Kaye, "and Patti wrote beautiful lyrics for it. We only did one take, as far as I remember, and at the end of it, there was this long space and my finger got caught in the swish as the last note was struck. Much later, when it came time to master it, I decided to do a little edit to fix this little 'mistake.' I saw Todd a month or two later and he just sort of looked at me, disapprovingly, and said, 'Oh, I see you shortened that little space.' Looking back, I think he was right. I should have just left it as it was. It was just that little touch of human anticipation before the last note, which would have been perfect."

Rundgren's final mixes were done relatively rapidly, as usual, and without the band present, although Kaye remained nearby for consultation. He admits that the band had problems with Rundgren's initial mix. "After a couple of hours," says Kaye, "Todd called me in and played back a mix of 'Frederick' at a really loud volume. I'm not sure what everyone was expecting to come off the tape, but it was just brightness central, with some pretty clattery drums. He asked me, 'What do you think?' So, I had my laundry list of, well, you know, 'Push this here, push this' and he seemed surprised: 'You wanna mix it again?' So he gave me maybe one or two more mixes and the rest of the record was mixed over the weekend. I brought it back to the band who, predictably, flipped out."

Daugherty recalls that, after listening to the mixes, it was agreed that Rundgren would take the tapes to a studio with an automated board, and attempt a more controlled remix. "Todd came down to New York City," says Daugherty, "and he remixed it in two days at Blank Tapes, up on 23rd Street, which was the only studio in New York at that time that had a computer for automation. I think that's probably one of the only reasons he agreed to do the mixes at all."

"This was before all the SSL automated boards," Kaye recalls, "and it was our first time with any kind of automated mix. Todd started on some Saturday in February, and we did 'Seven Ways Of Going' for about five, six hours, until it was perfect. I left to go do a radio interview at WPIX FM, and when I came back, another three songs were mixed. Then another four songs were mixed the next day. He worked quickly and the new mixes were all great. He didn't remix 'Revenge,' because he said that the compression on the drums was so perfect on his initial mix that he wasn't sure he could ever get it that way again. Actually, we still thought the drums in 'So You Wanna Be A Rock'n'Roll Star' were a little loud. But then, Keith Moon had just died recently, so we used that as a rationale for the louder drum sound."

Today, Smith still regularly works with Kaye and Daugherty, even though The Patti Smith Group is no longer operating by name. Looking back, Patti Smith holds many emotional memories associated with the *Wave* sessions and Rundgren. Still, when it was all done, she knew in her heart that it was time to wave goodbye. "As an artist, a human being, and as a growing person," says Smith, "I felt that I had reached a wall and needed to replenish, learn more, and study more. I just didn't think I had anything more to give the people until I learned more about myself. I had a true moment in 1979, after *Wave* and the subsequent tour. Our last concert was in a soccer arena in Florence [Italy] in front of 80,000 people, and the last thing we did was to turn over the stage to the people. We gave them the equipment and just said, 'It's all yours!'"

"I think, deep down, everybody realized we went out on top," says Lenny Kaye. "It was increasingly apparent that, in a certain sense that we had run our course in that configuration. On that last tour, we were playing all of the great venues, like the Winterland in San Francisco or the Palladium in New York. We were riding a wave, but there was nothing left to say. I look at Patti's long trail from the opening words of *Horses*, 'Jesus died for somebody's sins, but not mine,' to *Wave* and this beautiful walk on the beach with The Pope at the end – this is conciliation. *Wave* is also a farewell record, because Patti is on her way to the land of love. If you listen to some of the things on the record, a song like 'Broken Flag' is both anthemic and melancholic; and I really feel that things like 'Citizenship' or 'Revenge,' are really Patti Smith *Group* songs."

Smith recalls *Wave* as both a happy and painful journey. "It's funny," says Smith, "but before we were recording *Horses*, I never really thought I would ever even make one record. It was never one of my dreams. I just wanted to be an artist or to write a book or something. Then, they asked me to do more records until, by the time of *Wave*, I felt that I couldn't possibly have any more to contribute. And probably, at that time, it was everything that I knew or had to say."

Kaye also says he learned how to produce records by watching Rundgren. "I think you learn from all your producers," says Kaye, "but Todd's dictum, 'If you know what you want, I'll get it for you,' requires a lot of creativity. I don't think Todd is very visible on *Wave*; he just allowed it all to happen around him. When I produce a record, now, I want to be the man behind the curtain. And that's what I think Todd certainly did with *Wave*; he spoke through us. Todd had a great spirit of adventure and the record was definitely made in his reflection."

Rundgren says he probably gave Smith a much easier time in the studio than he would have if they weren't such great friends. "It's not my job to tell Patti Smith how to make music," he says, "but most of the album came together in the studio, eventually, and everyone seemed happy with the result."

In closing, Patti Smith recalls it all as a "miraculous time. You know, back when I first walked into the Woodstock Playhouse in 1970, never in my life did I imagine that, one day, he and I would do my album together. Yet, I got to do four records and to tour the world. I would have been happy that my last recorded effort was with Todd. He was never the record industry's pet. He's openly rebellious against the music business and fiercely independent. But for me, he was always just really supportive and really fun. I was always happy that, even though we had some ups and downs, I did that particular record with Todd, the first producer I ever met. So to wind up doing my last album of that period with him, was just the perfect bookend, a full circle."

Adventures In
Video And Healing

While 1979 saw the release of four Todd Rundgren audio productions – for The Patti Smith Group, Rick Derringer, The Tubes, and the Tom Robinson Band – his interests had already been diverted toward his newest pursuit, video production, by the time these records hit the shops. After the unexpected windfall from the sleeper success of *Bat Out Of Hell*, Rundgren finally had the capital to invest in and pursue cutting-edge video technology.

Rundgren had originally been commissioned by RCA SelectaVision to produce a VideoDisc presentation incorporating the musical track from Isao Tomita's interpretation of Gustav Holst's orchestral suite, *The Planets*. After Rundgren had sunk more than $150,000 into the project, however, RCA pulled the plug on the project, paying Rundgren only $30,000 and leaving him increasingly wary of the corporate world's lack of vision. After Gustav Holst's estate sought legal action to halt the Rundgren production – or even Tomita's audio recording – the project remained in limbo.

"I had been working, initially, out of Studio A at Bearsville Studios," Rundgren recalls, "doing the Patti album in one room and the Holst video in another, with all these little models and motorized cameras and things like that. It was kind of an improvised set-up and we wanted to move it into a real video studio, so we got another building."

Frustrated, Rundgren soldiered (and soldered) on, ordering more and more cutting-edge gear for Utopia Video Studios, which had now moved into a new 2,500 square foot building nearby. The company employed a staff of anywhere between ten and 30 people, depending on the project.

Journalist Bruce Pilato took a tour of Rundgren's video facility for a 1981 feature story in the US audio magazine *Mix*, and reported: "Utopia Video ... thus far has cost nearly $2 million. And according to Rundgren, it costs a staggering $40,000 to $50,000 per month just to keep open."

Today, Rundgren jokingly refers to the venture as "that money-hole thing," but he was still intensely committed to video technology as the 80s beckoned. In the *Mix* feature, Pilato had described much of the expensive, state-of-the-art video gear Rundgren had purchased and installed, including post-production effects and a computerized lighting system. Having just installed an Otari MTL 24-track audio recorder into Utopia Sound, Rundgren moved his trusty Stephens 16-track tape machine up to Utopia Video Studios.

According to house engineer Chris Andersen, Utopia Video Studios' Grand

Opening reception, early in 1979, was literally a blazing affair. "The place was packed with everyone from Woodstock and Bearsville," recalls Andersen, "but when we turned on a power amp, there were suddenly flames shooting out of this Klipsch speaker, right in the middle of this brand new television studio. I grabbed the flaming speaker, ripped the cord out of the wall, ran for the door and threw it outside, still fully ablaze."

In hindsight, the crash and burn of the speaker that night was an omen of things to come for the Utopia Video venture, but while it was not destined become one of his greatest success stories, Rundgren insists that, harsh financial truths aside, his goal for the studio was always more artistic than commercial. And indeed, the high costs associated with hiring an outside video studio meant that it was far more cost effective, per hour, to own your own place, as he had done with both Secret Sound and Utopia Sound. Among the video projects floated by Rundgren and Utopia Video were a political documentary series, to be titled *How To Run For President*, and a weekly television program to star Utopia, the band.

In the *Mix* feature, Rundgren complained that the financial drain of the TV production, and the early 80s economic slowdown, had presented him with a vicious cycle that forced him away from the video and back to audio production. "The day-to-day finances of the studio," Rundgren told Pilato, "the financial burden of keeping the studio open is so great that I can't even work in it ... I have to spend all my time producing records ... in order to get enough financial support to keep the studio going."

The shrinking economy was also behind Utopia's relatively scaled-back approach to touring in 1979. Instead of burning gasoline and traveling to many cities, they instead played a couple of residencies, including 14 shows over seven nights at the Roxy in Los Angeles and a similar run of eight shows over four nights at the Old Waldorf in San Francisco. There were also sporadic stadium events such as a Giants Stadium concert in June, a homecoming to Central Park in July, and a return to Knebworth in August, sharing the bill with Led Zeppelin's final performances.

When he wasn't doing video work or touring, Rundgren assembled the group to begin writing and recording *Adventures In Utopia*, which was ostensibly touted as the soundtrack to an imaginary "long running and successful" television series by the same name. "We didn't have an actual TV show," says Rundgren. "That was a bit of 'creative pre-visualization' on our part. While he had actually hoped to do a pilot for a series, it was more of the mythology of the album. We thought that if we imagined it, it would actually happen."

"Todd was thinking we could have a cartoon series," says Kasim Sulton, "and we could rule the world through television. But first, we had to kind of make believe that we had already done it. I think Todd even had a script that he'd written, floating around somewhere, but it never came to pass."

In Paul Lester's interviews for the liner notes to the 1999 UK reissue of *Adventures In Utopia*, Rundgren elaborated on what he called his "Tom Swift-y concept" for the show that never was. "The setting was very futuristic," he said. "We all had fabulous gadgets and we were computer scientists, not just guys sitting around a house with nothing to do. We had scripts, but this was pre-MTV, so the possibility of us getting on TV was extremely remote. The biggest issue as always was, was our music commercial enough? We were certainly able to handle the tools, but ... we weren't exactly racking up the Top 10 singles."

That year, Rundgren had also established a creative enclave known as the Neo-Utopian Laboratories Limited, or NULL, although quite what the labs produced may have been as ethereal as the 'television series.' Music was another matter, however, and as Utopia entered Utopia Sound in late 1979, Rundgren recalls the band was "really working well together." The sessions lasted just over three weeks. "On a good night," says Rundgren, "we were one of the best live bands going. We had strong live vocals, between Kasim and myself, and Roger and Willie harmonized with us well. Performance was never a problem in that band."

According to Sulton, genuine pop accessibility was aggressively pursued and encouraged for the first time, perhaps to get the band into a position where there would be real demand for a real television series. They even modeled their new songs on established hits to increase their familiarity with the pop audience.

"We wanted to make a record of original songs," Sulton admits, "that were reminiscent of the Top Ten songs on the radio and in the charts at that time. For example, in that time period you could not turn on a radio without hearing 'More Than A Feeling' by Boston. So Todd sat down and rewrote 'More Than a Feeling' as 'The Very Last Time.'"

While shades of the earlier Utopia informed the seven-minute 'Caravan,' and the opening section of 'Road To Utopia,' songs like 'You Make Me Crazy,' wouldn't have been out of place on The Cars' first album. With all material now credited with the line "Lyrics and Music by Utopia," Sulton was nonetheless happy to bring some unabashed pop hooks to his own contributions, from the Queen-meets-Beatles lilt of 'Love Alone,' to the Fleetwood Mac sound of 'Set Me Free,' which succeeded as the band's most commercially successful single.

"Stuff like 'Shot In The Dark' or 'Love Alone' was the kind of stuff I would write on my own," says Sulton, "and that was sometimes hard in Utopia because, unfortunately, they were extremely similar to the kinds of pop song Todd might write. And since he was a better songwriter, it was difficult for me to get my stuff in there and have it impress him. With 'Set Me Free,' though, Todd thought enough about it that he wanted to put it on the album."

Sulton still maintains that Rundgren and Powell's arrangement of the song made it come alive in the studio, however. "We actually recorded that song a little differently from other Utopia songs," he recalls, "because I played the electric piano on the basic track, with Willie playing drums, and then I overdubbed the bass part. It was rare that we pieced basic tracks together like that, but nobody else wanted to play the bass and Roger probably didn't want to play keyboards because it was my chord pattern, so I needed to lay it down. I have to say that Todd's rhythm guitar riff and those little pieces of ear-candy, like the horn arrangement, really go into making the song more memorable."

While 'Set Me Free' was a commercial success, Sulton found it ironic in that the lyric was literally a cry to Albert Grossman to release him from his Bearsville deal. "I was chomping at the bit to do a solo record," he recalls, "but Albert didn't feel I was ready yet and thought my demos weren't very good. He wouldn't let me out without paying him first. So 'Set Me Free' was kind of my pissed-off song to get out of the contract: 'If you're not gonna let me do a record, then set me free and let me go do it somewhere else.' I think it was probably another year before I did actually get to do a solo record, which came out on EMI."

Willie Wilcox recalls pushing for a more commercial direction for the band, and describes himself as "a pop guy" in the group, sometimes at odds with Rundgren's ideals for Utopia. "I was the edgy needle," he says, "always saying 'pop music, pop music, commercial, commercial.' I always wanted consistency in our band but, often, we'd all be at the mercy of Todd's schedule. He might go do a project, so in the off time we'd work on the music for the next record or do outside projects."

Roger Powell remembers the group's controversial video clip for 'Set Me Free,' which cast the band as newscasters over images of anti-nuclear demonstrations, hostage-taking incidents, capital punishment, and prison riots. "It had all kinds of political stuff in it," says Powell, "Kas, or one of us, was interviewing, like, the Shah of Iran I think. Corporate types didn't expect that from us, but I think our fans probably got it."

While Sulton felt vindicated when the single became Utopia's highest-charting Top 30 *Billboard* hit – backed with non-album song 'Umbrella Man,' recorded during the same sessions – he says he was dismayed by what he saw as Bearsville's lack of promotional push. "Bearsville pulled the plug on it," says Sulton, "right when it got to 23 or 28 on *Billboard*. There's no way to really judge what might have happened, or why it didn't happen. I've heard various stories over the years. Who knows? You can drive yourself crazy thinking what might have been."

Adventures In Utopia was released in late January 1980. In March, the band set out on the road across the USA for three months straight, taking a few weeks off in June to record another album before heading out again. The band also appeared on some real television programs such as *The John Davidson Show* and a national talk show hosted by Philadelphia's own Mike Douglas. For *The Mike Douglas Show*, the band appeared in their white one-piece costumes, with Rundgren playing his metallic 'Ankh' guitar and Sulton his similarly shaped bass, both dating back to the Ra tour, while Powell used his own Powell Probe keyboard (strapped on and held like a guitar). Willie Wilcox, however, showed off his new motorcycle-like electronic drum kit, the Trapparatus.

"We had taken an actual motorcycle frame," says Wilcox, "and then jerry-rigged this thing. I never used it in the studio, it was just a live thing, and it was really hard to play. The snare drum was actually a Syndrum pad, and the toms were Clavia Ddrums. We used my own drum samples that I triggered with the pads, and I remember going into the studio with Rick Kerr, who is not alive now but he was a really great engineer, and recording my drums together. All my special sounds were on cartridges and then got stuck into the 'brain' and so all the live sounds that you heard were coming off the Trapparatus."

That year, Powell released his long promised solo album, *Air Pocket*, and toured with David Bowie, appearing on Bowie's *Stage* and *Lodger* albums. According to Willie Wilcox, extracurricular activity was key to keeping the band intact, lest they sit on their hands waiting for Rundgren to call them. "We always left Utopia hanging," he says, "because we'd be at the mercy of Todd's other projects and his schedule. In the off-time we'd work on bits of songs for the next record, or other projects."

Rundgren had tried, when possible, to involve Utopia in his outside productions, such as the two songs he produced with Alice Cooper, 'Road Rats' and 'Pain,' for the soundtrack to a film, *Roadie*, that starred Meat Loaf. Utopia also backed Shaun Cassidy on Rundgren's production, *Wasp*, which was more or less a Utopia album with lead vocals by a teen idol, singing unlikely covers such as Ian Hunter's 'Once Bitten, Twice Shy,' Talking Heads' 'The Book I Read,' The Who's 'So Sad About Us,' and a disco-fied version of David Bowie's 'Rebel Rebel.'

While preparing the music for *Roadie* that spring, however, Rundgren had been asked to submit a song of his own. Perhaps the producers had been expecting either a *Hermit*-style piano-ballad or a fully-flanged Utopian raver, but what they got instead was 'I Just Want To Touch You,' a Beatles pastiche largely inspired by 'I Want To Hold Your Hand,' complete with Lennonesque harmonica bursts. It was fun, everybody loved it, but the film producers passed on it. Nonplussed, and probably not wanting to waste a good track, Rundgren couldn't shake the notion of a tribute to the Fab Four. He had, after all, copied not one but two Beatles songs on *Faithful*. This time, ever the conceptualist, Rundgren wanted to go one better. Why not follow up Utopia's biggest commercial success, *Adventures In Utopia*, with an entire album of original Beatles pastiche songs written by the band? According to Kasim Sulton, the rest of the band had their doubts about the concept, which, nonetheless, became Utopia's second release of 1980, *Deface The Music*.

"I think that if you ask Roger or Willie about it," says Sulton, "looking back, we'd say, yeah, it was an 'interesting' record to follow up *Adventures* with; but on the other hand, I think the band wanted to capitalize on the fact that we had sold close to 400,000 records with the last album, which was unheard of for a Utopia record. We really felt that it would be in our best interest to try and follow it up with a record that was just a little more consistent, style-wise. Maybe we'd sell 600,000 records the next time out."

Rundgren called a band meeting at his home to announce his 'Fab' idea. "We were shocked," says Sulton, "then he went on, describing how we were gonna rewrite all our favorite Beatles songs, and each song is gonna be identifiable with a Beatles song. We were just like, 'Ugh, you gotta be kidding me! We can't do that; it's suicide.' But, nobody was gonna argue with Todd, so we did what he wanted."

Roger Powell notes, however, that in a certain sense, following up a commercially successful album with a funny detour took some of pressure off. "Sure, it was mostly Todd's baby," he says, "and I'm still not sure why he had this burning desire to reinterpret Beatles music, but we all loved The Beatles so it was actually a fun record to make. Todd mostly saw Utopia as even more experimental than his solo albums, and that was why we kind of did these things that were all over the map. I mean, even in the space of a single album we'd run the gamut of styles."

Willie Wilcox recalls that by this time, June 1980, the band were not unlike Rundgren's version of Phil Spector's legendary Wrecking Crew, a tight and capable team ready to cop any style of music. "We could make a progressive record," he says, "or we could make a disco track or a conventional rock song, you know? Utopia was never all that genre based, so it wouldn't be unusual to say 'Let's make a Beatle record,' because we could. Musically, we were chameleons, but the 'Utopia' sound was more based on the various personalities of the four members. Of course, that allowed for bad business decisions too. And from a business or a fan base perspective, going to a Beatle album was very confusing. I have to say, though, from a musician's perspective, you only care that the band's making good music, and there are some great songs on *Deface The Music.*"

Utopia's deconstruction of the Beatles material had a light, comical touch that puts it more in the mold of Eric Idle's Beatles homage, *The Rutles*, from 1978. Beside the aforementioned 'I Just Want To Touch You,' other ersatz Fabs songs included 'Silly Boy,' which was imbued with the essence of 'From Me To You,' and Sulton's 'Alone,' in which he adopts a McCartneyesque lilt. Lennon's urgency inhabits Rundgren's vocal on 'Crystal Ball,' and the 'Eleanor Rigby' string quartet sound is represented by Powell's synthesizers on 'Life Goes On.' Rundgren's jangly guitar riff for 'Take It Home' perfectly approximates both 'Day Tripper' and 'Drive My Car.'

Wilcox remembers bringing in a lot of his own ideas for the songs, although most of the lyrics were by Rundgren with the material credited, once again, to Utopia as a whole. "It's pretty easy," he says, "to spot the influences. 'All Smiles' is obviously 'Michelle' and 'Hoi Poloi' or 'Always Late' was that sort of 'Yellow Submarine' era when they were having fun on their records. We were having fun doing it, too, because, as I say, it wasn't exactly something we did to further our career."

Fans who had been following the ongoing 'feud' between Rundgren and John Lennon could be forgiven for assuming that the sneeringly nasty lyric to 'Everybody Else Is Wrong,' from *Deface The Music*, was yet another salvo aimed at the ex-Beatle. Their battle had already included Rundgren publicly calling out Lennon as a limousine radical in 'Rock N Roll Pussy,' from *A Wizard, A True Star*. That move had culminated in Lennon, as 'Dr Winston O'Boogie,' writing the infamous "Opened Letter To Sodd Runtlestuntle," published in the *Melody Maker* in September 1974. After mildly excoriating Rundgren, Lennon did add that he had actually enjoyed 'I Saw The Light,' which he compared cheekily to The Beatles' own 'There's A Place.'

Rundgren insists, however, that there wasn't a great deal of seriousness about *Deface The Music*: "I don't think we really dwelled upon the deeper meanings of the songs. We only toured that album for a short time, as I recall."

Chris Andersen, who assisted Rundgren on the project, says the album was "knocked out" at a typically brisk pace, just as the early Beatles records had been. "I would basically run the sessions from the console," he says, "and I did that on a lot of Utopia records and quite a few of Todd's other productions as well. I was always one of the only people there for the final mixes, especially with outside bands."

Andersen describes Rundgren's typical mixing process, which he says remained unchanged throughout their time together at Utopia Sound. "We never had automation in that studio," says Andersen, "so we would pretty much always mix in pieces. It was very rare that we would mix a piece from beginning to end without cutting in little bits of it here and there. We'd do the intro and the first verse and then we'd stop and print that to tape. Then we'd set up for the next section, maybe the chorus or an interlude, and mix that and print that too. So we'd basically build the thing, piece by piece, splicing as we mixed each section. Todd might say, 'All right, we need to do a piece!' Then we'd redo that piece and splice it back into the master. Todd was a very good engineer. I don't really know where he learned all his tricks, since he never really worked with anyone else."

While *Deface The Music* sat in the can, awaiting an October release by Bearsville, Rundgren returned to his *Hermit* ways, holing up in Utopia Sound for days at a time to record his next solo album, *Healing*, assisted now and again by Mike Young and his pregnant partner Karen Darvin, as the couple prepared for the birth of their first son, Rex.

"*Healing* was an experiment, essentially," says Rundgren. "It wasn't meant to be one continuous piece, but two different things that were more or less about the same subject from two different angles. The first side was supposed to be like this little parable. Somebody discovers he has healing powers, and what the result of that is. It doesn't go into any sort of detail about the nature of those powers, or how they're administered, so it might just as well have been through some sort of musical mechanism as anything else. The second side was supposed to be a possible soundtrack to that story, as well as an experiment in actually trying to come up with some music that has, at least, a psychically salubrious effect, in that it won't necessarily make crippled people walk [laughs]."

Rundgren's music for the album was therefore designed to assist in this process. He adds that the idea of "sound healing," has roots in the time of Plato. "There are all sorts of other mystical disciplines," Rundgren notes, "where certain tones are attached to certain chakras and that sort of business. I just don't know if anyone had specifically done this sort of 'pop music' experiment before."

According to Rundgren, the central idea behind the music on *Healing* was that the most distressful things are essentially all in our minds. If one can evolve one's thinking, he asserts, one can heal oneself.

"It isn't the fact that you can't walk," says Rundgren, "it's how bitter you are about the fact that you can't walk. There's also that thing where people say that people who are blind from birth are almost luckier because they don't know what it's like ever to have seen. But when somebody goes blind, there's any number of ways to deal with it. You could just say, 'Life is not worth living if I can't see.' Or maybe you say, 'I'm going to develop, or utilize, my other senses to make up for the loss.' And then there's denial, where you just act like it never happened," he laughs.

Rundgren also claims to have heard from therapists who have used the album as a therapeutic tool, with great success, over the years since its release. "Some people took the experiment somewhat seriously," says Rundgren. "I think there have been some clinicians, psychiatrists, or mental hospital workers who have played it for some people who weren't necessarily tipped off about it and swear that it actually did have the intended effect. The scientific part of me wonders whether it's actually the music or the placebo effect. I suppose the only way to know for sure would be to spring it on somebody who doesn't know what it is and see if it helps them or not. If it were just a temporary, anesthetic effect then I think it would be considered a failure. Numbing is not healing."

Rundgren goes on to explain his use synthesizer drones in an attempt to mirror the sounds of the central nervous system. "It was all based on this 'om drone' thing," he says, "like in meditations. Most people don't really notice the sound of their own nervous system unless they get a fever or something. But if you listen, you can suddenly hear this high-pitched ringing in your ears. Just like a microphone, or any other kind of sensory apparatus, our nervous system has a 'noise floor,' or a point at which stimulus falls so low that the only thing coming out of it is baseline noise. It's easier to hear if you get into an isolation tank or something like that, but there is always input constantly stimulating your ears. It's the nature of the brain not to be blank, so if there is no noise, your brain will start creating it out of the noise coming out of your senses."

Since the time of *Initiation*, Rundgren had become intrigued by the way certain Eastern meditation disciplines employed a bell, or some other sound, to focus the mind. "Listen," Rundgren instructs in 'Healing,' as though leading the listener through a ceremony of sound. And while vocals, bells, and synthesizers make up much of the texture, Rundgren also made ample use of his newest toy, the Linn Drum computer, on the shorter song material such as 'Compassion,' 'The Healer,' and the dark music-hall number, 'Golden Goose.' He also made a lot of use of his crisp sounding Alembic guitar. And just as he had on *Hermit*, Rundgren played all these instruments himself, including the saxophone.

When *Healing* was originally released on vinyl, in February of 1981, the package included a bonus seven-inch, 45rpm single, featuring 'Time Heals,' backed with 'Tiny Demons.' "The single was Albert's idea," says Rundgren, "I think he recognized that, within the larger context of the *Healing* album, there was not a single *per se*. Though I think he also realized that it might have sounded a little weird if we had tried to shove one into the [album] running order, somehow."

Rundgren's video clip for 'Time Heals,' which he directed himself in the Utopia Video Studio, featured him dancing and superimposed against melting clocks, disembodied Rickenbacker guitars, and bowler-hatted Magritte gents. Released just in time for the summer 1981 launch of the MTV Network, 'Time Heals' became the second video ever aired on the network, right after The Buggles clip for 'Video Killed The Radio Star.'

"Second," says Rundgren, rolling his eyes in mock horror. "Second again! All I remember about that video was there was a lot of blue screen, and all these Dali images and other surrealist things. Up until that point, we used to do a lot of storyboarding, but for that one we did a lot of improvised set-up shots."

While Karen Darvin would give birth to a son, Rex, that November, any discussion of 1980 would be incomplete without at least touching on two significant non-studio events, both of which temporarily dampened Rundgren's otherwise positive outlook heading into the New Year. The first, and most personally affronting, had occurred on August 13, two months prior to Rex's birth, when four armed thieves staged a home invasion and threatened the lives of Rundgren, Darvin, their housekeeper, and some guests.

"This band of masked invaders came to our house waving guns," Rundgren remembers. "Bean [Darvin] was seven months pregnant and these cokeheads must have had it in their minds that we had a stash of drugs in the house. You know, 'He's a rock star! He must have drugs!' So they burst in looking for something easily disposable, like cocaine or some imaginary big money stash. They were convinced that there was a safe in the house. I said, 'I don't have a safe.' We gave them whatever of value that we could. At one point, one guy threatened to start cutting my fingers off if I didn't tell him where all the valuable stuff was. I just had to tell him, 'It won't do any good because whatever it is you're looking for, it ain't here!'"

Frustrated, the thieves trashed the house and left Rundgren, Darvin, and their guests bound in makeshift shackles. "They cut up all the electric cables and extension cords," says Rundgren, "so they could tie us up with wire, which isn't a great thing to tie up people with. It didn't take me long to just slip out of it after they left. But by then, the thieves were long gone and the police never found them. It was a horrifying violation and it started to make us feel kinda creepy about living up there. We never had a similar episode, but apparently there had been a wave of related criminal events in the Woodstock area, so were just 'lucky,' I guess, to be part of that particular spree."

While they were lucky also to have remained unhurt, with all fingers intact, Rundgren was, however, relieved of his current favorite guitar, the hand-made Alembic, in the incident. "*Healing* was probably the last album I used that guitar on," says Rundgren, "before it was stolen from me. You can hear it on the intro to the first song, that very crispy, crystalline sound. I got a lot of mileage out of that guitar and I never found another guitar that had that particular sound."

Miraculously, Rundgren managed to get the Alembic guitar back many years later, but it had been badly damaged. "It was unsalvageable," he says. "It looked like it had been through a fire. What happened was, a few years back, somebody tried to sell this guitar on eBay, and as it turns out, every Alembic has a serial number and I suppose the company regularly checks for hot Alembic instruments on the market. Somebody at Alembic saw the guitar, crosschecked the serial number and realized that it was mine. So we got the guitar back from whoever had had it, but it was in just horrible shape. I don't know if they got paid or whatever, it was a curious coincidence that it came back to me at all."

The final troubling incident of 1980 was the assassination of John Lennon, on December 8, at the Dakota apartment complex on Manhattan's Upper West Side. For the world at large, it was a day of infamy, but for Utopia, it provided an awkward backdrop for their just released *Deface The Music*. "Our record had just come out in October," says Kasim Sulton, "and it was already getting panned in the press because we'd disrupted some sacrosanct, unwritten law that you never, ever try to copy The Beatles. But then, after Lennon was assassinated in December, the last thing that people wanted to hear was a jokey Beatle parody record."

Creem magazine's Dave DiMartino, on the other hand, proclaimed it "the band's best album ever – it's one of the best pop albums of the year, something few critics bothered to mention while pulling Beatle quotes out of it like silly schoolkids." The critical savaging, however, paled in comparison to the knowledge, which would emerge over the coming year, that Lennon's killer, Mark David Chapman, had been equally obsessive about the music of Todd Rundgren, and had allegedly flipped a coin to decide which of his idols to murder first.

According to author Jack Jones, whose book, *Let Me Take You Down,* chronicles the killer's pathetic final days leading up to the Lennon murder, Rundgren's music had become the central soundtrack to the assassin's identity. In the book, the gunman confesses that he had memorized every word, sound, and moment from Rundgren's entire discography, and had told his wife that it was Rundgren, not Lennon, who had exerted the greatest influence on his worldview. "Right between the chambers of your heart," the killer told Jones, "[that's] how Rundgren's music is to me."

After slaying Lennon, the shooter was photographed in handcuffs wearing a *Hermit Of Mink Hollow* promotional T-shirt, while a subsequent search of his room at the Broadway Sheraton Hotel had turned up a copy of *The Ballad Of Todd Rundgren*, left behind "as a statement."

Healing was released in February 1981. In many ways, it was a cathartic record for Rundgren, a way of externalizing a roller coaster of personal emotions in a way that might even have been helpful to others. Today, Rundgren admits that it was one of the most satisfying albums he had made. As the year progressed, he continued with some outside productions, including an unreleased album for the band Touch, and

That's What Friends Are For, for the Irish punk group The Moondogs. Engineer Chris Andersen recalls that another album, *Walking Wild,* for the group New England, was completed in a mere ten days and was one of fastest projects he and Rundgren ever worked on.

In April, Rundgren emerged from the solitude of Lake Hill to head back out into an increasingly hostile world, as he and Utopia donned full camouflage fatigues and played songs from their last two albums, plus selections from *Healing*. The greedy 80s were barely a year old, and the political world had swung to the right, courtesy of the newly elected Republican President, Ronald Reagan, who had been sworn in on January 20. It was a violent time, and by March, another gun-toting madmen, John Hinckley, had attempted to assassinate the former actor.

Clearly, the inscription/mission statement from *Healing* couldn't have been timelier: "It's time to make the world a little wiser. There are enough destroyers and criticizers. The world needs a healer."

The Road To Dystopia

The year 1980 had been a particularly political one for Todd Rundgren. In October he had toured with musician Ian Hunter in support of the campaign of Presidential candidate John Anderson. While Rundgren had never been especially political, publicly, he claims to have backed Anderson because he was running as a third-party Independent (that is, neither Republican nor Democrat).

Now, in 1981, as Utopia made their way around the United States over April, July, August, and scattered dates in the fall, it was hard not to be drawn into fray. The so-called 'Reagan Revolution' had shifted the politics of the nation toward cultural and fiscal conservatism, and as Rundgren and the band convened for sessions at Utopia Sound, late in the year, the writing for their next album was on the wall. According to Kasim Sulton, changes in the country, in the band's career, and in their frayed relationship with Bearsville Records had fostered a new political anger within the group, extending far beyond their onstage camouflage outfits.

"It had been over a year since *Deface The Music*," says Sulton, "and we'd moved on. Since we never went into one record thinking about the previous one, it was always about the record we were doing right then. Todd wasn't particularly happy about Republicans taking over the White House, so it made perfect sense to get political in our songwriting at that moment."

The result was *Swing To The Right*, a record with lyrical themes light years away from the Fab escapism of the preceding Utopia collection. While the band was eager to get it out as soon as possible, the label bosses at Bearsville felt that it was too early to put another Utopia product onto the racks. If Rundgren had disapproved of the way his country was now being run, he and his fellow Utopians were unflinching in their disapproval of the way in which Bearsville, and parent company Warner Bros, was marketing their music. It was harder to keep morale up within the band when they weren't actively touring, and off the road, each band-member found other jobs to keep him occupied. While Powell pursued his instrumental music career, Sulton was finally laying tracks for his long-delayed solo album and Wilcox had begun a songwriting partnership with David Lasley, one of the three backing singers from the Faithful tour.

When *Creem's* Dave DiMartino interviewed the band in July 1981, *Swing* was already largely completed, even though it wouldn't see the light of day until the following March. After Rundgren had railed about Utopia's label issues, DiMartino changed gears and asked him what he'd be doing if he didn't need to work at music for a living. His answers were specific and prescient. "I'd be doing a lot of work in my video studio," he replied. "I do a lot of computer programming, which is gonna confirm a lot of people's suspicions that I'm some kind of technocrat, but I can't help it, it's something I enjoy doing ... but it's not as if I'm gonna stop making music. I have no intention of quitting making records. I don't know how directly I'll be involved in the business ... but there's some things that can only be expressed in musical terms, [so] I'll always resort to music if I feel I have to do that. But there are other things that are better expressed in other media. And the important thing to me is always the value of the expression, whether something is useful and important ... or fun to say. It doesn't always have to be earthshaking ..."

It was true. Rundgren was spending increasing amounts of time with new technology, having developed the Utopia Graphics System, among the first computer paint programs, designed to run on the Apple II computer with the Apple digitizer tablet. Eventually he would develop the Flowfazer program with David Levine, his partner in what would eventually become Utopia Grokware.

It was frustrating for Rundgren to have *Swing To The Right* kept on ice until the following March, especially because his own lyrics for it were packed with sharp political musings on Reagan's America, from the anti-war 'Lysistrata' to 'One World,' a hippie-friendly 'come together' anthem for the common man. Similarly themed originals like 'Only Human,' with music from Willie Wilcox, and the anti-greed screed 'Last Dollar On Earth' were augmented by a conceptually linked cover of The O'Jays' classic 'For The Love Of Money,' cast here as a cautionary call out to the prevailing capitalist myopia that wreaked havoc on Wall Street in the early 80s.

"*Swing To The Right*," says Kasim Sulton, "was kind of our anti-establishment record; our smart, smarmy, we-know-better-than-you record. And for some reason we had to petition Bearsville to even put it out. I think that it's possible that at that point, Albert was a little sick of Utopia and didn't want Todd to concentrate on the band; nobody did. They all thought Utopia was a distraction from Todd's solo work, which was much more successful and economically viable. But Todd told them this was what he wanted to do and if they didn't like it then maybe we should go somewhere else. Albert just said 'Well, I'm not gonna put this record out!' There was probably some animosity between the two of them as to whether the record should come out at all, but frankly I wasn't privy to any of their conversations. To be honest with you, I was gone for most of that period."

With Utopia in jeopardy, Rundgren kicked off 1982 by doing some solo dates with only a guitar and piano, as he waited out Bearsville. Finally, in March, the label relented and released *Swing To The Right* with little fanfare. Perhaps in reference to the backlash over *Deface The Music*, the Swing cover art referenced the Beatle bonfires, when the group's records were destroyed in protest at John Lennon's remarks about Christianity, in the Southern USA in the early 60s. Only now, the kids were burning Utopia albums. The destructive imagery wasn't entirely off the mark, as Utopia was going through upheaval outside the band and within it. With Sulton temporarily estranged from the group, and gone for "about six months," they enlisted Doug Howard, who had played bass in the band Touch, one of Rundgren's recent clients. Not one to sit still, Rundgren used the month of April to squeeze in a major production for the English group, The Psychedelic Furs (as detailed in Chapter 17).

After a few sporadic group dates by Utopia, and select Rundgren solo dates – including a trip to the UK where he appeared on *The Old Grey Whistle Test* – the band headed back into Bearsville Studios, with Howard still on bass, to begin their next album. By now Rundgren had wrested Utopia away from Bearsville – which retained him as a solo artist – and had secured a one-album deal for the group with Al Khoury's independent label, Network (not to be confused with Nettwerk Records).

Sulton recalls that when he eventually returned to Utopia, he found that the band had actually written and recorded several tracks for their Network debut, *Utopia*. "I finally begged, pleaded and cajoled my way back into the band," laughs Sulton, "and they had actually done some tracks with Doug Howard. But I finished the record, and I redid most of Doug's bass parts, although he may still be on some songs. What was interesting about that record was that we had a wealth of material for it, about an album and a half. That's why we said it had three sides."

Despite the rift in the band, which eventually healed, Sulton recalls a prolific time filled with seamless group collaborations and "happy accidents" which turned into songs. "A song like 'Call It What You Will' happened just like *that*," he says, snapping his fingers. "It was a real collaborative piece of music and everybody had a hand in it. Nobody took credit for anything, and even today I feel bad taking credit for any one particular piece of music in Utopia."

Utopia, technically the eighth album bearing the Utopia name (yet only the sixth to feature the long-running four-piece line-up), was released in August 1982.

Due to the label switch, it was their second (or second and a half) new Utopia album in five months. The light-hearted video that Rundgren directed for the single, 'Feet Don't Fail Me Now,' featured the band in cloth insect costumes superimposed on kitchen floors and sinks, and was 'new wave' enough to earn decent airplay on MTV. The rest of Utopia's year involved more touring, including a late November show at The Country Club, in Los Angeles, which was recorded for the first cable stereo simulcast, on the American USA Network television channel and over 120 radio stations across America. Selected audio portions of the show were also featured on a syndicated radio program, *The King Biscuit Flower Hour.*

Having fought with Bearsville over Utopia, Rundgren's next months as a solo artist with Bearsville would be his last. When the band wasn't working on the road, Rundgren withdrew to his Lake Hill sanctuary to work on "computer stuff" and track another solo album. He recalls taking a decidedly lackadaisical attitude towards the label as he roped together an atypically disjointed collection of songs for his tenth solo work, *The Ever Popular Tortured Artist Effect*, or *TEPTAE*, as it has become affectionately known to Rundgren fans.

Rundgren confirms that the title was a direct jab at Bearsville, whom he felt had largely given up on his "serious" album, *Healing*, the year before. "*The Ever Popular Tortured Artist Effect* was the album where I was my most 'just shuckin'.' I knew that the label was not taking, or promoting, my records seriously, so I thought, 'Why don't I do an album where I don't try as hard, and let's see if it makes any difference?' Thus the reference to a 'tortured artist.' I had to deliver an album, but I wasn't totally excited about the prospect."

Despite this devil-may-care attitude, his laid-back approach contributed to what is arguably his most unselfconsciously fun album in years. The styles Rundgren dabbled in on the record range from Nazz-ish power pop on his impassioned cover of The Small Faces' 'Tin Soldier,' to his most recent nod to Gilbert & Sullivan, 'Emperor Of The Highway.'

"With 'Tin Soldier,'" says Rundgren, "I was starting with a song I'd always loved ... I suppose it could have been tried on *Faithful*, but it was perfect for the mood I wanted for this."

Utopia Sound house engineer Chris Andersen recalls that his role on *TEPTAE* was not unlike the other records where Rundgren worked alone. "Typically, on the solo albums, I would set up the machine for him and make sure that everything was working right, then I'd just leave him alone. Then, about every week or five days or something, I would come back up to the studio and everything – all the synthesizers, all the microphones – would be on the floor and you couldn't walk through the control room. I would completely clean up the place and sort of reset everything and then he would keep going. He'd do all the vocals in the control room, on headphones. When he finally had mixes, I would sometimes sequence the album with him, and I would make all copies and deal with the project from then on."

Rundgren was now working heavily with the Linn Drum, augmented by live percussion here and there, for songs like 'Hideaway' and the prescient electro-disco of 'Chant,' both of which should have fitted in perfectly with the pop of the early 80s. Similarly, the *Hermit*-like numbers, such as 'Influenza,' 'There Goes Your Baybay,' and 'Don't Hurt Yourself,' would have surely pleased those disaffected fans yearning for the mid-tempo balladeer Rundgren of old. Yet, as it turned out, Rundgren's instincts were correct and these 'singles' never were, because Bearsville didn't release them as singles. In fact, the only near 'hit' from *TEPTAE*, 'Bang The Drum All Day,' created around a Linn kick and hi-hat program with a live snare drum, only caught on after it started to be played on the public address systems of various stadiums as a crowd-rouser at sporting events. Soon after, key radio stations began playing the song of their own volition. Rundgren laughs at the second life the song enjoyed, but says he'll take it.

"It may have turned out to be a 'cash cow' in the end," says Rundgren, "as a sports anthem and the like, for better or for worse. You don't want that to be the only thing people remember, but I suppose that's at least as good as a hit record. Still, it didn't come out contemporaneously with the album, and the label didn't release it as a single. I think they tried to put it out later, after radio started going with it. But by then, it was too late to fully capitalize on it. Still, I'm glad that it at least found some kind of life. 'Bang The Drum' was just a goofy song I dreamed and kind of captured pretty much verbatim as I dreamed it. For me, that album was just another self-fulfilling prophecy, you know? I didn't think the label would do a serious job of promoting me and they didn't."

Shortly after the album's release, in January 1983, Rundgren was commissioned by Channel Four in the UK to make a semi-autobiographical 90-minute special, also called *The Ever Popular Tortured Artist Effect*. It's Rundgren who used the term "semi-autobiographical," pointing out that the avant-garde, impressionistic film was in no way a literal interpretation of his life.

"I wouldn't make that close a connection to real life," he says. "The story in the *Ever Popular Tortured Artist Effect* video tried to tie events and songs from my history together in a way that made some degree of sense, but it wasn't necessarily biographically accurate."

Over the next year, Rundgren continued exploring computers and computer music. The Fairlight Computer Music Instrument had just been developed and Rundgren, naturally, took to it immediately. He also began doing film work in addition to more record productions. But before we go any further, however, let's go back to the previous spring for a deeper look at Rundgren's sessions with The Psychedelic Furs for their US breakthrough album, *Forever Now*.

17

The Psychedelic Furs *Forever Now*

"We're going to have a new producer next time," Richard Butler, singer for The Psychedelic Furs, told *Creem* writer John Mendelsohn in January 1982, "because there'd be no feeling of adventure in going in to do a third album with the same guy, using the same instruments. I've been listening to The Beatles a lot ... I'm keen to use cellos."

The Psychedelic Furs were formed five years earlier by Butler with his bassist brother Tim Butler, drummer Paul Wilson, sax player Duncan Kilburn, and guitarist Roger Morris. They had emerged on the London punk rock scene under various names before arriving at their final, misleadingly hippie-sounding moniker. After adding second guitarist John Ashton, and replacing Wilson with Vince Ely in 1979, the band made two fine records for Columbia: *The Psychedelic Furs* and 1981's *Talk Talk Talk*, both under the direction of hot new-wave producer Steve Lillywhite (XTC, Peter Gabriel).

Both were well received in alternative circles, but had barely dented the American charts. As the Furs toured the USA, internecine struggles within the band had resulted in the departures of Morris and Kilburn. Change was in the wind, and that wind was blowing in the direction of Lake Hill, New York, the home, and studio, of Todd Rundgren.

Richard Butler says that, while the band had appreciated Lillywhite, he and his bandmates were "very into the idea of stretching out a bit. We weren't necessarily looking for an 'American' producer, or anything like that, and there was really no pressure from Columbia to come up with a 'hit' producer."

"Sonically, we were just moving on," adds Tim Butler, "and getting more sophisticated in our arrangements, with these new songs written for cello and stuff. We definitely wanted a producer who could work well with strings."

Drummer Vince Ely had long been a fan of Todd Rundgren's work, both as an artist and as a producer, and felt that his experimental flair might appeal to the Furs. His bandmates, however, had their own candidates in mind for the job. "As I recall," he says, "John Ashton fancied bringing in Bill Nelson, out of Be Bop Deluxe, while Richard and Tim would have gone for David Bowie. Somehow, I convinced them to go with Todd."

Richard Butler says he had been impressed with how thoroughly Rundgren had adopted The Beatles' stylistic palette on both the *Faithful* album and Utopia's *Deface The Music*. "Vince was a huge fan," says Butler, "and he really convinced us that Todd might be a good direction to go in. And we figured Todd would probably be able to translate all of our 'strings' ideas better than most. Of course, that turned out to be exactly right."

Tim Butler recalls that, whereas the producer's work with such icons of cool as The New York Dolls and The Patti Smith Group strongly recommended him, there was controversy within the Furs over the fact that Rundgren had also produced Meat Loaf's less trendy *Bat Out Of Hell*. "There may have been some argument over that one," laughs Butler, "but I guess the Dolls and Patti Smith side won out."

Since the Furs were already touring in the Eastern USA at the time, they arranged to have their tour bus make a detour up Mink Hollow Road so they could meet Rundgren face to face. "So one drunken afternoon," Richard Butler recalls, "we got off the bus, exchanged greetings, looked around the place and then carried on that tour until late March, when it was time to go back to Utopia Sound to record."

Twenty-seven years after *Forever Now*, Todd Rundgren recalls that The Psychedelic Furs had come to him, like so many bands he worked with, during a transitional period. "It's funny," says Rundgren. "In some ways, this makes it easier for me in that they don't have some pre-set template that we have to work from. The Furs had undergone this radical personnel change – their sax player and keyboard player were both out of the group – so now they were a bit more stripped-down and open to a different sound that was not so dependent on the sax."

Both Butler brothers recall that, while they had extensively demoed the songs, they were still keen to avail themselves of Rundgren's celebrated arranging skills. Richard jokes that Rundgren's greatest assets were his ability to organize the band's wild ambitions and translate them into focused execution. "A lot of the record was already in our design," says Butler, "but Todd got to make a few changes, here and there, and he did the horn arrangements. And Todd really focused on John Ashton's guitar overdubs."

"On our first two albums," adds Tim, "Steve Lillywhite would let John do around six tracks of guitar and then comp the parts during the mixdown. But Todd wasn't having it, and told John to just figure out a part, then go in there and play it, on one or maybe two tracks."

Butler says that when the Furs returned to Utopia Sound, in late March, Rundgren was scrambling to finish another project, and instructed them to make themselves at home and get to know the neighbourhood. "Todd said he'd be done in a few days," remembers Tim Butler, "which stretched on a few more days. We took the time to rehearse, mostly, but we used to go down into the town of Woodstock and sort of carouse around, getting drunk and stuff. You'd drive into town and there'd be all sorts of head shops and bead stores, even though the actual Woodstock festival had been miles down the road, in Bethel. We used to drink down at the Tinker Street Café, and I seem to remember they had a guitar up on a shelf that was meant to be Bob Dylan's."

According to Rundgren, once he and the Furs actually commenced recording, on March 29, he became dismayed at what he felt was their undisciplined approach. "I think they were used to being in a more urban environment," says Rundgren, "so they'd wake up, go into town, drink too much and then show up at the session around one in the afternoon, already drunk. After a couple of days, I said, 'You know, we're not really accomplishing anything here, so let's do the drinking after the session.' After that, I think they finally settled down and started to get productive."

"Well, we were a bunch of English hooligans at that point," Richard Butler says, laughing. "Todd pulled us aside and said, 'Look guys, you need to take better care of yourselves. You don't want to find yourself wrapped around a tree halfway up Mink Hollow Road!'"

"He said we could either do a great album," adds Tim Butler, "or one of us could end up dead on the road and there wouldn't be any album.' Then he told us horror stories of other bands he'd worked with – I won't say who – but it straightened us up enough to turn the album out."

"A lot of their whole thing was this 'punky attitude' they'd adopted," Rundgren observes. "Attitude is fine if you put it in the music, but there was nowhere to go with that in the studio. It only took a couple days for everyone to settle down into something more serious."

Vince Ely somewhat defends the band's youthful indiscretions and chalks it up inexperience. "Give us a break," says Ely, laughing. "We'd only done two albums, none of us had been playing very long and we weren't very confident. Sure we liked to go to a party, you know? Really, though, we were just excited to be in America, and there wasn't much else to do up in old Woodstock other than misbehave, you know?"

Chris Andersen, who assisted Rundgren with engineering and managed a lot of the accounting for Utopia Sound recalls the aftermath of the Furs' time there. "They would come back from town," says Andersen, "and there'd be actual fistfights in the studio between the band-members. After the project was over, there was over $400 worth of repairs needed to the guesthouse."

As they settled down to work, Richard Butler remembers his apprehension about what they were in for with Rundgren who, rightly or not, had already earned reputation for being a heavy-handed control freak. "I had heard things," says Butler, "about Todd being controlling or ghosting different overdubbed parts over your tracks when you weren't around and stuff. But I didn't find any of that to be remotely true. In fact, I found him to be very open and transparent about everything."

"By time we went in," adds brother Tim, "we'd done our homework, so Todd didn't need to add a lot. Richard's lyrics were all pretty much written, so Todd wouldn't need to get involved there either. And Richard would have just have told him to get lost if he did!"

Ultimately, both Butler brothers found Rundgren to be on the same 'wavelength' as the group. "We'd heard some of his stuff," says Tim Butler, "like his remake of 'Good Vibrations,' so we thought 'Wow, we're gonna get more into some psychedelic things.' Todd's a very, very talented guy but he's also really out there, in a good way. The word 'genius' is really bandied around a lot but I think Todd really is a bit of a musical genius. He can either help you get the best out of yourself, and get what you want, or else he can perform it himself."

Among the credits for *Forever Now* is a thank you to "the man on the stairs," an oblique reference to Rundgren, who hovered above them in the loft control room at Utopia Sound. "Between takes," recalls Tim Butler, "he'd come halfway down the stairs or all the way down the stairs and give us comments; the distance depended on how much he had to tell us. So we kept thinking of him as 'the man on the stairs.'"

Andersen remembers that Richard Butler professed to be more comfortable singing at night, but Rundgren didn't like to work late. A compromise was arranged to provide Butler with total darkness and simulate evening by blacking out all the windows on the vocal booth. "I taped up a little flashlight," says Andersen, "and we gave him this unplugged SM57, purely as a prop, while we actually recorded him on a U87. He was convinced that he was hanging onto this streetlamp in New Orleans in the middle of the night when it was actually two in the afternoon."

As a result, Butler says he rarely saw the man on stairs while he was tracking his vocals. "I never knew what Todd was doing while I was singing," says Butler. "He was way up there, in the control room, so he couldn't see me either."

Rundgren says he admired Butler's live stage manner, which had reminded him, physically and musically, of David Bowie. He did, however, make a few suggestions about toning down his "raspy vocal thing," for some songs, most notably on the single, 'Love My Way.' "I had typically adopted this fairly aggressive sounding, ironic, and sarcastic hoarse tone in my voice," says Butler, laughing. "Well, Todd listened to the tape and said, 'Richard, I think this song could be a single, so we ought to approach the vocal in a softer way.' He suggested I lay back a bit on the vocals and make it a little more tuneful. And so we did. Up to then, we hadn't really considered that song as a single or anything. We didn't really think in those terms."

Vince Ely says that the whole band was impressed with Rundgren's swift pace in the studio. "He just arrived at a sound so rapidly," says Ely. "When we'd done the first two albums with Steve [Lillywhite] in London, I just remember sitting there, twiddling my thumbs, waiting. Any spontaneous ideas just got crushed. With Todd, on the other hand, it was rapid-fire record making. Todd was just such a great engineer, and of course, Chris Andersen was terrific, too."

Guitar always played a major role in songs like the title track and the ambitiously political, and vaguely metallic, 'President Gas.' Richard Butler, however, insists that any similarity to heavy metal was purely accidental. "For me," says Butler, "'President Gas' is more like Stravinsky's *The Rite Of Spring*, with all the powerful, grinding cellos. I really wanted that sound on the track, so we had [cellist] Ann Sheldon scraping throughout the whole song, pretty much."

Vince Ely, who says he tried hard to extend his "rhythmic vocabulary" on *Forever Now*, notes that, to this day, other drummers come up to him and ask about his drum patterns, including a particularly notable part on 'Love My Way.' "I do this fill coming out of the chorus and into the verse," he says, "where I just thought it would be nice to come down on a different beat than someone might usually come down. I don't think there's one track on the whole album, though, where the beats are 'exactly' the same. In most cases, I've changed the kick drum, or some aspect, to make them all slightly different. I also looked for sections where I could play nothing at all, such as on 'President Gas,' where I leave a gap for those cellos and it just changes the feel of the song. The guitars or the cellos can take up the rhythmic focus. Then, when I come back in, it feels more like a crescendo or something."

Midway through the sessions, however, Ely announced that he was to leave The Psychedelic Furs – upon completion of his drumming duties – to pursue an unspecified "outside opportunity." While working with Rundgren had no doubt enticed him to stick it out, Ely had said he found the working atmosphere within the band untenable at the time. There were, however, certain medical reasons behind his departure, including a case of Temporomandibular Joint Disorder or TMJ – a chronic inflammation of the joint between jawbone and skull – that Ely has never disclosed until now.

"I loved traveling," he says. "I just didn't particularly like touring with *them* at that point. I always kept my end up on the road, but it just wasn't working in the band for me. And there was also the fact that, during my last tour with the Furs, I had suffered from a severe case of TMJ, the cause of which was having undergone root canal work two days before traveling to the States from the UK for the start of the tour. I was not familiar with the term at the time and didn't know what on earth was happening with me. Everyone, apart from the specialists, was under the impression that I had nothing more than a headache. The pain was severe, to say the least, and I could not eat solids as my jaw was locked. Any free time on that tour was spent seeking out doctors, dentists, therapists, and the like for a solution to the problem."

Rundgren recalls Ely announcing his plans but assuring him that he would finish the job at hand. "It was probably a good thing," Rundgren notes, "that everybody knew, during the course of the record, that he was already leaving. That cleared the air and any interpersonal band issues were moot, which made it easier to get through it."

One particularly rough spot in the sessions occurred during the tracking of the song 'Aeroplane,' when John Ashton became frustrated with Rundgren over the guitar sounds he was getting. "Sometimes, John got extremely upset at my inability – or even the collective inability of the group – to see what he was going for," says Rundgren. "He was all about that 'guitar textures' thing, where it wasn't so much about 'what' you play as the kind of hazy texture of it. He practically came to tears at one point, because the sound I was getting was so far away from what he wanted. It seemed entirely subjective to me because there was probably very little that we would have needed to do to get it to how he wanted it. But he was very particular about those things."

Butler says that 'Aeroplane' – left off the album's 1982 release – was one of the weaker songs they recorded for the album. He blames a faulty synthesizer sequencer, borrowed from Roger Powell, which ruined the basic track; even with subsequent overdubs, the song never recovered. Asked today about the sequencer issues, Powell allows that Butler's story is entirely plausible, adding that synthesizer sequencers were still fairly unreliable in 1982: "I think we may have used one of my Moog step sequencers, the same stuff we'd used on the second side of *Initiation*. In those days, you had to print 16th-note clicks on a tape track and use special gear to read back and convert to voltage trigger pulses."

While The Furs no longer had a full-time horn player in the group, the band's Roxy Music influences frequently pointed to saxophone as a tonal color. As Chris Andersen pulled out his Rolodex to find local horn players, Rundgren pulled out his own saxophone and played the sax solo on 'No Easy Street' himself. "Todd and I did a bunch of tracking without the band even there," Andersen says, "and it took about 50 takes until he finally got one that he liked. I also brought in [sax player] Gary Windo, who had played with Pink Floyd. And since I had done a lot of work with [Bearsville Recording artists] NRBQ over the years, I called Terry Adams's brother, Donn Adams, from the Whole Wheat Horns, to play trombone." ("Apparently, they liked Gary so much that he ended up touring with them for a while after the album was done," Rundgren adds.)

While most everything on the *Forever Now* album had been written and demoed well before the sessions, the dreamy, Beatlesque 'Sleep Comes Down' was created, almost by chance, during the pre-album rehearsals in Lake Hill. "We rehearsed in this garage off Todd's guesthouse," Ely recalls, "and Tim and I were in there reasonably late one night, jamming. I had this rather simplistic drum beat and Tim was playing this very lilting bass thing over it."

"Well, I'd actually worked up the bass riff that night" adds Tim Butler, "based on something I'd been noodling with at sound checks on the Talk Talk Talk tour."

"Richard overheard it in his bed," says Ely, "and just sort of came down from his sleep, and then came up with the words for it. So I think the name 'Sleep Comes Down' comes from the fact that I think Rich was in his bedroom, trying to sleep, when he heard us down there playing that riff. In my opinion, when Richard added his bit, it really became quite a nice song."

"I just started plonkin' around on the piano," adds Richard Butler, "and we came up with the rest of the song right there in the studio."

Rundgren later suggested a Beatlesque orchestral rise for the outro section.

"That 'I Am The Walrus' type ending," says Tim Butler, still impressed, "the cellos and all that, was all Todd's idea. He was so 'musical.'"

Rundgren's methods, the bass player adds, sometimes strayed from the musical to the mischievous. "We were running through stuff in the studio," Butler recalls, "and I guess we were sort of playing a little sluggishly, you know? Well, Todd climbed out onto the studio roof and put firecrackers down the chimney, which opened out into the studio. That woke us up!"

"We all ran out to see what the hell was going on," adds Ely, "and there was Todd out on the studio roof! We were probably still a bit jet-lagged so he felt he had to motivate us somehow."

'Love My Way,' the first single from *Forever Now*, would become the proverbial firecracker that would motivate mainstream American to notice The Psychedelic Furs. A poppier departure from the band's earlier drones and dirges, the song featured some of the most Rundgrenesque touches on the record. From the bright and bouncy marimba hook – played by Rundgren himself – to the preening falsetto backing harmonies, evocative of T. Rex. Initially Richard Butler's idea, the marimba part was inspired by the instrumental hook from Orchestral Manoeuvres In The Dark's 'Souvenir,' although Rundgren strongly urged the band to employ genuine marimbas in lieu of the synthesizer patch they had used on their demo.

"Todd was quite adamant about it," says Butler, "but we were concerned that we'd have to get a marimba player all the way up to Woodstock to play them. I think we just said, 'Why don't you do it.' He said, 'Sure, I can play that!' So he went away and came back with this set of old marimbas, dusted them off, and played it himself."

Additionally, Rundgren recalls adding various other keyboard textures, here and there "Somebody would pick out these melodies on the keyboard, but, as simple as they were, they were maybe beyond the technical proficiency of anyone in the band, because they weren't keyboard players, so I had to play it. There was a piano on 'Sleep Comes Down,' and as I recall that was all Richard had, that little line, and the rest of it is a lot of pedaling. But that's the kind of thing that happens when you're making a record; you do whatever works to get it done."

Rundgren's most radical suggestion for the sessions was to bring in the singing duo of Howard Kaylan and Mark Volman, formerly of The Turtles, also known as Flo & Eddie. Rundgren had been a friend and fan of the team and felt that he might at last have a good excuse to have them lend their distinctive vocalizations to the Furs' ever-widening sonic tableau.

"It was late in the process," says Rundgren, "and I think we thought we were already done, but something was missing. I always loved those high-pitched textural things they had done on those T. Rex albums and, for quite a while, I had wanted to try this idea of using background voices as instrumental effect, where you were not supposed to hear them necessarily as voices, just part of a sound. But first, I remember, I had to sort of 'sell them' to the Furs."

Kaylan recalls getting the phone call from Rundgren about "this British band" that he felt might benefit from their vocalese. "Todd called me," Kaylan remembers, "and said, 'I'm hearing you guys singing on this.' This was over the holidays, so we were down in Manhattan, in from Los Angeles to do our annual Holiday shows at the Bottom Line. I think we were happy to make the trip up to Bearsville for Todd. I think the Furs, however, saw it as a radical idea to have us in at all."

Tim Butler recalls that his brother Richard was particularly dubious about having The Turtles, famous for the poppy 60s hit 'Happy Together,' on a Psychedelic Furs record. "Richard wasn't having it," Butler recalls. "He was like, 'Are you kidding us?' But Todd just said, 'We want them to sound like just another strange sounding instrument, like a keyboard.' And true enough, the backing vocals were fairly strange, they're not like normal backing vocals."

"I think," adds Rundgren, "I also made a point about Flo & Eddie's contributions to all those classic T.Rex records, like 'Metal Guru,' where they're singing really super-high and doing lots of that background kind of stuff. Since none of the guys in the band would really have the responsibility of singing [those parts] why not bring in these guys from the T. Rex sessions? I couldn't say 'Turtles' to the Furs, so I also made the point that they'd worked with Frank Zappa. That seemed to calm them down."

Kaylan felt that, before he and Volman arrived, the band had assumed that all tracking for the album was completed. "So you've got both Butler brothers," Kaylan recalls, "glaring over at Todd and saying 'Who the fuck are these old fucks from The Turtles?' We were anti-everything that they were going for. It was funny that our Zappa connection gave us 'street cred.' All of a sudden, they saw us as 'underground' figures. 'Hey, these guys are hip.'"

"Flo & Eddie were hilarious to work with," recalls Chris Andersen, "and they were telling us all these great stories about people they'd worked with. I actually recorded some of the headphone mix on a cassette, when they were adding voices to 'Sleep Comes Down.'"

"Frankly," says Richard Butler, "if you'd asked me then who 'Flo & Eddie' were, I wouldn't have had any idea. But since we very rarely had any backing vocals at all, I was concerned that it might be a bit too 'polished.' Todd said, 'Trust me on this. They're like singing machines. I promise that if you don't like it, we'll take it off.'"

Kaylan recalls that Rundgren had a specific vision for their vocal parts. "We worked them out and performed them, and he played it back for the band so they were able to see how we fit into the spectrum of sound, overall. Our voices just became part of the wall. One might have argued that the band didn't need more male voices, but in fact we were kind of doing more female-like parts, like on the T. Rex records. After we had done about four of five cuts, the band could hear that it was working and gradually came around."

Kaylan remembers one critical moment, just as he and Volman were getting ready to leave. "We had done about four or five songs," says Kaylan, "and we were done, heading out the door of the control room. I had my jacket on, and Mark had his car keys in his hand and Todd said, 'Before you guys drive back down to Manhattan, do you wanna hear the single?' So he rolls the tape of 'Love My Way,' which we hadn't sung on yet, for some reason. As we listened, Mark and I just sort of looked at each other and said, 'Hey Todd, do you know what this song needs? Us!' He seemed curious, stared us and said, 'Really?'

"So we took off our coats, went back out there, put on the headphones and sang exactly what we would have done had this been a Marc Bolan record. All those high, sustained, angelic voices, sort of made the thing 'celestial.' We tried one take in the studio, and Todd went, 'Holy fuck, this is gonna work!' So we did a few more takes, layering ourselves, I think, about four times. We played it back, I think it was the first time that he lifted the levels on the marimba loud enough that I could hear the juxtaposition of that instrument with the voices and it was unbe-fucking-lievable! I swear to God, when I hear that single today, I'll crank it in the car every time it comes on. It was an amazing sonic experience for us."

"I remember when were listening back to it," says Tim Butler, "we all agreed that Todd was right to bring 'em in; they were great. John was even more excited than I was about the T. Rex connection, because he was a huge Marc Bolan fan."

Rundgren's strict rule about keeping the band out of the mix sessions naturally rankled with some of the Furs at the time. But Richard Butler says he can see the wisdom of the closed-door policy. "On the previous two records we'd made," he recalls, "we'd all been part of the mixing process. And since we were such an argumentative bunch, it would take forever. Todd was so quick with the mixes, anyway. In less than an hour he'd call us in to listen to a mix he had done. He'd say, 'If there's anything you don't like about it, I'll change it.' And he honored that promise. It was always small stuff like turning the marimba up a bit louder or something or other. But seeing as we'd all been hearing the tracks build as we'd been doing the vocals and other overdubs, there was never anything that radical."

Forever Now was released by Columbia Records worldwide on September 25 1982 and gained wide critical acceptance in the UK and commercial inroads in the USA, where it rose to number 61 on the *Billboard* album charts. 'Love My Way' was a popular radio song, getting into the top 30 on *Billboard*'s Mainstream Rock Tracks chart and to Number 44 on their Hot 100 Pop Singles chart. *CMJ*, the American college radio magazine, ranked the album as Number 16 in their Top 20 Most-Played Albums of 1983.

The record also placed The Psychedelic Furs, for better or worse, into the vanguard of the first wave of video stars. They took full advantage of the newly launched MTV channel with a clip featuring the band miming the song in a shallow pool of water, with mercifully unplugged guitars and a set of marimbas in place of a drum kit.

Vince Ely, now living in Spain, looks back on *Forever Now* as the moment when The Psychedelic Furs began to mature into a world-class act, and he credits Rundgren for helping the band focus their potential. "Todd saw it through and finished it just the way he said he would," says Ely. "Surely, that's the job of a producer? To make things better and more cohesive, as he did with us. Mind you, he's got that sarcastic side too. He could hurt you if he needed to, but he's done well in his production career, and he's always chosen something more eclectic, hasn't he? I think he's always gone more for the hard option and he's been successful, whether it's been commercial or not."

In the end, both of the Butler brothers say that the band got what they wanted, and more, from their spring trip to Utopia Sound. "I remember getting back to London with the record under my arm," says Richard Butler, "and dragging people home from the pub to listen to it and being incredibly proud of it. We'd extended our sound, with Todd's help, advice, and additions, into something quite different from what our first two records had been. I was absolutely thrilled by it. So really, it was a great experience."

That may be so, laughs Todd Rundgren, who, as is his wont, throws a little cold pragmatism on this love-fest by asking, half-jokingly, if the Furs loved him so much, then how come they never called him to do a sequel? "You would have thought," says Rundgren, "that with the success of *Forever Now* and 'Love My Way,' they would have wanted to continue on that course. Still, there was no animus, as I recall; they just decided to move on to something else."

"You know," adds Tim Butler, "after the *Forever Now* album tour, Rich and I started living in New York and our next album, *Mirror Moves*, was even more influenced by America, even though we used a British producer, Keith Forsey. But all of that began with *Forever Now*, which I think of as the perfect Furs album. Todd was simply the best producer we ever worked with."

18

Cheap Trick
Next Position Please

In January 1983, Bearsville Records issued Todd Rundgren's tenth solo album, *The Ever Popular Tortured Artist Effect.* While Rundgren did a few scattered solo shows and select Utopia dates, most of his year was spent holed up in Utopia Sound, concentrating on production work. That month, in addition to producing *Watch Dog* for songwriter Jules Shear, Rundgren oversaw a two-day session with Stiv Bators's post-Dead Boys band, Lords Of The New Church, producing the single 'Live For Today.' Then, in March, he teamed up with Cheap Trick, the pride of Rockford, Illinois, for what would become *Next Position Please.*

Cheap Trick guitarist Rick Nielsen had first introduced himself to Rundgren as far back as 1969, in London's Marquee Club, while attending an early show by the progressive rock group Yes. "I thought the first Nazz record was really cool," Nielsen recalls, "and suddenly I'm sitting right next to Todd. I asked him about the Nazz and he told me they'd just broken up. I asked him how I could contact Mooney and Stewkey when I got back to the States, because I was actually looking for guys to play in my band. I asked him about their drummer, Thom Mooney. Todd said, 'He lives with his mother in Altoona, Pennsylvania.' So I said 'Oh cool. And what about Stewkey, you know that frail tiny little singer?' He says, 'He lives in Texas but whatever you do don't call him!' and I said, 'Well, how can I get in touch with you?' He said, 'I live with this guy named Paul Fishkin in New York.' He gave me his phone number and address."

Completely disregarding Rundgren's advice, Nielsen contacted the two ex-Nazz players and convinced them to join his band. They played a few shows, sometimes billed as Nazz and other times as The Grim Reapers. After Mooney left, Nielsen got in touch with Rockford-based drummer Brad Carlson, whom everyone knew by his stage name, Bun E. Carlos. Carlos joined Nielsen, Stewkey, and Tom Petersson, now trading as Sick Men Of Europe, until Stewkey left and the three enlisted singer Robin Zander, changing their name to Cheap Trick. Over time, the four-piece honed and perfected their Midwestern rock sound, which subtly blended crunchy rock guitars, four-on-the-floor backbeats and Beatlesque harmonies. After Aerosmith's producer Jack Douglas tipped the band to A&R man Tom Werman, they signed with Epic Records, which released Cheap Trick's self-titled debut, produced by Werman, in 1977. After another Werman-produced album, *In Color*, released later that year, the band and Werman followed up with the 1978 album, *Heaven Tonight*, which barely nudged into the *Billboard* Top 100, despite its infectious single, 'Surrender.'

In April of 1978, the band recorded a series of ecstatically received concerts at Tokyo's Nippon Budokan, which were subsequently released, in February of the following year, as the groundbreaking double-live album, *Cheap Trick At Budokan*. But by then, according to Bun E. Carlos, the band had grown to dislike Werman's production style. After a fourth studio album, *Dream Police*, they were ready to move on. "We'd done three albums with him," says Carlos, "and we fought a lot during *Dream Police*, but the label insisted we use Werman on every record. We were like, 'No, we don't like his production, we don't like his sounds.' Then the record company screwed with us and there were a few lawsuits going on."

Two years of big-name producer-hopping, from 1980's *All Shook Up*, with George Martin, to 1982's *One On One*, with Roy Thomas Baker, had failed to return the band to their Gold record Budokan heights. The bad blood between the band and CBS began to take its toll. As they prepared for their next album, Cheap Trick longed just to have fun in the studio again. "We were looking for a producer we felt comfortable with," says Carlos, "who would also be up to our standards. We'd worked with Jack Douglas (on *Budokan*), George Martin, and Roy Thomas Baker, you know? We wanted classic killer producers."

According to Nielsen, it finally occurred to them that Todd Rundgren, a peer and fellow guitar player who had also produced hit records, might be perfect for their next album. At very least, they figured, it might be fun. "I always thought," says Nielsen, "that Todd's production on Grand Funk's 'The Loco-motion' was one of the best sounding records of all time. And those early Nazz records sounded great, too, so we figured he's gotta be good."

Rundgren says that, knowing Cheap Trick, he was confident that they would have great material. "That's why it was such an easy call," says Rundgren. "My priority as a producer, first of all, is the material. Show me the music and then, of course, show me the money!" he laughs. "It's entirely down to songs, though."

"Epic Records was only concerned with hearing the 'hit single' on the record," Carlos adds, dismissively, "and they knew that Todd had actually produced hit singles so they weren't too concerned about him as our choice. That opinion changed later on, of course."

The band sent a demo tape to Rundgren containing around five songs. Some, such as 'I Don't Love Here Anymore,' were leftovers from the *One On One* material, which they had demoed back at Pierce Arrow Studio, in Evanston, Illinois. According to Carlos, Robin Zander's anthemic 'I Can't Take It,' which would become the album's energetic opener, was also among them. "It wasn't quite there yet," says Carlos. "The parts weren't all concrete, but we felt that it was ready and it was our idea of the single. Robin had also written 'Younger Girls' in like '75 or '76. We used to play that out live, so we also put that on the record."

Next Position Please was one of only a few Cheap Trick recordings not to feature bass player Tom Petersson; in his absence, the band employed Jon Brant. While refusing to elaborate, Nielsen will only joke, cryptically, that his good friend was temporarily out of the group "for medical reasons – he made us sick at the time." (He adds that being sequestered at Rundgren's woodland retreat in Lake Hill took the edge off what could have been a difficult time in their career.)

"It was great being up there in Mink Hollow," says Nielsen. "Every day all you could do was record, but we kept regular working hours, from around 11:30am to around 6 or 7pm. Then it was TV time and Todd would stop and go up to his house to watch the news. I'm a bit of news junkie myself so I loved it."

"Oh yeah," adds Carlos, "We were up on Cripple Creek there, in the Catskills, in that crappy little dumpy old farmhouse then we'd go up the hill and record at Todd's tiny A-frame studio."

Sometimes, Nielsen admits, cabin fever would set in. The band spent a few evenings in the town of Woodstock, "getting into trouble and hanging out with all the locals" at the Little Bear or the Big Bear. "But during the day," he adds, in a rare moment of seriousness, "it was great having a producer who can play everything, do everything, write songs and who actually liked our songwriting and us as people. I'd like to think Todd had fun doing that record, too."

During the sessions, Carlos was introduced to Rundgren's new favorite toy, the Linn Drum, and recalls the process of playing live drums to Rundgren's programmed beats. "Todd and Chris Andersen were big into the Linn thing back then. It was the 'latest and the greatest,' you know? I tried to learn to use it ... but that lasted about ten minutes."

With a keen memory for drums, Carlos describes his kit for the session: a Ludwig four-ply drumset, with white pearl finish, a 24-inch bass drum and 12, 13, 16, and 18-inch tom toms. He used 14-inch Zildjian hi-hats, a 17-inch medium crash, and an 18-inch crash, plus 20-inch ride cymbals. "I used a five-inch wooden snare drum," he adds, "although I probably brought a brass snare drum up there too."

While unconvinced by the Linn Drum, Carlos admits that the metronomic quality of the machine made it easier to play along with. "You could program in a snare, a bass drum, and a hi-hat and it would feel just like playing along with another drummer. You can really hear it on the 'hand claps' on 'Heaven's Falling.' At that time, that idea was brand new, so I was keen to give it a try, you know? 'Sure Todd, whatever you think!'"

Nielsen and Carlos both say that Chris Andersen played a "significant role" on the record. "Chris was one of the best engineers we worked with," says Carlos, "before or since. We could have made 80 to 90 per cent of this record with just Chris, you know? Obviously, Todd was running the show and was there to give it the Todd Rundgren Magic, but Chris was right there and ready to dial in a lot of the sounds, hand in hand, with Todd."

"There was just a great vibe in the studio," says Andersen, "and a genuine camaraderie between Todd and the band. Everything was fantastic, and I had the utmost respect for Robin, who was the consummate professional vocalist. He would go down, sing a vocal or two, then he'd come up [to the loft control room] and we'd go through the lyric sheet, line by line, and he'd underline all the parts he wanted to go back and redo. Then he'd go back down and we'd punch those things in. He was always friendly, very straightforward."

"Todd having Chris there, to do all the dirty work, made sense," adds Nielsen. "Any good producer always has a better engineer. Todd was a pretty terrific engineer himself."

According to Andersen, Rundgren used the Scholz Rockman for practically all guitar sounds. The small amplifier-simulator box had only recently been invented and marketed by guitarist/engineer Tom Scholz, leader of the group Boston. According to Carlos, both Nielsen and Rundgren were thrilled, at the time, by the new technology. "No more fucking around with guitar sounds," says Carlos, "if you'll pardon my French. It's like a compressor and a flange and all this other stuff built into one little box. You'd just dial up 'Setting number nine on the Rockman.' God, that Rockman was used on every track for all the guitar stuff. I remember hearing Robin play a bit of direct guitar at the start of 'Younger Girls' and thinking, 'Boy we're making a real dry record here.'"

Rundgren admits that he liked to record guitars and drums "nice and dry ... That way, I can essentially do anything I want to the sound, afterward in the mix. I also like to get a lot of isolation so that I can really amp up the snare and the toms. That sound, from both the Rockman and the Linn Drum, probably date the record somewhat."

While the group backing-vocals on *Next Position Please* seem to have certain Rundgrenesque flourishes, neither Carlos, nor Rundgren himself, can recall if he actually sang on it. "I suppose it's conceivable," says Carlos, "that he could have hopped down to do background vocals. I just don't recall it happening. We usually didn't need any help with the voices, because Robin and Rick would do all of that stuff. Although Jon Brant didn't do any backgrounds, so maybe Todd felt it necessary to fill in. I don't ever sing, though. As a rule, drummers look bad singing unless their names are Don: Henley or Brewer."

Nielsen says he had a hard time getting Rundgren to come down from the loft to trade guitar solos with him on the upbeat and energetic track, '3-D.' "If you've got Todd producing you," figured Nielsen, "you gotta get him to play a guitar, right? So that's him doing all that flanging and sweeping guitar solo stuff."

"I remembers we cut '3-D' in three pieces," says Carlos. "We cut the front end in one piece, the middle in another piece and everything after the solo is the third piece. There were all these rhythm changes in the middle like a 3/4 part or something, which was kind of odd. So Todd just looked up and said, 'We should just do it in parts.' He's the boss, so we said, 'Sure.'"

Nielsen's 'Borderline' could have been a Roy Orbison tribute, although Nielsen says he never considered it anything more than a good song. "I'm a songwriter and Todd's a songwriter," he says, "so we wanted to do some good stuff with him."

While Rundgren was happy with the material Cheap Trick brought in to the sessions, they nonetheless leaned on him to submit a song of his own for the album. "There was kind of this tradition," Carlos laughs, "where, if you cut a record with Todd, he would write you a song." Ever accommodating, Rundgren gave them a fast-paced, power-pop tune called 'Heaven's Falling.' A bright guitar rocker with an insistent machine tempo and ganged-up vocal harmonies, it was the kind of song Nazz might have done if they'd made it to era of the Rockman and Linn Drum.

"I had recorded the basic track for one of my own things," says Rundgren. "I think I submitted it for a film or something. I had the song all demoed before, so it wasn't *exactly* written for Cheap Trick."

Alan Robinson's liner notes for the 2007 Acadia re-issue of *Next Position Please* state that Rundgren had attempted to write the song in the mode of Def Leppard, in the same manner in which he had written Utopia's 'The Very Last Time' based on Boston's 'More Than A Feeling.' "Def Leppard was defining what heavy metal was, on the radio," Rundgren told Robinson, "so ... I wrote that to kind of fit in with that type of thing."

Carlos recalls the first time they heard the track, which Rundgren constructed while the band watched an NFL game on their Sunday day off. "After dinner," he remembers, "Todd goes off to work on the vocals. Then, at about 9 or 10 that night, he came in with this fully recorded demo. It could have gone on one of his records. Then, we went in and basically did a 'cover' version of his recording."

Rundgren can't recall exactly, but guesses that he probably played one or more of the guitars heard in the final mix. Nielsen appears to confirm Rundgren's guess. "I wouldn't use tones like that but that's what he does," he says. "And I think he'd kind of put the brighter main track down, that's him. I'm sure I probably played the same thing but you know the way he did it is cleaner and smoother then I would ever, or could ever, do it."

Carlos recalls begging Rundgren to show him 'The Fool,' the Gibson SG formerly owned by Eric Clapton. Shortly afterward, perhaps inspired by seeing the Clapton guitar, the members of Cheap Trick spontaneously set about recording a medley of songs by Clapton's former group, The Yardbirds. "Todd wasn't even in on this," says Carlos. "He was up at his house programming, so I went up to the studio with Chris, and Rick and Jon, one night. We just started recording this five-minute Yardbirds medley, with a verse each from 'I'm A Man,' 'Shapes Of Things,' 'Heart Full Of Soul,' and 'For Your Love.' Chris kind of produced it, but we only got to do the instrumental tracks and never got the vocals done."

While the Yardbirds medley was never intended for the *Next Position Please* album, it was almost included after they innocently played it back for Epic's Bruce Harris. Once the proper album was finished and mixed by Rundgren, Harris had come up to Utopia Sound to preview the results. Neither the band nor Harris were thrilled with Rundgren's initial mixes. Despite their feelings about the mix, however, Nielsen says that he never felt any friction between Rundgren and the band. "We were a good hard working band," he says, "and we knew we were good, and yet it was important to know that we also knew Todd was really good, too. Having mutual respect is the best way to get something done; it doesn't mean you always agree with everything, like mixes or guitar sounds here and there, because we didn't."

But then, just for kicks, they rolled the Yardbirds medley for Harris. That, says Carlos, was when everything started to get weird. "They thought it the coolest thing they'd heard, but it wasn't even on the album. We were like, 'Oh boy, here it comes.'"

Rundgren says that Epic Records' response – that they didn't hear a 'hit single' – was "typical" for a label, but he nonetheless wondered how they could have missed a couple of likely candidates from the album. "I thought 'I Can't Take It' would have been a great single," he says. "The trouble was that Epic, I think, wanted some variation of their big smash, 'I Want You To Want Me.' We didn't have a song like that on the record, so they sent the band back to the studio."

According to Carlos, two of the songs they recorded at Utopia Sound, 'Twisted Heart' and 'Don't Hit Me With Love,' also known as 'Hit Me With Love,' were removed outright by Epic Records and the band were advised to record two alternate selections. "Todd had refused to record any more," says Carlos, "but only because he was standing up for the record we'd made. He actually threatened to go to New York and kill somebody, or whatever. He was screaming at them, 'No fucking way,' and all that. Our manager really didn't stand up for us at all. In fact, Todd stood up for us more then *we* did."

Epic talked the band into recording a cover of The Motors' 1977 UK hit 'Dancing The Night Away,' telling them that The Motors were enthusiastic Cheap Trick fans who claimed to have written the song in their honor. "Yeah, but if they really loved us," laughs Nielsen, "they wouldn't make us do this song. Epic kept bugging us, saying, 'Didn't you get the tape? The Motors, uh, didn't you hear it?' Yeah, we heard it, but we didn't want to do it. We just hated it. Todd refused to do it because he knew it was crummy, too. Still, when push came to shove, we ended up being forced to do it against our wishes."

Carlos says that the band returned to Pierce Arrow studios, with engineer Ian Taylor producing, and cut 'Dancing The Night Away' and Nielsen's 'You Say Jump,' "which we just hated because it was the bastard son of 'I Want You To Want Me' and a piece of pop fluff."

Next Position Please, with the two non-Rundgren tracks added, was released by Epic Records on August 15 1983, and climbed to Number 61 on the *Billboard* album charts, where it languished for 11 weeks before falling off completely. Despite the label's lofty intentions, 'Dancing The Night Away' didn't connect in an especially big way with the pop charts or the band's fanbase. Although disappointing, it was a minor vindication for Cheap Trick, and for Rundgren, who had been against it all along. Scrambling to correct their mistake, Epic relented and rushed out 'I Can't Take It,' as the second single, but it was already too late. "The video for 'I Can't Take It' was pretty horrible too," adds Nielsen, "but the song is still good and we still play it and the fans love it."

Summing up their experience, Carlos says that the band were happy to just hang out with Rundgren in an environment of mutual respect. "We all loved the same bands," says Carlos, "like The Yardbirds and the British Invasion stuff, and we all hung out with the same people, going all the way back to Philly, and the Nazz guys. After our album came out, Todd showed up at a gig in Poughkeepsie and did 'Heavens Falling' with us ... occasionally, there'd be an onstage jam at various gigs."

"Todd was the guy who I listened to when I was in high school," says Nielsen, "so we couldn't let him down. He's a players' player, and to have that as your producer raises the bar."

In his superb liner notes for the 1996 Epic/Legacy box set *Sex, America, Cheap Trick*, *Trouser Press* founding editor Ira Robbins praised Rundgren's production of *Next Position Please,* describing it as "a warm, tuneful record, which favors songs, vocals, and ensemble performances over instrumental spotlights or conspicuous technology."

Today, Robin Zander says that, while neither the record company nor the record buying public at large had much time for it in its day, *Next Position Please* nonetheless represents much of what he loves about Cheap Trick. "Thanks to Todd," says Zander, "we were able to finish in record time and under budget. Maybe the first single was wrong, but we gave it a good shot with great songs worthy of any 'best of' Cheap Trick album."

"It was probably the most pleasure we'd ever had making a record, at that point," says Carlos, in closing. "Todd was a kindred spirit."

19

Beyond Oblivion

In addition to the Cheap Trick record, Todd Rundgren's produced a wide range of recordings in his personal musical factory, Utopia Sound, during 1983. And while his enthusiasm level varied from project to project, manager Eric Gardner kept a steady flow of artists rolling up Mink Hollow Road to work with him.

"The way it worked," says house engineer Chris Andersen, "was, if Todd was less invested emotionally in a project, I'd do a lot of the day-to-day running of sessions and basic engineering. Todd would still be there, of course, listening for things and occasionally making suggestions and making all final production choices and the mixes. But I could run most of the sessions based on his vision for a project. That was actually an amazing thing about Todd, he always had a clear vision, from the outset, of how a song was supposed to sound. I got the impression that the recording process was really paint-by-numbers for him, and we were just filling in the colors."

Songwriter Jules Shear says he was unsure about working with Todd Rundgren on his album *Watch Dog*, recorded in January of 1983. "I really liked Todd as a guy, and as a musician," says Shear. "I mean, he obviously knows a lot about making records, but my only question was: Should he be 'my' producer? He didn't seem like a natural choice, actually, but Gary Gersh, my A&R guy at Capitol Records, really thought so. They had sent Todd demos of about 30 of my songs – which I had recorded with Stephen Hague, from my old band The Polar Bears – and Todd liked them. At that point, I wasn't used to working with producers, but I thought, 'It's Todd Rundgren, we'll give it a try.'"

While Shear ultimately enjoyed making the album, with a stellar backing band which included Hague on keyboards, King Crimson's Tony Levin on bass, Rick Marotta on drums, Elliott Easton from The Cars on guitar, and Rundgren on everything else, he recalls feeling the producer's attention drifting away at times. "When we came to parts of the process that he wasn't interested in," says Shear, "he just didn't do them, and you could tell that Todd just wanted to get the thing done. Like, when I was tracking a vocal, Todd wouldn't let me try another take unless I could come up with a compelling reason why."

Those complaints aside, Shear says the three weeks of sessions ran relatively smoothly, with no serious run-ins between him and Rundgren. "I made a deal, before we started, that it was Todd's production and I was strictly 'the artist.' And Todd didn't really change anything radically from what Stephen and I had planned. 'Longest Drink,' for example, was pretty close to the vibe we had on our demo, although Todd did add some things, like the sound of water going into a glass that he'd miked up."

The *Watch Dog* sessions produced the debut versions of some great Jules Shear originals, including 'Whispering Your Name,' later covered successfully by Alison Moyet, and 'All Through The Night,' which became a worldwide hit when recorded by Cyndi Lauper.

Meanwhile, back in the video realm, Rundgren put together the *Videosyncracy* compilation, featuring visual presentations for the songs 'Hideaway,' 'Time Heals,' and 'Can We Still Be Friends,' all of which would later be bonus material on the DVD release of his long-form video, *The Ever Popular Tortured Artist Effect.*

That year, Rundgren also mixed tracks for *Dancing For Mental Health*, a record produced and written by Lynn Goldsmith, his photographer friend and one time Grand Funk co-manager, who was working under the project name Will Powers. Besides Rundgren, the record featured contributions from Steve Winwood, Sting, Nile Rogers, and The Thompson Twins' Tom Bailey. 'Kissing With Confidence,' a Rundgren/Goldsmith co-write featuring vocals by an uncredited Carly Simon, found minor chart success in the UK.

In June, Rundgren co-produced *Party Of Two,* an EP for the Californian power pop band The Rubinoos, now reduced to founding duo Jon Rubin and Tommy Dunbar and backed by Utopia. "I co-produced The Rubinoos thing with the other guys in Utopia," says Rundgren, "who were willing to sit with them while they nit-picked the music to death. They were really anal about everything, especially vintage microphones, and they had a list of all these microphones they wanted to get. I actually found them a vintage Neumann U47, which was a pain in the ass, because you'd wait so long for the power supply to warm up. I think I only used it myself on the cover of *A Cappella*, as a prop."

In August, Rundgren found himself commuting from Lake Hill to Danbury, Connecticut, to work with Laura Nyro, a songwriter he had admired since the Nazz days and the subject of his Runt-era song, 'Baby Let's Swing.' A publishing deal had left Nyro independently wealthy, and by 1983 she had built a recording studio in her own home. After working with other producers for months on an album, she abruptly scrapped it and brought in Rundgren to start from scratch. The situation was fraught with problems for Rundgren, who eventually withdrew from the project. It was eventually released – without Rundgren's name on it – under the title *Mother's Spiritual.* Chris Andersen remembers how it all came together, and fell apart, for Rundgren. "She had spent a lot of money on new gear," he says, "like two brand-new Studer machines and an API console. She got Todd producing the tracks in Danbury, but it was just taking forever to get it done. She won't be rushed and it's her own studio so eventually Todd wanted to either get it finished or get out of the whole thing."

An exit strategy was negotiated and Rundgren left the project to Andersen to finish: "I think that by the time it was done," says Andersen, "it had gotten so homogenized that Todd didn't even want his name on it anymore."

As Utopia wrote and recorded the songs for their next album, *Oblivion*, later that year, they found themselves drawn to paranoid and apocalyptic themes, which seemed to make sense as 1984 – the year prophesied in Orwell's classic anti-authoritarian novel – approached. Orwell's spirit inhabits songs like 'Welcome To My Revolution' and 'Winston Smith Takes It On The Jaw' which directly namechecks *1984*'s protagonist. Musically, the record sounds 'of its era' with new wave sounds suggestive of The Cars and even the flanged metallic echoes of Def Leppard. 'Crybaby' was of a piece with 'Heaven's Falling,' Rundgren's song from the Cheap Trick record, while 'I Will Wait,' stands out as one of the more emotionally direct songs on the set. Once again, a new album meant a new label, and *Oblivion* was released on Passport Records, where Utopia would ride out the remainder of their recording career.

Utopia only toured for a few weeks in the spring in support of *Oblivion*, but while they were still selling out halls they were playing to smaller houses and making less money. Morale in the band was beginning to suffer and Rundgren was spending more time working on video, computer programming, and outside productions like John Sloman's *Disappearances Can Be Deceptive* in June, and a record for Irish band Zerra I in July.

Over the summer, after performing a few well-attended shows with Utopia, in Chicago, New York, Philadelphia, and Columbus, Rundgren finally pulled the plug on his capital-depleting Utopia Video Studios enterprise. The cost of setting up the video studio was enormous in itself, but Rundgren soon found the monthly bills for routine maintenance and staff too draining on his depleted finances. He found himself constantly working on other jobs, and taking gigs he wasn't entirely keen on, just to support his video habit. So it had to go.

At the end of August, Rundgren returned to music production, flying out to San Francisco for a reunion with The Tubes. He and the band had both undergone myriad changes since recording *Remote Control* in Menlo Park, five years earlier. The Tubes had partnered with slick LA-based producer David Foster for *The Completion Backwards Principle* and *Outside Inside*, both of which had broken through to mainstream US radio with a smoothed-down approach that had translated to actual hit singles. Controversially within the group, Foster was also producing singer Fee Waybill's solo project, *Read My Lips*.

"David wanted to produce a third album with The Tubes," says The Tubes' Michael Cotten, "but entirely under his control, with only Fee singing, and with no other band members involved. That wasn't gonna go very far, with us, so he then changed the plan to do just do a Fee Waybill album, with this hit songwriting team behind it. Of course, it was a huge mega disaster, and in my Tubes documentary, you see David Foster admit: 'You guys were right, I was wrong.'"

According to Tubes guitarist Bill Spooner, after Waybill's album "went into the dumper," the band knew their days with EMI were numbered. "It would be like throwing good money after bad to promote the Tubes any more," says Spooner. "We were at the end of our contract and we were due to get around a half a million dollars just for re-signing. So they just said, 'Fuck this, this isn't gonna work.'"

Refusing to work with David Foster again, the rest of the band vowed that they would all be more involved with the recording process on what would be their swan song album, *Love Bomb*. "We knew EMI were gonna get rid of us anyway," says Cotten, "so we just figured we'd make it as weird and wild and as we could. And of course, we though, let's get Todd Rundgren back, because we knew we'd have a good experience with him. It was Todd's idea to take the album budget and buy a 24-track Otari tape machine, and spend a little money on renovating our warehouse and build a proper recording studio booth in it."

As he had done himself, first with Secret Sound and then with Utopia Sound, Rundgren had long advocated that, rather than 'throwing away' one's recording advance hiring outside studios, an artist should build 'a room of one's own.' Now, just as Grand Funk had heeded Rundgren's advice and refurbished the Swamp, The Tubes transformed their warehouse rehearsal spot, in San Francisco's Mission District, into Cavum Soni, also known as 'the Sound Hole.'

"The Sound Hole was an old, 8,000 square foot factory with sky lighting," says Cotton. "We had put in a dance studio for our choreographer, Kenny Ortega, and Prairie [Prince] and I had our art studio with a spray booth, where we'd make these wall-sized airbrushed backdrops. We already had everything based there, so we built the recording studio inside it. Recording equipment costs had come down at that point, so you could get a good 24-track machine for around $15,000. We were all really excited about the idea of artistic freedom, open-ended time, and working with Todd."

"Todd stayed up with us," says Spooner, "working many long nights, soldering cords and wires to get the place ready. So you gotta give him credit for that. Who else would do that with their band?"

"He helped us actually lay the floor in," adds Prince, "and Mike has footage somewhere of him carrying speakers in and setting it all up. The studio really was per his design, especially the control room. It was pretty primitive, but we had 15-foot high ceilings and I even had a trampoline inside. We also put in a lot of carpeting, so it was a pretty nice sounding room in the end."

Cotten recalls he was thrilled when Rundgren brought in a Fairlight Computer Musical Instrument for the sessions. "It was the first Fairlight I'd ever seen," says Cotten, "and it was kind of a revelation, because there weren't really samplers many around in those days, and certainly nothing that sophisticated. My god, a keyboard with a TV set on top of it and a touch screen, what's not to like? Of course, Todd let me play and run wild with it, and you can hear the results. There is totally ridiculous sampling madness on *Love Bomb*."

With their studio not quite ready, Rundgren and the band drove over the Bay Bridge to Berkeley's Fantasy Studios, home of hits by Creedence Clearwater Revival and others, to record the basic tracks. "We'd record at Fantasy all day," says Spooner, "just the basic stuff, and at the end of the day, we'd go back over to Cavum Soni to solder more wires and cords all night. It was kind of a 'round the clock' operation, trying to get our place ready to do the overdubs and stuff. But that was our plan."

In an interview conducted by Paul Wood for the September 12 1984 issue of the *Tubeland News* fanzine, Rundgren noted, among other things, that the band had around two albums worth of material, with "a large variety of stuff to choose from."

"As successful as their last two records have been," Rundgren said, "I think that they'd like to feel that, if the album is successful, it was because of something *they* did. The idea here is to make sure it sounds like The Tubes."

Love Bomb turned out to be The Tubes' last wild ride into the sunset. "Bill Spooner came up with the title," says Cotten, "and I thought it was genius. Prairie and I did that cover with the heart and the bomb. It's a dark record, all the songs, like 'Stella,' had this weird dark thing. I got to sing on 'Night People,' which is also very dark. He just let me do it straight out of my head, laughingly singing, completely as I did on my demo. He went ahead and put it on the record. It still shocks me to this day. And just before we did the record, Prairie and I had visited Bora Bora [an island in French Polynesia], where we got to meet King Tau Tu, who later stayed with me when he came to visit San Francisco. While he was here, we secretly recorded him talking and looped it into this song we'd crafted with authentic Polynesian rhythms, called 'Bora Bora 2000.' The King loved it, when he eventually heard it. Again, we were just so fortunate that Todd allowed that on the album."

Rundgren says he was also excited by an experiment wherein he and the band would make one side of the record a continuous suite of music all at the same tempo. "To accomplish this," he says, "we striped an entire reel of tape with MIDI time code and a click track from the Fairlight and programmed drum passages for each of the songs, which were later replaced by Prairie's actual performances, some of which were very lengthy."

'Piece By Piece,' originally written for Fee Waybill's solo album, became *Love Bomb*'s first single after Rundgren reworked it for the band. "That was a case where we said, 'Okay, we gotta at least try to do a single on here,'" Cotten says. "Fee and Todd pretty much did all of that, Fairlight effects [crunching glass] and all. I didn't have anything to do with it; I don't think Bill did either."

Rundgren was also keenly involved in the production of a computer-generated music video for 'Piece By Piece.' "Todd and I," says Cotten, "were both really big about this computer graphics convention they had every year called SIGGRAPH. We would both go and learn what was new in computer graphics and study all that stuff. So we got a little time in a studio and were able to do a demo that became the video for 'Piece By Piece,' which I directed, as weird and bad as it is. So that became another point of reference between Todd and I; we were both doing interesting things with Paintbox and early ADO video equipment. And of course Todd's history with video goes way back. And he did so many awesome things with computers too, like Flowfazer, that was just way ahead of its time, all these fractal patterns just playing on your screen. We all knew the same folks, through him mostly, like the people who did the first Video Toaster, and the guy who invented AutoCAD, or the guy who did the first video synthesizer. All just amazing geniuses."

"SIGGRAPH is put on by the American Engineering Society," Rundgren adds. "They have these Special Interest Groups, or SIGs, and this SIG was for graphics, specifically computer graphics. I started going to these conferences in the early 80s, when computer graphics were still pretty primitive and the biggest advance, at that point, was the movie *Tron*. The highlight and finale of the SIGGRAPH conference was this terrific hour-long film show packed with excerpts from all the latest experiments in computer graphics. One year, Pixar debuted their famous Luxor desk lamp animation at SIGGRAPH. So these were the people I was starting to get to know."

While Silicon Valley would impact Rundgren's career trajectory over the coming years, the entire *Love Bomb* experience was significant for two more reasons. One being that the album contained Vince Welnick's achingly romantic 'Feel It,' which Rundgren would later remake on his own *Nearly Human* album. The other being that the sessions marked Rundgren's first professional interaction with singer Michele Gray, The Tubes' live backing singer who would later become Michele Rundgren. According to Mrs Rundgren (whom we'll refer to herein as Michele Gray, to avoid confusion), their initial meeting had not gone well.

"I had been singing with The Tubes since around the Completion Backwards Principle tour," she says. "I had sort of met him on the Outside Inside tour dates on the East Coast but, to me, he was just some really bizarre, weird-looking guy standing in the corner against the wall with his hands behind him not really engaging with people. When the boys hired Todd to do *Love Bomb,* I kind of waited in the lobby, hoping I'd get called in to sing, but Todd never called me in. In fact, he never even spoke to me. I thought he was arrogant, I had no idea he was just socially inept," she laughs.

Perhaps feeling sorry for her, Michael Cotten snuck Gray into the studio when Rundgren wasn't there to record vocal parts for the song 'Muscle Girls.' As she recalls, however, "When Todd came in, next day, he wiped off my lead vocal and left the track instrumental on the record. So now I really hated the guy."

That would change within the coming years, but in the interim, The Tubes finished their final album without incident. Cotten admits that, while the band had vague hopes of reaching a broad audience while making the album, no one was under any illusions that *Love Bomb* would do the trick. "We always thought everything was just gonna be a disaster," says Cotten, "and it was always proven true. I've since learned that this is not the best way to approach life, but that's who we were. Still, we loved that creative crucible, and having Todd mixing the pot, and he just loved it too. He was our personal alchemist when it came to that stuff."

Upon completion of his Tubes duties, Rundgren returned home to Woodstock to mix the album at Bearsville Studios and prepared to enter Utopia Sound to make what would become Utopia's final studio album, *POV*. According to Kasim Sulton, the *POV* sessions found Utopia sadly lacking in the morale department, and their cherished band rule – that no one could disagree unless they had a better idea – was tested to the point of failure.

"Willie and Todd have a tumultuous relationship at best," says Sulton. "And I've always said that, while I think *POV* has a lot of great moments, like my song 'Wildlife,' it was really those guys butting heads that ended up breaking up the band. Willie wanted to do the record with drum programs but Todd wasn't so into that. Voices were raised, and Roger and I spent a lot of time staring at the floor. And, commercially, there was also the case of there being more supply than there was demand for; as a result, Utopia kind of fizzled out. We had a good run, though, and there was a constant flow of Utopia music from at least 1976 to 1985. But in the final analysis it was Todd saying he could not – would not – work with Willie ever again. So that was kind of sad."

"I had started writing a lot more," says Wilcox. "The thing was, when Todd wasn't writing his Todd ballads that people loved, I would try writing them. A song like 'Mated,' which I brought in for *POV*, was the kind of song that I wished Todd would write, but he didn't want to, at the time." He now looks back with mixed emotions at his career in Utopia, which he compares to a marriage. "Over the ten years we made records," he says, "I had pleasant and unpleasant experiences in the studio with Todd. Was it always great times? Nope. Were there some great times? Yep. I mean, we were together for a long time and I'd say, at the end of all of it, regardless of egos or clashing personalities, we made some good music together."

While Utopia would still tour behind *POV*, upon its release, the band would never produce another full album of original material. Meanwhile, Rundgren began working on his next solo album, *A Cappella*. He had been experimenting with multi-track vocal layering throughout his entire recording career, as far back as 'There Are No Words,' from *Runt*, and continuing with near a cappella pieces like 'Born To Synthesize,' from *Initiation*. Late in 1984, Rundgren finally felt he had developed sufficiently as a singer and arranger that he could pull of an entire album with just his voice.

"*A Cappella,*" says Rundgren, "was supposed to be my last record for Bearsville, but Albert just didn't want it to end, so he started pretending it wasn't my last album. Then, when that didn't fly, and the record was delivered, he simply refused to release it on the grounds that it wasn't 'acceptable.' He lied to me and told me he had sent it to Mo Ostin, from [Bearsville's parent company] Warner Bros, and that Mo had told him he didn't like it. Only that never actually happened; it was a total lie. We were at to the end of a contractual period and Albert could never stand the idea of you going forward without him getting a piece of you somehow. He wasn't managing me anymore and I was looking to move on from the label, and he just became completely unscrupulous with me. He held up *A Capella* up for about a year until I agreed to give him publishing on my next three records. In exchange for letting me go do a three-record deal at Warner Bros, Albert retained the publishing on those albums. At least, this way, it was allowed to come out at all."

According to Rundgren, 'Blue Orpheus,' a musical retelling of the mythological tale, was chosen to lead off *A Cappella* in order to "set the stage, thematically." He says that singing was the central part of the Orpheus story. "He can charm the birds out of the trees with his singing, except for the fact that he's lost his girlfriend to Satan, which makes him unwilling to sing anymore."

A Cappella was by no means strictly limited to corner doo-wop or conventional choral singing, and Rundgren fully explores the range of both his own voice, and 'voice' in general, with plenty of experimental textures, from disembodied voices and sound processing tricks to straight gospel and Middle Eastern influences. There are also some of Rundgren's most accomplished songs, such as the upbeat rhythm & blues of 'Something To Fall Back On' and the earnest ballad, 'Pretending To Care,' both of which would have been standouts on any Rundgren album. As this was one of Rundgren's last purely analog records, he naturally made good use of old-school tape manipulation, while also employing the latest technology, such as the Emulator sampling keyboard, which played an important role in generating chords and certain vocal-based percussion sounds.

"I realized at a certain point," he says, "that having a sampler would allow me to do this kind of record. It would have been a real pain in the ass previous to that, but the sampler made it easier, in some ways, even though I didn't have a sequencer. The drums were voice samples, often played out of pitch or really overblown, but they weren't sequenced, so I had to 'play' them manually, hammering on the keyboard all the way through a track like 'Something To Fall Back On.'"

On the Middle Eastern-inspired 'Miracle In The Bazaar,' Rundgren recalls using Vocoder, tape loops, and backward effects to achieve a wall of voices evocative of György Ligeti's atonal choral pieces. "On that track," says Rundgren, "I did some weird analog tricks. I built these long tape loops that I would run in the mix. On each of these loops, I would sing a note for as long as I could onto the quarter-inch tape and then I'd loop that, physically, with splice tape. Then I'd dub in five to eight minutes of that onto one track of the multi-track. Then I'd do another one, and another until I had, maybe, 12 tracks of me holding out a tone, constantly. Then, I'd play that with the faders on the board, like a glass harmonica or something, just moving the faders and building chords from the taped notes. I didn't have automated mixing in my studio either. I believe I was probably bouncing it down to another track somewhere, so if I got it wrong I could go back and do it again, or punch in somewhere."

According to Rundgren, the easiest part of the process was the singing itself. Since his earliest *Runt* sessions, Rundgren had recorded his own voice so many times that, by now, it took him very little time to set up and start tracking. "Once I get sort of warmed up," says Rundgren, "vocals become nearly production-line, in a way. I pretty much have an intuitive sense of the harmonies and if I'm familiar enough with the lead melodies, I can just sing the harmonies off the top of my head. The only setback is just the tediousness of singing these things over and over and over again. It's a lot of work, and a lot of breathing, so you get a little dizzy sometimes."

To capture his voice, Rundgren says he used a Gotham Audio version of a Neumann U87 microphone. "The only thing is," says Rundgren, "I need to do a particular EQ to smooth out my voice and I know exactly what that is. There's this lower mid-range component [to my voice] that needs to be ducked-down a bit. It'll depend sometime what environment I'm in when I'm recording it. It's just easy for me to get a sound I'm comfortable with a U87 style microphone, but I could do it with any number of microphones. Biggest problem is what happens when you're singing really loud, and what happens when artifacts like sibilants start to build up and how gracefully or ungracefully the microphone takes it. But I don't believe in dampening sibilant frequencies because sometimes that's the only way you can tell what people are saying. On the other hand, I've always had some sort of de-essing [limiter] available. Even back in the early days. As soon as I knew what a de-esser was, I had one."

Rundgren adopts a series of character voices on *A Cappella*, from the Middle Eastern inflection of 'Miracle In The Bazaar' to the old man of 'Lockjaw,' or the Irish dialect on 'Honest Work,' Rundgren's folk ode to unemployment, which was as timely in Reagan's America as it was in Obama's. "I wanted to give that song a kind of old-world, working man's sound," laughs Rundgren, "but it wasn't necessarily meant as a 'protest song.' I was thinking about the kinds of principal forms that utilize the voice in this unadorned way and I saw the song as going back to the old field-holler tradition, 'Oh Lord, my troubles is so …' that kind of thing. But again, it's evolved into something you might say was 'political,' in a sense. Like a song of the labor movement, I suppose, because of the idea that there is supposed to be the essential value of labor; the problem that the song is talking about is the lack of 'honest work' to do. So I imagine as unemployment continues to rise, in any era, the song will remain sadly relevant."

While Rundgren admits that 'Something To Fall Back On' was purposely recorded as a potential single, he was also compelled to record a cover of one of his favorite soul vocal hits from 1974, 'Mighty Love,' originally performed by The [Detroit] Spinners.

"I'm not exactly sure when I got the idea to do that song," says Rundgren, "but it sort of fit in and besides, I wanted to do something that people were somewhat 'familiar' with, since the rest of the songs on the record were originals. I intentionally gave it that churchy, Sunday morning, gospel quality. I think The Spinners also had that in mind when they did the original, but Thom Bell's production was so fully adorned that it took it out of church a little. I just decided to take it just a little bit more literally on *A Cappella*."

In late January 1985, with no word yet on when Grossman would allow *A Cappella* to be released, Rundgren produced an album for the LA band What Is This, assisted by Chris Andersen. The band was comprised of Alain Johannes, who would later play with Queens Of The Stone Age and Them Crooked Vultures, with Jack Irons and Hillel Slovak, who would both later play in Red Hot Chili Peppers. Also in January, Rundgren's partner Bean became pregnant with their second child, Randy, who would be born in September, just as Warner Bros finally released *A Cappella*, the first fruits of Rundgren's new three-album deal.

In March, Passport Records released *POV*, and Utopia put aside their differences and rehearsed for one last tour, over April, May, and June, supporting The Tubes, whose own final album, *Love Bomb,* had also just been released. According to Michele Gray, who was still singing with The Tubes at that point, the tour provided her with a chance to better get to know the "socially inept" man she'd met at the *Love Bomb* sessions. "On the road," she says, "Todd was actually really kind to me. As a result, I started to pay more attention to his music. I'd show up to listen to his set and I was like, 'Wow, this guy is amazing.'"

On September 13, Randy Rundgren was born. By now, Rundgren and Darvin, having been increasingly spooked by the home invasion five years earlier, had moved the family out of the Mink Hollow Road locale to a new house at 69 Sunshine Avenue in Sausalito, just over the Golden Gate bridge from San Francisco. While he retained the house in Lake Hill as part of the Utopia Sound compound, Rundgren was happy to be close to the emerging digital revolution in the Bay Area.

"Silicon Valley was still exciting back then," says Rundgren, "there was still a lot of the upstart about it. It didn't turn into a bunch of investment bankers in suits until the mid 90s, when it got insufferable. But when I first moved out there, the whole vibe was completely different and everything seemed wide-open. I was keeping up with all of these technological developments related to the computer, which was something I had a great fascination for but really hadn't applied much to music yet. I used to go to hackers' conferences and see these young guys dreaming up all these counter-culture type things, that few people understood, and working in a new area that seemed almost magical to me. It had a real 'mystique' about it until 'The Man' got involved, and then it got overblown."

With *A Cappella* in the shops, Rundgren toured behind the new album from October through December, backed by an 11-strong choir, featuring the voices of Kasim Sulton and Michele Gray, along with Rundgren's assistant Mary Lou Arnold among others, the extended line-up necessary to replicate the complex self-tracked harmonies on the album. Nobody knew at the time that not only was Rundgren's relationship with Bean falling apart, he and Michele Gray were becoming increasingly close.

"While we were on the A Capella tour," Gray reveals, "we were secretly dating, even though he was with someone else and I was married to someone else. I actually remember, I went to my parents' house to tell them, 'Oh my god, I fell in love with somebody besides my husband.' And I was trying to decide whether or not to get a divorce, and my parents were like, 'Oh, you shouldn't get a divorce.'

Then, in the mail, came a cassette. Todd had written this song called 'Parallel Lines' for us. So I put the tape in and, as we're listening to it, my mom is like, 'Okay, Get a divorce! I get it now, I totally get it!' She didn't know who Todd was but she was so impressed."

Aside from the inconvenient truth of their relationship, Gray recalled that performing Rundgren's music, in the 11-voice orchestra, was some of the hardest music she had ever sung. "I try never to speak for Todd," she adds, "because I never know what he's thinking, but I think he had so much fun doing the A Cappella tour that it inspired him to do the kind of soul music that became *Nearly Human* a couple of years later."

While a new baby, a new home, and a new relationship had shaken things up at the end of 1985, the beginning of 1986 was also marked by loss. Albert Grossman, from whom Rundgren had recently extricated himself, had died suddenly on January 25 1986, after a heart attack aboard a London-bound Concorde. The 60-year-old entrepreneur was buried in Woodstock, behind his beloved Bearsville Theater. Also that month, in an unrelated incident, arsonists razed the West Hurley, New York, warehouse containing several artifacts and items of musical gear belonging to Rundgren, Utopia, and other Woodstock musical entities. According to Roger Powell, almost everything they had stored in the warehouse – including Rundgren's Ankh guitars and Sulton's matching bass – was lost to the fire.

"Utopia weren't touring at the time," says Powell, "so we had put all of our equipment in there. I think I heard that someone sabotaged the warehouse; they had cut the gas line and started a small fire somewhere near. There was a big explosion and the roof blew 200 feet away, and all everything else, like my Moog synthesizers and a couple of prototype Powell Probes, just melted down to gray goo."

Fire and death aside, even one of the bright spots of Rundgren's year, if not his production career, became an arduous experience for both him and his clients, the English group XTC. Yet *Skylarking*, the album they began that April, would remain an artistic high point for all involved.

XTC Skylarking

One of Todd Rundgren's most notorious productions was *Skylarking*, his highly regarded 1986 album for XTC. Although the band recall that Rundgren was more or less 'thrust upon' XTC by their record label, Virgin, the 'shotgun wedding' paid off in one of the better albums by either party.

Quintessentially English, XTC had emerged from Swindon, Wiltshire, in the mid 70s and become part of the London-based post-punk scene. They were fronted by headstrong guitarist and vocalist Andy Partridge, who wrote and sang the lion's share of the group's material, along with bassist and singer Colin Moulding who, despite making fewer contributions, had managed to write some of the band's biggest hits, such as 'Making Plans For Nigel,' 'Life Begins At The Hop,' and 'Generals And Majors.' Affable guitar virtuoso Dave Gregory rounded out the band, which had had no full-time drummer since the departure of Terry Chambers in 1984.

XTC's earliest recordings had been snapshots of their live sets, characterized by a herky-jerky blend of angular guitars, buzzy electric organs, thundering drums, and stuttering vocals over songs imbued with the hand-made spirit of Captain Beefheart and the beer-soaked ambience of punk. As XTC became acclimatized to the recording studio, albums such as *Drums And Wires* (1979) and *Black Sea* (1980) grew progressively more complex, until *English Settlement* (1982), at which point XTC had become a largely studio-only band, after Partridge had steadfastly sworn off touring after suffering an onstage nervous breakdown in Paris.

For Partridge, as for Todd Rundgren, the recording studio provided a sonic sanctuary, a controlled environment where he and his band could stretch out and experiment. For a time, XTC flourished creatively, if not commercially, under Partridge's direction, which generally usurped the authority of their nominal producers such as Bob Sargeant, Steve Nye, and David Lord. "We'd had producers," says Colin Moulding, "but they were usually doing Andy's bidding. He was, shall we say, the 'executive producer.' If there was something the producer was doing that Andy didn't agree with, he'd let them know in no uncertain terms."

Yet, faced with diminishing sales returns from one XTC album to the next, Virgin Records had begun to doubt Partridge's instincts, feeling that the band needed a strong and objective outside producer at the helm to protect the band from their own self-indulgence. Shortly after the commercial disappointment of *The Big Express*, from 1984, Virgin's Jeremy Lascelles presented the band with a chilly ultimatum. They could work with the label and attempt to break the

American market, or leave the label altogether. Partridge recalls Virgin's suggestions for how to achieve the former.

"Virgin's idea," says Partridge, "was to find some American producer who could translate our 'yokel Englishness' to the American market. 'You know that thing you do so well? Could you not do that? In fact, could you be a poor imitation of an American group?' And if we didn't do this, they'd drop us. It was a simple as that."

Helpfully, Virgin drew up a list of recommendations for American producers, which is said to have included names such as Bill Bottrell, Greg Ladanyi and Bob Clearmountain. "You would have to be really 'inside' the industry," says Partridge, "or be a fan of Fleetwood Mac or Boston, to know some of these names. So I said, 'I pick none of them.' Then Virgin drew up a second list with the name 'Todd Rundgren' right at the bottom of it."

Rundgren's résumé seemed ideal for Virgin's needs. He was a legendary American 'name' producer who had a reputation for turning around troubled projects, such as Badfinger or Meat Loaf, and getting them to the charts on time and on budget. And unlike most of the other names on offer, XTC had actually heard of him.

"I think I had momentarily possessed a copy of *Something/Anything?*" Partridge recalls, "and I had liked a few songs, such as 'The Night The Carousel Burnt Down.' I'd also liked 'A Treatise On Cosmic Fire' [from *Initiation*]. Really, that's all I knew of Todd Rundgren. I think we also thought that, him being a bit of an Anglophile, he might 'get' us."

Unlike Partridge and Moulding, Dave Gregory was already an enthusiastic follower of Rundgren's work, having fallen for a cassette tape of *Hermit Of Mink Hollow* handed to him on a 1979 XTC tour. Gregory lobbied the rest of group, especially Partridge, to enlist Rundgren as their producer. "I reminded Andy that Todd had produced one of his favorite New York Dolls records." he says. "In the absence of any better alternatives, he agreed."

Moulding concedes that, at this point, XTC needed something – anything – to reverse the band's declining fortunes. "We hadn't had a hit in a while," Moulding admits. "So Virgin made Todd a financial offer, on the condition that we'd end up with something that was more commercially viable."

Todd Rundgren remembers his initial surprise when Virgin's head of A&R called in regard to XTC. "I usually don't get a call directly from a label about a 'veteran' band," he says, "so I knew something was up. The label was concerned about flagging sales."

Rundgren's familiarity with the band helped him immeasurably; their reputation for prolific songwriting had preceded them. "In most cases," he says, "while I listen up on a band's previous works to see what may have been lacking, I'm usually more concerned with their current material. Part of my job is usually to hector the songwriters to death before we start recording. *Skylarking* was one of those rare instances, however, where I was both familiar with the band's previous work and unnecessary as a 'songcraft agitator.'"

Moulding recalls that Partridge was less than thrilled about the forced abdication of his dominant role in the studio. "It was clear that we were meant to do whatever Todd wanted us to do, which didn't sit well with Andy."

Rundgren knew his work would be cut out for him, but took a pragmatic approach to the assignment. "I was aware of the band's reputation for wearing out their collaborators. I also knew that Dave Gregory had suggested me, that Andy and Colin likely had no opinion one way or the other, and that the label was pretty much forcing the band to accept a strong-handed producer they weren't very familiar with. I'm sure the fact that I offered our typical 'all-in' flat fee [one lump payment that included tape costs, studio hire, lodging, and producers fees] to complete the project probably appealed to [Virgin Records'] budget concerns."

As usual, Partridge and Moulding had written and demoed more songs than they needed in advance of the sessions. While not a songwriter, Dave Gregory had produced and played on Partridge's demos for 'Dear God' and a song then known as '(Drowning In) Summer's Cauldron' at his home that January. Another 20 songs were recorded by Partridge and Moulding, alone at their respective homes.

XTC's demos were dispatched to Rundgren in Lake Hill, who then dubbed and edited together only the songs he wanted to use, in a proposed album running order. "There were clear and remarkable stylistic differences," says Rundgren, "between Colin and Andy's songs, right down to the subject matter. Colin seemed to be in an especially productive period, so there were many more songs from him than usual. My initial challenge was to try to bridge the gap between Colin's 'pastoral' tunes and subject matter and Andy's 'pop anthems' and sly poetry."

Rundgren, the conceptualist, began to imagine certain songs fitting into a pattern, or song cycle, broad enough to include all the different styles and stories in the songs. He also suggested a working title, *Day Passes*. "The album could be about a day, a year, or a lifetime," says Rundgren, elaborating on his concept. "The evolutionary aspect of the theme allowed for transitions to different places, and there were songs that represented significant milestones along the way: birth, young love, family, labor, illness, death, sprinkled with moments of wonderment. Using this framework, I came up with a sequence of songs and a justification for their placement and brought it to the band."

A week later, Rundgren sent his *Day Passes* selections and concept back to England. Partridge admits that he was immediately put off, and somewhat threatened, by Rundgren's attempt to name their album. "I thought it was a crap title," Partridge laughs. "He'd even had a sleeve concept in mind; a couple of railway tickets that were 'day passes.' I actually have great respect for that because he tried to take this disparate set of songs that had absolutely nothing connecting them and make a concept album out of them. Although there's probably more of an actual 'concept' to *Skylarking* than, say, *Sgt Pepper*."

Rundgren says he understood why XTC had "about as much enthusiasm for the concept as anyone who had to endure a stranger pawing at their music would allow. But least they were willing to let me take the lead for the time being, which I thought was a milestone in itself."

Troublingly, for Partridge, Rundgren had picked more of Moulding's songs than typically appeared on an XTC record. "I was already feeling sort of pushed out by Virgin," recalls Partridge, "and forced to have this American producer, who now thinks more of Colin's songs. But, honestly, I think that was the best batch of material that Colin had ever offered up for an album and the atmosphere of his songs really suited the kind of record that Todd wanted to make."

Moulding, on the other hand, was thrilled. "I thought, 'Blimey, there's five of my songs in there! That was unheard of. I usually only get three, four at a push! Not having Andy calling the shots was obviously going to be beneficial for me."

Rundgren defends his song selection process, explaining that it was all about finding the 'conceptual center' of the bulk material. "For most artists," Rundgren explains, "putting out a record is an act of 'branding.' You're looking to make a record that, first of all, makes a strong coherent statement about where their band is at, musically. You find the center of all the songs and then draw a perimeter around it, like on a Venn chart. Some songs will fall inside or outside that perimeter, and that's how you know which ones should be on the record. It's also how you know if you're actually 'missing' something."

Despite his relative windfall, Moulding lamented that a few of his favorite songs still managed to fall outside of Rundgren's conceptual circle: "I was rather keen on 'Find The Fox,' and thought it was one of my better ones for the session, but it didn't fit the concept so that was a bit of a blow. Andy felt the same about his songs that were cut out, so we were both a couple of 'whingeing pommies.'"

According to Partridge, however, the completed song list for *Skylarking* didn't correspond 'exactly' to Rundgren's initial selections. "Originally," says Partridge, "Side two was to start with 'Let's Make A Den,' but to be honest, it was kind of argued to death. I also feel he didn't want any of my more 'political' songs, like 'The Troubles' and 'Terrorism,' which were also chucked out. A less political song, 'Little Lighthouse' was actually attempted, but it didn't make it. And of course we later redid that one with The Dukes Of Stratosphear.

Dave Gregory says that while he was generally happy to go along with whatever Rundgren had suggested, he was a little disappointed to find that, having labored for weeks over a string arrangement for Partridge's '1,000 Umbrellas,' the song had not, at first, made the cut. "To be fair, though," he adds, "Todd had only heard Andy's sparse vocal-and-guitar demo version." Rundgren would eventually be convinced of the song's value, and welcome it back onto *Skylarking*, after finally hearing it with Gregory's elaborate string arrangement.

On April 6, XTC boarded a Virgin Airlines flight to Newark, New Jersey – "probably the cheapest ticket at the time," Gregory laughs – and arrived in America in the dark of night, during a driving rainstorm. "Two crates containing our guitars had been shipped over separately," Gregory recalls with impressive clarity. "We'd sent ahead a Martin D35 acoustic, Wal Pro II and Epiphone Newport basses, a Rickenbacker 12-string, a Squier Telecaster, a Gibson ES-335, an Epiphone Riviera, an Epiphone Dwight, and a 1966 Stratocaster."

After Rundgren's long time super-assistant, Mary Lou Arnold, picked them up at the airport, XTC packed into the back of a camper van for the long drive up to Lake Hill, the rain beating down relentlessly the whole way.

"We were all very tired but in good spirits," Gregory recalls, "and as we finally left the freeway and ventured on to the dark country by-roads approaching Woodstock, the rain falling with ever-increasing intensity, it felt as if we were part of some opening sequence from an old horror movie – thunderclaps, forked lightning, the lot!"

Arriving at the guesthouse, the bleary-eyed band scrambled to claim bedrooms. In the room chosen by Dave Gregory sat a stereo turntable with a test pressing of Rundgren's *A Capella* album upon it. "Now it can be told," Gregory admits, "I liberated that disc and took it home with me."

When XTC awoke from their jet-lagged sleep, Arnold informed them that Rundgren had been detained in San Francisco, but was expected to return in a day or two. Gregory went to inspect the grounds of the Rundgren compound and found the door to Utopia Sound Studios wide open. Upon entering, he came upon a variety of dust-covered instruments and amplifiers, including a 1968 Vox Super Beatle amplifier, rented by Andersen for the sessions, and the 'actual' Story & Clark baby grand piano on which Rundgren had composed *Hermit Of Mink Hollow*. It was a fan's fantasy, come to life.

"There were also some Indian instruments," says Gregory, "hanging on the chimney-breast, including a sitar, and the much-vaunted Chamberlin, which we had been promised would be a suitable replacement for our absent Mellotron."

The self-confessed Toddhead stared, in awe, at the boxes containing the two-inch master multi-track tape reels from Rundgren's own recordings. On the wall behind the staircase to the control room he saw a blown-up painting of the 'wizard' cartoon from the back cover of *Runt*. His eyes grew wider, however, as he ventured into the control room and discovered 'Sunny,' Rundgren's celebrated Clapton 'Fool' SG, sitting in the corner.

"Clapton's sound with Cream," says Gregory, "had been among my biggest influences as a guitar player and to see the actual instrument he'd used right in front of me was a like a bolt from the blue. I decided that I'd finally reached rock heaven – all my musical dreams and aspirations were about to come true!"

With Rundgren absent, Moulding says the band took advantage of the time to get together in a circle and try and refresh their memories on the song structures: "We were told we'd better not rehearse too much in case Todd wanted to change the arrangements," he adds. "I didn't know the chords to half of these tunes."

In a few days, Rundgren returned to Utopia Sound and recording could begin in earnest. After reviewing the sorts of sounds the band were interested in, Rundgren decided that more instruments would be required. This necessitated a quick trip down to Manhattan and the fabled Manny's Music Store. "The long drive south and back again gave us an opportunity to get to know him a little better," Gregory says, "and we looked forward to getting down to some serious work. We came back from the city with a Prophet X synthesizer, like a double-manual Prophet V, a couple of tiples, which are small ukelele-type instruments from Mexico, and a big assortment of percussion."

The band was also pleased to learn that Rundgren had contracted Tubes drummer Prairie Prince for the album, although they were dismayed when they discovered that he would be overdubbing his drum parts later, in San Francisco. "We had assumed that Prairie was going to fly over and cut the backing tracks with us in Utopia Sound," says Partridge, "but we found out we were going to be recording the backing tracks to a click track, which just seemed really weird."

Rundgren's plan had been to map out all the song structures on the Fairlight CMI, tweak some arrangements, and then capture some essential band performances. Colin Moulding, however, refused to record his basslines without a real drummer in the room. "Todd had set up a click track and the chords [on the Fairlight]," he recalls, "but I'd never done that before and it just sounded alien to me. I wanted to put those bass notes right on somebody's foot. It was actually about three weeks into the sessions before I voiced my strong opinion that it was folly to go any further until we'd got the drum tracks down. Everybody else was of that opinion, too, so Todd eventually agreed."

"So we really just used Todd's Fairlight," Partridge adds, "for things like 'The Meeting Place,' to sequence all the Victorian industrial noise samples, like steam trains huffing away, and various engines clanking and grinding. We also did the rhythmic insect noises for 'Summer's Cauldron' as well. We'd choose, you know: 'OK, now bring the bee in, OK, more crickets.' It was like a more controlled version of The Beatles' 'Tomorrow Never Knows' tape-loop approach, but it was also a semi-naturalistic click track."

The entire production moved next to the Sound Hole, the San Francisco studio Rundgren had helped The Tubes to refurbish for their *Love Bomb* album. "We did all the drums and orchestral arrangements there," says Rundgren, "although we were going to return to Lake Hill, after the basic tracks, to finish the vocals and to mix. The band stayed in a condominium just a few blocks from my apartment in San Francisco."

Gregory, who kept detailed notes of the sessions, reports that the basic tracks had been recorded in the exact order they would appear on the record, a reel for each side. "And there was a third reel," he adds, "which may have contained 'extras' like 'Dear God', 'Another Satellite,' and 'Extrovert.'"

Partridge found it "rather quirky" that Rundgren had them perform the songs exactly in the order that they were to appear on the album, so saving tape. "We'd ask him, 'You're gonna do an edit on the tape, right?' And he shook his head and said, 'No, no, no. What you'll do is stop your instruments ringing there, at the end of "Summer's Cauldron" and we'll punch all the instruments in at the start of "Grass," right there.' To me it seemed rather stingy as far as cutting the precious tape, you know?"

Rundgren insists that his method had worked before, with Prairie Prince playing to Fairlight backing tracks, when they had done the final Tubes album at the Sound Hole, two years earlier. "But unlike on the second side of *Love Bomb*," Rundgren notes, "the tempos weren't all the same, so it didn't make as much sense. Still, there were several instances where songs might segue into one another, so we took a similar approach, laying down Fairlight drum tracks to be replaced by Prairie's actual performances."

Some songs, such as 'Earn Enough For Us,' didn't fit the system, so Rundgren consented to let the band record and perform them the old-fashioned way, beat combo style, live in the studio without computer backing. "The only instance of synthetic drums showing up in the final version of *Skylarking*," Rundgren adds, "was on 'Another Satellite,' a song which wasn't in my original running order, to be honest, because I never felt it belonged on the record."

XTC were impressed with how many ideas Rundgren brought to the table, and Rundgren himself acknowledges his increased level of collaboration in the project: "Since the label had mandated a change of direction, XTC were much more open to someone like me making such a significant contribution as orchestral charts and the like. I had appointed myself 'Keeper Of The Vision,' so I had a greater responsibility in realizing it."

"The whole thing was really difficult for me," Partridge admits, "because I was being instructed to behave, because you don't want to fuck up what this American is going to find in your sound that might to appeal to other Americans. Of course, the irony of it was that what he found in us was actually quite a lot more of our Englishness."

"But I also thought," says Moulding, "we'd paid a lot of money for a producer, so why shouldn't we give him 'carte blanche'? Andy kept coming to me in the first weeks of recording, saying 'I'm really not happy, you know?' This went on for ages, and he had a pretty bad time of it really."

Rundgren tried an experiment, on *Skylarking*, in which he instructed the band to collect images that would best represent feelings evoked by various songs. "We were all, myself included, to visualize the place the music was about," Rundgren explains, "and make that place as complete as possible. For example, I remember a certain picture of a lush, wild garden that became the setting for 'Summer's Cauldron.' Thus the sounds of cicadas, bees, and dogs in that track, or the factory whistle and hoof-clops in 'The Meeting Place,' and so on."

In some instances, relatively minor suggestions yielded significant results, as Rundgren recalls with Partridge's 'That's Really Super, Supergirl.' "Andy wanted to have something that evoked a presence streaking across the sky. So we put in this little eighth-note pattern, on a filter-swept keyboard, that created a subconscious 'Doppler effect', like a plane passing by. We also employed more literal orchestrations, such as string and horn parts, to evoke a time and place. And on that note, I should say that Dave Gregory's quartet arrangement in '1,000 Umbrellas' deserves special mention. Then, there was Andy's 'The Man Who Sailed Around His Soul,' which was in 7/4 time and had very 'jazzy' changes. Combine that with the panoramic scope of the lyric and it's just a short leap to James Bond and John Barry."

Partridge was pleased at how the swinging 'Man Who Sailed' had developed from his original, maudlin demo, which he described as "Leonard Cohen meets [German experimentalists] Can."

"It had this mechanical rhythm clunking along," he says, "to a strumming acoustic guitar. Todd had asked me how I wanted to approach it and I told him that, lyrically, the title suggests an ersatz Bond book title, like *The Man Who Knew Too Much*. Todd said, 'Do you fancy doing it like a piece of spy movie music?' So we ended up, between us, cobbling together this sort of existential spy film thing, you know, like *The Man Who Convinced Himself He Wasn't There*."

Gregory recalls that, one night, while executives from Geffen Records – XTC's American label – took the band out to dinner, Rundgren had stayed back at the studio to work on arrangements. "When we re-convened the following day," says Gregory, "he gave us a ticking off for not coming back to the studio after dinner – even though the restaurant had been 40 miles away, and we'd not returned until gone midnight. Then he switched on his sequencer and played us the parts he'd been working on. Strings for 'Sacrificial Bonfire' and 'Grass', the brass and woodwinds for 'The Man Who Sailed Around His Soul', in fact all the extracurricular decorative stuff we wouldn't be playing as a group. We couldn't believe he'd done so much work in so short a space of time."

"When this little combo of players came in to play through the arrangements," says Partridge, "I thought, Jesus this is perfect. Todd's arranging skill is frighteningly good."

Moulding was similarly impressed with Rundgren's flourishes for 'Sacrificial Bonfire.' "My demo was pretty primitive," says Moulding, "and used kind of prehistoric sounds, to sound 'druidish' or 'crumhornish.' Todd had this idea whereby in the second half of the song we should have an orchestra come in. I hadn't considered anything like that, but it made the last bars of the album more optimistic, which I think fitted into his original *Day Passes* concept. It was the dawn of another day. Of all the great arrangements he did, that was the one I remember where I thought he really did a great job and truly added something."

For Partridge's 'Mermaid Smiled,' Rundgren was asked to help 'jazz up' the tune, which he described as having had more of a "Middle Eastern feel" on the demo. "I asked Todd," says Partridge, "if we could make it more as if Bobby Darin or somebody might be singing it. I have a soft spot for really cheesy jazz – Martin Denny, Esquivel, Les Baxter – with goofy steel guitars and people singing 'zu, zu, zu' and stuff. The kinds of albums with the term 'Hi-Fi' on the label, and that come with instructions telling you where to sit 'for maximum stereo imaging.'"

According to Gregory, working with Prairie Prince in San Francisco was a boon to the group's flagging morale: "Prairie brought in a confident, aggressive rock attitude that took the album to another level and filled us with renewed vigor. And he seemed to love being there and playing these odd, British songs which he took to like a native. I think Prairie was the first musician to actually break sweat on the album. It was all sounding a bit flabby up to that point. Sure, there are some spirited vocals and moments of fiery playing elsewhere, but there's only so much 'performance energy' you can place on a track that doesn't have a real drummer on it."

Drummer Prince recalls that he recorded all the songs in the exact sequence they appeared on the final album, beginning with 'Summer's Cauldron' and on from there. "They had written out the song titles out on this big project calendar they had taped up on the walls, with all the instruments and the vocal parts they wanted to add. As things got recorded, they would check them off and make notes about what takes they were happy with. Andy would also do little drawings."

Musicians far and wide have long admired Prairie Prince's drum sound on *Skylarking*, particularly his trademark 'ringy' snare drum throughout. "I used a natural birch Yamaha kit," says Prince, "with a 22-inch kick, a 12-inch rack tom, and a 16-inch floor tom, and I used this beautiful-sounding, 1929 corroded-brass Ludwig snare drum that looks like it was from the Civil War. I got it for $500 in about 1980, at Charlie Donnelly's drum shop, in Hartford, Connecticut. Willie Wilcox called me and told me he already had one and that I should buy one, too. Todd just got such a great sound from it, left it really wide open, with a lot of ring. I've gotten more praise for the drum sound on that record, but I should say that Andy really knows how to compose parts for drums. I mean, I added a few of my own touches to the parts, like the little snare roll in 'Dear God,' which Andy loved, but most of the patterns were there on his demos. I'd listen to those and then make my own interpretation of them."

Rundgren says that in the case of 'Dear God,' he and the band arrived at an arrangement collectively. "We incorporated bluesy passages," he says, "that were intended to evoke George Gershwin and images of the Southern Bible Belt."

"The very last idea that would have occurred to any of us," Gregory says, "would be using a child, Jasmine Veillette, to sing the opening verse of 'Dear God.' Todd has such extraordinary ability and insight that you hesitate before querying what he's doing, or why he's doing it."

The string quartet on 'Dear God' was led by San Franciscan violinist Dick Bright, whom Prairie Prince had known since the earliest days of The Tubes. Bright worked well on the track and, as we will see, 'Dear God' would not be the last time Rundgren would hire Bright for a session.

Two of the less complicated songs on the album, 'That's Really Super, Supergirl' and 'Earn Enough For Us,' were also highly influenced by Rundgren flourishes. Dave Gregory recalls that Rundgren took a strong hand in 'Supergirl' after the band had attempted to record it another way. Partridge feels that the keyboard part Rundgren plays on the song has more in common with Utopia than XTC. "It's sort of the 'Todd' keyboard template," says Partridge, "and none of that is sequenced, by the way. In fact, Todd's keyboard technique was shockingly sloppy and primitive ... two fingers at a time."

"If Todd lacks one thing," adds Gregory, "it's patience. He really can't be bothered to listen over and over again to ham-fisted performance attempts and will often 'make do.' Many of our performances were at times sloppy, yet not so sloppy as to be unusable. I don't think Todd could see the value of replacing a part just to correct a minor kink. Sometimes Andy would want to replace one part with something 'better', but Todd would just look at him and say, "Andy, it won't necessarily be 'better' – it'll just be different.'"

Early on, back at Lake Hill, Partridge had asked Rundgren for an especially clangy and Beatlesque 'tang' for the snare sound on 'Supergirl.' "So Todd pulled out a multi-track tape from his library, put it on the reels, soloed a snare track and asked, 'Like this?' I said, 'Yeah, that's excellent, that's just spot on. What is this?' He said, 'Oh, this is the master tape for *Deface The Music*.' So the snare drum of 'Supergirl' is actually sampled straight off the multi-track of *Deface The Music*. Then, when we got to San Francisco, poor old Prairie had to play the bass drum and hi-hat around this sequenced snare sample, which must have been pretty hard."

Once in San Francisco, Dave Gregory treated himself to an afternoon of guitar shopping, purchasing a 1953 Gold Top Les Paul, which he subsequently used for "the rubbery arpeggios" on 'Dear God' and the *Skylarking* out-take, 'Extrovert.' Gregory also played a wide variety of other guitars on the album, and it just so happens he recalls every one of them. "Todd was very keen for us to use his black Ovation 12-string electro-acoustic," says Gregory, "and when we had a problem finding a [guitar] hook for 'Earn Enough For Us,' we used the Rickenbacker through a Scholz Rockman. Todd suggested re-introducing it over the final stanza, then playing four G5s over the end triplets. He then had me double-track it, and he may have beefed it up further with piano later. That was about as involved as he got with the guitars, but it did illustrate his strength as a producer, not interfering unless it was necessary, and always having something up his sleeve for when things didn't work."

Unable to resist, Gregory begged Rundgren to let him use the Clapton SG for his lead solo on 'Supergirl.' "Of course, it sounds more Todd than Eric, but that's okay. We recorded the solo in the control room, on the neck pick-up via the Rockman and whatever devices Todd used to produce that uniquely Utopian effect. That SG felt very comfortable to play, the neck has a nice profile, even with all the paint covering it. Later, I was listening to Utopia's *Ra*, at home, when Roger Powell's ascending trumpet lines in the middle of 'Magic Dragon Theatre' struck a familiar chord. Subliminally, I'd borrowed the same little five-note runs for part of my solo."

Gregory also shares an interesting story about the orchestral overdubs for 'Sacrificial Bonfire,' recorded in one six-hour session at The Sound Hole, on May 22. "The Coast String Quartet was led by John Tenney," says Gregory, "who was the musical director for a season by B.B. King at a hotel in San Francisco. The musicians therefore had to be back at the hotel for the evening show, which left them just the afternoon to do all the string parts and overdubs. They'd been given copies of the scores previously, so were able to fit in one rehearsal between their gigs with B.B."

Months after the sessions, Gregory was sitting at home listening to Joni Mitchell's *Ladies Of The Canyon* when he realized that the cellist on Mitchell's 'For Free' was the same Teressa Adams who had played on 'Bonfire.' "She was lucky that I was unaware of her history at the time," he says, "otherwise I would have spent most of the session grilling her for details [about Mitchell]."

Prairie Prince reveals that the booming tympani part on 'Sacrificial Bonfire' was, in reality, his 26-inch Yamaha kick drum, upended and played with mallets. "I put it up on one of those folding hotel luggage stand racks, with the heads facing up. It sounded big, like a tympani, and I tuned them to the track."

An often-fractious atmosphere hung over the sessions, but the tension wasn't strictly between Partridge and Rundgren, as one might have assumed. The pressure caused long simmering internecine tensions between Partridge and Moulding to boil over in San Francisco, culminating in Moulding storming out of the studio and temporarily quitting the group after a squabble over a bassline for Partridge's 'Earn Enough For Us.'

"Generally," says Moulding, "I didn't have any problem with Todd. My problems came with Andy because he was so unhappy and taking it out, a little bit, on me. I had just done what I thought was a spirited take, and Todd certainly thought so as well. Andy, however, suggested that it was not technically as good as it could be. I was of the impression that we were going more for the 'spirit,' but Andy wasn't backing down. I told him where to stick it, the session broke up and I went back to the hotel."

Partridge acknowledges that, in addition to homesickness and some actual medical illnesses, the problem with Moulding that day was strictly about the music. "Colin and Todd were taking the bassline into a more bluesy direction than I had hoped. It was my song, and I didn't want that. Colin, I think, was ready to snap anyway and used this moment to take all of the pressure that he was feeling and just blow up. Todd had to go over to where we were staying and talk him into coming back to finish the record."

To this day, Partridge refers to *Skylarking* as "the most difficult album XTC ever made in terms of stress level and infighting. I'd been told to shut up and obey someone who hadn't even written these songs. That was always going to make my hackles rise. Dave and Colin realized that if I resisted this, we'd get dropped off the label, so they urged me to shut it."

Nonetheless, Partridge continued to challenge Rundgren about the sounds he was hearing on tape. "He told Todd," says Gregory, "that if things didn't start to improve soon he would be packing up and leaving. Todd responded by telling him that he was not there to 'baby' us, and that he would continue to do the job he'd been hired to do by the record company, with or without Andy. A sort of stalemate ensued, though things improved a little after the drums and overdubs had been recorded."

"I hate sarcasm," says Partridge. "And Todd has got an enormous sarcasm muscle, which he would insist on flexing at every opportunity. Part of me thought it must be just how he wears you down so you would give in to his decisions. I'd tell him I'd like to go direction B instead of his direction A and he'd just say, 'Okay, I'll go back to the house, you can dick around with it for an hour, and when you realize it doesn't work your way, ring me up, I'll come down and we'll do it my way, the proper way.' You'd call it 'passive aggressive,' but this wasn't even passive."

Once again, it was Dave Gregory who provided a mediator's balance to the *Skylarking* session. Already a fan, he says he understood, perhaps more than the others, what Rundgren was trying to achieve for his band.

"Todd allowed us to follow our instincts," says Gregory, "until he heard something he didn't like; which actually didn't happen as often as one is led to believe. He has such extraordinary ability and insight that you hesitate before querying what he's doing, or why he's doing it. But it has to be said that this lack of personal interaction did have a negative effect. He was a bit remote, and unswervingly professional, unlike previous producers who nearly all became 'just mates' by the time the records were finished. I didn't really learn much about recording from Todd, other than what it was sometimes possible to get away with. So often it's in a record's flaws that much of the magic exists."

Gregory also recalls that, after final overdubs were completed in Lake Hill, Rundgren made the band promise not to hand over the two-inch master tapes to another engineer for re-mixing. "He must have had some premonition that we wouldn't like his mix," says Gregory, "because he didn't want us around when he was mixing."

Chris Andersen recalls that Rundgren had him rent a Mitsubishi digital two-track machine for the final mix. It was the first time either of them had used the new machine and this led to unexpected problems as they mixed *Skylarking*, at Utopia Sound, assisted by George Cowan. "When it was mixed," says Andersen, "we took the project down to Sterling Sound, in New York City, to be mastered by Greg Calbi. To our horror, we heard this audio dropout on this one song on playback. We thought it must be some digital code thing, because neither of us had worked with digital before. When we went and looked at the tape itself, though, you could see that there was a squished mosquito pressed hard onto it. We figured it must have flown in through the sliding doors at Todd's place and had gotten snared in there, mashed against the tape itself. Luckily, some technician at Sterling had some solvent that was safe for the tape and he got it off without destroying the data."

Unfortunately, the mosquito was the least of XTC's concerns with Rundgren's mixes, and Gregory recalls the band's horror upon hearing them. "It was cold, spiky, lacking in dynamics, and with a very narrow frequency range," says Gregory. "Probably perfect for radio, but not for XTC. Thankfully, the powers that be at Virgin agreed, and insisted he re-mix it. Weeks later, another mix arrived, improved slightly but covered with pops, squeaks, and digital dropouts. I thought, how could he not have heard them? Andy was furious, and ready to scrap the entire project. Virgin, however, were able to convince Todd that the master was faulty and refused to accept it."

Gregory recalls a rude awakening, at 3:30 one morning, by an urgent, transatlantic phone call from Mary Lou Arnold, who informed him that Rundgren was ready to re-mix the album but wanted to talk to the band first. "He came on the phone," Gregory recalls, "and very grumpily asked what we were expecting to hear from this re-mix. I explained about the dropouts, the distortion, and could we possibly hear some bass, please? He was far from happy about it, and said, 'You guys have got me doing what I *love* to do – *re-mixing*.'"

Partridge claims to have personally corrected many of the perceived shortcomings of the Rundgren mixes during his own intense mastering session with Greg Fulginiti at Artisan Sound Recorders in Los Angeles. Moulding, however, disputes whether Partridge's changes actually affected the overall album very much.

"Now, I know Andy took the record to the cut," Moulding explains, "and he said, 'We had to do a lot to it to get it to sound good.' Maybe that might have been true, you know, but it's not the first time that we've had to wrestle with tracks in the cut."

Skylarking was issued on October 27 1986, earning critical praise from Jon Pareles in the *New York Times*, who called it "a tuneful 1960s-tinged pastorale" and "a late-breaking reply to the Beatles' *Sgt Pepper.*" Similarly, David Fricke of *Rolling Stone* wrote of *Skylarking*'s "lush, bucolic allure," "earthy acoustic guitars, willow strings," and "playful paisley surrealism."

In the UK, the album was met with indifference, yet rose to a respectable Number 90 in the British charts. In the USA, *Skylarking* was a bona fide college radio hit and sold around a quarter of a million units, getting to Number 70 on the *Billboard* Top 200. 'Dear God,' issued originally as the B-side of the single 'Grass,' found its way to Number 37 on the *Billboard* Mainstream Rock Tracks chart, which hastened its inclusion in the album's subsequent pressings. Colin Moulding now says that, of all the records XTC ever made, *Skylarking* was their most pleasing, sonically.

"If you put a lot of these tracks on the radio," says Moulding, "they'd sound great. It's got a real hard, woody kind of center to it, which I find very appealing. It sounded very good on the radio and, now that most people listen to records through iPods and computer speakers, *Skylarking* just sounds even better."

For his part, Andy Partridge today praises Rundgren's "fantastic job" on the record, adding: "Todd is just a peerless arranger. He's staggeringly good and he's so quick and so thorough."

Fittingly, Rundgren fan Dave Gregory, who left XTC in the spring of 1998, gets the last word. "Quite simply," says the guitarist, "Todd Rundgren saved XTC's career. He did exactly what he'd been hired to do; against all the odds he'd gotten us a hit in America. 'Dear God' was released as a single, and a video was made which enjoyed heavy rotation on MTV and won some awards too. Very embarrassing for all the decision-makers concerned, and proving once and for all that the artist is not always the best judge of their own work."

21

Pursuing Happiness, Heading West

After the intensity of the *Skylarking* episode, Todd Rundgren returned to projects that, while no less complex, afforded him a bit more control over the proceedings. Regularly commuting between Woodstock and San Francisco, Rundgren was also making valuable contacts among the tech mavens of the emerging Silicon Valley scene. Indeed, the pursuit of technology would increasingly divert him from conventional record production over the coming decade. While composing and producing would always be a part of his overall workload, the golden age of the record producer was winding down and Rundgren was ready to embrace new frontiers.

Ever since *Initiation's* side-long instrumental, 'A Treatise On Cosmic Fire,' Rundgren had been interested in long-form instrumental music and the possibility of scoring for film. Now, in the latter half of 1986, after a new breed of directors such as Cameron Crowe had started using his songs in their soundtracks, Rundgren was at last commissioned to write actual scores. For television, he composed music for CBS's Saturday morning children's program, *Pee Wee's Playhouse*, and for NBC's gritty police drama, *Crime Story*, directed by Michael Mann, which debuted in the fall of 1986.

"Todd did *Crime Story* around the end of July," says Chris Andersen, who assisted Rundgren with the engineering. "It was a real grind, a weekly show with a relentless turnover schedule. Now, Todd likes to work fast, but this was crazy. The show's producers were very specific about where the 'cues' had to be and stuff like that. The overnight couriers were coming and going all the time and it was just madness around there. Eventually, Todd decided he really didn't like it."

For the cinema, Rundgren scored director John Stockwell's film, *Under Cover*, starring Jennifer Jason Leigh, which was released in the following year. With the demands of the film world, Andersen noted that Rundgren's interest in lower-profile band productions seemed to be waning. He recalls the two of them joking that a project for the Australian group Dragon, in August, would "drag on." And an unfinished record for emotionally troubled Canadian recording artist, B.B. Gabor, had left them concerned for their safety after Rundgren dropped out of the project.

In December, Rundgren went back on the road, backed only by MIDI sequencers, programmed by Roger Powell, for what was known as the Two Week Wonder tour – in actuality, it was closer to a month – culminating in a sold-out San Francisco 'homecoming' show, in January 1987.

Rundgren's enthusiasm for producing bands was briefly rekindled in the spring, when he was contacted by an outfit called Bourgeois Tagg, formed around the songwriting core of keyboard player Brent Bourgeois and bassist Larry Tagg, based in Sacramento, California. Their debut album for Island Records had been well received when, according to guitarist Lyle Workman, they approached Rundgren to tackle their sophomore set, *Yoyo*.

"We were all just huge Todd fans," says Workman, "as well as big fans of XTC's *Skylarking*, which had just come out. When we discovered that Todd was living in Sausalito, really near Sacramento, we had our management get in touch with him and send him our demos."

"He got right back to us," adds Tagg, "and said, 'I'll stop everything else I'm doing so we can do this right away.' He told us he wanted to change just a few things, but otherwise our demos were pretty 'sturdy' – that was his exact word. I remember he said that our demo for 'Stress' sounded like an Ohio Players B-side."

"He obviously had a great deal of respect for our musicianship," says drummer Michael Urbano, "but he was concerned with some of the lyrics. He pointed out a couple of songs on our demos and said, 'You can't sing about that, because it's jive and you haven't lived it.' This was at the meeting before he even really had the gig. He wasn't just kissing our asses, and I had a huge amount of respect for that. He also shared a little about his own career philosophy, and described how he was very honest with his fans: as a result, he can always go out and play for them because they know he's only ever sung his truth, you know? It was very illuminating and I think we were all inspired by hearing that."

Brent Bourgeois recalls visiting Rundgren in Sausalito, with Tagg, to discuss reworking the lyrics. "Todd kind of gave us a free pass on our 'musical' ideas," says Bourgeois, "but he was very interested in getting inside our lyrics. At the time, we'd been coming from a more observational, sort of Talking Heads point of view – there wasn't a lot of soul-searching in our lyrics. Todd cut right to the heart of that and, since he doesn't pull any punches, didn't have a lot of what you'd call 'tact.' One night, after one of these evaluations, I went home and wrote 'Cry Like A Baby,' in which the first line was 'What the hell do you want from me?' While he seemed pretty insulting to me, at the time, I've come to see that he was right. You really do have to kind of get naked with yourself, and get real; so that's something I've carried with me for the rest of my musical career."

Larry Tagg recalls Rundgren's key musical suggestion for 'Waiting For The

Worm To Turn.' "Todd came down to the band house one morning," he recalls, "and said, 'I've got it. I know how to make it "wormy."' He wanted it to sound like the inside of a watch, kind of a clockwork thing."

Urbano recalls that, at one point during the 'Worm' tracking session at Utopia Sound, Rundgren leapt down the stairs from the control room, waving his arms as he walked toward the drum booth: "He was shouting 'Stop, stop, stop! You're starting to sound just like a "professional session musician" in here, you got it all worked out don't ya?' I thought he was being complimentary, but he made it clear that professional wasn't necessarily fun or exciting and that he thought it just sounded too calculated. Then, he starts going around grabbing all this metal shit, like a saw blade and a cowbell, and he starts duct-taping these things all over my drum set. Then, he tells me to take a few cymbals off my kit, and to just bang these duct-taped metal pieces, at random, to make it sound 'like a Swiss clock falling down the stairs.' After a take using this approach, he says, 'That's it, you don't sound like a session player any more, you sound like an artist.' I actually get emotional recalling that moment, because it was life changing for me. To this day, if I'm in the studio and it's sounding uninspired or 'too professional,' I think of that moment."

According to Lyle Workman, Rundgren guided the sound design on every facet of the recording, including some unique guitar effects on 'Stress.' "Todd sent my guitar through a Vocoder and then he further changed the sound of my solo by mouthing these different vowel sounds using my signal. That was kind of fun, but he always had great ideas if we were stuck. And yet, he was really reluctant to merely 'dictate' parts. At one point, I remember handing him my guitar and saying, 'Dude, it's OK for you to just show me how to play it.' But he wasn't really about playing it 'for' us. Alternately, I must say that his greatest contribution to my song, 'I Don't Mind At All,' was to leave it pretty much alone."

'I Don't Mind At All' became Bourgeois Tagg's highest-charting single ever, climbing to Number 38 on *Billboard*, and featured an earnest lead vocal and lyrics by Bourgeois over a jangly acoustic guitar and string quartet motif composed by Workman.

"The *Yoyo* recording is pretty much identical to my demo," says Workman. "Brent and I wrote the string arrangement, and I can't say that Todd had a huge hand in that track. In fact, as I recall, he didn't think it really fit the rest of the tracks on the record. It was only later I realized that it might have been subconsciously influenced by Todd's 'Love Of The Common Man,' although I honestly wasn't thinking of it at the time."

According to Tagg, when the project shifted back to Sausalito's Studio D, for final overdubs, the band asked Rundgren to hire the Coast String Quartet, who had impressed them on XTC's *Skylarking*, to pour some strings over 'I Don't Mind At All.' "We had all loved '1,000 Umbrellas' on XTC's record," he recalls, "and since we were back in the Bay Area, where the quartet were also based, we had a hunch we could get them up to do it."

On April 22, Bourgeois Tagg appeared with Todd Rundgren at a benefit concert, Condomania, at San Francisco's DNA Lounge, intended to raise awareness of safe sex in the AIDS-ravaged city. Band and producer took a decidedly upbeat approach for their collaboration, reworking a few Rundgren originals for the occasion. According to reports, these included 'Love Of The Condom Man,' 'Rubber's The Answer,' 'Song Of The Trojan,' and 'Ramses Man.'

"First we did our own set," Bourgeois recalls, "but we had also learned a second set, performing as Todd's band for the night, and he gave us an opportunity to pick our favorite Todd songs, which was great. Todd came out in a rubber wading suit, basically dressed as a 'rubber.' That image will forever stay with me."

According to Urbano, Bourgeois Tagg took the invitation to back Rundgren as a sign of his respect for their musicianship. In fact, he says that this quiet validation was one of only a few direct compliments they ever got from him. "I'll never forget that feeling," he says. "Here I was, this 24-year-old kid from Sacramento, playing for the great Todd Rundgren, thinking 'I'm gonna play my heart out for this genius.' After a hot take, though, he might just look up from his magazine and say something like 'Well, that didn't bother me.'"

"But that was a classic Todd compliment," adds Bourgeois. "You'd learn to take little tiny doses of the smallest praise. I think he liked the way we played, especially our rhythm section, Larry, Mike, and Lyle, who all went on to work with him shortly after that – which was great."

Yoyo was released in August, but despite becoming Bourgeois Tagg's best selling album to date – largely on the strength of filmmaker David Fincher's high rotation video for 'I Don't Mind At All' – the band dissolved before making a third album. But just as Bourgeois said, it was not the last that certain members of Bourgeois Tagg would see of each other or Rundgren.

In the summer of 1987, the politically minded Rundgren staged the Vote For

Me / TR In '88 solo tour of America, a mock campaign for the US Presidency. After a New Year's Eve show with Bourgeois Tagg in San Francisco, Rundgren kicked off 1988 with a five-date Japanese mini-tour in January.

In July, he returned to Lake Hill to produce the Canadian group, The Pursuit Of Happiness (TPOH), whose leader and songwriter, Moe Berg, rivaled XTC's Dave Gregory in terms of being a Rundgren fan. TPOH's two Rundgren-produced albums – *Love Junk* (1988) and *One Sided Story* (1990) – were both amped-up rock affairs, with thunderous drums and raucous power-chording guitars over melodic, if mildly jaundiced, pop songs sweetened by two in-house female harmony singers. While Berg's lyrics veered away thematically from those of his mentor, it would be impossible to deny the impact of Rundgren's music on him. In truth, The Pursuit Of Happiness's long journey to Utopia Sound began ten years earlier in Edmonton, Alberta, when Berg first heard *Something/Anything?* in a local record store. Soon after that, Berg caught a Utopia date in Edmonton and rushed out to buy *Oops! Wrong Planet*.

"I was shocked that there could be music as amazing as this," says Berg. "I just couldn't believe it. A lot of the songs I was writing at that time sort of sounded like his, but to hear someone who could do it like a thousand, million times better than I was doing it was just ... wow."

Berg describes his first band, The Modern Minds, as "like if The Buzzcocks had listened to Todd Rundgren." But by 1985 he and drummer Dave Gilby had moved to Toronto, where they met bassist Johnny Sinclair and twin sister singers Tam and Tasha Amabile and formed The Pursuit Of Happiness. TPOH became the Canadian independent success story of 1986 with their self-produced video for the indie single 'I'm An Adult Now.'

By 1988, full-time backup singer Leslie Stanwyck and singing guitarist Kris Abbott had replaced the Amabile sisters. The band signed a major deal with US-based Chrysalis Records, who immediately asked Berg to put forth a list of 'dream producers' for their debut album. Half jokingly, he told them to get Todd Rundgren. "It was the answer to one of those 'What would you do if you had a million dollars?' kind of questions," says Berg. "Like the fantasy that you have after you buy a lottery ticket, you know?"

One night on tour in Winnipeg, however, the band's soundcheck was interrupted by a phone call: Todd Rundgren was on the line. "There was no preliminary discussion," Berg recalls, "Todd just launched right into this detailed critique of our material and my guitar playing and some inadequacies in the demos he'd heard. I went back to the band, shell-shocked, and told them Todd Rundgren was going to produce us."

After a 'bonding session' with the band – Rundgren had flown up to Toronto to see them in concert – TPOH and their producer were ready to make a record. "The great thing about meeting Todd ahead of time in Toronto," says Berg, "was that we got to ask him every 'fan question' I had ever wanted to ask him. Once I'd gotten all of that out of the way, I wasn't as star-struck any more, and it was easier to just get down to business and do the record. We also learned a lot about Todd's kind of 'dual personality' ... I don't think he seeks out social situations, yet when he's placed in one he can be unbearably charming. I've had many long, interesting discussions with him."

The Pursuit Of Happiness drove down to Utopia Sound in Lake Hill, New York, on July 1 1988, traveling directly from an afternoon Canada Day festival show in Toronto. "Our group morale was really high, at that point," says Sinclair, "so it was quite a fun trip, driving through the Catskills and finally getting to Lake Hill late that night."

"We got lost, looking for Mink Hollow Road," remembers Gilby, "so we had to call Todd for directions. We finally found it, and it was very exciting driving up this long, tree-lined rustic road."

For Berg, getting to walk around the grounds of Utopia Sound was "living the dream. I was thinking, 'I know this happens. I know bands do stuff like this all the time, but not my band, not me. I'm not really at Todd Rundgren's place, I'm not talking to him every day, and he's not producing my record!' You sort of think, this is what I always wanted, and this is what I'm doing."

That said, there was work to be done, and the band got right to it, setting up in the Utopia Sound live area after sleeping off their marathon drive of the night before. Berg, who had written all the songs, says that he was told in no uncertain terms exactly what obstacles he needed to overcome. "Todd told me bluntly," says Berg, "that he thought I was a crappy lead guitar player. It was his biggest complaint about our band, so I really had to practice."

"In my production work," Rundgren says, "there may sometimes be instances where I have little or nothing to contribute and, for the most part, that was the case with the first Pursuit Of Happiness record. They had played the material hundreds of times in concert, so there was no question about whether they knew it or not. It was just those lead-guitar solos that needed a bit more attention. My first thought was to make each one of the guitar solos interesting by goofing around with the sounds."

Rundgren assaulted Berg's guitar swith a battery of harmonizers, octavers, and fuzz boxes, then chorusing, flanging, and filtering the signal until it almost resembled his own. "He'd tease me," says Berg, "and say 'We'll put all these effects on your guitar and it'll sound like you're really great.'"

According to Berg, Rundgren played a strong role in the song selection process, choosing their inherently heavier rock songs over their sweeter, pop material, which Rundgren frankly dismissed as "twee."

"Somebody once described us," says Berg, "[by saying] 'If a van carrying AC/DC and a Volvo carrying ABBA had a car accident, it would sound like Pursuit Of Happiness.' Without Todd, we might have made a record where half the record was jangly pop and half the record was heavy and dark, and it wouldn't have made any sense."

Guitarist Kris Abbott recalls a "wow moment" while setting up her amplifier in a tape storage area at Utopia Sound. "I was standing back, kind of in a corner," she says, "with my Ibanez Paul Stanley guitar, and I'd turned around and read Patti Smith's name on these two-inch tape boxes. Over there was Cheap Trick. I realized that, all around me, were the masters for albums that I'd grown up listening to, just sitting on the bookshelves behind where I was playing my own guitar."

"Todd was not at all concerned about how slick you played," says bassist Sinclair. "It was all about feel. I accidentally played this little 'boing' on my bass at the end of one track, and when we listened back to the song, I said to Todd, 'Did you hear that?' He just said, 'Yeah, you should sticker the album, "Free Bonus 'Boing' with Record."' And that was it, you know, moving on."

Similarly, Rundgren wasted no time in capturing Kris Abbott and Leslie Stanwyck's signature vocal harmonies, recorded to a binaural microphone shaped like a mannequin head. "It was weird," says singer Stanwyck, laughing at the memory, "Kris and I sang a whole album's worth of parts into Todd's head microphone, standing six inches apart, over one or two days, tops."

"We could feel each other's hot, hungover breath on our faces," adds Abbott. "Les and I tended to sing really straight, long tones with no vibrato, more like keyboard parts. Todd may have fine-tuned the parts to some extent; he really pays attention to group vocals and was pretty demanding about enunciation. Moe had written backing parts, anyway, so the Todd influence was already there."

Berg, now a producer himself, says he learned a lot about recording from his work with Rundgren. "When I'm producing a band, I don't let them come into the mixing area either, at least until I've done a mix by myself."

"Todd's a virtuoso," says Kris Abbott, "so you might expect him to be very intimidating, because he is so smart and he's worked with so many people, but he really gets what music is about. That there's only so many notes, but it's what you do with them that really makes things magical."

Love Junk was released in Canada and the USA on October 26 1988, and was eventually certified platinum in their homeland, with more than 100,000 copies sold (plus another 100,000 units in the USA). "It is commonly accepted that early 70s mainstream rock was generally lame," remarked Andy Hurt in the UK rock bible *Sounds*. "It's only when you hear an album like *Love Junk* that you realize it wasn't *all* bad."

The Rundgren-produced remake of the TPOH single 'I'm An Adult Now' became a popular radio track in both countries and climbed to Number 22 on *Billboard's* Mainstream Rock chart and Number Six on the Modern Rock chart. While the video was initially banned from MTV, ostensibly for drug and sex references, the channel eventually saw sense.

Remarkably, after working with his idol, Moe Berg didn't only remain a fan – today, he continues to count Rundgren as a friend. "Todd Rundgren has been my lifelong passion," he says. "I'm still just such a huge fan, and I'm still in awe of him. To this day, when I've had the chance to just hang with him, it still blows my mind that Todd Rundgren is having a beer with me."

By the time *Love Junk* was pressed, Rundgren's life had changed again. Back in Northern California, he started to write his most emotionally direct songs since *Hermit*. To record them, he intended to take a bold step back to the olden days of recording, gathering a large ensemble of musicians in one high-ceilinged room to capture human performances, live to tape, with little or no overdubbing. In Rundgren's early vision, the record would be called *Time Marches On*, but by the time it was done, the project would be released as *Nearly Human*.

22

Very Suspicious Occasions

By the middle of 1988, Todd Rundgren's life had changed again. His relationship with Karen Darvin, the mother of his two boys, had collapsed, and he was now in an increasingly serious relationship with singer Michele Gray, although neither of them discussed it outside a close circle of friends. In June, he and Gray were spending much of their time in Sausalito when he decided it was time to make another album. To get the ball rolling, Rundgren selected the demo of the deeply personal 'Parallel Lines' and asked Gray to book a studio and round up some musicians. It was a pattern she would follow for the entire process.

"I'd ask him what instruments he needed," Gray recalls, "and he'd say 'This one has two guitar players, bass, and drums,' or 'I need a percussionist and a trombone,' or something like that. In addition to The Tubes, I had sung with different little bands in San Francisco, so I knew a lot of people in the Bay Area. Todd gave me the freedom to hire everybody out of our combined contacts."

According to Rundgren, his only concept for *Nearly Human* was to assemble and record a large ensemble the old-fashioned way, all at once, live in the studio, with little or no overdubbing. "It was a reaction to the sort of overly process-oriented way of making records," he says, "where everything is overdubbed and you have no idea what you've really got until you've finished the last overdub. When I'd first got into making records, they were made, more or less, live. Things were measured in three-hour sessions and it was 'get in, do it, and get out.' People were loath to do a lot of overdubbing. So this was an experience I hadn't had for a long time, to try and recapture that feeling that, while you're performing it in the studio, you're actually hearing the record the way the audience will hear it."

On June 26 1988, Gray booked Rundgren into a session at the Plant, in Sausalito, and invited a cast of musicians comprised of Vince Welnick and Prairie Prince from The Tubes, plus the members of Bourgeois Tagg. Gray also invited Nate Ginsberg along to play "harp synthesizer," plus a background vocal cast including herself and her friends Keta Bill, John Hampton, Melisa Kary, Scott Mathews, and Annie Stocking.

Bourgeois Tagg's Lyle Workman says he had found it hard to believe that not only had Rundgren produced his band, but he had now been invited to play a Rundgren session. "That was the most exciting moment in my life. I went over to his house to hear a demo of 'Parallel Lines,' and when he put the tape in, I was like, 'Don't cry, don't cry,' I was so moved by it. I'd been such a huge fan of his records for all these years, so I was just beside myself, getting to actually play on one."

The initial session, engineered by Rob Beaton, went well enough that Rundgren decided that he would continue recording one song at a time, in a similar live-in-the-studio fashion, until he'd accrued a whole album's worth of tunes. "It's kind of an incomparable feeling," says Rundgren of the live approach, "and it required a very unusual routine to get most of these fairly complex arrangements recorded with these armies of background singers and horns and/or strings. Since only some of the people participating were really adept at reading music, we were constantly striving to get to the point where everyone kind of just knew what we were going for and didn't have to refer to the sheet music, anyway."

Rundgren had also wanted to try to record the whole album to digital multi-track, a first for him, but found this limited his options in terms of studios in the Bay Area – at that time, anyway. "It wasn't like everybody was digital," says Rundgren, "so it was hard, but we ended up finding a 32-track Mitsubishi system at Fantasy Studios, in Berkeley."

Gray was given the official title of Production Manager, which basically amounted to finding out who was available and when, then calling Fantasy's Michael Rosen, who would also engineer the sessions, to see about availabilities. To book single days, as opposed to blocks of weeks, limited their choices to a variety of Sundays, during so-called 'downtime.' Thus, the next *Nearly Human* session wasn't until November 6, when Rundgren recorded the song 'Fidelity.' According to Gray, the song was based on the emotional upheaval she and Rundgren had endured when they first got together.

"That was written pretty early," says Gray, "back when I got my divorce, and around the time Todd moved his family to San Francisco. The lyrics are so direct and powerful, and he was starting to write more directly from his heart. You know, there are some Marvin Gaye influences all over *Nearly Human*, and Marvin was also one who wrote about true feelings. So, in a way, *Nearly Human* is Todd's version of Marvin's *What's Going On*."

On 'Fidelity,' Gray retained the core unit of Urbano, Workman, Bourgeois, and Tagg, along with Nate Ginsberg, conga player Michael Pluznick, clarinet player Peter Apfelbaum and sax player Bobby Strickland, who switched to flute on the session. "I had hired Bobby in a local band I had, called The Big Chill," says Gray. "He was just some kid who had auditioned to play sax in my band, and I had no idea that he could play everything. He was great on the flute, too."

According to Lyle Workman, his band Bourgeois Tagg had come to the point of disbanding only one night before they were to continue working with Rundgren in Berkeley. "When I got to Fantasy, I took Todd aside and said, 'You know, if there's a weird vibe in the room it's because we broke up the group last night!' Todd asked me, 'Why?' So I told him that Brent wanted to have a solo career. And, without missing a beat, he says, 'Oh great, just what the world needs, another Fee Waybill,' because that was how The Tubes had also broken up."

For backing vocals, Gray arranged to have singer Norman N.D. Smart, who had first worked with Rundgren as a drummer on *Runt: The Ballad Of Todd Rundgren*, to be part of a vocal ensemble with Kim Cataluna, Shandi Sinnamon, Cary Sheldon, Scott Mathews and Gray herself. "Todd's singing had truly come of age on *Nearly Human*," Smart recalls. "I always knew he had it in him before that, but now his singing was really quite something."

Over the next months, Rundgren says he developed a standard operating procedure for the Sunday sessions. "We'd have the rhythm section show up first, around noon, then I'd review the demo of the tune we were recording with them, if I'd made one. Those demos usually had just a keyboard, drum machine and bass, but if there were other things in the arrangement then I might have those on there too. If we had horn or string players in there, I would have to, with a great deal of effort, generate charts for them. After a listen-through, I would start showing everybody the basic keyboard, guitar, bass, and drum parts and whatever other instruments we had on any given date."

After a couple of hours, Rundgren's backing vocalists would arrive, and he would take them into an adjacent studio to run through their parts. "Most times, my little demo would not have had all of the vocal parts on it," says Rundgren. "In some cases, it didn't even have *my* vocal part on it, just the instrumental parts. I'd work out all background vocals with the singers and then leave them to rehearse that for a while. Slowly, I'd start to integrate all the elements until, about five hours into the session, I'd determine that we were close enough to start trying to get takes for a couple of hours, until my voice would start to go. If we'd done a bunch of takes, but constantly fucked up just one section, we'd go back to get a good one of that section in case we had to comp a bunch of different sections into one good take."

Once Rundgren was convinced he had at least one "somewhat correct" version of the song of the day, he'd call a break. "Then everybody would go off and get loaded," he laughs, "and we'd come back and do two or three of what I called 'mood-altered' takes, where everyone could stop thinking so much about it because we knew we already had what we needed in the can. You'd been struggling so hard all day long to learn this stuff, until everyone was too paranoid of screwing up to actually play it the way it needed to be played."

Rundgren says that many of these "mood-altered" takes became the versions used on the final album, "because we just played it with abandon. After having nailed it correctly, let's play it properly; that is, with all the excitement of a live gig. Since the vocals were live, too, it made a big difference for me, because I could stop worrying about anything else and completely focus on the singing. Until you're sure that everybody's got their parts down, though, you can't just abandon your responsibilities as producer and become your 'character.' You've always got to keep one ear on what's goin' down."

Recording with so many people, with competing volumes and frequencies, required a lot of separation and more than one isolation booth. "Sometimes we'd put the drums in the booth," Rundgren recalls, "or sometimes we'd just baffle the drums and put the string section [Dick Bright and John Tenney appear on some tracks] in the booth. It depended on what the instrumentation was for any given track."

On November 27, Rundgren recorded 'I Love My Life' with a huge line-up including Urbano, Tagg, Ginsberg, Workman, and Jimmy Pugh on the Hammond organ. The 22-voice choir Gray assembled for this date was the biggest on the album, and, in addition to the E Street Band's Clarence Clemons, Gray drafted most of the singers she knew from the San Francisco area, including Skyler Jett, Keta Bill, Vicki Randle, Scott Mathews, Jenni Muldaur, Shandi Sinnamon, and others. The choirmaster for the date was celebrated Bay Area record producer, and former Mahavishnu Orchestra drummer, Narada Michael Walden – one of only two guests specifically invited by Todd Rundgren himself for the record.

"I was close to Todd," says Walden, "and, while I consider him a genius, he's also just a kind, kind man. In the late 80s, Todd would come up to my place, Tarpan Studios, and educate me about the internet, which he was already way advanced on long before the general public was. I was not too sure why Todd asked me to be choirmaster, but he must have seen me conducting a choir at [San Francisco's] Glide Memorial [Church] or somewhere; but when he asked me would I conduct his choir on *Nearly Human*, I said, 'Of course.' Mainly, when I conduct, my whole thing is to get the spirit revved up and hot, and kind of contain that and get it on the tape. Of course, that's what Todd was after, too, so we just smoked it!"

Gray describes a party-like atmosphere for the session, largely she says, because "Narada was so funny, like a cheerleader director." She and Rundgren had originally contacted Bay Area singer Bobby McFerrin to conduct the choir. "Bobby would have also been perfect," says Gray. "We even went over to his house to ask him, but he didn't want to do it; I don't know why."

On December 2, Rundgren remade the Vince Welnick song 'Feel It,' which had been originally recorded for The Tubes' *Love Bomb*, four years earlier. While it wasn't Rundgren's intention to revisit old songs, some weeks had left him looking for established material in lieu of something brand new.

"We were doing pretty much one session a week," says Rundgren, "and I would write a song for each of them. Some weeks, however, I wouldn't have anything new so I either wouldn't call a session or else we'd do something else. In this case, since I figured Vince would be there, I decided to try and do 'Feel It.' On *Love Bomb*, we had actually tracked the song at a faster tempo than was probably optimal, to accommodate my tempo concept for that record. But if you knew anything about the lineage of the song, you knew it was supposed to be more of a Marvin Gaye slow-groove – which our version has – as opposed to the Barry White quality it had on *Love Bomb*."

Two days later, on December 4, Rundgren had some studio time but still had no new song ready, so he opted instead to record an old favorite, Elvis Costello's 'Two Little Hitlers.' Gray recalls Rundgren requesting a more stripped-down line-up for the session, engineered by Tom Size and featuring the Bourgeois Tagg rhythm section (Bourgeois, Tagg, Urbano, and Workman) with Paul Shaghoian on trumpet, Bobby Strickland on tenor sax.

While there were no background vocals needed for the session, Gray says she was surprised when Rundgren requested an accordion player. "I was like, 'Where the fuck am I gonna get an accordion player?'" she recalls. "Luckily, I called Vince Welnick and said, 'Vince? You don't happen to play accordion do you?' And he said, 'Are you kidding? I've played accordion since I was eight!' You know, they were laughing so hard before and after that session, it was goofy fun and I know they had a blast. Vince brought a lot to the project as far as nuance, tone, and pure keyboard ability. Todd's not strictly a piano player – he can't play even his own material perfectly and doesn't really use his middle two fingers – but when he showed Vince how he wanted a song to go, Vince could make what was in Todd's head sound a little better than what you expected it to be. Sometimes Todd would go over and say 'No, it's like this,' but once Vince was comfortable with a piano part it just soared."

On December 18, Welnick and Tubes bass player Rick Anderson joined Urbano, Workman, organist Jimmy Pugh, percussionist Gary Yost, and Bobby Strickland on baritone sax for the song 'Unloved Children,' with Rundgren joining on lead guitar. After breaking for Christmas, they returned to Fantasy Studios on January 12 1989, to record 'Hawking', along with ex-Journey bassist Randy Jackson, who later became famous as a judge on the popular *American Idol* television series.

According to Gray, the 'Hawking' session was "a little tough" for her, emotionally. "I didn't hire myself on the session, because I hadn't heard the music beforehand so I didn't know it would be such an absolutely gorgeous song. But also, for probably the first ten years of our relationship, Todd didn't like to be public about it, so he didn't want me to hire myself on every single song. In the end, I hired Skyler Jett and Keta Bill for that, and Keta's voice was just killer, way better than mine; but when they were cutting it in the studio, I was just crying, it was so beautiful. Later, when I did get to do it live, on the Nearly Human tour, it was hard for me to sing because I had to concentrate on the notes. If I concentrated on the content, my throat would close up."

On the session for 'Can't Stop Running,' on January 17, Gray arranged for a surprise mini-reunion of Utopia by bringing Willie Wilcox on drums, Kasim Sulton on bass, and Roger Powell on synthesizer, along with Prairie Prince, Mingo Lewis, Vernon 'Ice' Black, and the usual Bourgeois Tagg crew.

"I just thought it would be great to have all the Utopia guys come out," says Gray. "Todd had told me that he didn't want the same musicians on every song, anyway, and I know he wanted to have fun and to hear what everybody brought to the party. Todd didn't even know Utopia were coming until they popped round to Fantasy. I bet part of him was thinking, 'Oh my God, she's not gonna make this a Utopia record, is she?'"

Roger Powell recalls that by this time he was living in Colorado, working as a software engineer for the Wave Frame software company, when he got a surprise phone call. "None of us thought we were going to play together again, after our last tour. Todd certainly wasn't expecting us either. As I recall, I think Kas was already supposed to be there or something, but the surprise was that we ended up getting Willie and myself to come out there, too."

"When I heard that Todd was doing this record," says Kasim Sulton, "with a bunch of musicians playing live in the studio, I just thought it would be a great idea if Willie and Roger and I played on one song. So I kind of facilitated getting the three of us into the studio to surprise Todd. Todd doesn't like surprises, though, and you can sort of tell if you see the video footage on YouTube."

"While it was something of a surprise," Rundgren insists, "I would usually be aware of who's going to show up, or I'd know what the instrumentation was going to be on the date. So, if I didn't know it was going to be those particular guys, then there must have been something afoot, and someone had convinced me that someone else was going to show up. I'm sure everyone else knew about it, even if I didn't."

Gray also asked Rundgren assistant Mary Lou Arnold, a veteran of the 11-voice A Cappella tour choir, to join the background vocal chorus at this session. "She's always sung, and she's still singing. But Mary Lou is Todd's right hand man, and he needs her, too. I always say that if there's a plane going down and it's between me and Lou to get the only parachute, I'm giving it to her because she can take care of Todd and my family."

Lyle Workman, who plays the blistering guitar leads on 'Can't Stop Running,' recalls suffering from a bout of anxiety on his way to the session: "Todd's demo already had a great lead guitar solo on it, but now it was going to be 'me' soloing on the track, so the bar was set high, and I really practiced for it. When we cut it, I was set up in the control room, and I just put my heart and soul into it. Then, after we listened to one of the playbacks, Todd just looked back over at me with such an amazing look of approval on his face. I'd frankly never seen that look on him before. He was beaming and held his hand out to say, 'Gimme five.' Those moments are very rare, especially with Todd, and I have to say it was one of the greatest moments of my entire life."

Workman also alludes to a fascinating discussion he had with Rundgren about his song 'The Waiting Game' as they prepared to record it on January 27. "I asked him, 'How do you write something like 'Waiting Game,' with all these cascading, Fifth Dimension-style vocal parts and complex interplaying patterns? He said, 'I dreamed it. The whole thing just came out at once.'"

Gray recalls the exact morning, while staying at the Lake Hill house, when Rundgren had awakened from that dream and made a dash for the studio to make a demo. "He just woke up and said, 'I had the best dream last night. I heard this amazing song with, like, 20 parts and I have to go to the studio and record it before I forget it.' He went down and did 'Waiting Game.' He loved being in the studio in Woodstock, and he could be in that studio for sometimes 36 or 40 hours, without sleeping, if he had an idea he needed to get finished. I don't know how he does it. He would do that and write some songs at home, in Sausalito, and every time he got a new one, he'd say, 'I'm done now, can you book the studio and get it together?'"

The final session for *Nearly Human*, on February 6, was an auspicious occasion as soul great Bobby Womack came in to duet with Rundgren on 'The Want Of A Nail,' which would become the lead track and first single. According to Rundgren, he had originally invited Peter Gabriel, with whom he'd long been trying to collaborate, to sing on the track. "I thought that that would be a fun thing to do," he says, "but at that point, for whatever reason, Peter just couldn't make it happen. Might have been scheduling, or maybe he just didn't feel comfortable with the tune. But I had also been a longtime fan of Bobby Womack, yet it had never occurred to me that his voice and my voice could share the same space. He's got an extremely funky delivery, which I don't have, you know? I'm just … well, white. As it turned out, he was amenable and came up alone from LA. He was great, and really got into the 'mood-altered' take concept. By the end of the session he really threw himself into it; it was great. Ed Vigdor did a little video for the song, and asked Bobby, 'How do you feel about this auspicious occasion?' 'Very suspicious,' he says, 'This is a very suspicious occasion.' I loved that."

"Todd said he wanted some 'black chicks' singing on that track," Gray recalls, "and he needed two of 'em, because Bobby was also coming in. I called Keta and said, 'Quick, I need two black chicks but I only know one.' So we also got Vicki Randle, who's been the percussionist for Jay Leno's *Tonight Show* house band for years."

A sign of the times was that Rundgren's trombone player for the session was Jim Blinn, from Jet Propulsion Labs, whom Rundgren had met through the SIGGRAPH seminars. "Jim is a scientist," says Gray, "and so is Gary Yost, who played the tambourine. Having them on the record came directly out the fact that we were deep into the hacker scene in the Bay Area back then. Todd was a hacker, too, and that's how he met this new group of friends we had. They were just these scientist geeks and nerds, and they were all over at our house all the time. One day, Jim told us that he used to play trombone all the time in high school and college. So we had him come up and he was great."

"He'd played trombone in the marching band at USC," laughs Rundgren, "and still played in the Jet Propulsion Labs Band. So we wrote in a trombone part to give him the chance to pick up his trombone again."

Recording *Nearly Human* on multi-track digital tape presented Rundgren with certain challenges when it came time to do the mix, and after first having the masters edited – by Richard McKernan at Conway Studio in Hollywood – Rundgren mixed the album to two-track digital tape back at Utopia Sound. As was common for Rundgren, Greg Calbi did the album mastering at Sterling Sound, in Manhattan. With the album done, Rundgren didn't stop there, going back to Pixar to generate the images used on the album cover.

Despite all the digital gear involved, *Nearly Human* sounds just that, which was Rundgren's plan all along. "The idea was to create a body of work I could then go out and perform live in this sort of R&B revue context. It was important to be able to do that stuff live, even if I had taken a different approach to making the record. And, of course, as inevitably happens, you always wind up doing better later, and we did get the songs better on the tour."

Rundgren appeared at San Francisco's legendary Fillmore on March 3 with most of the players from the *Nearly Human* album, and Warner Bros released the disc that May. This line-up, one of the most lavish ensembles Rundgren had ever put together, toured with him throughout the months of July and August, and eventually made it as far as Japan in early 1990.

But first, Broadway, or Off-Broadway, at least, beckoned. Concurrently with the *Nearly Human* project, which came together over a protracted period of months, Rundgren had been composing songs for a musical production of *Up Against It* based on a 1967 Joe Orton screenplay that had been rejected by The Beatles as a follow-up to *Help!* In 1986, playwright Tom Ross had resurrected Orton's screenplay and adapted it for Joseph Papp's Public Theater Company and brought in Rundgren to write the tunes.

Despite the Beatles history in the piece, Rundgren wisely avoided the temptation to mount *Deface The Music, Volume 2*, drawing instead upon his familiarity with musical theater to craft original show tunes such as 'When Worlds Collide,' 'If I Have To Be Alone,' 'Love In Disguise,' and the Kurt Weill-esque 'The Smell Of Money.' A reworked version of 'Parallel Lines' was also added to the show, which was directed by Kenneth Elliott with musical arrangements by Doug Katsaros, when it opened at LuEsther Hall on November 14 1989. Theatre critic

Mel Gussow savaged the show in the *New York Times,* and it closed after only 16 performances, on December 17.

Rundgren, however, received a Tony Award nomination, Broadway's highest honor, for his effort, and today has mixed feelings about the whole episode. "*Up Against It* transpired over a series of years, I suppose," he recalls, "from the time it was first proposed to me, and I wrote the first couple of songs for it, to the time it got mounted, a lot of water went under the bridge. I got nominated for that Tony, though, so I suppose that was the only good thing that came out of the whole production."

Rundgren's next solo album would incorporate some of the songs from *Up Against It*, while continuing the live ensemble recording methods he had employed on *Nearly Human*. In some ways, *2nd Wind*, recorded before a live audience over a series of five dates at San Francisco's Palace Of Fine Arts, took Rundgren 'full circle' to the beginning of his production career, when he had engineered The Band's *Stage Fright* on the stage of the Woodstock Playhouse – only this time, Rundgren was in charge, and there was a paying crowd in the seats.

"Once we'd gone out and played *Nearly Human* in front of an audience," he recalls, "as we did here and in Japan, the songs had gone to yet another level. So we took a different approach with *2nd Wind*, and added that audience factor."

Rundgren reassembled most of the *Nearly Human* band, including Gray, Sinnamon, Muldaur, Strickland, Mathews, Powell, Welnick, and Workman, although bass player Ross Vallory, from Journey, took over from Larry Tagg, and Prairie Prince assumed the drum chair after Michael Urbano had a scheduling conflict. After the band had become familiar with Rundgren's demos, they embarked on a brief warm-up tour of California, beginning in Redondo Beach on June 19 and ending in Santa Cruz on July 2.

After a few days of dress rehearsals on the stage at The Palace Of Fine Arts, a mobile truck was brought to the venue and the shows, billed as "live recording sessions," took place over five non-consecutive nights: July 6, 7, 9, 11, and 12. This time Rundgren and his team employed a Sony 48-track digital system, another first for him.

According to Rundgren, the audiences "were told that they would be witnessing a recording session, so it wasn't going to be as socially interactive as a concert might be. Every night, I instructed them to not make any noise immediately after a take. I said, 'Don't yell out, don't whistle, don't make any noises during the course of the song,' because we wanted it to sound like a studio album, yet still retain that extra thing that only happens when you're playing for an audience."

Amusingly, Rundgren gave the audience a hand signal when it was all clear to applaud and let them vote on which hand signal they preferred. "They were really receptive to the concept of being a part of a recording session," says Rundgren, "and I think they found it amusing. It was like theater in some ways, but you were actually bearing witness to a 'real' recording session. If you had ever wanted to go to a recording session, here was your opportunity, as long as you behaved yourself."

While the album constituted the third of his three-album deal with Warner Bros, Rundgren notes that, in addition to the advance money, a good deal of the production expenses were funded directly by ticket sales. "I'm sure," he says, "that whatever money we made on ticket sales went to recording budget. On second thought, maybe I just pocketed it," he laughs.

Roger Powell was back working for a software company when he got the call to come up to San Francisco for *2nd Wind.* "Todd had actually written out all this music with some notation program," says Powell, "because, on that particular project, he was very strict about having everybody play 'exactly' what was written. Todd conducted some of the music with batons and everything, because it had a lot of tempo variation and was very challenging to pull off."

Michele Gray recalls Rundgren being "a little more uptight" during the *2nd Wind* dates than he had been during the relatively casual, and less public, *Nearly Human* sessions. "Todd is definitely the alpha male," says Gray, "and I think he *needed* it to be more difficult, and step it up a notch. Todd doesn't make records for anybody but himself, which is probably why he has such a cult following – they know he's really true to himself. But I was thinking, 'Oh my God, this is gonna be a nightmare.'"

Live audience expectations aside, Gray notes that inviting their combined families to the Palace Of Fine Arts likely added an extra layer of tension to the proceedings. "We were dumb," Gray laughs, "and brought my parents and Todd's parents down for the whole week of the sessions. I have to say, though, that this was a period where Todd really mended the relationship with his mom and dad. I was aware that he hadn't gotten along with his parents growing up, so it was very cool to see his dad, at the side of the stage, singing all the songs. His dad wasn't the sort who would ever have told him he did a good job, whereas on the other hand, Ruth, his mom, would go out and absorb the fan base and became the 'mother of Jesus,'" she laughs.

"It was really a family moment," Gray continues, "and he'd even written the song 'Kindness' about his grandmother. To top it off, we had Rex and Randy there too, so Todd had to wear a lot of hats and be the parent, son, son-in-law, master of ceremonies, singer, and producer. I was singing too, so it was a strange time for both of us to be real professionals on stage and then, backstage, have to discipline the boys for having a popcorn fight."

Never one to waste good material, Rundgren included the *Up Against It* songs 'The Smell Of Money,' 'If I Have To Be Alone,' and 'Love In Disguise' on the album. With so many family matters to attend to, Gray was just one of the backing singers, abdicating her Production Manager title to Joe Lamond.

Gray didn't even get to sing the featured duet with Rundgren on 'Love In Disguise,' a decision she says was mildly controversial around the dinner table at home. "Todd has such a problem with nepotism, so he didn't want anybody to think that I was getting preferential treatment or anything. We were having sushi dinner one night and he said, 'I'm gonna ask Shandi [Sinnamon] to sing the duet.' I said, 'Why? Do you think she has a better voice than I do?' He said 'No, but I don't want people to think it's the Steve & Eydie show.'"

On January 16 1991, *2nd Wind,* Todd Rundgren's second all-digital solo album, and his last for a major label, was released. To promote the work, Rundgren used cutting-edge technology to produce the video for the single, 'Change Myself,' employing the NewTek Video Toaster card for the Commodore Amiga 2000 computer.

As the 90s began, Rundgren was already moving away from conventional notions of what a rock producer or recording artist should be, and over the next two decades he would redefine those terms again and again. But the *Nearly Human* and *2nd Wind* productions could be said to have marked the end of an era. While Rundgren would continue to produce records for himself, and others, many of the innovative and individual technologies and business models he embraced and/or pioneered over the next 20 years would have such an empowering effect on future artists as to render redundant record producers, big studios, and even record labels.

"Obviously," says Rundgren, "these two records involved no computers at all, other than the fact that they were digitally recorded. The music was all performed live, with no sequencing of any kind. So I just started evaluating certain phenomena that were happening to music in general, and arriving at these conclusions that led me to believe that it was time for me to start putting some sort of 'technological spin' on what I was doing. There were things changing in music in general, like the fact that a degree of exhaustion, I guess, had found its way into the music scene to the point that, now, music was being recycled."

While there were other productions – including Jill Sobule's debut, *Things Here Are Different*, a follow-up album with The Pursuit Of Happiness, *One Sided Story*, in 1990, and a couple of albums for Japanese artist Hiroshi Takano in 1990 and 1991 – Rundgren was increasingly split between music and technology. Thanks to the computer revolution raging all around him, the next age would belong to the individual, and Todd Rundgren was never anything less than an individualist. The golden age of the studio producer may have passed, but Rundgren had proved his point. He'd been there, done that, and was hungry for new adventures.

There's Always More

"If it weren't for my musical career," Todd Rundgren once said, "I probably would have ended up attending college to become a computer programmer." Of course, Rundgren's career continued, and still continues, long after 1991; but the golden age of studio recording had given way to the digital age, where constant improvements in recording systems empowered the individual and downplayed the need for outside players or producers. As Rundgren's focus veered between his interests in new technology and live musical performance, his own self-recording experiments, which used to require bulky analog tapes, huge consoles, and racks of outboard gear, could be performed alone with nothing more than a personal computer.

Outside the studio, Rundgren briefly reunited with Utopia for a short Japanese tour, documented on the live album *Redux '92 Live In Japan: Utopia*, and performed as a member of Ringo Starr And His All Star band. Additionally, Rundgren and Gray had a baby son, Rebop, who was born in February of that year.

All through this era, whenever Rundgren came back to recording, he would constantly reinvent his methods. Having taken note of digital sampling and remixing, Rundgren paid particular attention to the phenomenon of UK acts such as The KLF and Frankie Goes To Hollywood, who managed to release multiple remixes of the same single, over and over. He was fascinated with the general public's acceptance of essentially reconstructed mixes, or whole singles, such as Vanilla Ice's 'Ice Ice Baby' or M.C. Hammer's 'Can't Touch This,' built out of samples from other records.

He also realized that people were beginning to hear music differently, and his response came in the form of an album written around the concept of listener interactivity, entitled *No World Order,* released by Forward, a subsidiary of Rhino, in May 1993. "Music was constantly being recontextualized," says Rundgren, "via sampling or remixing, into a product that was called a 'new song.' My thought was that, if the audience was responding to this, then this is something where you could use technology to actually emulate in real time. *No World Order* was written knowing that certain technological things had to be performed on it afterwards and that it would be presented in ways that might be recontextualized in real time. So before I could make the music I had to prove the concept first, to see whether such a thing was possible."

Rundgren contacted his programming partner, Aaron Dave Levine, with whom he had designed the Flowfazer screensaver, and set out to design the first interactive music CD. Fittingly, his next album would be credited to TR-i – the added "i" to announce the interactive factor. Encouraged at the time by news of the world's first CD-I player, developed by Philips, Rundgren offered to create a musical disc that could exploit the new interactivity.

"So I recorded some music," says Rundgren, "realizing that the song forms would necessarily be arbitrary. This forced me to think in terms of every piece of music having a discrete beginning and end, which could be cut out and pasted into a different context. There was a certain degree of technical challenge in that and it was also the first time I used sequencers to produce a significant part of the music. So much of the *No World Order* record was the process of tooling all of the sound that had been recorded to accommodate interactive technology. And, of course, it also came out in conventional record form but, by design, the record could have come out an infinite number of other ways. The only way to demonstrate this interactivity was to go to the logical conclusion of releasing it on interactive devices – that's why it came out on CD-I and CD-ROMS for both PC and Mac."

Unfortunately, Rundgren says that interactivity was such a leading-edge concept that many listeners, having only heard one version of the record, were taken aback by the approach. The rapping didn't help matters with some of his fans. "A lot of the fans didn't like the musical form at all," he says, laughing, "whereas I found it kind of liberating. The implicitly poetic nature of rap music made it easier to create these little modules that could be switched around and they would still have meaning, in spite of the reordering. Sometimes it would sound like rap of some kind, but then in a different context it could be [word jazz] like Ken Nordine, something like that. I wasn't thinking, 'Oh, I'm trying to gain validity as a rapper here,' I was thinking more in terms of the possibilities it afforded in this new experimental context."

To further demonstrate his concept, Rundgren had some of his producer friends – Jerry Harrison, Don Was, Hal Willner, and Bob Clearmountain – each contribute their own remixes of *No World Order*: "One producer picked a kind of central theme and then would branch off into some of these other musical themes but always return to this one theme. Another one's might be much more instrumental-oriented than either my version or any of the other producers' versions, and they might try to construct an instrumental suite with almost no vocalization in it. These producers' mixes became the basic versions, so you could start with their versions and apply various programmatic filters and stuff like that on it to change it into something you wanted."

While the Philips CD-I hardware never really caught on, Rundgren had, at the very least, proved that interactivity was viable. "In fact," he says, "it would be much easier with today's technology, and I have since rebuilt the system in other forms. I suppose if I was to put up a website where you could do this, we could gauge whether the audience has any level of interest in the concept. There are lots of [Pandora-style applications] nowadays, but they're always based on assumptions and you rate every song on a certain playlist – I 'like' this song or I 'don't like' this song – but there's nothing to say why you like it or don't like it. They make the assumption that you like a similar style, or a similar subject matter, but there could be a reason other than their assumption."

In 1995, Rundgren briefly returned to film composing with his original score for Peter and Bobby Farrelly's comedy, *Dumb And Dumber*, starring Jim Carrey. Also, from January 1995 to October 1996 he hosted the award-winning syndicated radio program *The Difference With Todd Rundgren,* interviewing and playing music by artists ranging from Joni Mitchell and Barenaked Ladies to Elvis Costello and Lou Reed.

Rundgren's next solo record, *The Individualist,* also credited to TR-i, was made with mostly synthesized sounds played and programmed by Rundgren himself, augmented by group vocals from Mary Lou Arnold, Ann Lang, Ed Bishop, John Ferenzik, Tom Nicholson, and Jesse Gress. This time, Rundgren experimented with musical structure as well as technology.

"If you go back and inspect the record," says Rundgren, "almost all of the songs are between six and eight minutes long – it was a kind of an experiment in long-form composition. I was focusing on the relationship of the bass or 'root' notes to the rest of what was going on. I had a specific vision in my head, particularly in the opening track, of trying to create this idea of flying over a landscape in an airplane, with the various features changing underneath you but with the constant thrum of the engine going on while everything else goes changing by. So a lot of the bass parts on the record have this unusual aspect of being the same thing over and over and over again, but you never notice it because everything else is constantly changing around it. And we sampled [former Republican Vice President] Dan Quayle [on 'Family Values'], so there's a highly political, somewhat apocalyptic note to that particular piece, too."

Released in November 1995 by Digital Entertainment, *The Individualist* was one of the first, and, according to Rundgren, last, 'Enhanced' CDs. When played in a conventional CD player, the disc operated as normal, but when inserted into a computer, the Enhanced content files would engage. "I remember it had a great effect on our release plans," says Rundgren, "because we were waiting for drivers from Microsoft to enable a PC to play an Enhanced CD. We had to essentially visualize the entire record and use the unused space on the CD to put all sorts of computer data and stuff like that."

Some time in 1996, Rundgren and his family left the Bay Area and relocated to the Hawaiian island of Kauai. In May, he stopped working at Utopia Sound for good. The Hermit of Mink Hollow was now the Hermit of Mahalo, and without a home studio for the first time in over ten years. In 1997, Japanese label Pony Canyon released a CD of the *Up Against It* music. The same year, during his worldwide tour behind *The Individualist,* Rundgren became one of the first Western artists to perform in Shanghai, China, backed by Prairie Prince, Larry Tagg, keyboardist John Ferenzik, and his new constant guitarist, Jesse Gress. Returning to Kauai, Rundgren was commissioned by Guardian, a subsidiary of Angel Records, to produce a curiously samba-friendly retrospective recording called *With A Twist*, which was released in September of that year.

"I had been hearing a lot about the size of the Latin music market," says Rundgren, "which is apparently 'humongous.' I had never really considered that market, or toured in Latin countries, so I began to think that maybe I'd like to do something with a Latin style. The people who released the project had originally wanted me to be part of a series of 'one-off' records by various artists who had fat catalogues, and everybody – such as James Taylor – was just doing acoustified versions of familiar songs. So I thought here's an opportunity to combine this Latin music idea with their agenda, which is to do the music in a different form."

Rundgren flew his band out to Kauai for two weeks so they could brush up on their bossa nova. "Actually," he says, "we'd been stocking up on stuff like Claus Ogerman, João Gilberto, and Nelson Riddle since the late 80s, when we'd been touring in Japan. It seemed to me that the Japanese were the first ones to kind of rediscover lounge music. This gave all of us a bit of a leg-up when it came time to learn that kind of bossa nova music or 'loungey' stuff."

Still with no home studio, Rundgren recorded *With A Twist* on location at the home of basketball star Kareem Abdul-Jabbar, overlooking Kauai's Secret Beach, accompanied by Prairie Prince, Kasim Sulton, John Ferenzik, and Jesse Gress. Rundgren played no guitar himself, concentrating instead on arranging and performing impressive feats of multi-tracked vocalese. "In fact, the hardest part was actually 'singing' this music, because it's way easier to sing loud than it is to sing that real quiet smooth stuff. It makes you dizzy, so it was something of a challenge in building the background vocals. It doesn't sound like hard work but it is!"

In addition to hosting an internet radio program, *Music Nexus*, Rundgren launched the With A Twist tour, starting in San Francisco in October 1997, which resembled a traveling Tiki Lounge. "I conceptualized this whole club-within-a-club thing," says Rundgren, still amused by the concept. "We'd have like three busloads of tourists come in during the evening. For us it was like we were pre-visualizing our retirement; this is what we'll all do when we're really old. I'll be like [Hawaiian singer] Don Ho, I'll have a little place somewhere here on the island and I won't tour anymore; tourists will come and see me play."

Apart from recording, Rundgren had continued to pursue emergent technologies and, in March of 1996, he launched, along with digital media consultant Kelli Richards, a company called Waking Dreams. It launched PatroNet, a prescient, subscriber-based internet music delivery system designed to eliminate the record company middleman and bridge the digital divide between recording artists and their fans. "The idea was to sponsor other artists to write material," says Rundgren, "in similar fashion to the way rich nobles would become patrons to Renaissance artists to create works for them." From the start, PatroNet jumped right in by uploading exclusive Rundgren content, including his first-ever internet-only 'single,' which featured 'Hit Me Like A Train' and 'Surf Talks.'

As for production work, May 1999 saw the release of an album for Splender, *Halfway Down The Sky,* and in October of the same year, he began his first 'all-digital' production, for legendary California punk group Bad Religion, entitled *The New America*. This was the first time Rundgren had recorded entirely on a Mac G4, using Line 6's Amp Farm amplifier simulators and Digidesign ProTools Mix124 system, which he had set up in Victor's Barn in Kauai, ostensibly to get a booming acoustic drum sound – one of the few sounds, apart from vocals, not created in the digital domain. "That entire project never ever left the computer," he says, "we had 16 inputs and I didn't use any outboard gear at all."

In July, Rundgren welcomed Minnesotan brothers Ryan and Ev Olcott – trading under the band name 12 Rods – to Kauai, and their album, *Separation Anxieties,* was released by V2 Records in June 2000, shortly after the Bad Religion record hit the racks. Additionally, Cleopatra Records released *Todd Rundgren: Reconstructed* – a compilation of remixes of Rundgren's music by outside DJs – in October.

As for live gigs, Rundgren launched the aptly named Power Trio Tour, joined by Kasim Sulton and drummer Trey Sabatelli, performing over 40 shows, from May through August.

In addition to patronet.com, Rundgren had launched his own web portal, tr-i.com, but by 2000 he had taken a break from active promotion of the PatroNet delivery system. He had arguably been too far ahead of the curve for mainstream acceptance of the idea, and he was also somewhat wary of newcomer Sean Fanning's Napster, a commerce-free file-sharing enterprise, which he felt was the antithesis of his artist-friendly 'patronage' based model.

Rundgren had railed about the state of file-sharing in a June 2000 interview with Jeff Brown, for Kansas City's *Pitch* magazine. "I'm not particularly an intellectual property freak," he said, "but the great hypocrisy of the whole issue is that most of these really abusive musical pirates are college kids who are going to go out and join some computer company, and their entire livelihood will be based on intellectual property. In ten years, they'll be dead set against anybody taking their software illegally, but right now, access to downloadable teen pop is their 'God-given right.'"

Temporarily discouraged, Rundgren reverted to a more conventional compact disc format for *One Long Year*, a compilation of selected PatroNet material, released in June 2000, by Artemis Records. According to Rundgren, the CD fulfilled a dual objective. "I had thought that I could build PatroNet's core service around me writing and recording one song a month and allow subscribers to listen to it at various stages, all the way up to completion, and then I'd do another song and another until we had a whole CD. The problem was I really didn't have the discipline to do that. And the nature of my inspiration was not such that I could just say, 'Okay, it's time to write a song this month.' So I would have spurts of creativity and then spurts where I wasn't creative. Also I was continuing to tour, so I'd be out on the road without the facility to record anything. So in the long run it turned out not to be a completely successful experiment, and it didn't amount to something that was especially charming."

Rundgren admits that the arresting bossa nova remake of 'Love Of The Common Man' on *One Long Year* was indeed a hold-over from the *With A Twist* sessions: "But I didn't think it particularly 'belonged' on *With A Twist*. As a matter of fact, at that time, we had the basic track but didn't put the other instrumentation or vocals on it. I just felt that from a subject-matter standpoint it didn't fit the rest of the record. That was the whole trouble with *One Long Year* – we had a song like 'I Hate My Frickin' ISP' alongside 'Yer Fast' alongside a bossa nova number, then an acoustic ukulele version of 'Bang The Drum All Day' ['Bang On The Ukulele Daily'] – so it was quite obviously a patchwork of things. These tracks were all fine on their own but it only works in the most completist sense as a record. I don't think it compares favorably with most of my other work."

In the summer of 2001, Rundgren was part of an ensemble gathered for touring show called *A Walk Down Abbey Road: A Tribute To The Beatles*, which also included, at various times, Ann Wilson from Heart, John Entwistle from The Who, Jack Bruce from Cream and producer/keyboard player Alan Parsons. Over the next few years, Rundgren continued to do solo tours, often opening for Hall & Oates and employing the headliners' backing band. Increasingly, Rundgren's stage guitar of choice was his 'Sea Foam green' Strat-style Fernandes, which he nicknamed "Foamy."

By late 2003, Rundgren had returned to the concept album form as he prepared his next solo album, *Liars*, working purely on his Mac G3 laptop, running OS 9.2 at the time, using plug-ins and software synthesizers to emulate the sounds of Hammond B3 organs and Wurlitzer or Fender Rhodes electric pianos. He was now running "Foamy" through Line 6 amp simulators and even employed Antares microphone modeling software to take the signal from his Beyer MCD100 digital dynamic mic and simulate the tone of his preferred Neumann 87. Gone, too, were the racks and racks of graphic equalizer units he had been accustomed to in his home studios of the 70s and 80s, replaced now by Channel Strip software plug-ins.

The record was released on April 6 2004 by Sanctuary Records. Rundgren told *Sound On Sound* magazine's Paul Tingen how it was created, using Propellerhead's Reason recording software and Pro Tools v5.1. "Reason is great," he said. "The virtualization of instruments and effects is something I can't go back from now. My virtual instruments were for the most part Reason's take on the classics. Also, I got used to the idea of not having to own Urei 1176 compressors any more. Instead I can have 20 of them virtually, if I want."

Looking back today, Rundgren admits that it took him longer than usual to compose the songs for *Liars* because he was especially mindful about having a set of coherent songs with thematically linked lyrics. Musically, he says he was also interested in exploring both the vintage soul sounds of his youth and the more contemporary club music and other electronica.

"It wasn't coming to me via club culture," Rundgren insists, "so much as from the 30-second or one-minute bits of drum'n'bass music used in TV commercials and the like. I started to figure out ways to incorporate some of that into what I was doing. At the same time, in some ways I was reconnecting with certain sonic aspects of these retro keyboard sounds, like the Wurlitzer and Rhodes piano or the B3 organ. Sure, I used all the techno techniques on something like 'Truth,' because that was supposed to be a techno track. But, for the most part, I avoided using purely synthetic sounds and most everything was supposed to sound like a real instrument; and I was also using orchestral samples and other stuff."

Liars enjoyed an unexpected wave of critical success as a new generation of musicians seemed to either name-check Rundgren as an influence or sample his music outright. Rundgren claims this approbation even came as something of a shock to him. "I was at a point where people hadn't even been paying attention to the records I was making, so I had no expectations of my audience when *Liars* came out. It essentially revitalized me, and my career, in a way."

Touring from spring to fall 2004, Rundgren was backed by 'The Liars' – Jesse Gress, Kasim Sulton, John Ferenzik, and Prairie Prince – who joined him in wearing extravagantly traditional 'religious' costumes and playing on an elaborate, aluminum-grid stage set. When the production simply proved too costly to justify continuing, Rundgren pulled the tour off the road and went out in a guitar and piano duo with songwriter Joe Jackson, backed by string quartet Ethel. It was, he says, "the only way I could make money."

Money continued to be an issue into 2006, when Rundgren was invited to join some original members of The Cars, Greg Hawkes and Elliott Easton, to do a tour and possibly record some new songs as The New Cars, assisted by Kasim Sulton and Prairie Prince. The move was controversial with both Rundgren's fans and those of The Cars, but Michele Gray says that former Cars frontman Ric Ocasek had personally suggested that Rundgren take his place.

"Everybody thought Todd went behind Ric's back," Gray explains, "but Ric just didn't want to tour anymore. But [as songwriter and owner of the group name] Ric still got a percentage of ticket sales for touring, so all of the press he did against it was really to promote it, because controversy generates interest. I remember we didn't think it was a good idea, at first, but we needed the money and Todd was told he'd likely make over a million dollars within one to two years. As it happened, we lost half a million instead of making two. We lost our shirts because the production company spent double what they were supposed to spend in putting the production together."

According to Rundgren, The New Cars tour and album, *It's Alive*, featuring live versions of Cars hits plus some new originals, seemed like "an opportunity to play some nice electric music and make some money, too. But it did not achieve expectations." Fate intervened when guitarist Elliot Easton broke his collarbone, delaying the tour by months. "So after Elliot's unfortunate accident," Rundgren says, "I had to go out and find something to do. I was already in a guitar-playing mode, so I decided to put a guitar quartet together and go tour around Canada for a few weeks."

Rundgren says that the guitar quartet, initially comprised of Rundgren and Gress on guitars, with bassist Tony Levin and drummer Jerry Marotta, was a hit with his fans and fun for him, too – so much so that he continued this format on tour into 2008, with various line-up changes here and there. "The positive response led me to conclude that, when I did make another record, I was gonna stay focused on the guitar aspect on it."

Released on September 30 2008, by Hi-Fi Records, *Arena* was recorded in much the same way as *Liars*. "In a sense it was still a 'concept album,' and I'm still working alone, with software amps and simulators for drums, because it's more important for me to create something that's thematically coherent and something that is within my control. Lyrically, whereas the theme of *Liars* was deception, the theme of *Arena* was gonna be courage and cowardice."

With all the rock guitar sounds up front in the mix, *Arena* was vaguely evocative of Rundgren's mid-70s work. Only now Rundgren can fit a Secret Sound's worth of gear into his laptop. As on *Liars*, he continued to use Reason software, augmented with Line 6 TonePort UX-8 (with GearBox), and Sonoma Wire Works' RiffWorks program synched to Reason using ReWire. He says he now relied less and less on ProTools, having been soured by problems he'd encountered with that system. Rundgren maintains that whatever format he records in, now or in the future, what will continue to matter most is the 'feeling' generated by a 'performance' – however he arrives at it.

"On *Arena*," says Rundgren "I was visualizing a band when I programmed it, because I knew I was going to have to play these songs live, at some point. Having been a drummer, if I'm gonna program drums, I'll write them the way a drummer would play. Those kinds of things are subliminal, in a way, but even a listener who doesn't have a lot of sophistication [about drumming] will be able to discern the difference between a synthesized performance and a live performance if the synthesized performance does not have that necessary attention to detail."

By 2009, Todd Rundgren's recording methods had almost come full circle. Just as he had in his heyday – the 70s and 80s – he went back to working alone, once more employing the best technology available to get him to the music in the straightest line possible, technical precision be damned. At the close of the year, Rundgren had a rare opportunity to go backward in time, grab something from the earliest days of his production career and drag it, screaming, into the 21st century: he was back producing The New York Dolls.

Since 2004, The Dolls – with only two surviving original members, guitarist Sylvain Sylvain and frontman David Johansen – had relaunched their brand as a modern recording act. They had added drummer Brian Delaney, guitarist Steve Conte, keyboardist Brian Koonin and bassist Sami Yaffa and, by 2006, had released a comeback album, *One Day It Will Please Us To Remember Even This*, produced by Jack Douglas, who had assisted Rundgren with their debut in 1973. Now, the Dolls were again knocking on Rundgren's door, a full 35 years after their hectic first sessions at the Record Plant, to record their 2009 release *'Cause I Sez So*.

According to Johansen, while the technology may have changed in those three-and-a-half decades, Rundgren remains the same. "Of course, his innate curiosity about sound hasn't changed either. The key difference being that today he's got all those years of exploration under his belt. He didn't want to go backward in time, and neither did we. Actually, in my observation, the cool thing about Todd, and what keeps him going, so to speak, is that he likes to throw everything out and start all over again or do something for the fuck of it."

Early in January 2009, the current New York Dolls, minus Koonin, convened at Rundgren's Hawaiian home, in the middle of the winter rainy season. "You can take the Dolls out of New York," says Johansen, "but you can't the New York out of the Dolls. I like the way Todd approaches record-making these days. We kind of evoked the sound of our first album but, I always say, we managed to drag it by the hair into the present day."

Rundgren continued his trend of tapeless recording for the Dolls album, running ProTools LE, which he describes as "a pain in the ass, as usual." Guitarist Steve Conte remembers some of the issues that Rundgren had with multiple software platforms, during the sessions, tracked mainly at a nearby rented house in Kauai. "Todd actually spent a few days transferring all the data into the Logic audio program he prefers to use. But, in the end, he had to get another ProTools system in to transfer back to, due to compatibility issues or something."

Conte admits that the sounds Rundgren found for the Dolls forever changed his mind about recording digitally. "For me, doing this record with Todd sunk that whole theory that 'digital is cold' and that you can't mix 'within the box.' I have spent so much money on my own records renting outboard tube stuff and going to tape to try to warm up digital tracks. All Todd needs to do is use his expert musician and engineer ears and place microphones in the right place, and the sounds mix themselves. 'We're mixing as we're recording,' he would say, and it was true."

A small mutiny was averted, however, after Rundgren had initially suggested they eschew amplifiers in favor of going directly into his preferred Line 6 amp simulators. "I always offer the possibility of recording the guitars directly," says Rundgren, "and using amp modeling plug-ins. This gives you the option of changing the amp sound after the performance is captured. I used that technique on the Bad Religion album, and they seemed fine with it. Syl and Steve, however, depended on too much feedback during the performance, so it was not as practical for them."

"We had a real attitude," says Conte in agreement, "about Todd's Line 6 combo amp, like, 'The New York Dolls do not use digital amp simulators; we use overdriven tubes and speaker cabinets.' When we heard how hard it was to rent good gear on Kauai, we brought in our own amp heads and pedals."

"We shipped all this stuff over," adds Syl Sylvain, "along with all our guitars, of course, and it cost us a fortune." With Rundgren's help, *'Cause I Sez So* reaffirmed The New York Dolls' reputation as a great rock'n'roll band with tons more to say and a uniquely swaggering way to say it. Johansen, as always, is philosophical on the subject of Todd Rundgren, with whom he believes he shares as 'psychic understanding.'

"I think that we can communicate almost better without words," says Johansen. "In more than a few ways, it was like that on that first album, 36 years ago. I don't think we said any more than a hundred words together the whole time we were together. We didn't need to."

In late 2009, and continuing into 2010, Todd Rundgren revisited another aspect of his past with a series of concerts where he performed his entire *A Wizard, A True Star* album live for the first time ever. He was joined by a who's who of Rundgren associates, including Kasim Sulton, Jesse Gress, Prairie Prince, Greg Hawkes, Bobby Strickland, Michele (Gray) Rundgren, and Roger Powell (replaced on later dates by original Utopian Ralph Schuckett). As the elaborately staged, multi-costumed *Wizard* show opened, Rundgren spacewalked out, through a smoke machine fog, wearing a NASA-style white Apollo spacesuit, to sing the opening lines from the opening song, 'International Feel.' "Here we are again," the spaceman sang, "The start of the end / But there's more."

After the final strains of 'Just One Victory' had died out, Rundgren returned to his studio-less studio in Kauai, to revisit a past even older than his own. Tapping into the same blues streak that had started him off as a young slide guitarist in Woody's Truck Stop, four decades earlier, Rundgren recorded and released a heartfelt tribute to the seminal songs of Robert Johnson. Always the frustrated comedian, however, he couldn't resist naming the album *Todd Rundgren's Johnson.* But that's Todd Rundgren in a nutshell: a serious thinker too smart to take himself seriously, pushing into the future while cracking wise about the past.

There's always more.

RUNTOLOGY: A SELECTED DISCOGRAPHY OF TODD RUNDGREN PRODUCTIONS

Compiled by Paul Myers

The following is a list of the major original works produced by Todd Rundgren. It includes a few notable exceptions where Rundgren was only credited as engineer or where only a few of his produced tracks made it to a final album. (Bill Traut was the producer of the first Nazz release, which is why it does not appear on the list.)

WITH NAZZ

Nazz Nazz (SGC 1969)
Nazz III (SGC 1971)

AS TODD RUNDGREN

Runt (Ampex/Bearsville 1970)
The Ballad Of Todd Rundgren (Bearsville 1971)
Something/Anything? (Bearsville 1972)
A Wizard, A True Star (Bearsville 1973)
Todd (Bearsville 1974)
Initiation (Bearsville 1975)
Faithful (Bearsville 1976)
Hermit Of Mink Hollow (Bearsville 1977)
Back To The Bars (Bearsville 1978)
Healing (Bearsville 1981)
The Ever Popular Tortured Artist Effect (Bearsville 1982)
A Cappella (Warner Bros 1985)
Nearly Human (Warner Bros 1989)
2nd Wind (Warner Bros 1991)
Up Against It (Pony Canyon (Japan) 1997)
With A Twist... (Guardian 1997)
One Long Year (Artemis 2000)
Reconstructed (Cleopatra 2000)
Liars (Sanctuary 2004)
Arena (HiFi 2008)
Todd Rundgren's Johnson (HiFi 2010)

AS TR-I

No World Order (Pony Canyon Japan 1992)
No World Order CD-i (Philips 1992)
No World Order (version 1.01) (Pony Canyon Japan 1992)
No World Order Lite (Pony Canyon Japan 1994)
No World Order CD-ROM (Electronic Arts 1994)
The Individualist (Pony Canyon Japan 1995)
The Individualist CD-e (Ion 1996)

WITH UTOPIA

Todd Rundgren's Utopia (Bearsville 1974)
Todd Rundgren's Utopia: Another Live (Bearsville 1975)
Ra (Bearsville 1977)
Oops! Wrong Planet (Bearsville 1977)
Adventures In Utopia (Bearsville 1980)
Deface The Music (Bearsville 1980)
Swing To The Right (Bearsville 1982)
Utopia (Network 1982)
Oblivion (Passport 1983)
POV (Passport 1985)
Trivia (Passport 1986)
Redux '92: Live In Japan (Rhino 1993)
POV, Oblivion, And Some Trivia (Rhino 1996)

SELECTED ARTISTS PRODUCED BY TODD RUNDGREN

American Dream *American Dream* (Ampex / Bearsville 1969)

The Band *Stage Fright* (Capitol 1970; engineer only)
Great Speckled Bird *Great Speckled Bird* (Ampex / Bearsville 1970)
Jesse Winchester *Jesse Winchester* (Ampex / Bearsville 1970)
Jericho *Jericho* (Ampex / Bearsville 1970)
Butterfield Blues Band *Live* (Elektra 1970)
Sparks (originally Halfnelson) *Halfnelson* (Bearsville 1971)
James Cotton *Taking Care Of Business* (Capitol 1971)
Butterfield Blues Band *Sometimes I Just Feel Like Smilin'* (Elektra 1971)
Badfinger *Straight Up* (Apple 1971)
Jesse Winchester *Third Down, 110 To Go* (Bearsville 1972; three tracks only)
Mark 'Moogy' Klingman *Moogy* (Capitol 1972)
Buzzy Lindhart *Buzzy* (Kama Sutra 1972)
Fanny *Mother's Pride* (Reprise 1973)
New York Dolls *New York Dolls* (Mercury 1973)
Grand Funk *We're An American Band* (Capitol 1973)
Badfinger *Ass* (Apple 1973; two tracks only)
Grand Funk *Shinin' On* (Capitol 1974)
Daryl Hall & John Oates *War Babies* (Atlantic 1974)
Felix Cavaliere *Felix Cavaliere* (Bearsville 1974)
The Hello People *The Handsome Devils* (ABC 1974)
The Hello People *Bricks* (ABC 1975)
Steve Hillage *L* (Virgin 1976)
Meat Loaf *Bat Out Of Hell* (Cleveland International/Epic 1977)
The Tubes *Remote Control* (A&M 1979)
Tom Robinson Band *TRB Two* (Harvest/EMI 1979)
Patti Smith Group *Wave* (Arista 1979)
Rick Derringer *Guitars And Women* (co-production) (Blue Sky 1979)
Shaun Cassidy *Wasp* (Warner Bros 1980)
Jim Steinman *Bad For Good* (Cleveland International/Epic 1981; co-production)
Moondogs *That's What Friends Are For (*Sire 1981)
New England *Walking Wild (*Elektra 1981)
The Psychedelic Furs *Forever Now* (Columbia 1982)
The Rubinoos *Party Of Two* (Warner Bros. 1983)
Cheap Trick *Next Position Please* (Epic 1983)
Jules Shear *Watch Dog* (EMI America 1983)
Lords Of The New Church 'Live For Today' (IRS single 1983)
The Tubes *Love Bomb* (Capitol 1984)
What Is This? *What Is This?* (MCA 1985)
Hunter *Dreams Of Ordinary Men* (Polydor 1986)
XTC *Skylarking* (Virgin/Geffen 1986)
Bourgeois Tagg *Yoyo* (Island 1987)
The Pursuit of Happiness *Love Junk* (Chrysalis 1988)
Jill Sobule *Things Here Are Different* (MCA 1990)
Hiroshi Takano *Cue* (Toshiba 1990)
The Pursuit of Happiness *One Sided Story* (Chrysalis 1990)
Hiroshi Takano – Awakening (Toshiba 1991)
Paul Shaffer *The World's Most Dangerous Party* (SBK 1993)
Splender *Halfway Down The Sky* (Columbia 1999)
Bad Religion *The New America* (Atlantic 2000)
12 Rods *Separation Anxieties* (V2 2000)
New York Dolls *'Cause I Sez So* (Atco 2009)

INDEX

Words *in italics* indicate album titles unless otherwise stated. Words 'in quotes' indicate song titles. Page numbers in **bold** indicate illustrations.

ACKNOWLEDGEMENTS

AUTHOR'S THANKS

This book would not exist without the music and determined vision of Todd Rundgren, who was remarkably accommodating during the interview process. His generosity and patience with my myriad questions was both admirable and impressive. I came into this process an objective fan of his work, but have left with a personal respect for him and for the sheer force of his creative will. I am also beholden to the kindness of the fabulous Michele Rundgren and the Most Valued Players on 'Team Todd' – Eric Gardner, Lynn Robnett, and the indefatigable Mary Lou Arnold – all of whom played important roles in enabling me to do the book. Thanks also to Jean Lannen for her dedicated eye. And there's no way I'm getting out of here without thanking Roger Linder at the TR Connection, Doug Ford at RundgrenRadio, Chris Andersen, Bud Scoppa, Marc Nathan, Peter Noble (for all kinds of things), Deborah Chesher, Dan Matovina (for the Badfinger stuff), Todd Bernhardt (for XTC help), Kelli Richards, Jonathan Wolfson, Meryn Cadell, and Billy James. Indirect thanks to journalists Barney Hoskyns and Paul Lester for their definitive Rundgren articles over the years.

Additionally, a shout out is in order to Dan Derbridge and Mark Palin, two childhood friends who first introduced me to the sounds of Todd Rundgren, along with lifelong friend Michael Phillip Wojewoda, from whom I learned the rest of what I know about recording.

My Jawbone Press experience began with Kevin Becketti, who is just an all around great guy, and continued with the assistance of Tony Bacon, Nigel Osborne, Tom Seabrook, and John Morrish.

As for the non-Todd interviews, my hat is off to ALL the subjects who deigned to discuss their artistry with me, often answering queries about work they did over 30 years ago. Particularly generous in this regard were Patti Smith, Lenny Kaye, Jay Dee Daugherty, Ivan Kral, Jim Steinman, Meat Loaf, Ellen Foley, Robbie Robertson, Kasim Sulton, Roger Powell, Willie Wilcox, Kevin Ellman, Moogy Klingman, Ralph Schuckett, John Siegler, Russell Mael, James Lowe, Earle Mankey, Daryl Hall, Andy Partridge, Dave Gregory (for the detailed notes and great photos), Colin Moulding, David Johansen, Sylvain Sylvain, Steve Conte, Rick Nielsen, Bun E. Carlos, Tim and Richard Butler, Vince Ely, Lyle Workman, Michael Urbano, Brent Bourgeois, Larry Tagg, Moe Berg, Kris Abbott, Johnny Sinclair, Leslie Stanwyck, Dave Gilby, Michael Cotten, Prairie Prince, Bill Spooner, Lynn Goldsmith, Don Brewer, Craig Frost, and Mark Farner.

PUBLISHER'S THANKS

Jawbone Press would like to thank Paul Cooper, Sarah Field, Dave Gregory, Jean Lannen, James Lowe, and Frank White.

PICTURE CREDITS

The photographs used in this book came from the following copyright holders, and we are grateful for their help. **Jacket front** Gijsbert Hanekroot / Redfern's; **2-3** James Lowe / Bearsville Records; **7** James Lowe (top); Ruth Rundgren (bottom left); Moogy Klingman (bottom right); **8** Bob Gruen / bobgruen.com (top); Bearsville Records (bottom); **9** Paul Myers (top left); Bob Gruen / bobgruen.com (bottom); **10** Fotos International / Rex Features (top); Bob Leafe / Frank White Agency (bottom); **11** Lynn Goldsmith / Corbis (main picture); Dave Gregory (inset); **12–13** Lynn Goldsmith / Corbis (main picture); Bob Leafe / Frank White Agency (inset); **14** Jean Lannen / jeanlannenimages.com (main picture); Dave Gregory (three inset images); **15** Jean Lannen / jeanlannenimages.com (both pictures); **16** Alex Sudea / Rex Features (top); Jean Lannen / jeanlannenimages.com (bottom).

"The math is not difficult to parse when you see that having a hit record equals all of your sexual frustrations being satisfied. So, in the end, it was also about getting laid and getting paid."
Todd Rundgren

Other books in this series:

MILLION DOLLAR BASH: BOB DYLAN, THE BAND, AND THE BASEMENT TAPES
by Sid Griffin

HOT BURRITOS: THH TRUE STORY OF THE FLYING BURRITO BROTHERS
by John Einarson with Chris Hillman

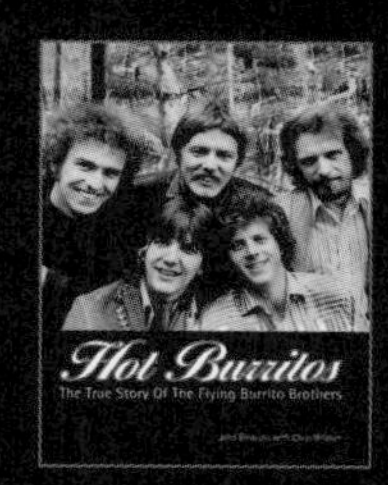

BOWIE IN BERLIN: A NEW CAREER IN A NEW TOWN
by Thomas Jerome Seabrook

THE AUTOBIOGRAPHY: YES, KING CRIMSON, EARTHWORKS, AND MORE
by Bill Bruford

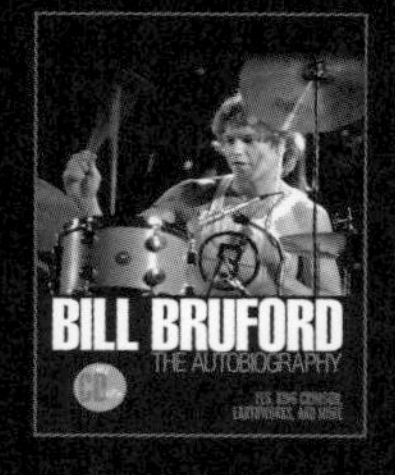

BEATLES FOR SALE: HOW EVERYTHING THEY TOUCHED TURNED TO GOLD
by John Blaney

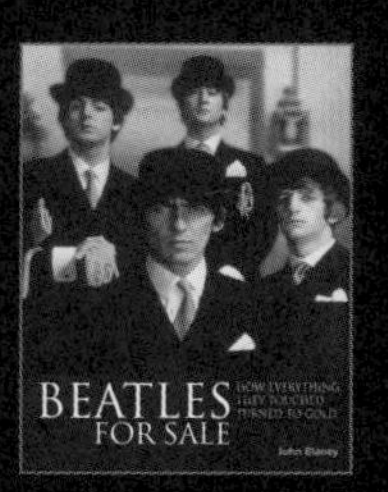

TO LIVE IS TO DIE: THE LIFE AND DEATH OF METALLICA'S CLIFF BURTON
by Joel McIver

MILLION DOLLAR LES PAUL: IN SEARCH OF THE MOST VALUABLE GUITAR IN THE WORLD
by Tony Bacon

THE IMPOSSIBLE DREAM: THE STORY OF SCOTT WALKER AND THE WALKER BROTHERS
by Anthony Reynolds

JACK BRUCE: COMPOSING HIMSELF: THE AUTHORISED BIOGRAPHY
by Harry Shapiro

SHELTER FROM THE STORM: BOB DYLAN'S ROLLING THUNDER YEARS
by Sid Griffin

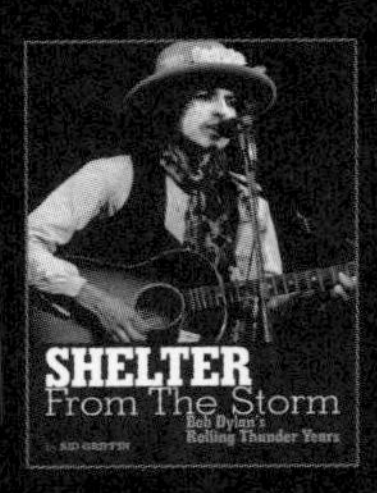

RETURN OF THE KING: ELVIS PRESLEY'S GREAT COMEBACK
by Gillian G. Gaar

SEASONS THEY CHANGE: THE STORY OF ACID AND PSYCHEDELIC FOLK
by Jeanette Leech

FOREVER CHANGES: ARTHUR LEE AND THE BOOK OF LOVE
by John Einarson